# SOUTHERN MEXICO
# & YUCATÁN GUIDE

## YOUR PASSPORT TO GREAT TRAVEL!

## ERIC HAMOVITCH

# OPEN ROAD PUBLISHING

1st Edition

Copyright 1995© by Eric Hamovitch
-All Rights Reserved-

ISBN 1-883323-11-8
Library of Congress Catalog No. 94-66041

Front and back cover photos courtesy of Mexican Government Tourism Office. Inside photographs by Eric Hamovitch.

# TABLE OF CONTENTS

# MAPS

# SIDEBARS

# 1. INTRODUCTION

Southern Mexico is a land of travelers' dreams. Millions go there each year, and everyone discovers something a little different. Some go just for the beaches, determined that nothing but sea, sand, and sun will fill their agenda, and they discover a tasty new dish, or a special drink, or some new friends who entice them with tales of what they've seen on an excursion the day before. Others go with a high-minded determination to cram as many visits as they can to Mayan ruins or colonial cities, and then discover the benefits of a day or two relaxing somewhere within earshot of the pounding surf. Yet others go with no preconceived ideas at all and just head where the spirit takes them, finding some little mountain hideout, or a spot where they can buy the most amazing weavings, or a quiet lagoon with thousands of exotic birds. Million of travelers bring millions of individual tastes, and the permutations on offer are so numerous that almost anyone can come away satisfied.

Southern Mexico is a vast place, in terms not only of geography but also of variety. Visitors will find an astounding range of mountain and jungle, of Indian and Spanish influences, of towns and beaches, of food and drink, of old and new. A beautiful thing about vacationing there is that it doesn't have to be a one-or-the-other decision. You want to bake on the beach, she wants to see an ancient Mayan city? You want to dive amid coral reef, he prefers to surround himself with colonial architecture? You can all come away happy.

This guide covers the southern part of Mexico, which accounts for a small portion of the country's total land area but a very large portion of its cultural and scenic wealth. This is not the Mexico of the quick cross-border shopping trip to Tijuana or the Mexico of the vast northern desert or the Mexico of booming industrial cities. Rather, it is a more genteel part of Mexico, a land of ancient cultures, of deeply felt traditions, of rugged mountains, of splendid beaches. We invite you to a voyage of discovery.

# 2. EXCITING SOUTHERN MEXICO & YUCATÁN! - OVERVIEW

This guide begins on Mexico's Caribbean coast and takes the traveler to the shores of the Pacific, across flatlands and mountains and several distinct cultural heritages. Here is a brief glance at some of the key attractions.

## MEXICO CITY

The Mexican capital lies outside the area covered by this guide, but we have provided a few pages of information for the benefit of visitors who plan to spend a day or two there on the way to or from the areas in the south and southeast of the country.

## THE CARIBBEAN COAST

With its crystalline sand, turquoise waters and vast array of comfortable hotels, **Cancún** has become almost synonymous with fashionable beach vacations. It has achieved nearly legendary status as the biggest and most popular of Mexican beach resorts. Poised near the northeastern tip of the Yucatán peninsula, it represents only the tip of what the Mexican Caribbean has to offer.

Beach-goers seeking something more casual and less expensive may be drawn to **Isla Mujeres**, a short ferry ride away, or to **Playa del Carmen,** an hour south of Cancún by road. Divers and snorkelers will be drawn to points further south, such as **Akumal** or to the more traditional resort island of **Cozumel**, with its reefs and other pleasures. Back on the mainland, **Tulum** is the site of heavily visited Mayan ruins which have the distinction of facing the sea. Tucked nearby are a series of small, secluded beaches with hotels to match. A short way inland are the less visited ruins of **Cobá**, much more dramatic than Tulum and surrounded by jungle. Finally, in the south, is **Chetumal**, gateway to Belize.

## CENTRAL & WESTERN YUCATÁN

The pancake-flat Yucatán peninsula has the unusual distinction of being generously washed with rain and yet having no surface rivers. All water moves underground. The Yucatán was the domain of an important branch of the ancient Mayan empire, and one of their most important cities was **Chichén Itzá**, whose spectacular ruins provide exciting glimpses of the past. Other archaeological sites in central Yucatán include **Uxmal**, south of the pleasant, colonial-era city of **Mérida**, with its plazas and museums, a good jumping-off point for several attractions.

A little further east lie **Izamal**, an intensely old-fashioned town where horse-drawn carriages are the only taxis, and **Valladolid**, another colonial town and a good base from which to visit Chichén Itzá and **Río Lagartos** on the Gulf coast to the north, a paradise for bird-watchers. West of Mérida lies the city of **Campeche**, an architectural mini-Havana with visible reminders of pirate days.

## CHIAPAS

Mexico's southernmost state, which shares a long border and many cultural traditions with Guatemala, achieved unwanted notoriety at the start of 1994 with the emergence of a previously little known rebel movement. In the north of Chiapas lie the ruins of **Palenque**, among the most beautiful in the Mayan world.

**POOLSIDE IN IXTAPA**

Further south is the cool highland town of **San Cristóbal de las Casas**, an utterly delightful spot filled with colonial-era buildings and a very pronounced Indian presence. Nearby are several ancient Indian villages, and the selection of handicrafts is excellent. The state capital, **Tuxtla Gutiérrez**, is a big and rather unattractive city, but it has a wonderful zoo and boat cruises through the spectacular Sumidero canyon. Toward the Guatemalan border are the **Lagunas de Montebello**, set in a heavily wooded national park. **Tapachula**, in the very south, is an important gateway to Central America.

## TABASCO & SOUTHERN VERACRUZ

The city of **Villahermosa** is modern and sprawling but nonetheless has several points of interest, including a fabulous outdoor museum with giant stone carvings from the ancient Olmec period. In the southern part of Veracruz state lie a cluster of three towns known collectively as **Los Tuxtlas** and each with its own special attractions, including cigar factories, an enchanting lake, and witchcraft rituals. Further north is the picturesque riverside town of **Tlacotalpan**.

## OAXACA

The city of **Oaxaca** is one of the most enticing spots in Mexico with its valley setting, gorgeous central plaza, abundance of colonial architecture, strong Indian influence and an array of museums and markets. Several ancient ruins lie nearby, **Monte Albán** in particular, and some of the neighboring towns and villages hold impressive weekly markets.

On the Pacific coast of Oaxaca state, **Huatulco** is an opulent new resort set around a series of nine bays, while **Puerto Escondido**, further west, is a casual and inexpensive spot to enjoy beaches, surfing and fine sunsets.

## GUERRERO

**Acapulco** is a name that became closely associated with glamour in the annals of twentieth-century travel. Although perhaps past its heyday, it is worth visiting for its spectacular setting, its beaches, and its active day-and-night pedestrian life along a main thoroughfare lined with restaurants, shops and hotels.

Further west lie the twin beach resorts of **Ixtapa**, with its row of modern high-rise hotels, and **Zihuatanejo**, older and more intimate, with several fine beaches. In the north of Guerrero state is the old silver-mining town of **Taxco**, partially frozen in the 18th century, with hilly, cobbled streets and, more recently, an abundance of jewelry shops.

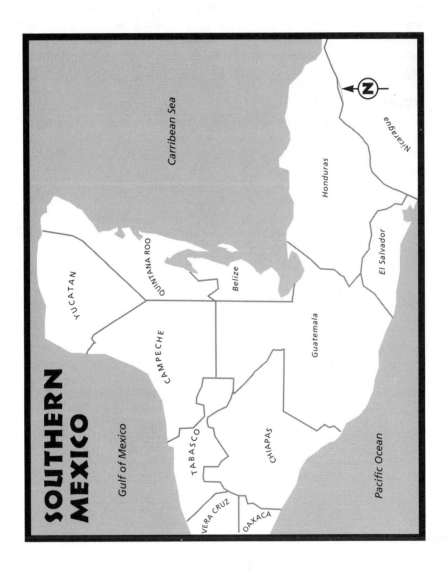

## OUTDOOR ACTIVITIES

A broad range of aquatic activities, from **scuba diving** and **snorkeling** in the Caribbean to **surfing** in the Pacific, are covered in this guide, as are **golfing**, **horseback riding** and **bicycling**. Perhaps surprisingly, Mexico has been slow to develop ecotourism (a term which causes many ecologists to shudder), but several environmentally conscious tour operators take visitors along quiet estuaries and lagoons for excellent **bird-watching**.

## FOOD & DRINK

Eating and drinking may not be the principal reasons for coming to Mexico, but they clearly add to the enjoyment. Certain regions, particularly the Yucatán and Oaxaca, offer distinctive local dishes in addition to the usual Mexican favorites.

# 3. LAND & PEOPLE

## THE LAND

Much of southern Mexico is mountainous, but the **Yucatán** peninsula is mostly flat. Although rainfall is quite abundant, the Yucatán is distinguished by its absence of surface rivers or large lakes. Instead, water moves through a network of underground aquifers, about which relatively little is known. In a few places the ground has collapsed, creating what amount to large open wells known as *cenotes* (pronounced say-NO-tays). Because the water they contain is filtered through layers of rock and sand, it is clean and safe for swimming.

Thus *cenotes* have taken on a vocation as swimming holes. In some places they are operated commercially, with a small entry fee and facilities that include access paths and ropes or ladders for bathers to lower themselves into the water without having to rely on slippery rock surfaces. Some *cenotes* also lead the way to networks of water-filled caves that have attracted adventurous divers; this requires a special type of expertise and can be quite dangerous.

The Yucatán faces the Caribbean on the east, the Gulf of Mexico to the north and west, Belize and Guatemala to the south, and Tabasco and Chiapas states to the southwest. It is divided between the states of **Quintana Roo, Yucatán**, and **Campeche**. The southern part of Campeche does not share the peculiar geological conditions of the rest of the peninsula.

Soils in the Yucatán are infertile except in some areas toward the northwest, and large areas are covered in scrubland. The center and south of the peninsula are very sparsely populated. An important traditional crop is *henequén*, or sisal, used in making rope. This industry has been in decline for decades.

**Tabasco**, southern **Veracruz**, and northern portions of **Chiapas** and **Oaxaca** states are fairly flat and lush, with heavy production of sugar cane, bananas and cocoa. Most other portions of Chiapas and Oaxaca are covered by various ranges of mountains, except for a narrow coastal plain along the Pacific, a handful of intermont basins such as the central valleys of Oaxaca, and the isthmus of Tehuantepec, a neck of land where the continent is at its narrowest anywhere north of Panama. Coffee is an important cash crop in both Chiapas and Oaxaca. **Guerrero** state is almost entirely mountainous except for the coastal plain.

Annual rainfall varies enormously between different parts of southern Mexico. The Yucatán has abundant rainfall, as do areas in the other states lying on the Gulf of Mexico side of the mountains as well as large portions of Chiapas. In contrast, central and southern Oaxaca, and all of Guerrero state, tend to be quite arid.

Nonetheless, climatic patters are similar, with a dry season running from November to April and a rainy season from May to October. The main difference is that showers are often more prolonged in areas with heavier rainfall. Even during the rainy season, it is common for skies to be clear in the morning, clouding over later in the day with rainfall concentrated between mid-afternoon and early evening, except in the rainiest areas.

There is little seasonal variation in temperatures, although December and January are slightly cooler, and April and May slightly warmer, than the rest of the year. On hot days, afternoon showers can cool the air in a hurry. Altitude is the main factor determining differences in temperature. Areas high in the mountains, obviously, are cooler than low-lying areas. **Mérida**, which lies near sea level but is too far inland to be cooled by sea breezes, has hotter weather than most other places covered in this guide, but even there temperatures rarely climb much above the mid-30s Centigrade (mid-90s Fahrenheit). The extreme temperatures found in Mexico's northern deserts are not encountered in the south.

## THE PEOPLE

On October 12, when the United States marks Columbus Day, Mexicans observe what is called *el Día de la Raza*, the Day of the Race. The arrival of Europeans in the final decade of the 15th century marked the beginning of the *mestizo* race, created by intermarriage between the indigenous population and the new arrivals. Today *mestizos* account for the great majority of the Mexican population. In the south they also form a majority, but the proportion of native Indians, referred to in Spanish as *indígenas*, is higher than in Mexico as a whole. In the eastern part of the Guerrero coast, in an area known as the **Costa Chica**, settlements were established in the 18th century by shipwrecked African slaves, adding yet another component to the racial mixture.

The largest indigenous group in the south are the Maya. Throughout their history, Mayans have tended to splinter into different groups, and there are notable differences in language and culture between lowland

Maya living in the Yucatán and their highland cousins in Chiapas. Because the Chiapas highlands were of little economic interest to most Europeans or *mestizos*, Mayans have been able to remain a majority there, although this is not reflected in the division of political or economic spoils. The introduction of large-scale cattle ranching in recent decades created new groups of dispossessed people, and this was a major factor in the 1994 uprising.

In Oaxaca state, Zapotec Indians form a large part of the population, and in the interior of Guerrero, **Nahuatl**, the language of the ancient Aztecs, is widely spoken. Again, these people have not been well represented among the political or economic elites (with the notable exception of 19th century President Benito Juárez, who was a Zapotec).

As elsewhere in Mexico, racial discrimination is not practised formally, but there are pervasive class differences that bear a strong correlation to skin tone. People with paler skins tend to be wealthier and better educated, and hence to control the reins of power. Southern Mexicans are darker-skinned and shorter in physical stature on average than their northern countrymen. They are also poorer. Most of the very wealthy live in Mexico City and the other big cities. The local oligarchies in the south are hardly in the same league.

**INDIAN MARKET IN CHILAPA**

# 4. A SHORT HISTORY

During the last Ice Age, Asians migrated to the American continent across a land bridge that later was submerged by the Bering Strait as the ice caps receded and sea level rose. Evidence suggests humans may have arrived in Mexico as much as 20,000 years ago.

Some 3,000 years before Europeans first set foot in that same territory, a succession of civilizations had begun to develop. By then agriculture had been practised for thousands of years, and maize had emerged as the most important staple crop.

## THE EARLY CIVILIZATIONS

One of the oldest and most mysterious civilizations was that of the **Olmecs**, which flourished for about 1,000 years and then disappeared several centuries before the birth of Christ. Some aspects of Olmec social structures, their far-flung trade routes, and some of the symbols they worshipped, including the god of maize and the feathered serpent, came to influence later civilizations. The most visible reminders of the Olmec period are the enormous carved stone heads found in what are now Tabasco and southern Veracruz.

Just as Olmec civilization was waning, a new civilization was being built by the **Zapotecs** at **Monte Albán** on a hilltop near the present-day city of Oaxaca. Monte Albán grew to become the biggest city of its era in Mesoamerica, and its intellectual achievements were important, including what may have been the first written calendar in the region. At about the same time, the religious center of Izapa, in the southern Chiapas lowlands, formed what many archeologists regard as a transitional civilization between the Olmecs and the Maya.

The **Maya**, in turn, achieved their greatest flowering between the third and ninth centuries A.D. when they built great cities in a wide arc extending from Honduras to Tabasco. These cities were dominated by high pyramids which served as temples and often as tombs for powerful rulers. The pyramids faced large plazas, and nearby were ball courts used for a highly stylized game whose outcome was believed to have oracular powers. Many of the stone surfaces were carved with elaborate figures, and finely worked pieces of pottery and jade have been found. The Maya also developed a highly sophisticated calendar using various combinations of periods and cycles that could be extended infinitely. Religious life was very important, tied into a series of rituals and beliefs about heavens and underworlds, with various animals and celestial bodies used as symbols. The Maya believed themselves to be descended from people made of maize, such was the central role played by this grain.

Nobody is quite sure what led to the collapse of Mayan civilization, although population pressures are thought to offer one explanation. The next several centuries saw only minor civilizations until the rise of the **Aztecs** in the 15th century, who expanded their empire from what is now Mexico City to encompass most of central Mexico and built trade networks extending far beyond.

## THE ARRIVAL OF THE SPANISH

The Aztec empire was utterly shattered between 1519 and 1521 by the ruthless trickery and brute force employed by Spanish *conquistador* **Hernán de Cortés**. In the following decades Spanish forces went on to subjugate most of what today is central and southern Mexico. The indigenous population declined rapidly as a result of harsh treatment from Spanish colonists who had been granted *encomiendas* (control over Indian settlements) and from epidemics of diseases to which they had no resistance. Franciscan and Dominican monks attempted to control some of the worst excesses but meanwhile set about destroying traditional beliefs and replacing them with at least a veneer of Christianity, thereby helping to consolidate Spanish control.

A rebellion intended to achieve independence from Spain was launched in 1810 by **Miguel Hidalgo**, a parish priest. The first attempt failed, but with Spain teetering from financial distress and Napoleonic invasion, the Spanish crown could not hold on much longer in the face of sporadic fighting, and formal independence came in 1821 with the establishment of a monarchy under **Agustín de Iturbide**, who had himself crowned emperor. Iturbide's empire reached from Costa Rica to California but collapsed in 1823 with the establishment of a republic in Mexico and the secession of the Central American provinces.

The next three decades were a period of extreme political instability. The dominant figure during this period was the buffoonish **General Antonio López de Santa Anna**, who led numerous coups and was commander of Mexican forces in a disastrous war and subsequent cession of land that allowed the United States to acquire a huge swath of territory extending from Texas to California. Santa Anna's final ouster came in 1855.

## JUÁREZ, DÍAZ, & THE MEXICAN REVOLUTION

Attempts at constitutional reform led to a dispute that was resolved in favor of liberal forces, who installed **Benito Juárez**, a Zapotec Indian from Oaxaca, as president in 1861. But Juárez inherited a country that was deeply in debt to the European powers, and his presidency was interrupted by French invaders, who named Austrian Archduke Maximilian of Hapsburg emperor of Mexico. This was a fleeting throne: Maximilian was defeated by forces loyal to Juárez and executed in 1867.

Back in power, Juárez undertook an ambitious series of reforms to the educational and legal systems, and stripped the Catholic church of much of its power. A few years after his removal from office in 1871 and his death in 1872, Juárez was succeeded in the presidency by fellow *Oaxaqueño* **Porfirio Díaz**, who was to remain in power for most of the period until 1910. Díaz modernized the Mexican economy, expanding the railway network and building other pieces of infrastructure, but he also ran a very repressive government and systematically favored the interests of the wealthy. This provoked growing unrest, and in 1910 Francisco Madero, who would be elected president the following year, issued a revolutionary proclamation.

Faced with military advances by rebel forces led by Pancho Villa in the north and Emiliano Zapata in the south, Díaz fled into exile in 1911. Fighting continued, at times with great intensity, until 1917, when a revolutionary constitution was proclaimed, and did not end completely until 1920. The new constitution, which remains in effect today, promised land to the peasants, weakened the power of the Catholic church, and forbad presidents from seeking re-election.

## MODERN MEXICO

The 1920s were a period of relative stability, marked later in the decade, however, by a violent reaction to anti-clerical measures imposed by the government. In 1929 President **Plutarco Élias Calles** established the political party which, under various names (currently, the **Institutional Revolutionary Party**, known by its Spanish initials **PRI**), has dominated Mexican politics ever since. **Lázaro Cárdenas**, president from 1934 to 1940, redistributed vast amounts of land to peasant communes and nationalized the oil industry in 1938 in reaction to provocations by foreign-owned companies.

The following decades were a period of steady economic growth and remarkable political stability, accompanied by strict limits on opposition to the ruling party. In 1968 hundreds of people were killed when government forces put down a student demonstration held to coincide with the Olympic Games in Mexico City. **Luís Echeverría**, president from 1970 to 1976, and his successor, **José López Portillo**, both led big-spending, blatantly corrupt governments which went heavily into debt and pushed Mexico into an over-dependence on oil exports. When world oil prices collapsed in 1981, Mexico faced a serious financial crisis and defaulted on international loans in 1982.

**Miguel de la Madrid**, president from 1982 to 1988, and **Carlos Salinas de Gortari**, elected under controversial circumstances to succeed him, both pursued policies of fiscal austerity and eased restrictions on imports, forcing Mexican industry to become more competitive. After years of harsh recession, the economy began to grow again in the late 1980s, but many people felt left out.

In 1994 Mexico became part of the North American Free Trade Agreement (NAFTA). At the same time a cry of desperation was heard in the southern state of Chiapas, where peasant rebels briefly seized four towns to press demands for greater political openness and fairer distribution of land. Later that year, **Ernesto Zedillo**, who was chosen to replace the assassinated **Luís Donaldo Colosio** as PRI presidential candidate, kept the PRI's winning streak alive.

## THE ECONOMY

Like modern Italy or the post-Civil War US, Mexico has a relatively wealthy, industrialized north and an economically backward, poverty-ridden south, with large areas dependent on inefficient agriculture and little hope of any immediate improvement.

The winds of economic liberalism that have swept Mexico in recent years, exemplified by the removal of countless regulations and a broad opening to international trade, have had scarcely any direct effect on the southern part of the country. The North American Free Trade Agreement, which came into effect in 1994, has principally benefited the north, with its proximity to lucrative US markets. Few investors have chosen to locate new industrial plants in the south, with its weaker road and railway networks and its lower levels of education.

Tourism is one bright spot for the regional economy, especially in the state of Quintana Roo, where the development of Cancún and newer resorts to its south have caused the population to multiply with the arrival of migrants from other parts of Mexico. Other parts of the Yucatán have felt a modest spinoff from Cancún.

Oaxaca has seen slow but steady growth in tourism, whereas the tourism industry in Chiapas was sent into a tailspin by the 1994 rebellion and appeared to be recovering at a lethargic pace. Guerrero state, which includes Acapulco, Ixtapa and Zihuatanejo, has long relied heavily on tourism. Some slippage in tourism from abroad has been compensated by the opening of a new highway from Mexico City.

Tourism alone, however, cannot serve as the base for a durable economy, and additional forms of development will have to be found if the people of southern Mexico are to gain new prosperity rather than to fall ever further behind their northern cousins.

**VISIT ONE OF COZUMEL'S MUSEUMS!**

# 5. ITINERARIES

Here are a few ideas for those of you planning to spend a couple of weeks in southern Mexico and can tear themselves away from the beach for part of their stay. These itineraries allow an easy pace and include some areas that are neglected by most organized tours. They provide a mixture of ancient and modern, of city and beach, and they allow you to choose between bus and car for your land travel.

Since you can set the pace yourself, you can add or subtract a day or two as the mood strikes you or as your schedule permits. And nothing should stop you from following them in reverse order should that work out better for you. You may decide you want to follow only part of an itinerary, or possibly to mix it with bits of the others.

These are self-guided tours that won't lock you into someone else's idea of how much time to spend at each place. Details on hotels and local points of interest will be found in other chapters of this book.

Cancún is chosen as the starting and ending point for some circuits for the simple reason that this is where many travelers first arrive in Mexico. You can adjust itineraries to your requirements if Cancún doesn't fit in well.

If you decide to travel by bus, try to store some of your baggage at your starting point if you intend to return there (most hotels provide this service for their guests) and take with you only what you really need. Two small bags may be easier to handle than one big one. You can do laundry along the way if you desire, so you won't need huge amounts of clothing.

## ITINERARY 1 - AROUND THE YUCATÁN PENINSULA

Cancún - Playa del Carmen - Cozumel - Cobá - Valladolid -
Chichén Itzá - Mérida - Uxmal / Izamal - Cancún
*Number of days:* 8
*Transportation:* By car or bus, with one side-trip by ferry
*Highlights:* Mayan ruins, beaches, colonial cities

**Day 1**

Go one hour south from Cancún to Playa del Carmen, a smaller, lower-priced and more easy-going beach resort. Settle in to a hotel room, then take a stroll along the beach and, in the evening, along the lively pedestrian-only main street.

**Day 2**

Catch the ferry to Cozumel. Take a brief walk around the center of town in San Miguel (the ferry leaves you right there) and then head by taxi to Chankanab Park for snorkeling, swimming or just plain relaxation. Ferry back to Playa del Carmen.

**Day 3**

You can stay longer at Playa del Carmen if you choose. If not, head south to Tulum, stopping briefly at the ruins (which are heavily visited by day trippers from Cancún and not all that interesting). Or skip Tulum and continue west to Cobá, whose ruins set in a jungle park are truly spectacular. You'll have lots of walking, so wear good shoes.

If you go by bus, there is a 10 am departure from Playa del Carmen that allows you five hours at Cobá for exploration and lunch before catching the last bus out. Baggage can be stored at restaurants near where the bus leaves you or at the entrance to the ruins. Then head north to Valladolid, arriving late in the day.

**Day 4**

Valladolid is an old colonial city with some interesting churches and *cenotes*, which are caverns filled with ground water and suitable for swimming. But most of all it is a good jumping-off point for the ruins of Chichén Itzá a half-hour west (hourly buses; get off in the village of Pisté). Go early in the day to avoid both the noon-time heat and the crowds from Cancún.

You can return to Valladolid or stay overnight in Pisté, which is a dreary place but closer to the evening sound-and-light show at the ruins, if that interests you.

**Day 5**

If you're an avid bird-watcher, you can do a day excursion north from Valladolid to Rio Lagartos (if going by bus, connect at Tizimín). Fishermen will take you by boat along an estuary to see flamingos, pelicans and cormorants. If this doesn't grab you, head west to Mérida and count one day less for your itinerary.

**Day 6**

Mérida, two hours west of Valladolid (frequent buses) is the capital of Yucatán state and a graceful city with many fine old buildings, several museums, and colonial plazas. You can devote the rest of your day to exploring the city.

**Day 7**

Two alternate excursions: (1) to the ruins at Uxmal and, if you wish, also to other archaeological sites nearby (see the section in this book on Uxmal and the Puuc Hills for details); or (2) to the town of Izamal, with its unusual church set near the remains of an ancient pyramid, and its very old-fashioned atmosphere, including horse-drawn taxis. Back early to Mérida.

**Day 8**

Return to Cancún (four hours; first-class bus recommended), or spend an extra day in Mérida. If you want to continue touring, you can pick up Itinerary 2 starting on Day 4. This will take you to Campeche and from there into Chiapas.

---

## ITINERARY 2 – YUCATÁN & CHIAPAS

*Cancún – Chichén Itzá – Mérida – Uxmal / Izamal – Campeche – Palenque – San Cristóbal de las Casas – Tuxtla Gutiérrez – Cancún*

**Number of days:** *10*
**Transportation:** *By car or bus, optionally by air on the last leg*
**Highlights:** *Colonial cities, Mayan ruins, Indian handicrafts, mountain scenery*

---

**Day 1**

Head west from Cancún toward the Mayan ruins at Chichén Itzá (2 to 2 1/2 hours). Set off very early to avoid the crowds and the mid-day heat. Buses leave hourly; get off in Pisté and go by foot or taxi from there; baggage may be stored at the entrance to the ruins. After seeing the ruins, continue west to Mérida, arriving in late afternoon. *For more of the Yucatán, see Itinerary 1, which reaches Mérida on Day 6.*

**Day 2**

Enjoy the day exploring Mérida with its colonial plazas, churches and museums.

**Day 3**

Head out for the day to Uxmal or Izamal (see Itinerary 1, Day 7), or spend an extra day in Mérida.

**Day 4**

Travel southwest toward Campeche (2 1/2 hours, frequent buses), an old port city that still has some of the ramparts that protected it from pirate attacks. This is a picturesque place with several small museums. If you're in more of a hurry, you can skip Campeche and head straight on to Palenque (8 1/2 hours, direct bus leaving Mérida at 8 am).

**Day 5**

From Campeche, continue to Palenque (six hours). If you're traveling by bus, the day will get off to a leisurely start; unless schedules have changed, the only direct day-time bus goes at 10:45 am, arriving late in the afternoon.

**Day 6**

A visit to the ruins, of course. Minibuses run frequently between the town of Palenque and the ruins. There is a museum on the way to the ruins that is also worth a visit. If time permits later, consider a visit to the falls and natural pool of Misol-Ha in a dramatic jungle setting, reachable by minibus (with some walking) or by taxi.

**Day 7**

Onward to San Cristóbal de las Casas (six hours, frequent buses). Points of interest along the way include a cascading series of waterfalls and pools known as Agua Azul (hard to reach by bus except for organized trips from Palenque) and the dramatic ruins of Toniná (reachable by taxi from Ocosingo, about mid-way between Palenque and San Cristóbal).

Or you may prefer to head directly to San Cristóbal and spend some extra time there. As you approach, altitudes are higher and temperatures are cooler. There is good mountain scenery along the highway.

**Day 8**

San Cristóbal de las Casas is a delightful colonial city with many streets lined by traditional low-slung buildings. It is also an important center of contemporary Mayan life and a good place to shop for handicrafts. Its museums and churches are worth visiting, as are several of the outlying villages. Many people come to San Cristóbal planning to spend only a day or two and end up staying much longer. The place really does have a very special atmosphere.

### Day 9

Stay another day in San Cristóbal if you can. If not, head west (and downhill) 1 1/2hours to Tuxtla Gutiérrez (fine mountain scenery, frequent buses). Unlike San Cristóbal, Tuxtla is hot and ugly, but it boasts a fabulous zoo, a decent archaeological museum and, from nearby Chiapa de Corzo, boat trips through the dramatic Sumidero canyon.

### Day 10

Time to head back to Cancún. There are overnight buses if money is tight. By car, count on a day-and-a-half. Otherwise, the airplane is recommended (it makes two stops on the way). There are also daily flights from Tuxtla Gutiérrez to Mexico City, Oaxaca, and several other spots.

## ITINERARY 3 - TABASCO, CHIAPAS, OAXACA

*Villahermosa - Palenque - San Cristóbal de las Casas - Tuxtla Gutiérrez - Huatulco / Puerto Escondido - Oaxaca*
**Number of days:** 12
**Transportation:** *By car or bus, optionally by air on some legs*
**Highlights:** *Ancient ruins, colonial cities, Indian handicrafts, beaches, mountains*

### Day 1

Arrive in Villahermosa, the capital of Tabasco state, by car, bus or air. Buses serve Villahermosa from Mexico City and from most parts of eastern and southeastern Mexico. Air service is available from Mexico City, Oaxaca, Tuxtla Gutiérrez, Mérida and Cancún.

If you arrive early, visit La Venta museum-park, which features large archaeological pieces, including huge Olmec heads, set in a big park with an easy self-guided trail. Baggage can be checked at the ADO bus terminal. Then head southeast to Palenque by car or bus (2 1/2 hours, buses every couple of hours).

### Days 2 to 5

Palenque, San Cristóbal de las Casas, and Tuxtla Gutiérrez. Same as Days 6 to 9 of Itinerary 2. Please see above.

### Day 6

An all-day trip to the Oaxaca coast (a through bus leaves Tuxtla

Gutiérrez at 9:10 am; overnight service is also available; other buses provide connections at Salina Cruz  a truly awful place). There's good mountain scenery as you descend from Tuxtla Gutiérrez, but much of the trip is through hot, un-scenic scrublands.

An alternative is to fly from Tuxtla to Oaxaca, visiting Oaxaca city first and then heading to the coast.) The two main choices along the Oaxaca coast are the swank new upscale resort town of Huatulco or the more laid-back and lower-priced resort of Puerto Escondido, two hours further west.

### Days 7 and 8
Time to relax on the beach and enjoy the Pacific waves. If you're feeling energetic, tours are operated from Puerto Escondido to nearby nature reserves. Or you can do an excursion on your own, about midway between Puerto Escondido and Huatulco, to the fishing and naval port of Puerto Ángel (bus connections at Pochutla, frequent service), continuing on to the nude beach at Zipolite (served by bus) and the turtle museum at Mazunte (a few minutes by taxi or an hour's walk from Zipolite).

### Day 9
Head north to Oaxaca city. From Huatulco there is the gentle route via Salina Cruz or a more scenic route via Pochutla. From Puerto Escondido the route via Pochutla makes the most sense. There are fine mountain vistas along the way. Trip time is about six hours. Most buses are second-class. Daily flights run to Oaxaca both from Huatulco and Puerto Escondido, but fares are quite high.

Oaxaca is a colonial city of great beauty and serenity, with a substantial Zapotec Indian presence. After checking into your hotel, the first place to head is the *zócalo*, the almost magical central plaza, which is especially lively in the early evening.

### Day 10
Time to explore Oaxaca and its surroundings. Besides the *zócalo* and some of the surrounding streets and markets, there are several museums and churches to see. Also, you won't want to miss a visit to the dramatic hilltop ruins at Monte Albán, just outside Oaxaca.

### Day 11
Continuing your stay in Oaxaca, you may want to visit one of the weekly Indian markets in an outlying town. *See the Oaxaca chapter for information on which days of the week to go.* Or you may choose to visit the ruins at Mitla east of Oaxaca.

**Day 12**

It is now farewell time. Buses and planes connect Oaxaca with Mexico City and points stretching as far east as Cancún. If you're planning also to visit Acapulco, it would make sense to go to Oaxaca city first and the coast afterwards.

---

### ITINERARY 4 – GUERRERO & OAXACA

*Mexico City – Taxco – Acapulco – Puerto Escondido/ Huatulco – Oaxaca*

*Number of days: 10*

*Transportation: By car or bus, with the last leg optionally by air*

*Highlights: Beaches, colonial cities, mountain scenery*

---

**Day 1**

From Mexico City head south to Taxco (2 1/2 hours, hourly buses). This hilly, cobbled former silver mining town is a visual delight and an important center of jewelry production. It is a fine place simply to stroll (and also to shop). Its churches and museums are worth seeing. Try to avoid Saturday and Sunday, when the town is crowded.

**Day 2**

Continue south to Acapulco (three hours by road, buses every couple of hours). Acapulco needs little introduction. It is known for its beaches, nightlife and shopping.

**Day 3**

If today is Sunday, double back north part way and then east to Chilapa (bus connections at Chilpancingo), where the weekly market draws thousands of vendors, including handicrafts makers, from surrounding towns and villages.

Otherwise, enjoy another day in Acapulco, perhaps making the short excursion to Pie de la Cuesta for a change of pace.

**Day 4**

A six-hour trip along the rather un-scenic highway to the Oaxaca coast (buses at least hourly), ending at the casual beach resort of Puerto Escondido or, two hours further east, at the newer and more upscale resort of Huatulco. Then enjoy a fabulous sunset. This trip can also be done by overnight bus.

**Days 5 to 9**

Puerto Escondido or Huatulco, and Oaxaca. Same as Days 7 to 11 of Itinerary 3. Please see above.

**Day 10**

Stay longer in Oaxaca, if you wish. If you are moving on, planes and buses connect Oaxaca with Mexico City and with points as far east as Cancún.

**Note:** If Chiapas is in your plans, you can go by road or air from Oaxaca to Tuxtla Gutiérrez and then follow Days 6 to 9 of Itinerary 2 in reverse order. From there you can also continue east to the Yucatán peninsula (Days 1 to 5 of Itinerary 2, again in reverse order). Or if you prefer to head straight to the Yucatán, fly directly to Mérida, from where you can follow portions of Itineraries 1 or 2. If your trip starts in the Yucatán or Chiapas, you can tack this itinerary onto the end of one of the others.

You may have noticed that these itineraries have some overlapping portions. Here are the day counts for several combinations:

Itineraries 1 and 2 combined: 14 days
Itineraries 2 and 3 combined: 16 days
Itineraries 1, 2 and 3 combined: 20 days
Itineraries 1 and 4 combined: 17 days
Itineraries 2 and 4 combined: 19 days
Itineraries 3 and 4 combined: 17 days
All four itineraries combined: 24 days

# 6. PLANNING YOUR TRIP

## WHEN TO GO

The most popular time for travel to Mexico is during the northern winter, and this makes perfect sense. From November to early May, southern Mexico has pleasant, mostly dry weather, in rather obvious contrast to large parts of North America and Europe.

As in most tropical zones, there are only two seasons, the dry season and the rainy season, with only small differences in temperature. Southern Mexico's rainy season begins during May and usually runs until late October. On the Caribbean coast September marks peak hurricane season, but dangerous storms are rare.

If you're thinking about traveling during the wet period, the rain shouldn't really stop you. It rarely rains for prolonged periods. Rainfall often comes in the form of brief but intense showers, usually in the middle or late afternoon, although it may occasionally rain at other times of day.

Even during the rainy season there can be many rainless days, and most of the time you'll get at least some sunshine. Acapulco sees at least some sun an average of 360 days a year. In Cancún and surrounding areas the weather can sometimes turn a little cooler and cloudier in December and January if north winds come in.

Unless you're going on a package tour, you should probably think twice about traveling during the Christmas or Easter periods. The week preceding Easter is a big holiday period for Mexicans, while the period around Christmas and New Year's is peak travel time both for Mexicans and foreigners.

If you've got confirmed hotel bookings and aren't planning to move around very much, you'll probably do all right, but if you're the sort of traveler who prefers a more casual approach you could run into problems. Hotels jack up their rates and even so are often booked solid. Airplanes and buses go full, especially at the start and the end of the holiday period (though in between it's easier to find space). Even with arrangements are in order, you may find that beaches are more crowded and that restaurant service suffers because of heavy demand.

Many hotels, and some airlines, charge higher rates at certain times of year. High season rates at resort hotels are sometimes double the low season rates. Seasonal rates kick in on different dates in different spots, though high season rates generally apply from mid-December to mid-April, and in many places may also apply during the school break in July and August when families are traveling with children. Some hotels charge extra-high rates at Christmas. Low season rates apply during the northern spring (after Easter) and throughout the autumn.

November and early December are good times to visit southern Mexico. The weather is dry and not excessively hot, the crowds haven't arrived yet, and prices are lower. In January and early February rates are higher, but things aren't yet as crowded as they get from mid-February to Easter. During Holy Week, as the pre-Easter period is called, it is better to avoid the resort areas, but it is a good time to visit Mexico City. Many people get the week off, automobile use drops considerably, the air is clearer, and everything (except religious sites) is less crowded.

## HOW TO ARRANGE YOUR TRIP

Decisions, decisions! How will you decide where to go? How are you going to make your travel arrangements? Do you want to arrange everything in advance, or do you prefer to play it by ear? Do you want to travel on your own, or in a group? These are some of the questions you may be asking, and many others are bound to arise.

As for deciding where to go, this guidebook can provide many of the answers. Whether your interests lie in beach resorts or archaeological sites or any number of other domains, you will find plenty of suggestions. We have gone a step further here and proposed sample itineraries, which appear in a previous chapter. These are not meant to be followed to the letter, but they do offer ideas which can be useful to anyone planning a trip.

Before deciding how to arrange your trip, think about what kind of trip you find most appealing. Do you want just to relax by the sea, or do you want to travel around? Are you prepared to make your own travel arrangements? How much flexibility do you want to allow yourself? Think about these points, and read on.

### Limited Package Tours

Many visitors to Mexican beach resorts go on limited package tours that include air fare, hotels, transfers between airport and hotel, and, in some cases, meals and sporting activities. These are not the same as escorted tours: participants are left pretty much on their own after they arrive. Tour packages often provide a choice of hotels at each destination offering different levels of luxury. The tour wholesalers who assemble these packages buy air and hotel space in bulk and offer lower prices than individuals can normally obtain at comparable hotels. Another advantage is simplicity, both for travelers and for travel agents.

The disadvantage, for some people anyway, is that they end up stuck in a single spot for their entire vacation, except perhaps for some short excursions. An interesting compromise (and not all tour wholesalers allow it) is to book lodgings for only part of your stay. For example, you could request a package that gives you a two-week stay in Mexico but only one week's prepaid accommodations at a resort hotel, leaving you free to wander at will during the second week. Ask your travel agent.

### Escorted Tours

For those who want to travel around and see more of the country but who don't feel adventurous enough to do it on their own, or who simply like being with a group, many escorted tours are available. A good travel agent (and not all travel agents are equally good) will have information from different tour operators, allowing you to choose the itinerary and the dates that suit you best.

Variations in price usually reflect group size, the quality of hotels and meals, and whether any flights are included. It is important to read the small print and learn, for instance, how many meals are included in the price and whether there are any hidden taxes or service charges that will have to be paid later. Again, travel agents can advise you.

### Self-guided Travel

If you do feel capable of handling things on your own, you'll have to decide how much of it you want to arrange in advance. For many travelers, an air ticket is sufficient. They're quite happy to make other arrangements after arriving, although this is not always so easy during peak holiday periods. Others may prefer to book a hotel for their first couple of nights and to play it by ear after that.

Even if you prefer to map things out more precisely, do try to allow for a degree of flexibility in case you decide you want to spend a day more, or a day less, at a certain place, or to go somewhere you hadn't though of before. The more tightly things are arranged, the more complicated it becomes to alter your arrangements.

Bear in mind that some travel agents prefer to deal with familiar international hotel chains, and their computer databases include very few of the smaller or more economical hotels. You would have to contact these hotels on your own, by mail, fax or phone. Also, travel agents can arrange flights and car rentals but are not likely to have bus information.

When making hotel reservations on your own, consider doing it by telephone even if this involves expensive long-distance charges to Mexico.

This way you can learn right away what's available and how much it costs. Alternately, try to seek information or confirmation by fax; if you don't receive a rapid reply, follow it up with a phone call. Letters are usually too slow; they may go unacknowledged for weeks or even months and are probably best limited to establishments where you are already known.

Sometimes a hotel will request a deposit. This may simply involve providing the number of a credit card which can be billed for the first night's lodging to protect the hotel if the traveler fails to show up, or it may involve sending a "cash" deposit. Actual cash should never be sent; payment should be by international money order, preferably sent by registered mail or some equivalent. In some cases a hotel will send a form asking you to authorize charges to a credit card; make sure the amount is clearly stated. You should not agree to pay any deposit covering more than a small fraction of your expected stay.

## GETTING THERE

For obvious reasons of geography, most foreign visitors to southern Mexico arrive by air. The busiest international entry points are Mexico City and Cancún. International flights also serve Cozumel, Mérida, Huatulco, Acapulco and Ixtapa-Zihuatanejo. If you're headed elsewhere, you'll probably have to continue by connecting flight or by road.

Scheduled or charter flights are available to all these points from many places in the US and Canada. Scheduled international service from the US is provided by Aeroméxico, Mexicana, American, Continental, Delta, United, USAir, Northwest, America West, Lacsa and Aviateca. From Canada, connections are available on several of these carriers and direct flights on Canadian Airlines. Many charters operate to the beach resorts mentioned here, although some run only on a seasonal basis.

From Europe and from Central and South America, many scheduled airlines serve Mexico City. There are also scheduled and charter flights to Cancún and the occasional charter to other beach resorts. Travelers from Europe may occasionally find it cheaper or more convenient to reach Mexico by way of the US. Cut-rate tickets are available through some consolidators in Europe.

Charter flights usually provide cheaper fares than scheduled flights even without a long advance purchase, and they offer direct point-to-point service without going through a hub airport. On the other hand, they run less frequently, often only once a week, and they offer almost no flexibility: it can be difficult or impossible to change dates after tickets are issued. Furthermore, schedules may be less convenient and seating less comfortable, and frequent flyer points are rarely offered. Take these factors into account when deciding if a charter flight is for you. Charter tickets normally are issued only through travel agents and not directly by the airline.

Passengers on scheduled flights often have an array of fares to choose from, with the cheaper fares fettered by many restrictions and usually requiring an advance purchase. If you want a flexible return date, check to see what penalty applies for changing dates on the ticket. It may pay to buy a ticket in a higher fare category if the penalty is lower.

Southern Mexico is also reachable by bus or car from the US and from Central America, although the journey is a long one. From eastern Texas border points, buses skirt the Gulf of Mexico through Veracruz state, with connections to all of southeastern Mexico. To or from more westerly points, there are countless connections in Mexico City. And from the California border, there is direct bus service from Tijuana along the Pacific coast all the way to Acapulco and into Oaxaca state.

## ENTRY REQUIREMENTS

Citizens of the US or Canada need only proof of citizenship to enter Mexico. A valid **passport** is preferred but not required. (Passports do make it easier to exchange travelers' checks in Mexico or to obtain cash advances with a credit card.) Acceptable proof of citizenship includes an expired passport, a birth certificate accompanied by photo identification, a US voter registration card, or a Canadian citizenship card. A driver's license is not considered proof of citizenship. If you have any doubts, contact a Mexican consulate or a Mexican government tourism office.

Citizens of most western European countries can enter Mexico without a visa but do require a valid passport. The same applies to citizens of Australia, New Zealand, Japan, South Korea, Israel, and certain countries in Latin America and the Caribbean. Citizens of most other countries require consular visas. Regulations can change at short notice. Again, if in doubt, check with a Mexican consulate beforehand. At the time of writing, French citizens required consular visas.

All visitors must fill out a tourist card and sign both copies on the back. Tourist cards are available from most airlines that fly into Mexico and are normally distributed to passengers at check-in or aboard the aircraft. They may also be obtained at some travel agencies, at Mexican government offices, and at land borders. The traveler must retain one copy of the tourist card for presentation to an airline clerk or immigration officer when leaving Mexico.

Upon arrival, an immigration officer will mark the maximum number of days that a visitor may stay in the country. For most nationalities a stay of 90 days is granted routinely and a stay of 180 days may be requested. Extensions may be obtained at immigration offices inside Mexico provided the total stay does not exceed 180 days. The tourist card does not grant the right to seek employment. Immigration officers rarely ask to see onward tickets or proof of financial solvency but are more likely to do so with visitors who have a scruffy or unconventional appearance.

No vaccinations are required to enter Mexico except for visitors who have recently been in a country where yellow fever is endemic.

## CUSTOMS

### Entering Mexico

Customs forms are distributed aboard aircraft and at entry points. Visitors to Mexico are allowed to bring with them a reasonable quantity of goods for personal use, including camera equipment and electronic goods, three liters of alcoholic beverages, 200 cigarettes, and up to $300 in gifts. Firearms and narcotics are prohibited. Customs inspections are conducted on a random basis.

### Returning Home

US residents may bring in up to $400 worth of goods duty-free, including one quart of liquor and 200 cigarettes. Receipts can be helpful if the value of any goods is questioned.

Canadian residents are allowed to bring in $300 (Canadian funds) worth of goods duty free once a year if they have been outside the country at least seven days and $100 worth of goods any number of times after a 48 hour absence. These limits include 1.14 liters of liquor and 200 cigarettes.

Residents of other countries should check before leaving home.

## TRAVEL COSTS IN MEXICO

For years Mexico had the reputation of being a cheap place to travel. Sharp devaluations of the Mexican **peso** in the early and middle 1980s led to highly favorable exchange rates for anyone holding US dollars or other hard currencies, bringing bargains galore for most visitors. But then for a few years the peso scarcely slid in value against the US dollar even tough inflation remained higher than in the US, resulting in less buying power for dollars.

At the end of 1994, the peso slid sharply once again, making a variety of goods and services cheaper for foreign travelers. Although not as cheap as a few years earlier, prices for holders of dollars have fallen from their peaks of the early 1990s. Luxury resorts are a notable exception; many have set their prices in dollars rather than pesos.

Mexico is a country of contrasts, and the price gap between luxury and budget travel is broad. Top-category hotels tend to cost as much as similar lodgings in the US, but cheaper hotels often are quite a lot cheaper. The same is true of restaurants: plusher establishments may have prices approaching European levels, but it's quite possible to find eating places that offer delightful meals at modest cost.

In transportation, similar tendencies apply. Air travel and car rentals are regarded as luxuries, and this is reflected in pricing. Unrestricted air fares on domestic routes in Mexico are often a bit lower than on US routes of comparable distance, but roundtrip excursion fares offer only small discounts and in many cases cost more than in the US.

**Car rentals** often cost double what they do in the US. Fuel is also more expensive, and highway tolls are outlandish. Buses, on the other hand, offer excellent value. Some of the newer intercity buses are more comfortable than anything Greyhound has on the road, and most fares are substantially lower. For travel in urban areas, taxi fares are usually much lower than in the US, and urban buses cost just a fraction of US levels.

If you are asking how much you should expect to spend while in Mexico, the answer is: it depends largely on you. Two people traveling together can easily spend $200 a day per person if they insist on five-star comfort, fancy restaurants and lots of air travel. Or they can hold the line at $20 a day each if they're willing to accept modest though by no means slummy surroundings and if they don't move around too much.

Most readers will fall somewhere in between. If you've traveled recently in the US and you're a high-end sort of traveler, you should expect to pay just as much in Mexico or maybe even a little more. For mid-level travel, costs should be somewhat lower than in the US, while budget-minded travelers can enjoy themselves for substantially less.

Because of variations in personal habits and exchange rates, we hesitate to attach any dollar amounts or percentage figures to these observations. Remember, of course, that solo travelers have nobody to share hotel or taxi costs and will pay more per person than couples. Remember also that certain places, Cancún in particular, have above-average price levels.

A rule of thumb for travel to any country is to bring half the clothing and twice the money you expect you'll need. Once you've been in Mexico several days, you should have a pretty good idea of what your average expenses will be. If necessary, you can cut back a little and seek less expensive hotels or scale back your itinerary. Conversely, if you're in the lucky position of being under budget, you can allow yourself a few extra treats. Whatever the case, put aside a small extra reserve for unexpected costs or for additional gifts.

## WHAT TO TAKE

Let's just repeat that basic rule of thumb: take half the clothing and twice the money you expect you'll need. If you expect to be staying put during most of your stay, then by all means pack that extra outfit or those heavy books.

But if you expect to be moving around a lot, that extra weight may become quite burdensome.

Think carefully about how much you really need to take with you. Take into account that reasonably cheap, same-day laundry service is widely available in Mexico not laundromats, where you lose hours doing the wash yourself, but full-service laundries that will return everything neatly folded. With that in mind, changes of clothes for about 10 days should be more than adequate for most travelers.

Consider also that you will be spending most of your time in tropical places, which all but eliminates the need for heavy clothing. If you expect to be in Mexico City, San Cristóbal de las Casas, or some other spot at a high altitude, remember to pack a sweater. But you won't want to be lugging around your winter overcoat and boots. Try to leave those at home if you can get to your flight without them.

> *When planning your travel wardrobe, try to strike a balance between the formal and the outrageously informal. Formal clothing will rarely, if ever, be necessary unless you are traveling on business, while clothing that reveals more than the usual amount of flesh is fine for the beach but less acceptable elsewhere. Aim for something in the middle. In more traditional places in Mexico, adults who wear shorts in public places are sometimes regarded as slightly ridiculous.*

Other things to take include a **toiletries kit** (again, eliminate items you don't really need; the weight can add up), a small **first-aid kit**, any **prescription drugs** you normally use (do not put these into checked baggage), a **sunhat** and **sunscreen**, a **camera** and **film** (film is readily available in Mexico so you need not take huge amounts), a reasonable quantity of **reading material** (consider taking things you won't mind giving away to lighten your load along the way). If you are a news buff, you might want to take a small **short-wave radio**.

If you can limit your baggage to carry-on items that you can take with you aboard an aircraft, you can save yourself plenty of time and trouble, not only at airports but also after you arrive, especially if you are doing any bus travel. Try, though, to leave a little extra space for any items you decide to purchase during your trip.

## MEXICAN REPRESENTATIVES ABROAD

Mexican **Government Tourism Offices** can provide helpful information regarding all aspects of tourism in Mexico. They may not always have answers to specific queries, but they seem to be up on many general points, and they have a good selection of leaflets. Embassies and consulates can help with information about entry requirements and with entry documents, but they normally cannot answer questions relating to other aspects of tourism except in cases where they have tourism attachés.

## MEXICAN GOVERNMENT TOURISM OFFICES
### In the US
- **Chicago**: *70 E. Lake St., Suite 1413, phone (312) 606-9015, fax (312) 606-9012*
- **Houston**: *2707 N. Loop W., Suite 450, phone (713) 880-1833, fax (713) 880-5153*
- **Los Angeles**: *10100 Santa Monica Blvd., phone (310) 203-8191, fax (310) 203-8316*
- **Miami**: *128 Aragon Ave., Coral Gables, phone (305) 443-9160, fax (305) 443-1186*
- **New York**: *405 Park Ave., Suite 1401, phone (212) 755-7261, fax (212) 753-2874*
- **Washington, D.C.** (tourism attaché, Mexican Embassy): *1911 Pennsylvania Ave. N.W., phone (202) 728-1750, fax (202) 728-1758*

### In Canada
- **Montreal**: *1 Place Ville Marie, Suite 1526, phone (514) 871-1052, fax (514) 871-3825*
- **Toronto**: *2 Bloor St. W., Suite 1801, phone (416) 925-0704, fax (416) 925-6061*
- **Vancouver**: *999 W. Hastings St., Suite 1610, phone (604) 669-2845, fax (604) 669-3498*

### In Europe & Asia
- **Frankfurt**: *Wiesenhuettenplatz 26, phone (69) 25.34.13, fax (69) 25.37.55*
- **London**: *60-61 Trafalgar Square, phone (071) 734-1058, fax (071) 437-6265*
- **Madrid**: *Calle Velázquez 126, phone (1) 261.18.27, fax (1) 411.07.59*
- **Paris**: *4, rue Notre Dame des Victoires, 2e, phone (1) 40.20.07.34, fax (1) 42.86.05.80*
- **Rome**: *Via Barberini 3, phone (6) 482.71.60, fax (6) 482.36.30*
- **Tokyo**: *2-15-1 Nagata-Cho, Chiyoda-Ku, phone (3) 580-2962, fax (3) 531-5539*

## MEXICAN EMBASSIES & CONSULATES
### In the US
Mexico has an embassy in Washington, DC, and consulates blanketing most of the country, especially in areas near the border. There are Mexican consulates in Albuquerque, Atlanta, Austin, Boston, Brownsville, Calexico, Chicago, Corpus Christi, Dallas, Del Rio, Denver, Detroit, Eagle Pass, El Paso, Fresno, Houston, Laredo, Los Angeles, McAllen, Miami,

Midland, New Orleans, New York, Nogales, Oxnard, Philadelphia, Phoenix, Sacramento, St. Louis, Salt Lake City, San Antonio, San Bernardino, San Diego, San Francisco, San José, San Juan (Puerto Rico), Santa Ana, Seattle and Tucson.

### In Canada
Mexico has an embassy in Ottawa and consulates in Montreal, Toronto and Vancouver.

### In Europe
Mexico has embassies or consulates in Athens, Barcelona, Belgrade, Berlin, Berne, Bonn, Brussels, Budapest, Copenhagen, Dublin, Frankfurt, Hamburg, Helsinki, Lisbon, London, Madrid, Milan, Moscow, Oslo, Paris, Prague, Rome, Seville, Stockholm, The Hague, Vienna, Warsaw.

### In Asia, Africa, and Oceania
Mexico has embassies or consulates in Algiers, Ankara, Bangkok, Beijing, Cairo, Canberra, Harare, Hong Kong, Jakarta, Kuala Lumpur, Manila, Nairobi, New Delhi, Rabat, Riyadh, Seoul, Singapore, Sydney, Tehran, Tel Aviv, Tokyo, Wellington and Windhoek.

### In Latin America and the Caribbean
Mexico has embassies or consulates in Asunción, Belize City, Bogotá, Brasilia, Buenos Aires, Caracas, Guatemala City, Havana, Kingston, La Paz, Lima, Managua, Montevideo, Panama City, Port au Prince, Quetzaltenango, Quito, Rio de Janeiro, San José (Costa Rica), San Juan (Puerto Rico), San Pedro Sula, San Salvador, Santiago, Santo Domingo, Sao Paulo, Tecún Umán and Tegucigalpa.

## GETTING AROUND SOUTHERN MEXICO & YUCATÁN
Some people for whom the airplane-and-car-rental routine is almost second nature may want to reconsider when traveling in Mexico, first, because car rental rates can be very high and, second, because high-quality bus services often provide a good alternative.

With few exceptions, trains in Mexico are slow and uncomfortable. Airplanes are a good choice for longer distances, though service on some routes is infrequent and overpriced.

### By Air
For years Mexican airline companies, especially Aeroméxico, were notoriously unreliable, with frequent delays. This has changed dramatically, and in recent years they have posted enviable on-time performances. It also used to be that domestic fares were very cheap. This, too,

has changed dramatically. On most routes fares in dollar terms rose to double or triple what they had been in the middle 1980s, though it is possible to find the occasional bargain. Unrestricted fares for one-way or round-trip travel tend to be somewhat lower in Mexico than on most US routes of similar distance, but excursion fares offer only very small discounts. Certain short-haul fares are very high.

Mexico has been part of the liberalizing trend in airline services, and a proliferation of new carriers has broken the traditional duopoly of **Aeroméxico** and **Mexicana**. (The government sold its holdings in the two airlines, and both later came to be controlled by the same company.)

Some of the new entrants, such as the ambitious **TAESA**, fly jet aircraft over far-flung route networks. Others, such as **Aviacsa**, also fly jets but over a smaller territory. Still others fly propeller planes, mostly on short routes. Information on air services appears at several places in this book, but bear in mind that things are in a state of flux and details quickly become outdated. Travel agents can provide up-to-the-minute information on routes, schedules and fares on most airlines, although a couple of the smaller ones do not appear in their reservations systems.

Most airports in Mexico look as though they were designed by the same architect, with the same marble flooring and similar furnishings throughout – although the **Huatulco airport** is a notable exception with its open plan and lofty thatched roofing. On the whole they are clean and pleasing in appearance, although seats in the waiting areas are often uncomfortable. Most have restaurants and shops, and most (Mexico City is an exception) have minibus services providing door-to-door service at economical rates.

### By Bus

Buses are far and away the most commonly used form of transportation between cities and towns. Buses go almost everywhere, and on some heavily traveled routes they operate at surprising frequencies, often with two or more companies competing for your business. Of course on quieter routes service is less frequent, but it's still far easier to get around by bus in Mexico than in many other countries, particularly the US.

Don't let a bad Greyhound experience sour you on bus travel. Some of the newer buses in Mexico are quieter and more comfortable than anything you're likely to encounter on scheduled routes in the US, and they attract a more representative cross-section of society. Buses can be almost as fast as driving, and they're certainly more restful and economical. Although fares have risen in recent years, they remain a bargain.

Mexican buses are fabled for the colorful rural services with live chickens sharing scarce space with tightly packed human passengers. These still exist, but they form just a tiny part of the total picture.

Mexican bus services vary enormously in quality and comfort, running the gamut from wretched minibuses that stop constantly and cram passengers into seats suitable only for small children, all the way up to luxury express coaches with wide, well-cushioned armchairs and leg rests, heavy curtains, refreshments on board, film showings, and special lounges in the terminals.

Buses in Mexico used to be designated simply as **first–class** or **second–class**, with first-class providing reserved seating, relatively comfortable vehicles and fewer stops. These distinctions still exist, but some second-class services also provide reserved seating, and first-class services have recently been supplemented on many of the busier routes by one or more categories of **luxury service**, often provided by the same company operating under different brand names.

These new luxury categories still don't have fixed designations, and they don't all provide the same comfort and amenities. Relative fare levels should give you some idea of what to expect. The **top luxury category** offers three-across seating rather than the usual four-across, and on the Mexico City-Acapulco route some buses have attendants serving drinks and snacks.

At the **next level down** you're back to four-across seating, but you still get center armrests and a self-service bar at the rear stocked with coffee, tea and soft drinks. You'll also find air conditioning, on-board toilets and video screens for movies, amenities that are often, though not always, provided on the regular first-class services. The movies, by the way, are a mixed blessing because of the blaring sound. You can expect mostly to see some of Hollywood's weaker efforts, dubbed or subtitled in Spanish.

As always, you'll have an easier time if you travel light. If you're carrying only a small suitcase or knapsack, you can take it on board with you. This saves hassles when you disembark and reduces the chance of theft (which in any case is rather small). Some bus companies issue baggage checks, and this provides extra reassurance.

Printed timetables are not available, but fares and departure times are usually posted at ticket counters. If you're going more than a short distance, particularly at weekends or holiday periods, it's often a good idea to buy tickets a day or two in advance. Tickets show reserved seat numbers and are valid only at the time and date indicated, so be sure to show up. Some bus companies have computerized reservations systems that make it possible to reserve seats for return or ongoing trips. Seating charts are often shown to help in your selection. Seats on the right are often preferable, especially at night to avoid the glare of oncoming headlights.

Buses referred to as *de paso* originate at other points; often tickets are not sold until the bus arrives and the driver presents a seat count. If a bus is designated *local*, that means it originates locally; it does not mean it makes all local stops. Buses designated *directo* tend to make the fewest intermediate stops. On some short hops, or on more lightly traveled routes, you may have to depend on second-class services, often with older, noisier vehicles and many stops. It's all part of the experience.

---

### WHICH BUS SERVICE TO CHOOSE?

*Often you have a choice between competing bus lines.* **ADO** *is the biggest and most respected bus company in eastern and southeastern Mexico, and its services come highly recommended.* **ADO GL** *is a separate division offering slightly more comfort, and* **UNO** *is the top-of-the line luxury division.* **Cristóbal Colón**, *now controlled by ADO, has a strong presence in Chiapas and on some routes in Oaxaca state; its service is much improved from a few years ago.*

*On routes in Guerrero state, notably to and from Acapulco,* **Estrella de Oro** *used to be the top choice but, in frequency of service and the state of its fleet, it has been eclipsed by* **Estrella Blanca**, *which also operates under the names* **Flecha Roja, Turistar, Cuauhtémoc,** *and* **Gacela**. *This group used to have a poor reputation, but they have really pulled up their socks. As in anything else, use your common sense, and don't be too dogmatic in your choice of bus lines.*

---

Now a word about safety. There can hardly be a newspaper reader who has not seen the occasional item about a Mexican bus crash. Some roads in Mexico are hazardous, and the enormous number of buses means there will be more accidents than in countries with few buses. But the vast majority of bus drivers are safe and conscientious. In the unlikely event that something terrible does happen, your chances of survival are better in a bus than in a car. Try to sit back and relax.

### By Train

Despite heavy cutbacks, there are still some decent passenger trains in Mexico. Unfortunately, none of them operates in the territory covered by this guide. For the most part, rail services in southern Mexico are uncomfortable and preposterously slow. The last remaining sleeping-car services have been chopped. One or two trains still convey *primera especial* (special first-class) coaches with air conditioning and reclining seats, but most provide only a single, spartan class of service. Fares are cheaper than on the bus, though, and there's plenty of baggage space. Some trains may be of interest to railway buffs and will be mentioned elsewhere in this book (see "Trains" in the Index).

## By Car From the US or Canada

The regions of Mexico covered in this guide lie a long way from the US border, but even so it is not unusual to see US or Canadian license plates. The long drive evidently is worth it to people who are planning a prolonged stay and who want ready access to a vehicle without paying exorbitant rental fees.

If you're considering this option, be sure your vehicle is in top mechanical shape. There are plenty of good mechanics in Mexico, but the language barrier can add to the distress of a breakdown.

Only a limited range of car models are sold in Mexico, and the availability of parts can be a problem. Toyota parts, for instance, are few and far between, and parts even for some GM, Ford, and Chrysler models can be hard to find.

Motorists entering Mexico must buy **automobile insurance** at the border. Policies issued outside Mexico are not valid. There are insurance dealers at most border crossings, and the process usually takes just a few minutes.

If you belong to an automobile club, contact them when planning your trip to see if they have any special advice. The American Automobile Association urges members to budget several hundred dollars extra to cover Mexico's stratospheric highway tolls. The AAA rates the new toll roads highly and says they are preferable to the narrower, slower and more hazardous free highways. Many two-lane highways have no shoulders. In the Yucatán, for instance, jungle vegetation often comes right to the edge of the roadway.

The AAA also advises against driving at night along two-lane highways because of hazards posed by defective headlights on some oncoming vehicles, disabled vehicles parked along dark stretches of road, or wandering livestock.

In Guerrero and some western states, there is also a threat from bandits.

### SPEED LIMITS

*Speed limits on four-lane toll highways are set mostly at 110 kilometers an hour, equal to 68 miles per hour. On many two-lane highways the speed limit is set at 90 km/h, equal to 56 mph. These limits tend not to be rigidly enforced.*

**Petroleos Mexicanos**, the government-owned oil company commonly known as Pemex, holds a monopoly on fuel sales. Lead-free gasoline is readily available throughout Mexico. Gasoline prices are somewhat higher than in the US. In some parts of Mexico gas stations are spaced far apart; it is a good idea to top up your tank when you can. There are no self-service stations. Gas station attendants do not receive salaries and depend entirely on tips for their income.

## By Rental Car

Car rental rates are high in Mexico, often double what they are in the US. They also vary enormously from place to place and from one season to the next. Within the Yucatán peninsula, for instance, rates are moderate in Mérida, expensive in Cancún, and sky-high in Chetumal. Rates drop substantially during the low tourist season.

US-based car rental companies including **Hertz, Avis, Budget, National** and **Dollar** are well represented in Mexico. They sometimes charge less when reservations are made in the US or Canada. Lower-profile local companies compete directly with the big boys in most cities and often undercut their prices.

When comparing rates, ask if insurance, taxes, and free kilometers are included. Ask also about the deductible amount on any insurance plan; it is often quite high. The free insurance provided with some gold credit cards may not be valid in Mexico; check with your card issuer before leaving home. Charges for returning a car to a station other than where you rented it can be downright extortionate. By far the cheapest car to rent is the ever-popular Volkswagen beetle, known in Mexico as the Sedan, but it is not known as a particularly comfortable or safe vehicle.

When renting a car you must present a **valid driver's license** and a **credit card**. Often the fuel tank is almost empty when the car is delivered to you, and it is anticipated that you will return it in similar state. Don't put in too much fuel unless you're feeling very generous, but try not to cut it too finely either. See the previous section above on night driving, speed limits, and gasoline.

## By Motorcycle or Bicycle

These means of transportation require a hardy spirit on Mexican highways. Large motorcycles do command a certain respect. Rural people sometimes travel along highways by bicycle, but most Mexican highways are bereft of shoulders. If you are on a bicycle and heavy vehicles are approaching in both directions, you had better watch out! With careful planning long-distance cycling can be enjoyable, but it is recommended only for the most experienced of riders or for those traveling in well organized groups. Bicycles are most widely used in the Yucatán.

## By Taxi

Taxis can be almost indispensable within cities and sometimes make sense for out-of-town excursions. If you expect to be gone only a few hours, a taxi may cost less than renting a car, and you save the trouble of driving, navigating and parking. But you'll have to bargain before you set out. The price should reflect the number of hours you expect to be away and the distance you plan to travel. Check to see if the tires and other parts of the vehicle appear to be in reasonable shape. Taxis based at the fancier hotels are often costlier than taxis flagged on the street.

## HOTELS

From fabulous luxury resorts to dreadful dives, Mexico has the full panoply of lodgings. Many of the familiar international chains are present, and Mexico has its own home-grown luxury hotel groups including **Camino Real**, **Presidente**, and **Fiesta Americana**. But you'll also find many independent hotels, many more than in the US, especially in the middle and lower price ranges. It's also much easier to find appealing city-center hotels in these ranges. As a general rule, the less expensive the hotel, the less likely you are to find English-speaking staff.

The term *motel* is less widely used in Mexico, in part because it often refers to spots where couples go for quick trysts. Budget chains such as Motel 6 or Super 8 have no Mexican equivalent, but independent hotels serve this part of the price range admirably. Rooms in the lower ranges are less standardized than in the US. You may well find quirky bits of decor as well as unexpected services such as bellhops, but you are less likely to find such amenities as carpeting or ice dispensers. Trailer parks and campgrounds are not very numerous in Mexico.

Unless you're traveling at a peak holiday period or during some local festival, you can usually find something suitable without advance reservations. Late morning is the best time of day to conduct a search because that's when hotels are likely to have the greatest number of unoccupied rooms. If you prefer to book ahead, travel agents or toll-free telephone services can handle the chain hotels and the more expensive independent hotels, though you'll have to contact the less expensive hotels directly by mail, fax or telephone.

The Mexican government has a rating system based on stars. **Two-star** and **three-star** hotels provide moderate levels of comfort, while four-star and five-star hotels are more luxurious. The top categories are *gran turismo* and *categoria especial* hotels. You should try not to let yourself be guided too much by the number of stars. The system tends to be influenced more by room size and physical amenities than by quality of service or attention to decor. A hotel with a pool and air conditioning inevitably gets a higher rating than a perfectly charming place that may happen not to offer these amenities.

Also, it is rare for inspectors to make return visits. A hotel can retain a multi-star rating even if it has deteriorated badly in the intervening years. European visitors may find the Mexican ratings rather generous; by subtracting one star you often come closer to the European rating.

Hotels mentioned in this guide have all been visited by the author. Unless otherwise indicated, all offer private (as opposed to shared) bathrooms, hot water and good standards of cleanliness. All prices shown here include tax.

### What the Hotels Don't Tell You About Rates

Hotels in many parts of the world – and Cancún and other Mexican resorts provide perfect examples – publish what are called **rack rates** or *tarifas públicas* which bear little resemblance to what most guests pay. These are comparable to full fares on the airlines: some suckers end up paying them, but most passengers travel on discounted fares. Generally speaking, the bigger and more lavish the hotel, the more likely it is to engage in this ruse, and the more likely it is that most guests are paying less than the rack rate.

You need only look at some of the tour packages sold in the US or Canada to see that, even with air fare included, prices may be well below the hotel's published rates. What happens here is that tour wholesalers who purchase hotel rooms in bulk are getting rates far below what the hotel quotes to the public. Most of this saving is passed on to customers.

On the other hand, most medium-priced and budget hotels lay it straight on the line: the price you see is the price you pay. There may be low-season discounts, and you may occasionally get a reduction for longer stays, but these are not hidden from the public, and in most cases everyone at the hotel is paying pretty close to the same rate.

Even at the more expensive hotels, it rarely hurts to ask for a promotional rate, or *tarifa promocional*. You're not likely to get a favorable response during peak holiday periods, but if you show up without reservations at a moment when things are a little slow and the hotel has a large inventory of unsold space, desk clerks may be advised by the sales manager to offer discounts to anyone who asks. Rates will still tend to be higher than what tour wholesalers are getting, however, and such discounts are far from a sure bet.

Many of the bigger or more exclusive resort hotels in Mexico belong to groups which have toll-free reservations lines for customers in the US and Canada. If you know what hotel you want to stay at, it may sometimes pay, first, to get a quote from a travel agent for a particular date, then to hear what rate the toll-free service is quoting and, finally, to call the hotel directly.

If the hotel itself offers the most attractive rate, you can book immediately. If you get a lower rate from the travel agent or the toll-free line, you can call back and you will have been billed for only one long-distance call. Remember to ask if any meals or extras are included.

Remember also that your local travel agent can issue you a prepaid voucher on the spot and offers the most security.

Most of the time, though, you can get the best hotel rates in resort towns as part of an air-and-hotel package, purchased through a travel agent. This is not to be confused with a guided tour where you are thrown together with a bunch of strangers and led around like sheep. You will be issued an air ticket, a hotel voucher and, often, vouchers for additional services such as transfers between the airport and the hotel. Then you will be on your own. If you want a hotel room for one person, you can expect to pay a hefty supplement. Most rates are based on double occupancy.

One drawback of these packages is their relative lack of flexibility. You will have to stay a minimum length of time (usually one week), and dates will be tied into the operating dates of charter flights or of regular flights on which the tour wholesaler has obtained a group fare. Often, though not always, you can get a package that will allow you, say, a two-week stay with a comfortable hotel room provided for the first week, leaving you free to wander as you please for the second week. As usual, a good travel agent (and not all travel agents are good) is a valuable ally.

## BEWARE THE TIME-SHARE PITCH!

Time-share salesmen (in Mexico they are usually male) are a scourge in some resort areas. You'll have no trouble finding them. Their representatives will be out luring you with assorted freebies. Once they have, you will be subjected to an insidious and unctuous.sales pitch.

What they are selling is the use of a hotel suite or condominium unit for a week or more each year for a period of several decades, typically 30 years. In some other cases, title may remain with the buyer in perpetuity but with access for only a short period each year.

Normally the salesmen work in teams. The first salesman will vaunt the delights of the resort development to which you have been enticed and try to convince you that this is where you really want to spend your vacations for decades to come. If you are not convinced, he will produce a glossy catalog showing an assortment of glamorous spots where you, as a future time-share owner, will have exchange rights.

When you ask about cost, he will scoot off and whisper something into the ear of another salesman, who will then introduce himself and start scribbling numbers onto a large notepad. He usually will start by telling you how many dollars it would cost to rent that same unit at standard rates, multiplying by the number of years and coming up with a figure well into five digits. He then will chop the figure roughly in half and tell you that for this relatively modest sum you can have your vacation lodgings in paradise paid for up front, and you won't have to worry about hotel bills for decades to come.

At this stage, some gullible customers succumb to the salesman's idiotic grin and sign on the dotted line, putting themselves on the hook for a sizable sum. If they hesitate, the salesman will show how small a portion of their total income this represents over the period in question, and he will offer various high-interest financing schemes. If he senses his prey are interested but he can't quite persuade them himself, the closer will be called in and the pressure will become even more intense.

Time-shares aren't always a bad deal. Some people are quite happy with what they get, especially if they have friends who stay nearby at the same time of year. But for every satisfied customer, there are probably several who wish they had never got involved. Time-share units can be resold, but the market often is not very liquid, and the seller may have to accept a steep loss.

Here are a few questions to ask yourself before signing any document or making any commitment:

You are being asked to fork out a large sum of money up front. This is excellent for the developer's cash flow, but not as good for your own. Do a calculation. If you put the same amount of money into an account or a safe investment providing an annual return of, say, five per cent, your money would more than quadruple in 30 years. Of course, if you take some of it out each year to spend on hotel bills or whatever else, it won't grow as quickly. But don't let any salesman have you believe you are getting something at half price.

Maintenance fees and other service charges can be quite staggering, representing a sizable portion of what you might pay to rent similar accommodations at standard rates. Take this into account when calculating the cost of a time-share unit. And remember that these fees can increase year by year, sometimes to truly unconscionable levels. Learn if there is any written protection against steep fee increases, and don't take a salesman's word for it.

The first unit you visit may bear little relation to what you actually get. You can expect to see a lavishly furnished apartment with a splendid ocean view or a choice site at the edge of a golf course. Other units may be less enticing, facing a parking lot or located several floors up in an elevator-less building. And you may have to arrange well in advance to get the use of your unit on the dates you choose. Sometimes, few dates are available at high season.

If the development is in an unfinished state, you may want to check on the developer's financial solidity. Even if the developer looks solid, it cannot always be assumed that all promised amenities will, in fact, materialize. And you will want to know about future development plans: a vacation in the middle of a construction site is not much fun. Also, bear in mind that the character of an area can change over the years.

For most people, buying a time-share unit represents a significant outlay of funds. You wouldn't buy the first car a salesman shows you without at least giving it a test drive. Stay a few nights to see if you really like it. Compare prices with what you can find elsewhere. And remember that you can always go back. Unless you are really confident of your judgment, you may want to talk it over with friends or advisers at home before buying. Also, poke around to see if anything is available on the secondary market. Somebody who has already bought and wants to sell may offer you a better deal.

## IS ALL-INCLUSIVE RIGHT FOR YOU?

Club Med pushed the concept decades ago by stressing the notion that if you're on vacation you shouldn't have to be fumbling for wallets or fiddling with signatures at every turn. What people in the travel industry call the all-inclusive formula has existed in various guises almost as long as hotels have been around, but Club Med put a new spin on it by broadening the range of activities included in its rates and by introducing gimmicks such as glass beads as a cash substitute to pay for bar drinks.

All-inclusive has caught on in a big way, and many resort hotels that formerly operated on a pay-as-you-go basis have jumped onto the bandwagon. The appeal is quite simple: for a set price, you get not only a hotel room but also copious meals and a broad selection of activities ranging from sailboard instruction to glittery evening shows. In many cases these rates also include bar drinks. The range of activities that are included can vary, but volleyball and aerobics are invariably free while golf and scuba diving normally cost extra unless you buy a special package in advance.

Both formulas all-inclusive and the more conventional itemized approach have their pros and cons. While the all-inclusive formula may look enticing, it is not for everyone, and there are a few things to consider before deciding if it is really for you.

### Advantages of the All-Inclusive Approach

• It is an effective way of controlling costs. There are not many surprises. You may pay a large sum up front, but with a little care any additional spending will be minimal. Try to set something aside, however, for telephone calls, in-room minibars, laundry, or for those few activities that aren't included in the price. Your spending can also rise if you wander outside the hotel (or to gift shops inside the hotel).
• Unless you are very abstemious in matters of food, drink and athletic pursuits, you will probably fork out less than you would with the pay-as-you-go formula. The all-inclusive approach enables hotels to achieve economies of scale which would be impossible if they weren't assured, for instance, of having captive markets for their restaurants. It also

enables them to cut down on the bureaucratic costs of keeping itemized accounts for each guest or of collecting cash at every turn. Mass-market tourism is a competitive business, and these savings tend to get passed on to consumers.

• Hassles are kept to a minimum. You can eat, drink and be merry without worrying about any additional strain on your wallet (but do take it easy at the buffet table to avoid strains on your health). You can also participate in various activities which might never have occurred to you or which you might have shunned because of money bothers. You will be in a safe, cocoon-like atmosphere where most of your needs are looked after with little effort on your part. You can also be left alone, if you choose. Although Club Med and some of its imitators push rather hard to get guests involved in group activities, this is not the case at most all-inclusive resorts.

**Disadvantages of the All-Inclusive Approach**

• You will have spent several hours on an airplane to reach an interesting and exotic place. What a pity if you found yourself isolated from your surroundings and largely confined to the grounds of your hotel. Although there may be no physical barrier to stop you from heading off on your own and sampling, say, a local restaurant, the fact that you have already paid for your meals does tend to act as a disincentive.

• When food is offered in large quantities, quality can suffer, especially with hotels under competitive cost pressures. Also, if you're going to be eating at the same place day in and day out, you are bound to see some repetition. No matter how lavish the spread, and no matter how creative the kitchen staff in trying to vary the food, after a few days you may start suffering flashbacks to your high school cafeteria. Most hotels try to offer variety by such devices as adopting different national or regional themes at each evening buffet or by offering the option of some *à la carte* meals at separate restaurants, but this is not the same as being able to choose any restaurant in town.

• Although all-inclusive hotels tend to offer good value for money, they are not cheaper for everyone. If you don't take advantage of the various activities and the "free" drinks, you may, in effect, be subsidizing your fellow guests. Also, the all-inclusive formula is offered mostly at upper-category hotels with lavish grounds and big, air-conditioned rooms. No matter how you slice it, this will probably end up costing more than staying at more modest establishments. In addition, the cocoon-like atmosphere may be fun for some people but not for others who have a greater sense of independence.

These are just a few points to take into account. Select the type of hotel that suits your preferences, but try to be aware of what you are getting into. Rates at all-inclusive hotels (as at other resort hotels of similar category) are often much lower if you book through a travel agent before leaving home, especially as part of a package including air fare. This, however, may require a minimum stay, which typically is seven nights. Some packages sold within Mexico offer three-night or four-night stays.

## TOURS FOR BIRD-WATCHERS

Several tour companies in Puerto Escondido offer excursions to see the bird life and the relatively unspoiled vegetation of the Manialtepec lagoon and the more distant Chacahua lagoon. Some of these tours are worthwhile even for non-birders. Prices average about $30 per person.

Especially recommended are the tours conducted by Michael Malone, a biologist formerly with the Canadian Wildlife Service. Reservations can be made through **Turismo Rodimar**, *Avenida Pérez Gasca 905, phone (958) 20734 or 20737*. Malone conducts both early-morning and sunset cruises of the Manialtepec lagoon several times a week from mid-December to early April. He has run these tours since 1985, and says there are more birds in the morning. Some people have trouble getting up early enough, though. Malone also offers tours to **Chacahua**, but he prefers Manialtepec. Although Chacahua is officially designated a national park, bird life is less abundant there, and several hours are wasted on the road.

On one recent excursion to **Manialtepec lagoon**, on a date chosen at random, participants were able to see the pied-billed grebe, least grebe, brown pelican, olivaceous cormorant, anhinga, yellow-crowned night heron, green-backed heron, tricolored heron, little blue heron, cattle egret, snowy egret, great blue heron, bare-throated tiger heron, northern jacana, spotted sandpiper, laughing gull, royal tern, Caspian tern, turkey vulture, black vulture, grey hawk, common black hawk, osprey, white-winged dove, orange-fronted parakeet, white-fronted parrot, ringed kingfisher, belted kingfisher, Kiskadee flycathcher, tropical kingbird, magpie jay and great-tailed grackle. These are just some of the more than 200 species which can be found at the lagoon.

Along with his expert commentary, Malone provides binoculars to all participants. The boat cruises slowly past mangrove forest and over lily-covered expanses of water (the water-lilies are denounced by naturalists as intruders and weeds), along the lagoon and up minor inlets. The boat goes slowly enough to avoid creating waves that could disturb some nests.

Even so, there is time to stop for a swim at a sandbar by the sea. Some fishermen can be seen at work in the lagoon, which is sealed from the sea by the sandbar during the dry season. Here and there are patches of destruction wrought by would-be cattle ranchers, who slash and burn the vegetation to clear land for pasturage or cultivation and discover too late how poor the soil is. Committees have been established to try to obtain official protection for this zone.

Other companies offering excursions to Manialtepec and Chacahua lagoons include **Agencia de Viajes Erickson**, *phone (958) 20126 or 20849*, and **Viajes y Excursiones García Rendón**, *phone (958) 20057*. Both have offices along Avenida Pérez Gasca.

It is especially important that tour operators show a suitable degree of ecological sensitivity. So-called ecotourism can become quite destructive otherwise.

Several other areas mentioned in this book offer interesting bird-watching possibilities. These include **Isla Contoy** (p. 122) and the **Sian Ka'an Nature Reserve** (pp. 162-163) on the Caribbean coast, and **Río Lagartos** (pp. 176-177) and **Celestún** (p. 200) on the Gulf coast of the Yucatán peninsula. These latter spots are richly endowed with flamingos, pelicans, and cormorants.

# 7♦ BASIC INFORMATION

## ELECTRICITY

Mexico uses the 60-cycle, 110-volt system, the same as in the US Appliances sold in North America can be used without voltage adaptors. Most wall outlets take only the old-style two-pronged plugs, however. If you're bringing anything with three-pronged plugs you may need a plug adaptor, which is easy to find at hardware stores and some supermarkets in Mexico. European appliances require voltage adaptors.

## EMBASSIES & CONSULATES IN MEXICO CITY

Following is a partial list of foreign embassies and consulates in Mexico City. They can help citizens of their countries who are in distress and provide visas and other documents for people who are traveling to their countries. Most also have commercial sections to help with trade and investment matters. Where there are consulates in places other than Mexico City, these are indicated in the corresponding Practical Information sections in later chapters of this book. All telephone numbers below have the city code 5.

The **United States Embassy in Mexico City** is housed in a prominent building at *Paseo de la Reforma 305. The main phone number is 211-0042.*

Other embassies include:

- **Australia**: *Jaime Balmes 11, 1st floor, Plaza Polanco, Tower B, phone 395-9988*
- **Austria**: *Campos Eliseos 304, Colonia Polanco, phone 540-3415*
- **Belgium**: *Musset 41, Colonia Polanco, phone 280-0758*
- **Belize**: *Thiers 152-B, Colonia Anzures, phone 203-5642*
- **Britain**: *Río Lerma 71, Colonia Cuauhtémoc, phone 207-2449*
- **Canada**: *Schiller 529, Colonia Polanco, phone 724-7900*
- **Costa Rica**: *Río Po 113, Colonia Cuauhtémoc, phone 525-7764*
- **Cuba**: *Presidente Masaryk 554, Colonia Polanco, phone 280-8039*
- **Denmark**: *Tres Picos 43, Colonia Chapultepec Morales, phone 255-3405*
- **El Salvador**:.*Paseo de las Palmas 1930, Lomas de Chapultepec, phone 596-3390*

- **Finland**: *Monte Pelvoux 111, 4th floor, Lomas de Chapultepec, phone 540-6036*
- **France**: *Alexandre Dumas 16, Colonia Polanco, phone 281-4338*
- **Germany**: *Lord Byron 737, Colonia Polanco, phone 280-5409*
- **Guatemala**: *Explanada 1025, Lomas de Chapultepec, phone 540-7520*
- **Honduras**: *Alfonso Reyes 220, Colonia Hipódromo Condesa, phone 515-6689*
- **Israel**: *Sierra Madre 215, Colonia Lomas de Barrilaco, phone 202-7939*
- **Italy**: *Paseo de las Palmas 1994, Lomas de Chapultepec, phone 596-3655*
- **Japan**: Paseo de la Reforma 395, phone 211-0028
- **Netherlands**: *Montes Urales Sur 635, 2nd floor, Lomas de Chapultepec, phone 202-8453*
- **New Zealand**: *Homero 229, 8th floor, Colonia Chapultepec Morales, phone 250-5999*
- **Nicaragua**: *Ahumada Villagran 36, Lomas Virreyes, phone 540-5625*
- **Norway**: *Avenida Virreyes 1460, Lomas de Chapultepec, phone 540-3486*
- **Panama**: *Campos Eliseos 111, Colonia Polanco, phone 250-4229*
- **Spain**: *Parque Vía Reforma 2105, Lomas de Chapultepec, phone 596-1833*
- **Sweden**: *Plaza Comermex, Ávila Camacho 1, 6th floor, phone 540-6582*
- **Switzerland**: *Hamburgo 66, 4th floor, Colonia Juárez, phone 533-0735*
- **US**: *Paseo de la Reforma 305, phone 211-0042*

Other countries with embassies or consular representatives in Mexico include: Albania, Algeria, Argentina, Bangladesh, Bolivia, Brazil, Bulgaria, Chile, China, Colombia, Côte d'Ivoire, Cyprus, Czech Republic, Dominican Republic, Ecuador, Egypt, Ethiopia, Greece, Haiti, Hungary, Iceland, India, Indonesia, Iran, Iraq, Ireland, Jamaica, Korea (South), Lebanon, Madagascar, Malaysia, Morocco, Pakistan, Paraguay, Peru, Philippines, Poland, Portugal, Rumania, Russia, Saudi Arabia, Senegal, Serbia, Slovakia, Surinam, Thailand, Tunisia, Turkey, Uruguay, Venezuela and Vietnam.

## HEALTH

Everyone gets sick in Mexico, or so we often hear. A more accurate assessment is that *some* people get sick in Mexico. The fact is, most visitors to Mexico do *not* get sick, and a commonsense approach improves your chances of staying healthy.

**Water** is the biggest problem. Tap water in most places has high bacterial levels and is not safe to drink without being boiled or filtered. Ice cubes made with unpurified water, or raw vegetables rinsed in unpurified water, will carry these same bacteria. The most common symptom of bacterial disorder is a mild case of diarrhea. This usually isn't serious but it's always annoying, and it's something you'll want to avoid. Different people have different levels of tolerance. If your tolerance is weak, or if you're not sure, it won't hurt to err on the side of caution. If you're staying and eating at a comfortable resort hotel, you probably don't have much to worry about. Purified drinking water will be readily available, ice cubes and salads will be prepared hygienically, and you'll generally be kept out of harm's way (though there are never any airtight guarantees).

But not everyone does all their eating and drinking at fancy hotels. If you're at a restaurant that doesn't cater heavily to foreigners or to well-off Mexicans, things you may choose to avoid include drinks that don't come bottled, drinks with ice cubes, raw seafood (cooked seafood is usually safe), salads, and fruit that may have been rinsed. As for street stalls, some items may be stored without refrigeration or kept warm at unsafe temperatures.

If you have lived or traveled much in tropical places, you may have developed a resistance to certain types of bacteria and can probably let your guard down a bit. Many foreigners (including the author of these lines) come to Mexico and eat at some very humble spots and still avoid getting sick. Everything in life carries a risk, but it never hurts to be aware of the potential hazards.

If you do get diarrhea, Pepto-Bismol is a simple and often effective remedy. Pharmacists can suggest other remedies as well. If it goes on more than a few days, consider seeking medical help.

If you come down with something more serious, ask your hotel to recommend a doctor. If you doubt their judgment, ask another hotel for a suggestion. In bigger cities and the more developed resort areas, it is usually possible to find English-speaking doctors.

In warm climates it is a good idea to drink plenty of water. Bottled water is readily available in Mexico. Heavy alcohol consumption can cause dehydration. When very thirsty, drink some water before hitting the beer. If you plan any serious drinking, take water both before and afterwards. Among other things this can lessen the discomfort from a hangover.

One of the bigger risks faced by many vacationers is sunburn, which is caused by ultraviolet rays. Many doctors also warn that heavy exposure to sunlight increases the risk of skin cancer later in life.

To lessen both these risks, use sunscreen and try to do most of your sunning in the early morning or late afternoon, avoiding the stronger mid-day rays, especially your first couple of days when your skin is most sensitive. Even in a shaded spot you may be bombarded by reflected rays from the sand or water. Remember also that cloud cover provides only partial protection against ultraviolet rays.

No vaccinations are required to visit Mexico unless you have traveled recently in a country where yellow fever is endemic. Malaria risk is quite remote in the towns covered by this guide but, if you are in jungle areas at night, insect repellent, socks, slacks, long sleeves and mosquito netting offer extra protection.

Most pharmacies in Mexico carry a broad range of medicines, and some drugs that are sold only by prescription in the US, including basic antibiotics, are available over the counter. If you are a regular user of prescription drugs, bring a good supply with you, and carry it in your hand baggage on the airplane. A small first-aid kit can also be useful.

## LANGUAGE

**Spanish** is the sole official language of Mexico and is spoken nearly everywhere. In certain areas Indian languages are also widely used, and in some villages only a minority of inhabitants speak Spanish. English is the most widely understood of foreign languages. In the principal resort areas, most hotel clerks and restaurant waiters speak at least some English, and bilingual menus are often available.

Once you step outside the cocoon of a tour group or resort hotel, you will almost certainly be thrust into situations where a knowledge of Spanish is useful. That doesn't mean you'll be totally lost if you don't know Spanish. It does mean you'll have to show patience, grace, good humor, and the odd bit of ingenuity. Sign language combined with a few key words is often useful, and having pen and paper at the ready can help in some situations. A tiny handful of North Americans still perpetuate the nineteenth-century notion that, if you speak loudly enough in English, anybody will understand you. Fortunately, most people are more sensible than that.

A pocket dictionary can help you read signs or menus, and it won't hurt to spend a couple of hours with a phrasebook trying to memorize a few lines. Key words you must learn include *por favor* (please), *gracias* (thank you), and *de nada* (you're welcome).

In a few places in this book, pronunciations of some difficult words or names are shown phonetically, with accented syllables shown in upper case. "A" is pronounced as in cat, "ay" rhymes with day, "ee" rhymes with see, "oo" rhymes with too, and "ow" rhymes with cow. The "ah" sound does not exist in Spanish; some people imagine, mistakenly, that it makes them sound erudite. The letter "j" (as well as "g" when followed by an "e" or "i") has a guttural sound not found in English; "kh" will be used here to show that sound.

## LAUNDRY

Same-day laundry service is available in most towns and cities in Mexico at reasonable cost. We are not talking here about laundromats, but full-service laundries that return your clothes neatly folded and wrapped in plastic. The charge goes according to weight, and usually there is a minimum. Count on spending $1 to $2 per kilo (roughly 50 cents to $1 per pound).

When clothes are brought in, they are placed on a scale, and the customer is given an invoice showing the amount to be paid when the clothes are picked up. Clothes brought in by mid-morning will usually be ready by late afternoon or early evening. Try to plan ahead and have your clothes washed in a town or city where you expect to spend at least two nights. And make sure you know the closing hours of the laundry.

The more expensive hotels provide laundry service for guests. This is the most convenient way to have clothes cleaned and also the most expensive, with a separate charge for each item.

The addresses of laundries in some towns are provided in this book. To get the address of a laundry close to where you are staying, you can ask a hotel clerk or housekeeper, but at some hotels they may try to steer you to the hotel's own, more expensive service. The Spanish word for laundry is *lavandaría*. A dry cleaner is a *tintorería*.

## MONEY & BANKING

Mexico introduced a new currency at the beginning of 1993. The **new peso** (*nuevo peso*) is equal to one thousand old pesos. Prices in Mexico now are shown by the letter "N," followed by the dollar sign (which is also the peso sign) followed by the amount. For example, N$4.50 means four pesos and fifty centavos.

In late 1994, after the latest devaluation, the new peso was worth about 21 US cents. Note that, although prices are shown here in dollars, many establishments will accept payment only in pesos. Some prices will no doubt be lower than those shown in this guide. Note that, although prices are shown here in dollars, many establishments accept payment only in pesos.

Banknotes come in denominations of 10, 20, 50, 100, 200 and 500 new pesos, while coins come in denominations of 5, 10, 20, and 50 centavos and 1, 2, 5, 10 and 20 new pesos. The very lowest and the very highest denominations of coins are seen only seldom. Coins of 1, 2, and 5 pesos are similar in appearance (silver-colored rims with brass-colored centers) and should be examined carefully to be sure amounts are correct. High-denomination coins are really worth something and should not be treated casually.

There are three series of banknotes in circulation, including a new series introduced at the end of 1994. The very old notes of 10,000, 20,000, 50,000 and 100,000 pesos are almost identical in appearance to the middle-issue notes and are used interchangeably. Simply ignore the last three zeros. Some old 2,000 and 5,000 peso notes were also circulating but most had given way to coins. Among old coins still circulating were those of 100 old pesos (equal to 10 new centavos), 500 old pesos (equal to 50 new centavos), and 1,000 old pesos (equal to one new peso). This can make for a confusing array of coins and notes, but the old denominations seemed set to disappear almost completely within a couple of years.

Old habits die hard, however, and some people still insist on giving prices in old pesos. If a taxi driver quotes you a fare of 10,000 pesos, you need not panic. What he really means is 10 new pesos, which is equal to $2.10 US.

### Changing Money

The US dollar is by far the easiest currency to exchange in Mexico, whether in cash or travelers' checks. In some resort areas, especially Cancún, it is widely accepted for direct payment of many goods and services.

There are a few things to watch for, however, when changing dollars to pesos. Exchange rates can vary enormously, and if you get a poor rate it means everything you pay for in pesos is costing you more than it should. Rates are normally more favorable in Mexico than in the US or other countries, but it is a good idea to obtain a small quantity of pesos before leaving home in case the exchange counters are closed when you arrive in Mexico. In the US, the best rates can normally be found in towns along the border or in places with big Mexican communities where pesos are heavily traded and competition is keen.

In Mexico, rates at airport exchange counters are often poor, though not always. At the airport in Mexico City, rates vary greatly from one counter to the next. Rates are poorest in the international arrivals area but tend to be better further along the concourse toward the domestic departures area. When changing large amounts of money it pays to shop around. The situation is worse at most other airports. Hotels tend to pay the poorest rates of all.

When shopping for the best rate, check both the buying and selling rates for dollars. If they are only 3 or 4 per cent apart, then you are getting an acceptable rate. We have seen spreads as high as 15 per cent, which means the exchange dealer is making a killing at the customers' expense. If you arrive first in Mexico City, it is probably a good idea to obtain plenty of pesos there before heading elsewhere in Mexico. Exchange rates are generally poorer in most parts of southern Mexico, although we found decent rates in Mérida and Acapulco. Oaxaca and Chiapas states were particularly dismal for currency exchange.

Banks sometimes offer better rates than *casas de cambio* (exchange dealers), but they tend to have longer lines, shorter hours and more complicated procedures. Most bank branches in Mexico are open only from 9 am to 1:30 pm, Monday to Friday only, and some branches exchange dollars only until 11 am. Some do not handle travelers' checks, and others do not deal in foreign exchange at all. You must be careful to go to the correct wicket (usually marked *cambios* or *dólares*), and if you are changing travelers' checks you may sometimes need authorization first from an assistant manager (*subgerente*).

*Casas de cambio* are open longer hours and are usually easier to deal with. Unless there is a sizable gap in exchange rates, they may be a better bet than banks. Among the banks, we found Bancomer offered the best rates in most towns, though not everywhere. Banks tend to pay similar rates for cash and travelers' checks. Some *casas de cambio* pay slightly less for travelers' checks than for cash and a few pay slightly more! Passports are usually required when changing travelers' checks.

Try to change unspent pesos back to dollars before leaving Mexico. Coins are usually impossible to change in other countries, and even notes may fetch poor rates.

Large amounts of money, whether in cash or other forms, should not be kept in trouser pockets or purses. Before leaving home, check at a department store or travel outfitter for a pouch that can be worn under the clothing. Although awkward at first, this keeps money and other valuables more secure.

If you carry travelers' checks, the issuer should provide you with instructions for reporting loss or theft. Make a careful note of any telephone numbers that are given, and keep the sales record separate from the checks themselves.

Canadians and Europeans bound for Mexico are strongly urged to take US dollars, in cash or travelers' checks or both. Although Canadian dollars and some European currencies can be exchanged in some places in Mexico, rates are usually disappointing. People from other parts of the world are already well accustomed to the idea of traveling with US dollars.

**Bancomer** and **Banamex** are the two biggest banks in Mexico and have the biggest branch networks. Both also have good networks of banking correspondents in other countries, as does the number-three bank, **Serfín**. With more liberal regulations coming into effect, several foreign banks were preparing to set up retail banking operations in Mexico, joining long-established Citibank.

### Credit Cards

**Visa** and **Mastercard** are widely accepted at hotels, shops, restaurants and airline counters throughout Mexico. **American Express** is also useful but a little less so, while **Diners Club** is recognized only at a smaller number of establishments. The **Discover** card is virtually unknown in Mexico; you *can* leave home without it.

## CREDIT CARD ABBREVIATIONS USED IN THIS BOOK

*In this book, we use the following credit card abbreviations:*

**VI** = *VISA*       **MC** = *MasterCard*

**AE** = *American Express*      **DC** = *Diners Club.*

Some hotels will ask you to sign a credit card voucher at the time of check-in with the amount of the transaction left blank. This is disconcerting for some visitors, but it is rarely abused. To protect yourself against unauthorized charges or loss of the voucher, jot down the number appearing in the upper right-hand corner; in extreme cases, you can then advise your credit card issuer not to accept this voucher.

If you have concerns about the exchange rate on your credit card transactions, check with your card issuer before leaving home and then compare the rate quoted for Mexican pesos with the interbank rate found in the financial pages of most newspapers. Both these rates change constantly, but if there is only a small gap between them on any given date, you know you will getting a good deal. On the other hand, if rate gap is broad in percentage terms, you may want to limit the use of your credit card in Mexico.

Credit cards and **automatic teller machine** (**ATM**) cards provide alternative means of obtaining pesos while in Mexico. To get a cash advance (*disposición en efectivo*) at a bank, first present your Visa or Mastercard plus your passport to an assistant manager for authorization and then go to a teller. Many banks in Mexico offer this service; look for the credit card logo on the door. Remember that you will probably have to pay interest starting the day you obtain the cash advance, but even so this will sometimes be a cheaper way to obtain pesos than exchanging dollars on the spot.

Most automatic teller machines in Mexico are linked to international networks such as Cirrus or Plus, but you cannot be certain your credit card or ATM card will work. If you think you may want to use this service, check with your bank before leaving home to find out about card acceptance, transaction fees and exchange rates. Visa International has announced plans to introduce prepaid cards which can be used for ATM withdrawals and has pledged to offer favorable exchange rates. This looks like a promising development and could eventually replace travelers' checks.

If you're short of cash and your credit card is near its limit, money from a friend or relative at home can reach you via a cash advance or ATM withdrawal. Funds deposited to a credit card account or to an ATM-linked savings or checking account are available right away. This is faster, cheaper and more reliable than wiring money. If you think you may want to use an American Express or Diners Club card to obtain cash in Mexico, check with one of their offices before leaving home.

## NEWSPAPERS, TELEVISION, & RADIO

Mexico City has an enormous profusion of Spanish-language daily newspapers, including two financial papers, plus one English-language daily, *The News*, which tends to toe the government line but provides a good roundup of Mexican and international news (with a heavy US emphasis) as well as stock tables and sports results. *The News* can be found in most bigger cities in Mexico, though sometimes not until afternoon. There is also a small English-language daily in Cancún containing brief news summaries, distributed free at many hotels.

Foreign newspapers are hard to find, though two or three US papers are sold in a few spots in Mexico City and Cancún. US magazines, on the other hand, are readily available at hotel gift shops and elsewhere. Regional newspapers in Mexico tend to be rather dismal. The papers in Mérida are better than most and circulate in much of the Yucatán. In some resort areas there are monthly or quarterly magazines in English with entertainment and restaurant listings; these are often placed in hotel rooms.

Televisions at some hotels can pick up only the Mexican channels, but many other hotels offer one or more American channels on cable, usually drawn from among **CNN**, **ESPN**, and a couple of the movie channels.

If you expect to be somewhere beyond the reach of cable television or of readable newspapers and you want to keep up with the news, your best bet is to take a small short-wave radio and tune in to **BBC World Service**, **Voice of America**, or some other international service. Reception is best at night. when it is often possible to pick up US commercial stations on the AM band. In Mexico City there is one English-language radio station, called **Radio VIP**, which broadcasts on the FM band.

## TAXES & TIPPING

Nearly everything you'll be paying for in Mexico is subject to a **value-added tax** which, at the time of writing, stands at 10 per cent. Most of the time you won't even notice this tax because it will already be included in the price. When you buy something at a shop or eat at a restaurant, the amount that appears on the price tag or the menu is the price you pay, and it includes the tax.

There are some exceptions to this. Lower- and medium-priced hotels nearly always include the tax in the rates they present to the public, but most upper-range hotels add it on top, which can sometimes make for an unpleasant surprise when you receive your bill. We find this practice deceitful, even if it is common in many countries. *All hotel prices we show in this book have the tax already added.*

The same applies in the field of transportation. Intercity bus fares always include the tax, but advertised airfares do not. Besides the 10 percent value-added tax, there is an **airport tax**. International air tickets purchased in Mexico, and tickets to or from border towns (including Chetumal and Tapachula), are taxed at a lower rate.

A **departure tax** applies on international flights ($11.50 at the time of writing). This is often added when you purchase your ticket but sometimes isn't. If you see the letters "XD" next to an amount in the fare calculation or tax boxes on your ticket, that means the tax has been paid. If not, set aside a sufficient amount in pesos or US dollars to cover this at the airport. Car rental rates sometimes include the tax but sometimes don't. Check before signing the contract.

### Tipping

Taxi drivers do not expect to be tipped, but if they help you with baggage or take you to a remote or hard-to-find spot, a tip will be highly appreciated. Porters should be tipped according to the volume of baggage and the distance they carry it, but usually no more than $2 unless your baggage is quite voluminous or something heavy has to be hauled up steps. Chambermaids are poorly paid and can put small tips to good use.

Waiters at bars and restaurants should get tips equal to about 10 per cent of the bill, but offer more if the bill is for a small amount, or if the service has been especially good, or if you are charging the tip to a credit card (in which case management may retain part of it). At all-inclusive resorts, tips are usually included in your room rate.

## TELEPHONE, FAX, & POST

*Teléfonos de México*, the monopoly telephone company, has been the darling of foreign shareholders and the despair of public telephone users. For years it seemed that the higher the share price rose the worse the service became on the ground. Long-distance competition was set to become reality at the end of 1996, and there were fond hopes that this might lead to lower rates and improved service.

Mexico has many types of public phones, and this can be confusing. Some operate with **credit cards** (but they accept only cards issued by Mexican banks). Others operate with **coins**, while a few older telephones are free but provide only local calls.

Still others operate with **prepaid plastic cards** (called *tarjetas Ladatel*) of the sort common in much of Europe. These phone cards are often hard to find, and there are two different types, one imprinted with a magnetic band and a newer type with a silicon wafer. Most card phones in Mexico

City take only the newer type, while phones elsewhere that take the older type are being phased out one city at a time. Some phones accept prepaid cards as well as credit cards. Are you confused by this? Most Mexicans are.

Adding to the annoyance, you often won't find the type of phone you need in a given place. Rest assured, however, that, at any given moment, a majority of public phones will be out of order. It is often possible to spot those that work by the lines of people waiting to use them.

To place a long-distance call either within Mexico or to another country, you have several options. If you want to pay on the spot, the simplest but most expensive choice is to call directly from your hotel room; this will entail a hefty surcharge. Another option is to visit a *caseta telefónica*, a small shop with several telephone booths and an operator who will place your call and collect your money when you are done; this entails a lower charge, though rates vary from one *caseta* to the next.

Coin phones accept coins of up to five new pesos. First enter the first few digits of your number and a small panel will display the cost of the first minute. Prepare a mixture of large and small coins. The phone will not make change, but it will return any unused coins when you hang up. Prepaid cards are the best bet if you expect to be making several calls because you're not having constantly to fuss with coins. Unused or partly used cards cannot be refunded, but they are appreciated as gifts or tips.

## INTERNATIONAL CALLS FROM MEXICO

*If you are calling collect or billing a call to an account at home using a telephone calling card number, enter 09 at a public phone to speak to an international operator. You won't always reach the operator on your first attempt. Hotels and casetas will also handle these calls for a fee.*

*An easy alternative is to place the call through the long-distance carrier you subscribe to at home. Here are toll-free numbers to call from any telephone in Mexico:*

**US residents:**

| | |
|---|---|
| *AT&T subscribers* | *95-800-462-4240* |
| *MCI subscribers* | *95-800-674-4000* |
| *Sprint subscribers* | *95-800-877-8000* |

**Canadian residents:** *95-800-010-1990*

*You will be connected with an operator in your home country and billed at the rate charged by your long-distance carrier, usually with a surcharge of $2 or more. Although this service is convenient, it normally costs more than paying with coins or a prepaid card. If you live outside North America or subscribe to another long-distance carrier, you can check with your phone company before leaving home to see if this service is available to you.*

Fax service is available at most *casetas* and post offices and at many stationery shops. Most hotels also provide fax service, but ask first about service charges.

**Calling Instructions**

Mexico's international calling code is 52, and each city in Mexico has a calling code of one, two or three digits. The biggest cities have seven-digit local numbers, many mid-sized cities have six-digit numbers, and smaller centers have five-digit numbers.

---

## INSTRUCTIONS FOR PLACING CALLS TO, FROM, OR WITHIN MEXICO

*Instructions for calls to Mexico:*

| | |
|---|---|
| *From inside Mexico:* | *91 + city code + local number* |
| *From the US or Canada:* | *011 + 52 + city code + local number* |
| *From other countries:* | *international access code + 52 + city code + local number* |

*Instructions for calls from Mexico:*

| | |
|---|---|
| *To elsewhere in Mexico:* | *91 + city code + local number* |
| *To the US or Canada:* | *95 + area code + local number* |
| *To other countries:* | *98 + country code + city code + local number* |

---

**Fax**

Many hotels provide fax service, both for sending and receiving. When sending fax messages, it is sometimes cheaper to go outside the hotel. Some stationery shops provide fax service, as do some post offices and telegraph offices. Rates may vary widely. At Mexico City airport, fax service is available at the Telecomm office near the domestic arrivals area.

**Post**

Unless you're on a very long holiday, postcards and letters should be sent soon after you arrive in Mexico to have a reasonable chance of reaching your loved ones before you return home. Service can be very slow. **Post offices** (marked *Correos* or *Servicio Postal Mexicano*) are found in central areas in all towns and many villages. The larger post offices are normally open 8 am to 6 pm on weekdays. Some also have Saturday or even Sunday hours. There is a post office at Mexico City airport near the domestic arrivals area.

## TIME & BUSINESS HOURS

All areas covered in this guide remain on **Central Standard Time** year-round. This is one hour earlier than Eastern Standard Time, two hours earlier than Eastern Daylight Time, and six hours earlier than Greenwich Mean Time. It is one hour later than Pacific Daylight Time and two hours later than Pacific Standard Time.

Office hours in southern Mexico run roughly from 9 am to 2 pm and then from 4 pm to 7 pm, with some variations. Some government offices are open continuously from 8 am to 3 pm and then close for the rest of the day. Banks open from 9 am to 1:30 pm, Monday to Friday only. Lunch hours are considerably later than in most other countries: two or three o'clock is the norm. Many shops close for lunch and reopen later in the afternoon, often staying open until well into the evening.

Punctuality in southern Mexico isn't always what might be desired. When going to a business meeting, bring reading material so that time spent waiting can be put to use.

## TROUBLE - AND HOW TO AVOID IT!

Crime rates in southeastern Mexico tend to be reasonably low, but use common sense. Do not flaunt expensive jewelry on the street. Don't take large amounts of money or valuable documents to the beach, and don't leave them in hotel rooms either. Most hotels provide safekeeping service.

When on the move keep your valuables in a spot where they cannot easily be snatched. Be cautious about wandering into crowds: this can be an invitation to pickpockets or bag-snatchers. At night avoid empty beaches and dark streets. And never forget that recreational drugs can land you in prison.

## WEIGHTS & MEASURES

The metric system is firmly established in Mexico. Accordingly, distances in this book will be shown in kilometers (abbreviated as km). One km is roughly equal to five-eighths of a mile, and one mile equals approximately 1.6 km. If you see "500m" on a road sign, that means 500 meters and not 500 miles! There are 1,000 meters in a kilometer. Speed limits on Mexican highways are shown in kilometers per hour (km/h).

Other measures you'll need to know include include the kilogram (kg), equal to 1,000 grams or 2.2 pounds. In common speech kilogram is often shortened to kilo. One pound equals 454 grams, or a little under half a kilo; an ounce is equal to about 28 grams. The liter (*litro* in Spanish) is used to measure liquids and is slightly bigger than one US quart. Temperatures in Mexico are given in degrees Centigrade (sometimes called Celsius). Zero on the Centigrade scale is the freezing point of water, 20 degrees is room temperature and 37 degrees (equal to 98.6 degrees Fahrenheit) is normal body temperature.

## METRIC CONVERSIONS

| Distance conversions | | Temperature conversions | |
|---|---|---|---|
| 100m | = 110 yards | 0ºC | = 32ºF |
| 500m | = 550 yards | 5ºC | = 41ºF |
| 1km | = 0.62 mile | 10ºC | = 50ºF |
| 2km | = 1.24 miles | 15ºC | = 59ºF |
| 5km | = 3.1 miles | 20ºC | = 68ºF |
| 10km | = 6.2 miles | 25ºC | = 77ºF |
| 15km | = 9.3 miles | 30ºC | = 86ºF |
| 20km | = 12.4 miles | 35ºC | = 95ºF |
| 30km | = 18.6 miles | 40ºC | = 104ºF |
| 50km | = 31 miles | 50ºC | = 122ºF |
| 100km | = 62 miles | 100ºC | = 212ºF |

# 8. FOOD & DRINK

It's easy to fall into stereotypes. Yes, some Mexican dishes are hot and spicy. Most, however, are not. At mealtime you will often see bottles or bowls of hot sauce on the table. You are free to use it or not, as you choose. At restaurants that cater heavily to foreigners, even some traditionally spicy dishes are toned down to suit delicate palates. In the afternoon many restaurants offer a *comida corrida*, a full-course meal at a set price that is often an excellent value. This is less common in some resort areas.

Restaurants in the big resort hotels tend to be more expensive than those outside, which in turn are often more expensive than restaurants away from tourist areas.

**Tortillas**, those soft, flat cornmeal disks, accompany all traditional Mexican meals, although now they are sometimes displaced by crusty dinner rolls or on rare occasions, horror of horrors, by sliced white bread. Most Mexican meals are also accompanied by **black beans** (*frijol*), prepared in dozens of different ways and as common as potatoes are in more northerly climes.

Main dishes are often preceded by a hearty soup, of which some examples are *sopa de verduras* (vegetable soup), loaded with freshly boiled vegetables; *sopa de ajos* (garlic soup), with a chicken base, plenty of garlic and often a raw egg; and *sopa de tortillas* (tortilla soup), a dark, rich broth laced with pieces of fried tortilla, avocado, soft white cheese and smoked chipotle pepper. A specialty of Guerrero state is *pozole*, really a meal unto itself, filled with mounds of large-grained corn and slices of pork or chicken, to which various condiments are added.

## MEAT & CHEESE DISHES

Everybody is familiar with *tacos*, which are bits of meat or other fillings usually seasoned with herbs and onions and wrapped in a tortilla. If the main filling is cheese, it becomes a *quesadilla*. *Tacos al pastor* are made from a tasty mystery meat cut in thin slices from a spit. *Enchiladas* are chicken tacos baked in a tangy tomato-based sauce and coated with melted cheese.

*Tortas* are the classic Mexican sandwiches consisting of a dinner roll stuffed with slices of meat or cheese topped with avocado, tomato, onion and hot pepper. *Torta cubana* contains slices of roast pork, ham and cheese  tasty, but not something you'll find in Cuba. These dishes and others like them are collectively labeled *antojitos* (pronounced an-to-KHEE-tos).

Now we come to the more serious dishes. A classic Mexican dish is chicken *mole* (pronounced MO-lay), with a dark, rich sauce whose primary ingredients are unsweetened chocolate and hot peppers. This is an acquired taste; many varieties are served in Oaxaca. Chicken (*pollo*, pronounced PO-yo) comes in countless other preparations. *Pechuga* is a breast of chicken. *Puerco* and *cerdo* both mean pork, while *carne* can refer either to beef or to meat in general. *Carne de res* refers specifically to beef.

American-style cuts of steak are found on many menus, while *carne tampiqueña* (usually less expensive) is a thin steak accompanied by savory side items. *Milanesa* means a thin, breaded piece of meat (usually beef, occasionally pork, only rarely veal). *Pok chuk* is a tasty Yucatán regional specialty consisting of marinated loin of pork grilled on charcoal. Other Yucatán specialties include *cochinita pibil* and *pollo pibil*, suckling pig or chicken, respectively, marinated in a sour orange sauce and baked in banana leaves.

## FISH & SEAFOOD

If you're anywhere near the coast, or even if you're not, you won't want to miss out on fish and seafood. Often the simplest preparations can be the most satisfying. In many of the humbler beach resorts you can find simple beachfront restaurants, often consisting of little more than a crude thatched shelter, offering extra-fresh fish and seafood dishes. Some of them (though by no means all) offer truly wonderful food.

*A la plancha* means it is grilled with almost nothing added, *al ajillo* or *al mojo de ajo* means garlic is added, *a la veracruzana* means tomato, onion and olives are added. Among preferred fishes are *huachinango* (pronounced wa-chee-NAN-go), or snapper, and *róbalo* (sea bass). *Mojarra*, which has no direct translation, is a smaller fish that is often served whole. *Ceviche* (pronounced say-BEE-chay) is a cold dish, popular as an appetizer or light meal, containing fish or seafood, marinated and served in its marinade with bits of tomato, onion and herbs.

Shrimp (*camarón*) is offered in an amazing variety of preparations both hot and cold. *A la diabla* means it comes with a peppery, tomato-based sauce. Squid (*calamar*) is an interesting option; when prepared *a la romana*, it is cut into thin rings and fried in egg batter. Octopus (*pulpo*) is found on many menus and is not as rubbery as you might expect; it is sometimes offered *en su tinta* (in its own ink). Crab (*cangrejo*) has a lovely, subtle taste but needs lots of work to get it out of its shell. Lobster (*langosta*) is usually very expensive in Mexico.

## VEGETARIAN POSSIBILITIES

Vegetarians sometimes have a difficult time in Mexico. Certain towns do have restaurants specializing in vegetarian dishes, and many ordinary restaurants offer suitable dishes, especially for those who eat cheese or eggs.

But the variety can be slim, and in a society whose poorer members struggle to get hold of meat even once a week, the very concept of vegetarianism can seem baffling. Nonetheless, strict vegans will be pleased to know that tortillas and beans together provide a complete protein, and many restaurants prepare dishes of boiled vegetables or elaborate fruit salads which can be recommended even for carnivores.

## BREAKFAST FARE

Breakfast fare at many restaurants centers around eggs, with the usual *huevos fritos* (fried eggs) and *huevos revueltos* (scrambled eggs) often outshone by *huevos rancheros* (fried eggs with a tomato-based sauce) and *huevos a la mexicana* (scrambled eggs with bits of tomato, onion and hot pepper. *Huevos motuleños*, originally from the Yucatán, are an everything-but-the-kitchen-sink concoction containing eggs, ham, tortilla, peas, fried banana and tomato sauce. Many restaurants offer enchiladas or chilaquiles: *chilaquiles*, often served at breakfast, contain layers of tortilla baked in a spicy tomato-based sauce along with bits of chicken or cheese. and fruit salads often provide a tempting option.

---

### MEAL TIMES

*Mexicans traditionally have a hearty breakfast (desayuno) early in the morning and then don't eat again until mid-afternoon, when they tuck into the comida, the main meal of the day. It rarely begins before two o'clock and usually not until three o'clock. It may be followed by a nap (siesta), after which the work day resumes until early evening. The evening meal is a light affair often consisting only of sweet rolls and coffee or tea.*

*This is the traditional meal pattern, but it's not iron-clad, and some Mexicans are choosing to eat more lightly in the afternoon and to have a full meal at night. Restaurants do a roaring evening trade, and not just with foreigners. Many towns have all-night restaurants.*

## WATER & JUICE

Water is the most basic and perhaps the healthiest of beverages. While tap water is generally to be shunned, **bottled water** is readily available in countless shops all over Mexico. In warm weather it's a good idea to keep some on hand. Freshly squeezed **orange juice** is offered at many restaurants, especially at breakfast, and is also available from street stalls (usually safe, but insist on a straw; a disposable cup is more hygienic than a glass).

Other fruit juices are offered fresh at specialized juice bars or in cans and bottles at shops and restaurants. *Licuados* are slices of fruit mixed in a blender with water or milk.

## SOFT DRINKS

As for soft drinks, the usual international brands are ubiquitous. Soda water is called *agua mineral* (mineral water) even if it doesn't come from a natural source. Lightly sweetened **apple soda**, variously called **Sidral** (the best), **Manzanita**, or **Extra Poma**, is a Mexican original. **Grapefruit soda** is also quite popular, especially in the Yucatán; **Squirt**, a leading brand, is less sugary than its US namesake.

## BEER & WINE

Mexico is known for its beers, ranging from the light and frothy **Corona** to the dark, rich **Negra Modelo**. Promotional efforts in recent years have been steered heavily to the more watery brews, which are cheaper to produce though less pleasing to the palate.

Visitors accustomed to light US-style beers can choose from among **Corona**, **Sol**, **Carta Blanca**, **Tecate** and **Superior**, while **Dos Equis Lager** and **Modelo Especial** are slightly richer in taste. **Victoria** and **Bohemia** are fuller-bodied brews. **Montejo**, a regional brand in the Yucatán, also has a richer taste. Finally, **Negra Modelo** (a national brand) and **León Negra** (in the Yucatán) will satisfy many lovers of dark beer.

Mexico is less well known for its wines, but some producers have made good strides. The varietal wines of **L.A. Cetto** are among the better choices. Imported wines tend to be expensive, although some Chilean and Spanish wines are moderately priced.

## THE HARD STUFF

**Tequila** is truly the signature drink of Mexico. Mexicans usually drink it straight up from shot glasses, sometimes followed by a chaser. The ritual involving the licking of salt and the sucking of lime is not often observed.

Most visitors prefer tequila in cocktails such as the Texan-invented margarita (mixed with lime juice and orange liqueur and served in a salt-rimmed glass) or the tequila sunrise (mixed with orange juice and truly a tourist drink).

## RUM & BRANDY

**Mezcal**, like tequila, is a cactus-based liquor, but it is made from a different type of cactus and usually contains a tiny worm at the bottom of the bottle (something about enhancing the flavor). Tequila is produced mostly in western Mexico, mezcal mostly in Oaxaca state. Rum and brandy are highly popular. A common rum-based cocktail is *piña colada*, made with pineapple juice and coconut milk. Mexican-made liquor is taxed very lightly and costs about the same in supermarkets as in duty-free stores. Imported liquor is pricier.

# 9. MEXICO CITY - A BRIEF GLANCE

**Mexico City** is one of the biggest, smoggiest, most baffling, most fascinating cities in the world. Nobody is quite sure how many people live in the metropolitan area, but recent estimates point to around 20 million. Mexico City is a place of amazing contrasts: 16th century churches stand guard an easy walk from audacious modern towers; fine museums, restaurants and cultural spectacles await those with the patience to get through car-choked streets; wealth and poverty mingle in as stark a fashion as you'll see anywhere. Just about anything you might desire can be found here but, alas, all sorts of things you wouldn't desire are also present.

The Mexican capital lies outside the geographic area covered by this book, but we have added this short chapter for the guidance of those who are passing briefly through the city en route to or from somewhere else, with information provided in very condensed form. We think many visitors will want to return some day and get to know it better.

## ARRIVALS & DEPARTURES
### By Air

Mexico City's international airport (airport code MEX) lies well within urban boundaries in the northeastern part of the city. In light traffic a taxi to the city center takes about 20 minutes; in heavy traffic it can take much longer. A new extension to the terminal building provides bright, spacious surroundings for international passengers. Unfortunately, passengers connecting between international and domestic flights may face a long walk.

No baggage carts are available outside the Customs area, but there are porters to help with baggage. They should be tipped according to the number and size of bags. For two large bags, $2 should be about right.

The older part of the building, with its marble floors and broad array of shops, is well laid out and offers a wide array range of facilities, including a post office and telecommunications office at the far end beyond the domestic arrivals area. Baggage storage is also available. Several currency exchange booths are scattered along the main concourse. Rates tend to be more favorable in the domestic departures area than in the international arrivals area.

When heading into the city, use only authorized taxis. Fares are set according to distance. To the central part of the city they are $10 to $12. Tickets sold in the baggage area and near the taxi marshaling points are accepted by drivers as full payment, although a small tip is always welcome. Avoid "independent" drivers. There have been too many accounts of passengers being subjected to overcharging and worse.

If you have only light baggage and have a clear idea where you're going, there's a subway (*metro*) station at the edge of the airport just 100 meters beyond the domestic arrivals area. Take the train marked Pantitlán and connect there for trains to the central part of the city. This is very economical, only 12 US cents at the time of writing, but it is not suitable for everyone. Large pieces of baggage are not allowed aboard the subway.

***From the US:*** Most big US airlines serve Mexico City, and Mexico's two biggest airlines, Aeroméxico and Mexicana, operate many nonstop flights to the US. Cities without direct service can be reached through connecting flights.

United Airlines serves Mexico City with nonstop flights from Los Angeles, San Francisco, Chicago, Washington and Miami. Delta flies from Los Angeles, Dallas-Fort Worth, Atlanta, Orlando and New York. Continental flies from Houston, Newark, San Diego, San Antonio and McAllen, Texas. American flies from Dallas-Forth Worth, Miami and Chicago. Northwest serves Mexico City from Detroit, America West from Phoenix, and USAir from Philadelphia and Tampa.

Aeroméxico's routes to Mexico City include New York, Miami, Houston, Dallas-Forth Worth, Los Angeles and Ontario, California. Mexicana flies from Newark, Miami, Chicago, Los Angeles and San José, California. LACSA of Costa Rica, Avianca of Colombia and Malaysia Airlines also serve the busy Los Angeles-Mexico City route, while Air France flies between Houston and Mexico City. Newcomer TAESA connects several US cities to Mexico City with intermediate stops.

***From Canada:*** Canadian Airlines flies from Toronto and Japan Airlines from Vancouver. A multitude of connections is available via the US.

***From Europe:*** Aeroméxico flies from Madrid, Paris, Frankfurt and Rome. The following European carriers serve Mexico City: Iberia from Madrid, Lufthansa from Frankfurt, KLM from Amsterdam, Air France from Paris, British Airways from London, and Aeroflot from Moscow. Many connections are available via the US.

*From Asia:* Japan Airlines flies from Tokyo to Mexico City via Vancouver. Malaysia Airlines flies from Kuala Lumpur via Taipei and Los Angeles. Many connections are available via Los Angeles or San Francisco.

*From Latin America:* Service from Central America is provided by United, Mexicana, KLM, Aviateca of Guatemala, TACA of El Salvador, LACSA of Costa Rica (with stops in El Salvador or Guatemala), and COPA of Panama (with stops in Nicaragua or Honduras). LACSA and COPA provide connections from points in South America and the Caribbean. Aerolineas Argentinas, LAN Chile, Ladeco (also of Chile), Varig of Brazil, AeroPerú, Avianca of Colombia, Avensa of Venezuela and Cubana all serve Mexico City. Mexicana flies from Bogotá, Havana and San Juan, Puerto Rico. Many connections from South America and the Caribbean are available via Miami.

*Within Mexico:* Aeroméxico and Mexicana (now under common ownership) both have comprehensive route networks covering most parts of Mexico. TAESA, an ambitious newcomer, offers a lower-cost alternative on several routes. Aerocalifornia connects Mexico City with points in western and northwestern Mexico, while Aviacsa serves the southeast. Aeromar operates propeller aircraft on some shorter routes from Mexico City.

## By Bus

Mexico City has four major bus terminals, one for each cardinal point of the compass. The two biggest terminals are the **northern terminal**, serving buses from most of northern and western Mexico, and the **eastern terminal**, serving the territory to the east of the capital. Both are huge, modernistic structures, bigger and busier than all but the world's biggest airport terminals. The **southern terminal** serves the states of Morelos and Guerrero (as well as some points on the Oaxaca coast), while the **western terminal** serves points in Mexico state and Michoacán.

The division of territory used to be quite rigid, but recently some more heavily traveled routes have been served from more than one terminal to save connecting passengers the trouble of getting from one terminal to another. Most of the areas covered in this guide are served from the eastern or southern terminals.

Each bus line has its own ticket counters, and on some routes there are several competing companies. This may entail some running around to compare departure times and fares. All seats are reserved on long-distance buses from Mexico City, and it is possible the departure you want may be sold out. It's first come, first served.

On routes to eastern Mexico, ADO is the biggest and most respected bus company. Cristóbal Colón is the main option to Chiapas state. To

Acapulco and other points in Guerrero state, as well as to Puerto Escondido, the best choice is Estrella Blanca, which also operates under other names including Cuauhtémoc and Flecha Roja. This company has greatly improved its quality of service, overtaking direct competitor Estrella de Oro.

*From the eastern terminal:* The eastern terminal, often called by the initials TAPO, is situated next to San Lázaro subway station on line number 1. UNO, the super-deluxe division of ADO with wide seats and refreshments on board, provides overnight services to Oaxaca ($36), Villahermosa ($54), Coatzacoalcos ($51) and Tuxtla Gutiérrez ($60). There are also daytime and overnight services to Veracruz ($20). ADO plus its GL division, which provides slightly enhanced service, have departures as follows:

Campeche (21 hours, $47-$56) six times daily; Cancún (27 hours, $57-$65) five times daily; Catemaco direct (8 hours, $23), twice daily; Chetumal (23 hours, $53-$59) five times daily; Mérida (24 hours, $49-$60) six times daily; Oaxaca (9 hours, $18-$23) hourly from 7 am to 8 pm and every 15 to 30 minutes until midnight; Palenque (16 hours, $39) twice daily; Playa del Carmen (28 hours, $58) three times daily; San Andrés Tuxtla (8 hours, $22-$24), eight times daily; Tlacotalpan direct (7 hours, $21) once daily; Tuxtla Gutiérrez (19 hours, $40-$44) twice daily; Tulum (29 hours, $63) once daily; Valladolid (26 hours, $63) once daily; Veracruz (6 hours, $16-$20) at least once an hour from 7 am to midnight; Villahermosa (14 hours, $33-$40) one to two hours apart from 7 am to 11 pm, every 30 minutes from 3 pm to 8 pm.

Cristóbal Colón and its deluxe divisions have departures as follows: Comitán (23 hours, $51-$58) twice daily; Huatulco (14 hours, $36) once daily; Oaxaca (9 hours, $20-$22) 7 times daily; San Cristóbal de las Casas (21 hours, $42-$52) three times daily; Tapachula (20 hours, $41-$50) nine times daily; Tuxtla Gutiérrez (19 hours. $40-$49) eight times daily.

Second-class services are provided by AU and Sur, including 17 daily to Oaxaca ($16), three to Catemaco ($20), three to San Andrés Tuxtla ($21), three to Villahermosa ($29) and many to Veracruz ($14).

*From the southern terminal:* The southern terminal (Central Camionera del Sur), is situated next to the Tasqueña subway station at the southern end of line number 2.

Estrella Blanca, operating under the names Flecha Roja, Cuauhtémoc, Turistar and Futura, offers frequent service to Acapulco. The longest gap without a departure is from 2 am to 5 am. Service at other times operates at least once an hour. Fares range from $22 to $37, depending on the level of comfort. Three daily departures labeled Turistar Ejecutivo have extra-wide seats and refreshments on board. Travel time is a little over four hours. To Taxco (2 hours, $7-$10), there are hourly departures from

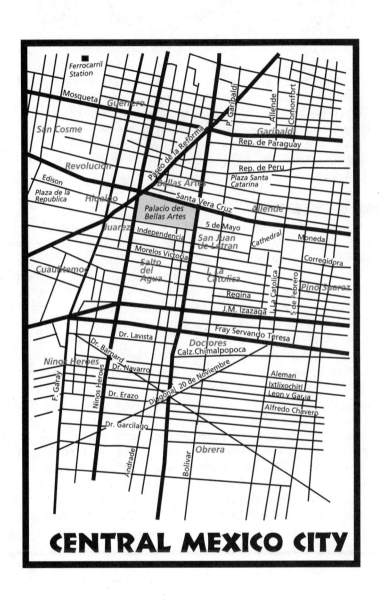

CENTRAL MEXICO CITY

7:30 am to 8:30 pm To Chilpancingo (3 hours, $13), there are buses every 40 to 60 minutes through most of the day. To Zihuatanejo (9 hours, $27-$36) there are four direct departures, most going overnight. There are two overnight departures to Puerto Escondido (11 hours, $37) and Huatulco (13 hours, $42).

Estrella de Oro has more than 20 daily departures to Acapulco (4 hours, $20-$39), three of them in Diamante class with extra-wide seats and attendants serving refreshments. This company also has five buses a day to Taxco, 12 to Chilpancingo and six to Zihuatanejo.

*From the western terminal:* The western terminal (Terminal de Poniente) is situated next to the Observatorio subway station at the western end of line number 1. Autobuses Zinacatepec has five daily second-class departures to Zihuatanejo on the slow but scenic route via Ciudad Altamirano, two of them going overnight.

## ORIENTATION

Mexico City is gigantic. The old part of the city, called the *centro histórico*, lies toward the eastern side of the city's central area. It is centered around the **Plaza de la Constitución**, known commonly as the *zócalo*, a vast open plaza facing the **Metropolitan Cathedral** on its north side and the **Palacio Nacional**, the seat of government, on its east side.

To its west the streets are lined with many handsome old buildings. The **Palacio de Bellas Artes**, a beautiful art deco theater, lies just a bit further along, facing Avenida Juárez. To its west is the **Alameda Central**, a lively urban park. Avenida Juárez meets at an odd angle with the **Paseo de la Reforma**, a broad tree-lined boulevard and the most important thoroughfare in the city, lined with office buildings and hotels and running through the very extensive **Chapultepec park**, which includes a zoo and several museums.

About midway along the Paseo de la Reforma and to its south lies the *zona rosa*, a smart area about five blocks square with many restaurants, boutiques and hotels. One corner of it is crossed by **Avenida Insurgentes**, which bisects the city from southwest to northeast. There are many *casas de cambio*, or currency dealers, along Reforma near the *zona rosa*. If you are changing a large sum of money, check the rates at several of them.

## GETTING AROUND TOWN

Short-term visitors may find taxis the most useful way of getting around. Most taxis in Mexico City are metered, and fares tend to be quite cheap. The exceptions are the taxis at the airport and some of the bus terminals, and the large sedans parked in front of major hotels, which have fixed rates. The very abundant metered taxis you can flag in the street are usually less expensive.

From the airport or the eastern bus terminal, buy a ticket near the taxi stand, valid for full payment to your destination. Tickets can also be purchased at the southern bus terminal, but drivers there try to get passengers to double up, and this can mean a long wait. Instead of buying a ticket, turn left when leaving the building and flag a taxi on the street.

The city has an extensive subway (*metro*) system, with nine lines in operation. Lines 1, 2, 3 and 8 pass through the central part of the city. Line 5 passes by the airport. Fares are very cheap (only 12 US cents at the time of writing), trains and platforms are clean, and service is frequent, but at certain hours the trains on some lines can get exceedingly crowded. Large items of baggage are not permitted aboard. Users should take precautions against pickpockets.

There are two types of buses in Mexico City, the big diesel buses and trolleybuses with set fares (exact change required), and minibuses, called *peseros*, with fares that vary according to distance (drivers provide change). It is not always easy to figure out the routes. Most parts of Mexico City are safe for pedestrians during daylight hours, but if you are going at night to an unfamiliar area or to the *centro histórico*, taxis are a better idea.

Renting a car is not really a good idea unless you are planning excursions outside the city. The density of traffic and the expense of parking will pose problems, and you would have to take an awful lot of taxis before you paid as much as you would to rent a car.

## WHERE TO STAY

There are more than 500 hotels in Mexico City, from the super-deluxe to the downright insalubrious. The list below is, quite obviously, far from comprehensive. Apart from the airport hotels, it emphasizes middle-priced hotels, with a few budget choices as well.

### Airport hotels

**HOTEL CONTINENTAL PLAZA AEROPUERTO**, *linked by pedestrian bridge from area B of the terminal building, phone (5) 785-0505, fax (5) 785-1034; 600 rooms, $198 single or double, VI - MC - AE - DC.*

Formerly the Fiesta Americana, this hotel is built around a huge nine-story atrium with hanging vines. Rooms are big and comfortable, many with views of the runways. Amenities include bars, restaurants, a pool, health club and business center.

**HOTEL RAMADA AEROPUERTO CIUDAD DE MÉXICO**, *Boulevard Aeropuerto 502, phone (5) 785-8522, fax (5) 762-9934; 312 rooms, $149 single or double, VI - MC - AE - DC.*

Formerly a Holiday Inn, this hotel is separated from the airport by a busy highway, but guests are served by a courtesy van. This long, low-slung building extends deep inside, away from the highway. Rooms are quiet, comfortable and nondescript. Some face the garden and pool, others face a parking area. Amenities include restaurants, bars, a night club, pool, gym and business center.

**HOTEL J R PLAZA AEROPUERTO**, *Boulevard Aeropuerto 390, phone (5) 785-5200, fax (5) 784-3221; 121 rooms, $99 single or double, VI - MC - AE.*

This hotel lies across the highway from the airport, but guests are served by a courtesy van. Rooms in this big orange building are elegantly furnished, with hardwood floors, area rugs and big bathtubs. Rooms facing the highway can be a little noisy, but aviation buffs get runway views from the upper floors. There are a restaurant and bar but no pool.

**HOTEL AEROPUERTO**, *Boulevard Aeropuerto 318, phone (5) 785-6928 or 785-5888, fax (5) 784-1329; 52 rooms, $42 single, $51 double, VI - MC.*

By far the least expensive hotel near the airport, this beige and white building lies across the highway, and guests have to make their own way. Leaving the airport by the domestic arrivals area and walking past the *metro* entrance, there is a pedestrian bridge over the highway, although it may not be advisable to use it at night. Receptionists hide behind a sheet of dark glass, but rooms are bright, modern and comfortable. Those facing the highway are noisier. Runways are visible from the upper floors. There is a restaurant and bar.

### Hotels near the zócalo

**HOTEL MAJESTIC**, *Madero 73, phone (5) 521-8600, fax (5) 6262; 85 rooms, $86 single or double, VI - MC - AE - DC.*

This Best Western affiliate has an impressive, tile-lined lobby. Many rooms are set around a seven-story atrium. Some have majestic views of the *zócalo*. Rooms are big, attractive and comfortably furnished.

**HOWARD JOHNSON GRAN HOTEL**, *16 de Septiembre 82, (5) 510-4040, fax (5) 512-2085; 125 rooms, $101 single or double, VI - MC - AE - DC.*

Formerly the Gran Hotel Ciudad de México, this hotel has an enormous four-story art deco atrium lobby with a stained glass roof. Rooms are spacious and decorated in shades of blue and beige, some with views of the *zócalo*, but some of the carpeting needs to be replaced.

**HOTEL RITZ**, *Madero 30, phone (5) 518-1340, fax (5) 518-3466; 140 rooms, $72 single or double, VI - MC - AE - DC.*

This Best Western affiliate has an air of faded elegance, with worn Persian carpets and murals in the lobby, which also serves as a dining room. Rooms are decorated in old-fashioned style.

**HOTEL JUÁREZ**, *1er Callejón 5 de Mayo 17, phone (5) 512-0568; 38 rooms, $16 single, $20 double, no cards.*

Set in a refurbished colonial building on a quiet side street, rooms are simply but pleasantly furnished. Many face the interior of the building.

**HOTEL WASHINGTON**, *5 de Mayo 54, phone (5) 512-3502 or 521-1143; 47 rooms, $18 single, $20-$23 double, VI - MC.*

Some rooms in this friendly spot are quite tiny, but they are simple and well arranged, with TV and phone.

**HOTEL BUENOS AIRES**, *Motolinia 21, phone (5) 528-2137; 63 rooms, $11-$13 single, $15-$24 double, no cards.*

Rooms are quiet and face a bright, three-story covered courtyard, but inside they are plain and rather dark.

**HOTEL CANADÁ**, *5 de Mayo 47, phone (5) 518-2106 or 518-2107, fax (5) 512-9310; 84 rooms, $27 single, $30 double, VI - MC.*

Rooms vary in size and are simple but reasonably comfortable. Some face an internal shaft.

**HOTEL PRINCIPAL**, *Bolívar 29, phone (5) 521-1333, fax (5) 522-8083; 94 rooms, $17 single, $18 double, VI - MC.*

Rooms are dark but spacious and moderately comfortable. The street side can be noisy. A few tiny rooms with shared bath go for $8. Some areas are a bit shabby.

**HOTEL GILLOW**, *Isabel La Católica 17, phone (5) 510-8585; 102 rooms, $30 single, $36 double, VI - MC - AE - DC.*

We mention this hotel only because it is recommended by some guidebooks and shouldn't be. The place is dirty and the service surly.

### Hotels near Paseo de la Reforma

**HOTEL MARÍA CRISTINA**, *Río Lerma 31, phone (5) 566-9688 or 566-9129, fax (5) 566-9195; 150 rooms, $50 single, $56 double, VI - MC.* Situated several blocks north of the *zona rosa*, rooms here are small but quiet and comfortable. What makes this hotel especially popular are its lawns and gardens and its very appealing public rooms, including a pleasant bar and restaurant.

**HOTEL STELLA MARIS**, *Sullivan 69, phone (5) 566-6088, fax (5) 592-5904; 114 rooms, $48 single, $56 double, VI - MC - AE - DC.*

Situated a few blocks north of the *zona rosa*, this hotel is popular with business travelers. Rooms are comfortably furnished, the lobby is bright and spacious, and service is friendly. It has a restaurant, bar, and pool.

**HOTEL DE CORTÉS**, *Hidalgo 85, phone (5) 518-2181, fax (5) 512-1863; 29 rooms, $93 single or double, VI - MC - AE - DC.*

This gorgeous, 18th century building, facing the Alameda park, has a big, partially covered courtyard. The courtyard restaurant is quite lovely, with musicians in the afternoon. Rooms are carpeted but otherwise have a colonial ambiance, with wall hanging, wooden furniture and warm colors.

**HOTEL CALINDA GENEVE**, *Londres 130, phone (5) 211-0071, fax (5) 208-7422; 320 rooms, $119 single or double, VI - MC - AE - DC.*

This *grande dame*, with its large, comfortable rooms, has recently been renovated. Set in a handsome building in the heart of the *zona rosa*, it has a very pleasant courtyard restaurant, now run by Sanborns.

**HOTEL IMPERIAL**, *Reforma 64 at Morelos, phone (5) 705-4911, fax (5) 703-3122; 60 rooms, $141 single or double, VI - MC - AE - DC.*

This old but fully renovated hotel has elegantly decorated rooms, refined service and a sparkling, triangular atrium lobby.

**HOTEL BAMER**, *Juárez 52, phone (5) 521-9060; fax (5) 510-1793; 111 rooms, $33-$51 single, $36-$54 double, VI - MC - AE - DC.*

Prices at this hotel, which faces the Alameda park, vary according to room size and represent good value. The small rooms are adequate, while the big rooms are huge. Furnishings are somewhat gaudy.

**HOTEL REGENTE**, *Paris 9, phone (5) 566-8933, fax (5) 592-5794; 138 rooms, $37 single, $40-$50 double, VI - MC - AE.*

The less expensive rooms are quite small, but all are freshly renovated and pleasantly furnished. A few face an interior shaft. This friendly spot is situated near the intersection of Paseo de la Reforma and Avenida Insurgentes.

**HOTEL PREMIER**, *Atenas 72, phone (5) 563-2700, fax (5) 703-3304; 88 rooms, $41 single, $45 double, VI - MC - AE - DC.*

Rooms are cheerful and brightly furnished.

**HOTEL PARADOR WASHINGTON**, *Dinamarca 42 at Londres, phone (5) 566-8648; 37 rooms, $24 single, $27 double, VI - MC - AE.*

This older hotel faces a small plaza and has a distinguished-looking curved exterior with red gables over the windows and an arched entranceway. The interior is somewhat shabbier, with big, sparsely furnished rooms. Still, this represents good value.

**HOTEL VASCO DE QUIROGA**, *Londres 15, phone (5) 546-2614, fax (5) 535-2257; 50 rooms, $51 single, $55 double, VI - MC - AE.*

This old-fashioned spot has a big salon with a lofty ceiling next to the lobby. Rooms are carpeted and decently if conservatively furnished, but they are showing their age.

**HOTEL MAYALAND**, *Antonio Caso 23, phone (5) 566-6066, fax (5) 535-1273; 100 rooms, $36 single, $39-$42 double, VI - MC.*

Rooms are small and reasonably furnished. Some face an interior shaft.

**HOTEL CAN CUN**, *Donato Guerra 24 at Reforma, phone (5) 566-6488, fax (5) 592-0397; 100 rooms, $35 single, $44 double, VI - MC - AE - DC.*

Small, bright rooms are garishly furnished but reasonably comfortable and quiet.

**HOTEL EL EJECUTIVO**, *Viena 8, (5) 566-6422, fax (5) 705-5476; 118 rooms, $41 single, $53 double, VI - MC - AE - DC.*

This 15-story building has big, modern rooms, somewhat starkly furnished.

## WHERE TO EAT

The restaurants in the **SANBORNS** department stores are popular with Mexico City residents and visitors alike. Some people turn up their noses at the thought, but these restaurants are comfortable, moderately priced and authentically Mexican, with broad menus and service from early morning to late evening. A house specialty is *enchiladas suizas*, sort of a Mexican version of cannelloni, with chicken wrapped in cornmeal tortillas and smothered in tomato sauce and melted cheese. There are Sanborns branches scattered around the city. The landmark **central branch**, with a huge, lofty dining room, *is situated in the Casa de los Azulejos (the house of tiles), on Avenida Madero east of the Palacio de Bellas Artes.* Another, *in the Hotel Calinda Geneve on Calle Londres in the zona rosa*, has a handsome, colonnaded dining room with plenty of natural light.

The old part of the city, or *centro histórico*, is replete with restaurants serving full-course Mexican meals at inexpensive prices, especially on weekday afternoons. There are also a few more elegant spots, including the century-old **LA ÓPERA**, *on Avenida 5 de Mayo one block east of the Palacio de Bellas Artes*, with plenty of dark wood paneling, frosted glass, a massive bar and a full menu. On Sunday afternoons they sometimes have trouble coping with the crowds. **CAFÉ TACUBA**, *one block north on Tacuba street*, is decorated in colored tiles and offers a wide selection of traditional Mexican dishes.

The Sunday buffet offered atop the **HOTEL MAJESTIC** *facing the zócalo* is noted for the choice of dishes and for the view over the central plaza. **EL NUEVO ACAPULCO**, *on Calle López just south of the Palacio de Bellas Artes*, has excellent fish and seafood dishes at moderate prices. It closes early. For something casual, **SALÓN FAMILIAR** *on Calle Bolívar near Madero* has a big choice of tacos, including superb *quesadillas*, and very good draft beer.

In the *zona rosa*, **DELMONICO'S** and **BELLINGHAUSEN**, *both on Calle Londres*, present Mexican and European dishes in a traditional ambiance, with prices toward the high side of moderate. **CAFÉ KONDITORI** *on Genova between Londres and Hamburgo* pushes a Danish theme. Both the sidewalk terrace and the indoor dining room are pleasant. The open-faced sandwiches make good snacks. The main courses are more Mexican.

**YUG**, *on Calle Varsovia just off Reforma*, offers superb vegetarian dishes at modest prices in pleasant surroundings. It closes at 9 pm. **LA LANTERNA**, *further west along Reforma around the corner from the immense Seguro Social building*, offers authentic Italian dishes at fairly high prices.

**LA GÓNDOLA**, *on Genova near Hamburgo*, is another spot for Italian food. **MESÓN DEL PERRO ANDALUZ**, *with a big terrace on pedestrian-only Copenhague street*, is a delightful spot for Spanish cuisine. **LES**

**MOUSTACHES**, *Rio Sena 88 on the other side of Reforma*, is a classic French restaurant and very expensive.

There are several Japanese restaurants in or near the *zona rosa*. The quality of Japanese cuisine in Mexico City is quite high. The same does not apply to Chinese cuisine.

## ENTERTAINMENT & NIGHTLIFE

The weekly magazine *Tiempo Libre*, sold for $1 at newsstands throughout Mexico City, contains comprehensive listings of movies, plays, concerts, art exhibitons and other cultural presentations. American **films** are usually shown with subtitles rather than dubbed, keeping them intelligible for English-speakers.

One spectacle not to be missed if you are in Mexico City on a Wednesday evening or a Sunday morning or evening is the **Ballet Folklórico**, a lively and colorful spectacle of traditional music and dance from different regions of Mexico. It is presented *at the Palacio de Bellas Artes*, giving you an opportunity to see the interior of this magnificent theater. Tickets should be purchased in advance at the theater.

**Bullfights** are held Sunday afternoons at 4 pm *at the Plaza México, toward the south of the city just off Avenida Insurgentes*. The main season runs from November to April. The bullring is easy to reach by taxi or bus, and there's no need to buy an expensive package from a tour agency.

Every evening, **mariachis** serenade passersby *at Plaza Garibaldi (served by metro line number 8), situated off Avenida Lázaro Cárdenas a few blocks north of the Palacio de Bellas Artes*. They charge by the song and it can be expensive, but it doesn't cost anything to listen to them serenading somebody else. There are many eating and drinking places around the plaza. The back streets around here are dangerous.

There are many **nightclubs** in and around the *zona rosa*, usually offering a mixture of singing, comedy and striptease. Most have cover charges. To save yourself a nasty shock, check drink prices before ordering too many.

## SHOPPING

Handicrafts from all over Mexico can be purchased in Mexico City. There is a small handicrafts market *in the zona rosa on Londres between Genova and Amberes*. A much bigger market, with a broader selection and lower prices, *can be found across from the ciudadela, or citadel, near the corner of Balderas and Ayuntamiento, near the Balderas metro station where lines 2 and 3 intersect*. The *zona rosa* has many fashionable shops with Mexican and imported goods. The **Sanborns department stores** have some interesting gift items as well as broad selections of magazines.

## SEEING THE SIGHTS

The **Plaza de la Constitución**, known more commonly as the *zócalo*, is a vast, open public square whose sides are each equal to 2 1/2 city blocks. Apart from an enormous flagpole in the center, it is almost totally bare and has become a favored spot for official ceremonies and public demonstrations. *Facing it on the north* is the immense **Catedral Metropolitana**, erected in stages beginning in the 16th century. It displays several architectural influences, and its 14 chapels are decorated in various styles. *Just to its right* is the churriguresque **Sagrario Metropolitano**, a small church with an intensely carved façade.

*Next door* is the recently unearthed ruins of the Aztecs' main temple, or **Templo Mayor**, which is actually a series of temples superimposed on one another at the heart of the ancient city of Tenochtitlán. There are a raised walkway around the site, a fountain containing a brass model of Tenochtitlán showing its many canals, and a museum, the **Museo del Templo Mayor**, displaying artifacts discovered at the site and presenting various exhibits related to Aztec life. *The site and the museum are open Tuesday to Sunday from 9 am to 5 pm. Admission is $5, but free on Sunday. There is a $3 fee for the use of still cameras and $8 for video cameras.*

**METROPOLITAN CATHEDRAL**

*The entire eastern side of the zócalo* is occupied by the **Palacio Nacional**, Mexico's seat of government, erected beginning in the late 17th century and built of a reddish volcano stone. It is worth visiting this building to see the dramatic murals by Mexican artist Diego Rivera in its interior courtyards and stairways. The church of **Santo Domingo**, *several blocks north near the corner of República de Venezuela and República de Brasil*, is among the most beautiful of the many churches in the old part of the city and a fine example of 18th century baroque architecture. The small plaza it faces is surrounded by several other fine colonial buildings.

*A few blocks west* is the wonderful art deco **Palacio de Bellas Artes**, with its flashy exterior and marble-clad foyer, which leads to the main theater as well as to a small museum, a café, and a bookshop. It is flanked by the lively and verdant **Alameda** park, whose pathways form a series of Union Jacks. *To the east, on Calle Tacuba*, is the **Museo Nacional de Arte**, with an excellent selection of Mexican painting and sculpture. *It is open Tuesday to Sunday from 10 am to 5:30 pm. Admission is $3, free on Sunday.*

If you have time to visit only one museum, make it the **Museo Nacional de Antropolgía**, *on the northern side of Chapultepec park*. This superb, spacious museum houses a vast trove of priceless treasures from archaeological sites in different parts of Mexico plus many displays devoted to ethnology. *It is open Tuesday to Saturday from 9 am to 7 pm, admission $5, and Sunday from 10 am to 6 pm, admission free. It is closed Monday. The museum is situated near the Auditorio station on line 7 of the metro and can also be reached by many buses going along Reforma.*

Also in Chapultepec park, and within easy walking distance of the anthropology museum, are two museums of contemporary art. The **Museo Rufino Tamayo** centers its collection around the Mexican and foreign works gathered and donated by the renowned Mexican painter for whom the museum is named. It is also the site of many temporary exhibitions. *The museum is open Tuesday to Sunday from 10 am to 6 pm Admission is $3, free on Sundays.*

The **Museo de Arte Moderno** concentrates on Mexican painting and sculpture. *Opening hours and admission are the same as the Museo Rufino Tamayo.*

## PRACTICAL INFORMATION
**Airlines**
• **Aerocalifornia**: *207-1392*
• **Aeromexico**: *228-9910*
• **Air France**: *627-6060*
• **American Airlines**: *203-9444*
• **America West**: *264-8222*
• **Aviacsa**: *566-1955*

- **Avianca**: *566-8550 or 566-8560*
- **British Airways**: *785-7669 or 785-8714*
- **Canadian Airlines**: *208-1883*
- **Continental**: *280-3434*
- **Delta**: *202-1608*
- **JAL**: *553-5515 or 535-5516*
- **KLM**: *202-4444*
- **Laca**: *208-4654 or 208-4691*
- **Lufthansa**: *202-8866*
- **Malaysia Airlines**: *511-8984*
- **Mexicana**: *325-0990*
- **Northwest**: *202-4444*
- **TAESA**: *227-0700 or 758-1487*
- **United**: *627-0222*
- **USAir**: *682-0580*

Several other airlines also serve Mexico City. Information on routes appears in the "Arrivals & Departures" section in the front of this chapter.

## Car Rentals

Most major car rental companies have counters in the international arrivals area of Mexico City airport. Car rental offices are also situated in several of the bigger hotels and in the *zona rosa*. For trips within Mexico City, however, taxis are a simpler and cheaper way of getting around.

## Currency Exchange

Most exchange dealers, or *casas de cambio*, offer rates comparable to those at the banks for both cash and travelers' checks with less waiting, less fuss, and longer hours. There are many *casas de cambio* along Pasco de la Reforma and on the *zona rosa*. If you are changing a large sum of money, it pays to compare rates at several of them. At the airport, *casas de cambio* in the domestic departures area tend to pay better rates than those in the international area.

## Embassies & Consulates

Listings are found in the *Basic Information* chapter, pp. 56-57.

## Newspapers, Magazines, & Books

Outdoor newsstands are dotted liberally around the city. Most carry a braod range of local newspapers, including *The News*, an English-language daily providing Mexican and international news. Among the numerous Spanish-language dailies are two financial papers, *El Financiero* and *El Economista*.

All branches of Sanborns department stores carry a broad range of American and other foreign magazines, and some branches also carry a small selection of American daily papers, also availalbe at newsstands at the airport. Along Avenida Madero in the old part of the city are two or three bookshops with good selections of books in English.

## Telephones

All phone numbers shown here have the city code 5.

## Tourist Information

Mexico City's main **tourism office** *is situated in the zona rosa at the corner of Amberes and Londres and is open from 9 am to 9 pm.* Staff can speak English, and a variety of brochures is offered. The national tourism office at Avenida Presidente Masaryk 172 in the Polanco district north of Chapultepec park is bureaucratic and unfriendly. Maps of the city and of different regions of the country can be purchased at many bookshops and at the Sanborns department stores.

# 10. THE MEXICAN CARIBBEAN

Names such as **Cancún** and **Cozumel** have become an almost automatic part of the world's tourism lexicon. People come not only for sea, sand, sun, and that other S-word but also, in the case of Cozumel, for extraordinary diving and snorkeling and, in the case of Cancún, for the glitter and glamour of one of the biggest and most modern resorts on earth. Both have wonderful beaches of fine white coral sand (far more extensive in Cancún), turquoise waters, comfortable accommodations, warm tropical climates, and excellent dining and shopping.

But there is more to Mexico's Caribbean coast than Cancún and Cozumel. **Isla Mujeres** and **Playa del Carmen** are each just a short hop from Cancún. Each offers lower-priced lodgings near the beach and a casual ambiance. The 131 km of coastline between Cancún and **Tulum**, particularly the portion south of Playa del Carmen, are being turned into a tourism corridor, with several new resort developments under way. Tulum is noted mostly as an archaeological site but has become a beach resort in its own right, with small hotels spreading along isolated stretches of coast. A short distance inland are the dramatic Mayan ruins of **Cobá**, set in a jungle park. In the very south is **Chetumal**, the gateway to Belize.

The Caribbean coast of Mexico forms the eastern fringe of the **Yucatán peninsula**. (The Yucatán faces the Gulf of Mexico to its north and west.) It is contained within the state of **Quintana Roo** (pronounced keen-TA-na ROH), which occupies the eastern third of the peninsula. The area away from the coast is unsuited to agriculture and is very sparsely populated.

Until a generation ago, even the coastal area was occupied mostly by small Mayan communities that lived from fishing, subsistence farming and the sale of copra, the dried kernels of coconuts. In the last three decades, Quintana Roo has been the fastest growing Mexican state in proportionate terms, and this is due almost entirely to tourism. Cozumel caught on in the 1960s, and Cancún followed a decade later, undergoing a huge boom in the 1980s. Now this boom is spreading. Chetumal is the capital of Quintana Roo, but Cancún is the biggest city in the state.

# CANCÚN

*Cancún lies near the northeastern tip of the Yucatán peninsula. It is linked by many flights and by a new four-lane highway from Mérida.*

**Cancún** has developed quickly into Mexico's busiest, glitziest, most dazzling beach resort, and it's not hard to see why. First there is the water, with its remarkable turquoise hue and its amazing clarity. Then there is the bright white crystalline sand, soft on the toes and never too hot to walk on. And then there are the easy airline connections to some of the most heavily populated and winter-weary parts of North America.

Add a string of five-star hotels, offer a slew of decent restaurants plus some high-tone shopping centers and high-decibel discotheques, and you've got the formula for what many people regard as close to paradise. Being near some of the world's finest diving and snorkeling and to millennium-old Mayan ruins simply puts the icing on the cake.

It was not always thus. A generation ago Cancún was merely a gleam in the eye of tourism authorities. Then it was just a long sandbar shaped like the numeral seven, with a quiet lagoon on one side and the azure Caribbean on the other. What would soon be Cancún was almost devoid of human presence, home only to a handful of fishermen and their families. Puerto Juárez, just to the north (and today a suburb of Cancún), was the only nearby town.

Cancún was born as the result of a government decision that drew solid support from the private sector. It was planned and nurtured by a government body called Fonatur (an acronym in Spanish for national tourism development fund) which put in the roads and other basic infrastructure and kept tight control over all aspects of planning. Private investors began pouring cash into hotel construction in the early 1970s, slowly at first but with increasing alacrity as occupancy rates stayed high.

With only a brief hiatus following the devastation wrought by Hurricane Gilbert in 1988, Cancún's story has been one of relentless growth, coupled with more than a touch of architectural gimmickry. Many hotels have been built in bold shapes, with the Mayan-inspired pyramid theme dominating. Viewed from the air, the hotel zone came to look like the pieces from a curious puzzle.

By 1994 Cancún could offer visitors an array of 19,000 hotel rooms, more than many big US cities can boast. Even so new hotels were still being built, but a slowdown was on the horizon as people both in government and among the citizenry began to voice concerns about overdevelopment, a recognition that some visitors and residents felt was overdue.

People did not actually live in Cancún until 1974, making it the youngest big city or the biggest young city in the western hemisphere. In the early 1990s its resident population passed the 300,000 mark, but virtually every adult came from elsewhere! The only people born locally were still children or adolescents.

Most residents live on what, for obvious reasons, is called the mainland. The hotel zone, or *zona hotelera* in Spanish, is situated on a narrow isthmus linked at either end by short bridges. Cancún is hardly the only spot in the world where tourists and residents are physically separated, but this *de facto* segregation is highly noticeable.

Cancún, we should hasten to add, is not for everybody. It is perhaps not the ideal place to go for quiet seclusion, although it remains possible to find tranquillity at some of the more exclusive hotels. It is not somewhere to look for cultural vitality: in the absence of a long established local population, there is little by way of local color or local artistry. And it is definitely not the place to escape the consumer culture of North America, which Cancún exhibits with an enthusiasm unmatched elsewhere in Mexico. Nor is it kind to pedestrians, at least in the very suburban-inspired hotel zone: buildings are spaced well apart, narrow sidewalks abut a busy high-speed roadway with few safe places to cross, and hotel architecture often seems meant to intimidate anybody with the temerity to approach by foot. Even downtown, some intersections seem designed more to menace pedestrians than to help them across.

But many among Cancún's annual average of two million visitors like it just as it is. For Americans it can feel like a home away from home, overlaid with a gentle glimmer of exoticism. US dollars circulate as commonly as pesos, staff at most tourist establishments speak at least some English, the plumbing works well, and the food isn't too spicy.

Something else we should hasten to add is that prices in Cancún tend to be well above average Mexican levels. As customers even at familiar-looking fast-food joints can attest, prices are often substantially higher than in the US. For some people this doesn't really matter because they come on prepaid package tours, often staying at hotels that include all meals and many activities in the price of the room, and out-of-pocket expenses after arrival can be held down with a little care. Others master money-saving techniques such as loading up at breakfast buffets and eating lightly the rest of the day.

Visitors who arrive with slim wallets and without prepaid hotel rooms may face a nasty shock unless they are willing to accept low-comfort accommodations far from the beach. If you're in this situation – if your international flight arrives in Cancún and you just want a reasonably economical place to spend a few peaceful days by the sea – you may do well to catch a ferry to Isla Mujeres or a bus to a resort town down the coast such as Playa del Carmen, where prices are lower and the atmosphere more relaxed. But if you decide to stay in Cancún and you end up in a hotel far from the beach, remember: all beaches in Mexico are public property and that, however much some of the big resort hotels may try to make it look as though the beach belongs to them, anyone is allowed there.

Not surprisingly, most visitors to Cancún do arrive on package tours, and usually they pay just a fraction of posted hotel rates. Competition-crazed North American and European tour wholesalers with their many thousands of eager customers can drive tougher bargains with hotel managements than individual travelers could hope to, although it never hurts to ask for a promotional rate outside the peak holiday periods. Air and hotel packages are offered from elsewhere in Mexico, but sometimes not very cheaply, with the result that a week's stay, air fare included, may cost less from Montreal than from Monterrey.

Even so, Cancún does draw Mexican tourists, accounting for about one-quarter of the total. South American traffic is growing, and Japanese are starting to follow. But people from the US still comprise by far the biggest group, accounting for more than 60 per cent of the visitor total, including Mexicans, and for around 80 per cent of all foreign visitors.

Here, then, is an introduction to the swank blend of natural splendor and human vision that is called Cancún. Part of the attraction, as we mentioned, is the variety of places to which easy excursions can be made. These will be outlined a little further along.

## ARRIVALS & DEPARTURES
### By Air
Cancún's international airport (airport code CUN) is the second busiest in Mexico; only Mexico City's is busier. Service on international and domestic routes is offered by many scheduled and charter carriers.

From the US, direct scheduled service is provided year-round by American Airlines, Mexicana and Iberia from Miami, Northwest Airlines from Tampa and Memphis, Aeroméxico and Lacsa from New Orleans, Continental and Aeroméxico from Houston, American from Dallas-Forth Worth and Raleigh-Durham, Mexicana from Chicago and Los Angeles, and Mexicana, Lacsa and Continental from New York.

Scheduled flights from most other US cities involve stops or connections. Some of the above-mentioned cities and many others are served by charter carriers. Charter flights tend to operate less frequently, with tickets normally sold only through travel agents, but fares tend to be low and the flights are usually direct.

From Canada, scheduled service to Cancún involves connections in the US or Mexico City, but there are many charter flights, some of them operating year-round. From Europe, some Aeroméxico flights to Mexico City from Madrid, Paris, Frankfurt, or Rome stop first in Cancún. Connections between Europe and Cancún are available on many airlines via the US, and there are charter flights from several European cities.

From Central America, Aviateca flies to Cancún from Guatemala City and Flores (near Tikal), and Lacsa provides service from Costa Rica and Honduras. Trans-Jamaica flies from Jamaica, Grand Cayman and Belize. Aerocaribe was preparing to serve Flores and Belize. From South America and Cuba, scheduled service is provided by Ladeco of Chile, and charter flights are available on several routes.

Within Mexico, frequent service from Mexico City to Cancún is offered by Mexicana and Aeroméxico, with less frequent service (but lower fares) on TAESA and SARO. Mexicana flies direct from Guadalajara and Aviacsa from Monterrey. Aviacsa and Aerocaribe (a Mexicana affiliate) both fly from Oaxaca, Tuxtla Gutiérrez, Villahermosa and Mérida. Aerocozumel (part of the same company as Aerocaribe) flies at two-hour intervals from Cozumel using propeller-driven aircraft. They also serve Chichén Itzá. Service from Chetumal, near the Belize border, is provided by TAESA or Bonanza.

International and domestic flights are served from separate but adjacent terminal buildings. The airport is situated about 20 km south of downtown Cancún. It is somewhat nearer the very spread-out hotel zone, but distances vary.

### From the Airport to Town & Back Again

**From the airport**, some tour groups are met by buses, and some individuals choose to rent cars. Otherwise, your main choice will be the collective taxis (mostly 8-passenger Chevrolet Suburbans) that run the length of the hotel zone and then downtown, making all requested stops. The fare is $6 per passenger. If you want one of these vehicles to yourself, the fare is $25. If you're going somewhere besides Cancún, fares can be exorbitant. There is no regular bus service to or from the airport.

An alternative for passengers without heavy baggage is to walk just beyond the airport perimeter, past the parking area and the guard box, and to flag a city taxi that is returning empty (they aren't allowed to pick up passengers on airport property). For two or more passengers, this will be cheaper and faster.

**From Cancún to the airport**, taxis are your main choice and should cost $10 to $12. A budget alternative from downtown Cancún is to take a bus bound for Playa del Carmen and ask the driver to drop you at the airport road ($1 fare). From there a taxi for the last 4 km should cost $3. Look for taxis heading to town from the airport.

**By Bus**

In some places in Mexico, bus terminals are monuments to civic pride, but not in Cancún. Mexico's glitziest city has one of its shabbiest bus terminals, consisting of three small structures in the center of downtown Cancún near the intersection of Tulum and Uxmal avenues. One of these structures, around the corner from the other two, serves some of the first-class bus lines and is air-conditioned. Despite the general raggedness and confused layout of the terminal, high-quality services are available on many routes. Each bus line has its own ticket sellers.

*Southbound:* For Playa del Carmen, three companies – Interplaya, Playa Express and Oriente – each offers frequent service. Travel time is about one hour, and the fare is $2. Interplaya has the most frequent service but the least comfortable buses. The first departure is at 4 am and the last at 10:30 pm. Through most of the day there are several buses per hour, and some of these continue south to Tulum, with highway drop-offs for intermediate points such as Xcaret, Puerto Aventuras, Akumal and Xel-Ha. Second-class buses to Chetumal, including those operated by Caribe and Pioneros, make these same stops. Buses calling on Playa del Carmen stop near the ferry pier for Cozumel.

For Chetumal (and connections to Belize), there are a variety of first-class and second-class services, including some premium services. Fares range from $11 to $14 and travel time averages about five hours. First-class buses run by Caribe or Oriente leave at average intervals of about two hours from 6:30 am to 7 pm, with overnight services in addition. Second-class services are provided by Caribe and Pioneros, with departures starting at 4 am and filling some of the gaps in the first-class schedules.

*Westbound:* Oriente provides second-class service to Valladolid ($3.50), Chichén Itzá ($4.50) and Mérida ($7) with departures hourly from 5 am to 7 pm and some overnight services as well. Most buses to Chichén Itzá do not go directly to the ruins but stop in the village of Pisté at a point about 15 minutes' walk (or three minutes' taxi ride) from the main entrance. Return trips leave hourly on the half-hour from a small terminal in Pisté. Travel time between Cancún and Chichén Itzá is about 2 1/2 hours each way.

Oriente offers regular first-class express service to Mérida ($10) with hourly departures from 6 am to 8 pm plus overnight runs, and premium first-class service ($11) nine times daily. Express buses take about 3 1/2 hours between Cancún and Mérida. Caribe has a total of 17 premium first-class services daily. ADO has seven daily first-class trips to Mérida via

Valladolid, five regular first-class nonstops to Mérida and five premium service nonstops ($11). UNO, the super-deluxe division of ADO, has two daily departures to Mérida for $18 with three-across seating rather than the usual four-across.

To Tizimín with connections to Rio Lagartos, Autobuses del Noreste has nine daily departures, including three first-class runs. To Campeche, ATS, Caribe and ADO between them a total of four departures. If none goes at a convenient hour, there are fast and easy connections in Mérida. ADO has two overnight trips to Villahermosa, with one continuing to Veracruz and the other to Mexico City ($65, about 21 hours).

**By Car**

A new four-lane toll highway runs west from Cancún to Valladolid, Chichén Itzá, and Mérida, with the trip time to Mérida now shortened to a little over three hours. Tolls are very high, however, with the result that most traffic continues to move over the old two-lane Highway 180, which is slower and more crowded.

Highway 307 runs south to Playa del Carmen, Tulum, and Chetumal (near the Belize border). This highway narrows to two lanes a short way south of Cancún, but there were plans to broaden it to four lanes as far south as Tulum. Playa del Carmen is the terminal for passenger ferries to Cozumel. Road travel from the US to Cancún takes several days.

**By Ferry**

Passenger ferries to and from Isla Mujeres operate from Puerto Juárez, just north of downtown Cancún. Two companies compete on this route. The slow boats take 45 minutes and cost $1.35. The fast boats take 20 minutes and cost $3. Between them they provide service from Puerto Juárez every half-hour from 8 am to 8:30 pm. From Isla Mujeres service begins at 5 am and the last departure is at 8 pm.

Car ferries operate from Punta Sam, a little further north. The fare is $9 per car plus $1.50 per passenger. Departures are every two to three hours. From Punta Sam the first ferry leaves at 7:15 am and the last one at 8:15 pm. From Isla Mujeres service runs from 6 am to 8:15 pm.

Passenger ferries for Cozumel leave from Playa del Carmen. The bus-ferry combination between Cancún and Cozumel works quite well. The bus terminal and the ferry pier in Playa del Carmen are just a couple of minutes' walk apart. See the Playa del Carmen section of this book for more details.

**By Rail**

There is no railway to Cancún.

## ORIENTATION

Two main areas constitute Cancún, the "**mainland**" which includes the downtown area, or *centro*, and the **hotel zone** (*zona hotelera*) which is shaped like the numeral seven with the Caribbean on one side and the saltwater **Nichupté lagoon** on the other. The hotel zone stretches 26 km and is connected to the mainland at either end by short bridges.

**Boulevard Kukulcán** is a four-lane divided roadway that runs the entire length of the hotel zone and, indeed, is the only road of any importance there. A long string of hotels lines Boulevard Kukulcán like beads on a necklace, nearly all of them on the Caribbean side, although from the upper floors of most hotels the lagoon is plainly visible. Shopping centers, restaurants, amusement areas, and a convention center also lie along Kukulcán, many of them on the lagoon side or along the median in places where it broadens.

**Punta Cancún** is the area near the upper right tip of the numeral seven; home to several big hotels, it lies just off Kukulcán. **Punta Nizuc**, a small protrusion toward the base, marks the southernmost area of development. Further south, the road narrows and curves westward, crossing the main north-south highway (Route 307) and continuing another 4 km to the airport. To reach the downtown area from the airport you can either take the highway straight north or, as passengers in collective taxis will discover, take a long loop through the hotel zone.

The urban zone of Cancún also falls under the aegis of Fonatur, the coordinating body in charge of Cancún's development. Although Fonatur has had only limited success in preventing the appearance of shantytowns along the western and northern fringes, it has been able to impose its master plan in the layout of the downtown area and the recognized residential areas, which are divided into numbered zones called *supermanzanas*, or superblocks. If you see, for instance, an address ending in SM28, this means it is situated in "supermanzana number 28." These numbers are shown on some maps, although few tourists are likely to wander into areas where they are a required part of the address.

The main avenues in downtown Cancún are named after ancient Mayan cities. Some of them meet at odd angles: planners wanted to get away from a rigid grid pattern. The most important is **Avenida Tulum**, bordered by banks, supermarkets, hotels, restaurants, shops and flea markets. Several of the neighboring side streets, some of them U-shaped, are also lined by restaurants and hotels, When tourists head downtown, this is usually where they go, especially the stretch of Avenida Tulum between **Avenida Cobá** and **Avenida Uxmal**. Avenida Cobá is the road leading to the hotel zone. One point of interest beyond the main tourist areas is the neighborhood market in Supermanzana 28, home to several

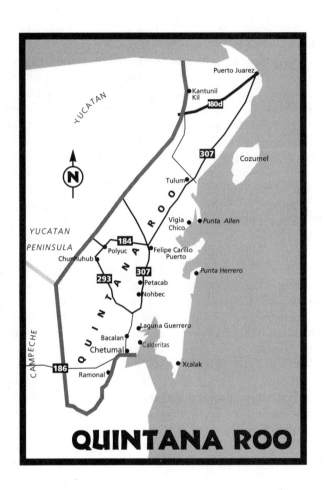

QUINTANA ROO

good restaurants. It is usually referred to as **Mercado 28** (pronounced mehr-CA-doh vayn-tee-O-cho). Taxi drivers all know it.

The airport lies about 20 km south of downtown Cancún. **Puerto Juárez** and the ferry terminal for **Isla Mujeres** lie 3 km north of downtown. The bus terminal is right downtown near the intersection of Avenidas Tulum and Uxmal.

## GETTING AROUND TOWN

Cancún is simple in its layout, but distances can be long, especially in the hotel zone. Though the downtown area is walkable, you'll need some form of motorized transportation to get between there and the hotel zone or, indeed, between most points in the hotel zone. Fortunately, nearly everything in the hotel zone is set along or near Boulevard Kukulcán.

### By Bicycle or Scooter

A **bicycle path** extends from the edge of downtown Cancún about 10 km into the hotel zone. Ask at your hotel about rentals. Cycling in the tropical heat is not everyone's cup of tea, but it will appeal to a select handful. **Motor scooters** are also available for rental.

### By Bus

There is a frequent and efficient **bus service** along Boulevard Kukulcán, continuing into the downtown area. These buses are used daily by thousands of visitors, including many who would never dream of taking a bus at home. Any bus marked *Hoteles* or *Zona Hotelera* will take you from Avenida Tulum downtown and along the hotel zone almost to the far end. Buses turn around just before the Westin Regina Hotel and just a few minutes' walk from the Club Med. All other big hotels lie directly along, or very near, this bus route. Although there are marked stops, buses can be flagged almost anywhere. Service is very frequent – every couple of minutes from early morning to mid-evening, and somewhat less frequent until midnight.

The fare is the equivalent of 75 US cents, high by Mexican standards, but the quality of service is also high, and drivers provide change.

### By Rental Car

**Rental cars** are a more conventional option, but rates are high. It may make sense to limit your use of rental cars to excursions out of town. Unless you get a cheap weekly rate, you would have to take an awful lot of taxis within Cancún before spending what you would to rent a car. Even for excursions out of town, buses often provide a suitable alternative. There are car rental counters at most of the big hotels, at the airport, and downtown.

**By Taxi**

**Taxis** also are abundant, but they are not metered. Fares are fixed and usually are reasonable for the distance traveled. A few drivers have been known to take advantage of visitors, but most are honest. Trips within the downtown area cost under $2. Between downtown and the hotel zone fares run mostly between $6 and $10, depending how far you are going. To the airport count on $10 to $12. Taxis that park in front of some hotels or by the bus terminal may charge somewhat higher fares. It is sometimes a better bet to flag a taxi in the street.

## WHERE TO STAY

At last count Cancún had 116 hotels, with a majority of rooms falling into the four-star or five-star category and some even higher. Most big hotels, and most of those in the upper categories, are situated in the hotel zone and lie directly along the beach. Most of the more modestly priced hotels are located in or near downtown Cancún, far from the beach though linked by frequent buses. There are a couple of luxury hotels downtown and a handful of less pricey hotels along one stretch of the hotel zone, but the general rule is: hotel zone expensive, downtown relatively cheap.

A great majority of foreign visitors stay in the hotel zone, and most arrive on tour packages which, through the magic of bulk buying by wholesalers, can give them five-star amenities at prices they can actually afford to pay. For an explanation of how this works, please see Chapter 6, *Planning Your Trip*, pp. 49-50. If you do arrive without prepaid reservations, you may be in for a shock, and if money is tight you may be happier going to Isla Mujeres or Playa del Carmen.

Without neglecting the upper categories, we are going to concentrate here on more moderately priced lodgings in Cancún. The reason is simple: if you stay somewhere with an official rating of four stars or higher, you have a pretty good idea beforehand of what to expect, whereas hotels rated three stars or lower are less predictable and guidance can be more useful. Most visitors staying at upper-category hotels tend to book ahead through travel agents, either directly or as part of a tour package, and a description of amenities and location is normally provided. The cheaper hotels usually don't even appear in a travel agent's database.

In virtually all the big hotels in Cancún's hotel zone, you can expect a vast lobby, often extending skyward to suit the architect's fancy; plenty of well-trained, bilingual staff; big, bright, comfortably furnished rooms with large beds, central air conditioning, cable TV and views of the ocean or lagoon (except on the bottom floors in a few hotels); at least one pool but usually several, including a big one by the beach; deck chairs and umbrellas at poolside and along the beach; lavishly landscaped grounds, with pools carefully integrated; several restaurants ranging from casual to formal; a lobby bar, a pool bar and usually at least one other bar; a tour desk, a car rental desk, and at least one gift shop; and salons for special events. Maybe we've forgotten something, but this should give you the general idea. Despite differences in architecture and decoration, there is much that is similar. This is a formula that has worked and which continues to attract millions of visitors.

Truly top-of-the-line hotels offer larger staffs and more attentive service, more artwork and fancier furniture in the bedrooms, plusher towels and extravagant toiletries in the bathrooms, and more refinement in restaurants and bars. Prices will reflect this and more, but the basic formula is still the same.

### Upper Range in the Hotel Zone: A Sampling

Hotels mentioned here are chosen either because they are typical of Cancún hotels as a whole or because they offer some special distinction in terms of architecture or luxury. A great many hotels are similar in price, amenities and general layout. Contrasting them can become an exercise similar to comparing the menus at different branches of McDonald's. Some hotels have gone to the all-inclusive formula, with room rates including all meals and most drinks and sporting activities. Rates shown here are rack rates, which are like full fare on the airlines: most people end up paying less. Discounted rates are often available.

Kilometers shown in addresses along **Boulevard Kukulcán** mark the distance from downtown Cancún. This helps set bearings in relation to shopping areas, restaurants, and so on. From kilometer 9 on down, the beach faces the **Bahía de Mujeres** and the ocean is very placid. At the higher numbers the waves are bigger but still tolerable for all but the most timid. At the very lowest numbers the beach may be somewhat rocky.

**HOTEL OASIS CANCÚN**, *Blvd. Kukulcán, km 15.7, phone (98) 850867 or 850752, fax (98) 850131, US reservations 800-446-2747; 960 rooms, $132 single or double garden view, $143 lagoon view, $149 ocean view, $154 ocean front; rates lower in the spring or autumn, higher in the peak winter season; all-inclusive packages available at extra cost; VI - MC - AE - DC.*

With 960 rooms, this hotel is the biggest in Cancún. Part of the Spanish-based Oasis group, it is distinguished by an intricate series of pools extending 500 meters (nearly one-third of a mile) and a beachfront 800 meters (half a mile) in length. Rooms, all freshly renovated, are spread over four pyramid-shaped buildings, with two separate lobbies.

**HOTEL MELIÁ CANCÚN**, *Blvd. Kukulcán, km 15, phone (98) 851160 or 851114, fax (98) 851085, US reservations 800-336-3542; 450 rooms; single or double, high season $272 (higher at Christmas), low season $187; suites available; VI - MC - AE - DC.*

Another architectural spectacle, the building is pyramid-shaped with bold geometric extrusions, including a glass and steel pyramid atop to the huge eight-story atrium with its hanging vines and tropical forest below. Rooms are elegantly furnished in shades of ivory, pink and pale blue.

**HOTEL FIESTA AMERICANA CONDESA**, *Blvd. Kukulcán, km 16.5, phone (98) 851000, fax (98) 851650, US reservations 800-223-6800; 502 rooms; singe or double, high / low season: ocean front $198 / $154; ocean view $187 / $143; partial ocean view $171 / $132; suites $215-$462 / $165-$413; VI - MC - AE - DC.*

This hotel stands out for its dramatic architecture, starting with its red marble-clad lobby roofed with enormous superimposed conical palapas. Rooms are housed in a trio of seven- and eight-story buildings forming a U shape around a vast atrium with hanging vines and a tropical forest and stream. Building exteriors form an intricate pattern of recesses and promontories painted yellow, beige and ochre. Rooms are well appointed in hues of dark blue and turquoise, but are not quite as special as the exterior. Near the beach are a series of connecting pools and palapa bars.

**HOTEL FIESTA AMERICANA CANCÚN**, *Blvd. Kukulcán, km 9.5, phone (98) 831400, fax (98) 832502, US reservations 800-343-7821; 281 rooms; single or double, high / low season: standard $248 / $149; deluxe $264 / $165; VI - MC - AE - DC.*

Part of the same group (there are three Fiesta Americana hotels in Cancún) but separately owned and managed, this building also has a very pleasing appearance with multiple nooks and gables, looking almost like part of a medieval European town rising five stories in shades of yellow, beige, and ochre. The rooms are pleasant but rather ordinary, which makes them a little disappointing in comparison. The hotel is situated near the Plaza Caracol shopping center and the convention center.

**HOLIDAY INN CROWNE PLAZA**, *Blvd. Kukulcán, km 18.5, phone (98) 851022, fax (98) 850313, US reservations 800-465-4329; 363 rooms; high season $303 single, $430 double (higher at Christmas); low season $204 single, $286 double; VI - MC - AE - DC.*

This is one of a growing number of hotels that has adopted the all-inclusive formula. Prices include all meals, snacks and bar drinks (except from the in-room minibar), a variety of sporting activities, evening shows, tips and taxes. Food, offered buffet-style throughout the day, is above average for this type of operation; full table service is available at two additional restaurants in the evening. All rooms have ocean views, with balconies. This eight-story building features a high curving atrium with a lush tropical garden below. There are four pools and a wide variety of sporting amenities.

**HOTEL ROYAL SOLARIS CARIBE**, *Blvd. Kukulcán, km 20.5, phone (98) 850100, fax (98) 850354, US reservations 800-368-9779, Houston 713-*

*266-9797; 480 rooms; high season $190 single, $320 double; low season $150 single, $260 double; children $60; VI - MC - AE - DC.*

This is another all-inclusive hotel and combines what previously were two hotels. Management has attempted to give separate characters to the two buildings, one a conventional slab-like structure where many activities are centered, and the other "Mediterranean-style" with a terraced exterior, which is meant to be quieter. The two are similar in decor. On offer are the usual sporting and relaxation amenities such as sunfish sailing, pedalboats, kayaks, snorkeling, windsurfing, scuba demonstrations, bicycles, jacuzzis, a gymnasium, aerobics, tennis, and indoor games. There are a total of seven restaurants and five bars. About 60 per cent of rooms have ocean views.

**THE RITZ CARLTON,** *Blvd. Kukulcán, km 14, phone (98) 850508, fax (98) 851015, US reservations 800-241-3333, US fax 305-446-9082; 369 rooms; single or double, high / low season, standard $303 / $259, ocean view $330 / $286, ocean front $358 / $314, suites $523 and up / $495 and up; all rates higher at Christmas; VI - MC - AE - DC.*

Opened in 1993, one of Cancún's newest hotels is also one of its most traditional in terms of architecture. With its understated pink-beige exterior, it looks like a grand old European seaside hotel but on a larger scale. From the chandeliers and well-stuffed armchairs in the lobby to the spacious corridors with their acres of Persian carpet and old-fashioned oil paintings, this hotel breathes Victorian elegance. Rooms are big, with blue and pink decor, fine wooden furniture, comfortable armchairs, balconies, and marble-clad bathrooms. Suites are enormous, and very Victorian. The dining rooms and bar look like they might have been lifted from one of the better English hotels.

**LA CASA TURQUESA,** *Blvd. Kukulcán, km 13.5, phone (98) 852924 or 852925, fax (98) 852922, US reservations 800-634-4644; 31 rooms; single or double, high / low season: poolside $308 / $275, ocean view $385 / $325, superior suite $550 (year-round), royal suite $2,420 (year-round); VI - MC - AE - DC.*

This small and very exclusive hotel is about as close as you'll get in Cancún to a discreet hideaway. Rooms are big and exquisitely furnished in hues of pink, blue and grey, with marble floors. Each has its own jacuzzi on the balcony. A bright, comfortable lobby faces the sea; its features include a curving stairway and stone carvings with Maya motifs. The hotel has a restaurant, 24-hour room service, CD and video libraries, and concierge service to handle tours, sporting activities and special requests.

**HOTEL VILLAS TACUL,** *Blvd. Kukulcán, km 5.5, phone (98) 830000 or 830080, fax (98) 830349, US reservations 800-842-0193; 76 rooms in 23 villas; high season / low season rates: garden view room $143 / $110; ocean view* *room $187 / $149; two-bedroom villa $396 / $275; three-bedroom villa $594 / $429; VI - MC - AE - DC.*

One-story and two-story villas, some consisting of individual units, some with several rooms, are scattered over four hectares (ten acres) of sprawling, landscaped grounds. This is rather a change from the high-rise hotels that typify Cancún. Some units have kitchens. There are a pool and a broad stretch of beachfront. Rates are higher at Christmas.

### Moderate Range in the Hotel Zone

Hotels that we call moderate here would seem high-priced almost anywhere else in Mexico, with the notable exception of the youth hostel mentioned below. These hotels are situated in the portion of the hotel zone nearest to downtown Cancún. Beaches here are more than adequate but not quite as broad or sandy as some of the beaches deeper in the hotel zone.

**HOTEL CAROUSEL CANCÚN**, *Blvd. Kukulcán, km 4.5, phone (98)830778 or 830513, fax (98) 832312; 150 rooms, high season $127 single or double, low season $83, VI - MC - AE - DC.*

This four-story hotel has a pleasant garden and pool area, as well as tennis courts and two restaurants. Rooms are air conditioned with fairly ordinary decor. All have sea views.

**HOTEL PLAYA BLANCA**, *Blvd. Kukulcán , km 3.5, phone (98) 830344, US and Canada reservations (800) 528-1213; 161 rooms, high season $121 single or double, low season $88, VI - MC - AE.*

Promotional rates are often available at this hotel, situated near a marina. Besides air conditioning, TV and phone, all rooms have minibar, comfortable armchairs and balconies. About one-third have sea views.

**HOTEL AQUAMARINA BEACH**, *Blvd. Kukulcán, km 4.5, phone (98) 831344 or 831425, fax (98) 831751; 200 rooms, high season $105 single or double, low season $94, VI - MC - AE.*

Rooms are air conditioned and fairly ordinary, about three-quarters with sea views and many with kitchenettes. The grounds include a pool, a mini-golf course and two restaurants.

**HOTEL CALINDA BEACH**, *Blvd. Kukulcán, km 4.5, phone (98) 831600, fax (98) 831857; 470 rooms, high season $121 single or double, low season $88, VI - MC - AE - DC.*

This hotel caters heavily to package tours and, at certain times of year, has large numbers of young people among its guests, generating a party atmosphere. With standard-issue slab-style architecture and standard amenities, it projects a certain anonymity.

**VILLA JUVENIL CANCÚN**, *Blvd. Kukulcán, km 3.2, phone (98) 831337; 350 beds, $9 per person; 150 camping spaces, $5 per person; no cards.*

There is no age limit at this government-run youth hostel, which is open to all. Members of the International Youth Hostels Federation get a 10% discount. Lodging is provided in eight-bed dormitories, segregated by sex and spread over a series of three-story buildings, which appear not to be well maintained. They face a somewhat unappealing beach, although better beaches are only a few minutes' walk from here.

### Downtown Hotels

Most tourists come to Cancún for the beach, and if you're staying downtown, you're not anywhere near the beach. Virtually all moderately and budget-priced lodgings are in the *centro*, however. Take heart, because buses run every couple of minutes to the hotel zone with its fine beaches, and all beaches in Mexico are public property. You can beachcomb by day even if you have to return downtown at night. You can go to **Playa Chac-Mol**, a public beach 10 km inside the hotel zone, or you can plant yourself in front of one of the big resort hotels. They may pretend to own the beach, but they don't.

Downtown hotels are concentrated in two main zones, one along **Avenida Tulum** and some of the neighboring streets, including **Avenida Uxmal**, and the other a little further north in the area around **Avenida Yaxchilán**, which is not quite as touristy but which does also have a selection of restaurants.

**HOTEL ANTILLANO**, *Tulum at Claveles, phone (98) 841532 or 841132, fax (98) 841878; 48 rooms; high season $39 single, $45 double; low season $33 single, $39 double; VI - MC - AE - DC.*

This friendly downtown hotel is one of the best values in Cancún. A few rooms are a little dark and others get some street noise, but all are pleasantly furnished, spotlessly clean and cooled by central air conditioning, a luxury in a moderately priced hotel. Rooms also have TV and phones. There is a small pool in back.

**HOTEL PLAZA CARRILLO'S**, *Claveles 35, phone (98) 841227 or 844833, fax (98) 842371; 43 rooms, $39 single or double, VI - MC - AE - DC.*

Rooms in this friendly and central spot are small but pleasantly furnished, with air conditioning, TV and phone. There are open-air lounges on each floor and a small pool. The hotel faces a quiet side street.

**HOLIDAY INN CENTRO**, *Nader 1, phone (98) 874455, fax (98) 847954; 248 rooms, high season $116 single or double, low season $93, VI - MC - AE - DC.*

Situated on a quiet side street at the edge of the city center, this four-story hotel faces inward toward a pool courtyard and is the most comfortable in the downtown zone. It has a pale orange exterior, a lobby with a big domed atrium, and rooms decorated in pastel shades with white tile floors, air conditioning, TV, phones and, in most cases, balconies. Amenities include a pool, tennis courts and gym.

**HOTEL NOVOTEL,** *Tulum 75, phone (98) 842999, fax (98) 843162; 41 rooms; high season $39 single, $48 double; low season $32 single, $40 double; VI - MC - AE.*

This quiet but central two-story hotel has an enclosed courtyard and big, bright air conditioned rooms, with stucco walls painted beige and pale blue.

**HOTEL PARADOR,** *Tulum 26, phone (98) 841922 or 841310, fax (98) 849712; 66 rooms, $36 single or double, VI - MC.*

This three-story hotel has a long, narrow garden courtyard with a pool and small, simple rooms, which are fairly quiet despite its location near a busy intersection. Rooms have air conditioning, TV and phone..

**HOTEL CANTO,** *Yaxchilán 31 near Tanchacte, phone (98) 841267, fax (98) 849262; 23 rooms, $21 single, $24 double, VI - MC.*

This friendly spot is a bargain. Large, bright, simple rooms have air conditioning, TV and phones.

**HOTEL REAL DEL CARIBE,** *Uxmal at Nader, phone (98) 842028, fax (98) 849857; 23 rooms, high season $50 single or double, low season $42, no cards.*

Set on bright, spacious grounds with a garden and pool, this hotel offers quiet rooms with kitchenette, air conditioning, TV and phone but rather ordinary furnishings. Painted tiles and Mayan-style glyphs add a little atmosphere.

**HOTEL PLAZA CARIBE,** *Uxmal at Tulum, phone (98) 841377, fax (98) 846352; 140 rooms, high season $80 single or double, low season $56, VI - MC - AE - DC.*

Situated directly across from the bus terminal, this Best Western affiliate looks a bit tacky from the outside but feels like an oasis inside, with a pool, garden and palapa-shaded restaurant. Rooms each have two double beds, air conditioning, TV, phone, white tile floors and white stucco walls, but they are quite small and many have uninspiring views.

**HOTEL MARGARITA,** *Yaxchilán 22, phone (98) 849166, fax (98) 841324; 100 rooms, high season $63 single or double, low season $56, VI - MC - AE - DC.*

Quiet, decently furnished, marble-floored rooms have air conditioning, TV, phones, refrigerators and work tables. The pool area is pleasant.

**HOTEL KOMVASER,** *Yaxchilán 15, no phone; 36 rooms, high season $18 single or double, low season $15, VI - MC - AE.*

Rooms are large, bright, fan-cooled and simply furnished. There is a pool.

**HOTEL TULUM,** *Tulum 119, phone (98) 841890; 22 rooms, $33 single or double, no cards.*

Rooms in this central hotel are big and equipped with air conditioning, TV, phones and small refrigerators. Decor is more pleasant than the garish orange and white lobby would suggest. Rooms in back are quieter.

**HOTEL COLONIAL BERNY**, *Tulipanes 22, phone (98) 844 861 or 841535; 46 rooms, $23 single or double with fan, $26 with air conditioning, no cards.*

This three-story hotel has a pleasant garden courtyard with exuberant vegetation, but rooms are small and plainly furnished.

**HOTEL POSADA LUCY**, *Gladiolas 25, phone (98) 844165; 16 rooms, $24 for up to four people, $39 with kitchenette, AE.*

Rooms are small but pleasantly furnished, with air conditioning.

**HOTEL CARIBE INTERNACIONAL**, *Yaxchilán at Sunyaxchén, phone (98) 843999, fax (98) 841993; 80 rooms; high season $53 single or double, $90 for junior suite with kitchenette; low season $45 for regular room, $66 for junior suite, VI - MC - AE.*

This friendly hotel has a pleasant pool area and rather ordinary rooms with white and pink painted stucco, air conditioning, TV and phone. There is some street noise. Transportation is provided to the beach.

**HOTEL PLAZA KOKAI**, *Uxmal 26, phone (98) 843666 or 843218, fax (98) 844335; 48 rooms, high season $60 single or double, low season $45, VI - MC - AE - DC.*

Rooms here are somewhat small and nondescript, with air conditioning, TV, phone, desk and marble floors. The hotel has a pool and provides transportation to the beach.

**HOTEL PLAZA DEL SOL**, *Yaxchilán 31, phone (98) 843690, fax (98) 843478; 81 rooms, high season $60 single or double, low season $40, VI - MC - AE.*

This handsome, pale orange three-story building has a pleasant pool area and an attractive restaurant. Rooms are comfortably furnished with air conditioning, TV, phone and refrigerator, but some rooms are a little dark or have poor views.

**HOTEL AMÉRICA**, *Tulum near Brisa, phone (98) 847500 or 875080, fax (98) 841953; 177 rooms, high season $70 single or double, low season $50, VI - MC - AE - DC.*

Situated just outside the downtown area, this hotel consists of a pair of six-story buildings with a pool, restaurant, bar and transportation to a beach club. It offers big, bright rooms with air conditioning, but views are uninspiring and elevator service is slow.

**HOTEL RIVEMAR**, *Tulum 49, phone (98) 841708 or 841199; 36 rooms, $20 single or double with fan, $24 with air conditioning, VI - MC - AE.*

Rooms are big and quiet but plainly furnished and rather dark. Decor in the hallways is on the funky side.

**HOTEL CANCÚN HANDALL**, *Tulum near Jaleb, phone (98) 841412, fax (98) 841976; 50 rooms, high season $44 single or double, low season $40, VI - MC - AE - DC.*

This two-story hotel just outside the downtown area offers air conditioning, TV and a pool, but rooms are small and musty, with tired furnishings.

**HOTEL VILLA ROSSANA**, *Yaxchilán 68, no phone; 10 rooms; high season $20 single, $26 double; low season $14 single, $20 double; no cards.*

Rooms are large and plain, with fans.

**HOTEL VILLA MAYA CANCÚN**, *Uxmal 20, phone (98) 841662; 15 rooms, high season $27 single or double, low season $24, VI - MC - AE - DC.*

Simple, fan-cooled rooms here are a little scruffy.

**HOTEL COTTY**, *Uxmal 44; phone (98) 840550 or 841319; 28 rooms; high season $24 single, $29 double; low season $21 single, $26 double, VI - MC - AE.*

Rooms in this friendly but scruffy motel-style spot are simple and a little musty.

**HOTEL ALUX**, *Uxmal 21, phone (98) 840662; 32 rooms, $20 single, $27 double, no cards.*

Rooms in this handsome, four-story building near the bus terminal are small, pleasant and air conditioned, but staff seem unfriendly and some street noise intrudes.

**HOTEL GALERÍAS MAYA**, *Claveles 7, phone (98) 871965; 51 rooms, $29 single, $35 double, VI - MC - AE.*

This central hotel is better avoided. Rooms are bright and air conditioned, but furnishings are plain, upkeep is poor, and staff are not helpful.

## WHERE TO EAT

The restaurant scene in Cancún is a faithful reflection of the glitter and the high prices that characterize the place generally. Fancy decor and gimmickry sometimes take precedence over quality of food, and many restaurants that purport to offer authentic Mexican dishes tone down the seasonings to suit foreign tastes.

As with hotels, prices and offerings are more extravagant in the hotel zone and more economical downtown. One way to get around high meal prices in the hotel zone is to take advantage of the all-you-can-eat breakfast buffets offered at many of the bigger hotels. These tend to be costly, often $12 to $15, but you can find good varieties of American and Mexican breakfast dishes, including fresh fruit, and since the quantities are unlimited you won't have to bother with lunch. Not even fast-food restaurants are reliable places to eat cheaply: if you head to McDonald's or KFC, you're likely to find it more expensive than at home.

Starting in the hotel zone, **CASA ROLANDI**, *situated in Plaza Caracol along Boulevard Kukulcán at km 8.5*, has a Swiss-Italian menu featuring pastas and Italian-influenced fish and beef dishes. It offers Mediterranean decor and, although it is not cheap, it offers good value for money. **TRATTORIA DE ARTURO**, *just off Boulevard Kukulcán near km 3.5*, is a more elegant and expensive spot with classic Italian specialties and a good wine list.

**GRIMOND**, *in the hotel zone at Avenida Pez Velador 8*, is another expensive spot, with French rustic decor and an interesting selection of classic French and Mexican-accented French dishes. For wretched excess, **PLANET HOLLYWOOD**, *near km 11*, is just the place for an $8 hamburger or an $11 portion of pizza. This heavily hyped spot, partly owned by Hollywood heavy Arnold Schwarzenegger, is strong on glitter, with extra-planetary architecture and plenty of brass and marble in its multi-level interior. **PETE'S EATS**, *in the food court of the Plaza Flamingo shopping center at km 11*, is a small take-out restaurant with chicken tacos, grilled chicken breast and grilled beef at prices well below the Cancún average.

---

### AN HONEST MEAL AT AN HONEST PRICE

*Avenida Tulum in downtown Cancún has a number of tourist-oriented restaurants that are stronger on contrived atmosphere than on food, where you can run up a hefty bill just for a couple of beers and a plate of tacos. But there are other spots where you can get an honest meal at an honest price. Check the menu before entering and don't be afraid to say no to the obnoxious touts employed by some restaurant. On some of the side streets, and in the area around **Avenida Yaxchilán**, the pickings are better.*

---

**CARRILLO'S**, *Claveles 12 just off Avenida Tulum*, is a cheerful terrace restaurant with good seafood and fish at reasonable prices. **LA DOLCE VITA**, *Cobá 87*, offers pasta and Italian-influenced seafood dishes at an indoor dining room and an outdoor terrace. *Along Avenida Uxmal, a block-and-a-half past the bus terminal*, **VALLADOLID** and the next-door **RINCÓN YUCATECO** both offer Yucatán specialties such as *cochinita pibil* and *pollo pibil*, pork or chicken cooked in banana leaves with a tangy citrus flavor, as well as fish and other dishes. Prices and decor are modest. *A few doors down*, **LAS TEJAS** has a good variety of grilled meats and tacos, as well as *frijoles charro*, beans with meat. Decor is simple but cheerful, and prices are moderate.

Going along Avenida Uxmal in the other direction from Avenida Tulum, **YAMAMOTO**, *Uxmal at Rubia, between Nader and Bonampak*, offers an assortment of Japanese dishes at reasonable prices. **BELICEÑO**, *on Avenida Tulum two blocks east of Uxmal*, well outside the tourist zone, serves Belizean dishes such as rice and beans with chicken. Decor is simple, and prices are low. **THE FISH MARKET**, *on Avenida Cobá*, has persuaded many taxi drivers to bring customers; food is poor and overpriced.

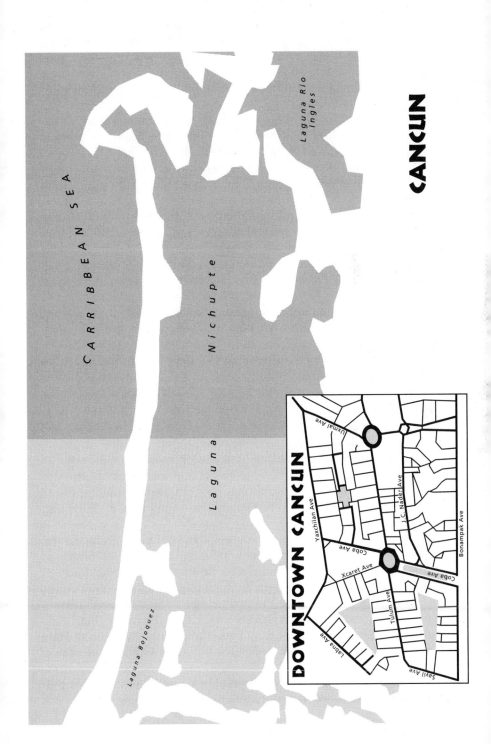

There are several good and inexpensive restaurants *along Avenida Yaxchilán near the corner of Sunyaxchén*: **LA ESQUINA**, for Spanish dishes, and **MARISCOS CANCÚN** (closes early), for seafood, both offer good value. Nearby is **LA PARRILLA** for grilled meats and *tacos al pastor*, made from that delicious mystery meat carved from spits and topped with onion and herbs.

Well away from the tourist zones lie several public markets frequented mostly by local people. One of these markets, known as **Mercado 28** (pronounced mehr-CA-doh vayn-tee-O-cho) for the *supermanzana* where it is situated, has a cluster of restaurants offering generous servings of authentic dishes at prices a fraction of those in the hotel zone. Decor is nothing fancy, menus are usually in Spanish only, and most of these restaurants are open only until late afternoon. *Mercado 28 lies some distance from Avenida Tulum and can be approached by Avenidas Sunyaxchén and Xel-Ha.* The best bet is to go by taxi, just $2 from Avenida Tulum. This area has started to catch on among visitors: a small but toney shopping center has sprung up next to the market. Among the restaurants at the market, **LOS JAROCHOS** is highly recommended: it offers Veracruz-style seafood cocktails and *arroz a la tumba tumba*, a wonderful dish of seafood and rice. **LA CHIQUITA DEL CARIBE** is another spot for seafood dishes. **ACAPULCO** specializes in cocktails, fried fish and *pozole*, a hearty soup of large-grained corn and meat. **ROSTICERÍA LA JAROCHITA** has chickens roasting on spits.

## SHOPPING

Shopping is one of the favorite activities of visitors to Cancún, and you have to wonder why. Certainly, there is no shortage of glittery shopping malls offering climate-controlled comfort and an array of famous brand-name boutiques, but prices and selections of imported goods are less interesting than what you can find in any big North American city, and Mexican handicrafts are costlier than in most other parts of the country.

One of the most popular items seems to be the big, embroidered, broad-rimmed *sombreros* of the sort worn mostly by rodeo performers or mariachis. It is possible, of course, to find a much broader range of handicrafts, including weavings, ceramics, glassware and leather goods.

Shopping centers in the hotel zone, all of them along Boulevard Kukulcán, include **Plaza Kukulcán** *at km 13*, **Plaza Flamingo**, big, bright and extravagant, *at km 11*, the giant **Plaza Caracol** and the adjacent **Plaza Lagunas**, *at km 8.5*, and the rather less prosperous **Plaza Nautilus** *at km 3.5*.

There are many tourist-oriented shops along **Avenida Tulum** in downtown Cancún selling T-shirts and handicrafts. On the opposite side of the street, near **Avenida Uxmal**, is a flea market offering many of the same goods at lower prices, but you must be prepared to bargain. Also along Avenida Tulum are two big supermarkets, **San Francisco de Asís** and **Comercial Mexicana**, with groceries and general merchandise.

# ENTERTAINMENT & NIGHTLIFE

The **folkloric ballet** presents brilliant costumes, elaborate choreography and exuberant musicianship in lavish versions of traditional dances from the Yucatán and other regions of Mexico. In several parts of Mexico, the local folkloric ballet troupes put on their shows in theatrical settings.

In Cancún, the folkloric ballet is presented as a dinner show, with the cost running near $50 including a full meal, drinks, tax and tip. The **Hyatt Regency Cancún** has been the venue for many years. *For information and reservations, phone (98) 831234.* A second troupe has been presenting shows at the **Hotel Continental Villas Plaza**, *phone (98) 831022.*

In the last week of May, Cancún becomes home to an annual **jazz festival**, with many of the performances presented on the beach.

**México Mágico**, *Boulevard Kukulcán km 12.5, opposite the Sheraton Hotel*, is a colorful amusement park with six commercially-oriented national theme areas, each with restaurants and shops. *Open evenings from 5 pm to 12:30 am; admission is $6 (discount coupons available at some hotels), and a dinner show costs an additional $20.* Dancers, singers, and other entertainers are featured, with a special emphasis on Mexican folklore.

Cancún lies well outside traditional **bullfighting** territory, which is centered in western Mexico, but the red capes come out every Wednesday at 3:30 pm at Cancún's **bullring** *(plaza de toros)*. Some tour companies offer packages with transportation and tickets, but it is far cheaper to go by taxi and buy tickets at the bullring itself, *Avenida Bonampak at Sayil, phone (98) 845465 or 848248.*

Cancún has a full complement of **discotheques**, including **Christine** *at the Hotel Krystal, Boulevard Kukulcán, km 9*, **Tequila Rock** and **Dady'O** *nearby*, and **La Boom** *at km 3.5*. All have cover charges.

**Azúcar**, *next to the Hotel Camino Real at Punta Cancún off Boulevard Kukulcán near km 8.5*, presents bands performing salsa, merengue and other tropical beats. There is a cover charge. **Batacha**, *in the Misión Park Hotel, km 10.5*, has Cuban or Dominican bands most evenings, also with a cover charge. **Méjico 1800**, *downtown on Avenida Yaxchilán near Uxmal*, presents salsa, merengue or cumbia bands from 8 pm to 4 am with no cover charge. **La Candela**, *on Avenida Tulum near the Hotel Antillano*, presents salsa most evenings.

For jazz, as well as food and wine, try the **Bistro** *on Tulipanes near Tulum*. **Cat's**, *Avenida Yaxchilán 12; opens at 10 pm with a cover charge*, offers late-night reggae.

## EXCURSIONS

With its vast number of visitors and its limited cultural attractions, Cancún generates heavy demand for excursions. A whole industry has emerged to cater to this demand, with all manner of buses and boats mobilized to move people around. Visitors can choose between organized tours and the usually cheaper do-it-yourself variety.

First, here is information for do-it-yourselfers. To the ruins of **Chichén Itzá**, the trip by car takes about two hours each way. There are also daily flights with Aerocaribe and hourly second-class buses (see Arrivals and Departures section above). These are slower and less comfortable than tour buses operating on the same route, but they are considerably less expensive and enable you to spend the number of hours you choose at the site.

To the ruins of **Tulum**, the trip by car takes two hours, to **Cobá** about 40 minutes longer. From Cancún to Tulum there are frequent second-class buses and occasional first-class services. To Cobá, a connection is required at Playa del Carmen or Tulum, with infrequent service. There is a departure from Playa at 10 am, leaving Tulum at 11 am, and allowing a little over three hours in Cobá before the return trip. It is possible to visit both sites in the same day with an early morning departure for Tulum.

Visits to spots between Playa del Carmen and Tulum, such as the **Xcaret** water park, **Akumal** for diving, **Xel-Ha** for snorkeling, or remote beaches in between, can be done easily by car or by second-class buses bound for Tulum. In some instances, bus passengers may face a considerable walk from the highway drop-off point to the final destination.

To **Cozumel**, there are frequent flights with Aerocozumel, and the more economical bus-ferry combination via Playa del Carmen is quite simple. The ferry pier in Playa del Carmen is just a couple of minutes' walk from the bus terminal. There are about 25 crossings a day in each direction, running until mid-evening, with two ferry companies competing. Resist the temptation to buy a joint bus-ferry ticket. It will lock you into using a particular company and may entail extra waiting. **Isla Mujeres** is a short hop by ferry from Puerto Juárez, just north of downtown Cancún (see Arrivals and Departures section above) for ferry information.

Now for some of the organized excursions. A group called **Los Amigos de Sian Ka'an** organizes regular visits to the huge **Sian Ka'an** nature reserve south of Tulum. Information on Sian Ka'an appears in the Tulum section of this book. *The group's office is in Cancún (3rd floor, Plaza América, Avenida Cobá 5), phone (98) 849583 or 873080.* Day tours cost $115 per person from Cancún, including a boat trip along remote canals and lagoons. Groups normally vary between four and nine persons.

Tour agencies at the bigger hotels and elsewhere around Cancún handle reservations and tickets for a variety of excursions by bus and boat.

Bus tours operate to most of the points mentioned above, and bus-and-ferry tours operate to Cozumel with snorkeling or diving included in the price. Tours are also run by air to Chichén Itzá or Cozumel.

Many kinds of short cruises are offered in the waters around Cancún, some with visits to **Isla Mujeres**. Some are evening cruises with dinner and entertainment included. These vary in price depending on length, on the lavishness of meals, and on whether drinks are included. Other cruise operators use smaller vessels to tour mangrove channels and lagoons on Cancún's inland side or semi-submersible vessels to see reef areas.

Further afield, excursions of two or more days can be made by air from Cancún to **Tikal** in Guatemala or to **Havana** in Cuba. (The US Government has placed severe restrictions on travel to Cuba by US citizens, but Cuban authorities do not stamp US passports, leaving no telltale evidence of travel there.) Travel agencies in Cancún can sell full tour packages or air tickets alone to either of these destinations.

## PRACTICAL INFORMATION

### Airlines

It usually isn't necessary to reconfirm North American flights, but it can be helpful. Some charter airlines or tour operators require reconfirmation. They normally give passengers an information sheet with a phone number for this purpose. Flights to most other countries must be reconfirmed at least 72 hours before scheduled departure time.

- **Aerocaribe** and **Aerocozumel**: *Tulum 29, phone (98) 842000; airport: (98) 860162*
- **Aeroméxico**: *Cobá 80, phone (98) 843571 or 841097; airport: (98) 860018 or 860094*
- **American Airlines**: *airport, phone (98) 860055 or 860151*
- **Aviacsa**: *Cobá 55, phone (98) 874214 or 874211*
- **Aviateca**: *Tulum 200, phone (98) 843938 or 871386; airport: (98) 860150*
- **Continental Airlines**: *airport, phone (98) 860006 or 860169*
- **Iberia**: *airport, phone (98) 860244 or 860243*
- **Lacsa**: *Bonampak at Cobá, phone (98) 873101 or 875101; airport: phone (98) 860014 or 860008*
- **Mexicana**: *Cobá 39, phone (98) 874444 or 872769; airport: phone (98) 860120*
- **Northwest Airlines**: *airport, phone (98) 860044 or 860046*
- **TAESA**: *Yaxchilán 31, phone (98) 874314 or 874315; airport, phone (98) 860206 or 860175*

### Car Rentals

Vehicles ranging from Volkswagen beetles to Jeeps are available all over Cancún, at the airport, in town and in many of the hotels in the hotel zone, with many firms represented. Despite the competition, rates are substantially higher than in the US, although they do tend to come down somewhat during the low season. Weekly rates often provide a sizable saving. All phone numbers shown here have the 98 city code.

- **Hertz**: *at the airport (860150), Camino Real (830634), Conrad (853121), Marriott (852000), Oasis I (850867), Oasis II (850752), Plaza Mayfair (833624) and downtown on Avenida Yaxchilán (841524)*
- **Budget**: at *the airport (860026), Marriott (852000), Hyatt Regency (830966), Hyatt Caribe (830044), Royal Solaris (850100), Mayfair (832612), at the convention center (830660) and downtown on Avenida Tulum (844612)*
- **National**: *at the airport (860152), Omni (850714), Cancún Marina (831999), Presidente (830200), Holiday Inn Crowne Plaza (851020), Vista Playa de Oro (851366), Meliá Cancún (851114), and on Avenida Uxmal (840097)*
- **Dollar**: *at the airport (860133), Sheraton (831988), Paraíso Radisson (850112) and Condos Salvia (833621)*
- **Avis**: for locations, *call 860222 or 830803*

Other car rental companies with Cancún agencies include **Monterrey Rent, Caribbean Rent, Elite Renta de Autos**, and **Economóvil**.

### Consulates
- **Canada**: *Plaza México, Tulum 200, phone (98) 843716*
- **United States**: *Nader 40, phone (98) 842411, 846399 or 848222*

### Currency Exchange
A number of exchange dealers (*casas de cambio*) are scattered around the hotel zone and the downtown area, but rates are often poor and some charge extra commissions. Better rates are found at the banks downtown.

The main branch of **Bancomer** *on Avenida Uxmal* operates a *casa de cambio* next door to the bank itself with fast service and better-than-average rates. Many hotels exchange dollars but at unacceptably low rates.

### Golf
The 18-hole **Pok-Ta-Pok** course *is situated behind Laguna Bojórquez off Boulevard Kukulcán near km 6. Phone (98) 830871 for information.* The **Hotel Meliá Cancún**, *at km 15, has a nine-hole course. Phone (98) 851114.*

### Newspapers& Books
**Fama**, *on Avenida Tulum near Tulipanes downtown*, carries a small selection of US newspapers and magazines and also sells tourism guide-books in several languages. Shops at some of the bigger hotels also offer reading material in English, including newspapers and magazines. A newssheet with a brief summary of world news and US sports scores is published daily in Cancún and distributed free at certain hotels.

**Tourist Information**

The **state tourism information bureau** *is located in downtown Cancún on Avenida Cobá near Avenida Tulum, next to Rolandi's Pizza; open daily from 9 am to 9 pm.* Staff appear eager but not very knowledgeable.

# ISLA MUJERES

> *The island is just 8 km long and as little as 300 meters wide in places. It lies just 5 km offshore from Cancún, to which it is linked by a frequent ferry service.*

Many people take vacations in Cancún to get relief from the winter cold and the rigors of daily life back home. Some come to **Isla Mujeres** to get relief from the glitter and the costliness of Cancún. Here they will find a more casual ambiance and a decent choice of moderately priced lodgings near the beach.

Isla Mujeres (literally, *island of women*) may have gotten its name from the female clay figures Spanish sailors first saw when they arrived during a Maya religious ceremony. It is a relaxed place, with fine beaches, good snorkeling and a bit of sightseeing, including visits to **Isla Contoy**, a bird sanctuary. The illuminated skyline of Cancún, with its strange pyramid shapes, is clearly visible at night, but it seems a world away.

Most visitors stick pretty close to the charming, beach-lined town that covers the northern tip of the island. This town has a rustic atmosphere, a range of services, and a cluster of middle-priced and lower-end hotels. Nearly everything is within walking distance. Taxis provide transportation to other parts of the island. There is also an hourly bus going as far as Playa Paraíso about 5 km south. A tourism office facing the *zócalo*, or central plaza, keeps irregular hours.

## ARRIVALS & DEPARTURES

**By Air**

There is a small airstrip on the island but no regular air service.

**By Ferry**

Passenger ferries connect Isla Mujeres town with Puerto Juárez, just north of downtown Cancún. Two companies compete on this route. The slow boats take 45 minutes and cost $1.35. The fast boats take 20 minutes and cost $3. Between them they provide service from Puerto Juárez at least twice an hour from 8 am to 8:30 pm. From Isla Mujeres service begins at 5 am. The last departure is at 8 pm.

Car ferries run from Punta Sam, north of Puerto Juárez. The fare is $9 per car plus $1.50 per passenger. Departures are every two to three hours. From Punta Sam the first boat is at 7:15 am and the last one at 8:15 pm. From Isla Mujeres service runs from 6 am to 8:15 pm.

## WHERE TO STAY

Most hotels in town offer accommodations in the middle and lower parts of the price range; several upscale hotels are found south of town.

### Hotels in town

**HOTEL NA-BALAM**, *Zazil-Ha 118 near Playa Norte, phone (987) 70279, fax (987) 70593; 19 rooms, $66 single or double, VI - MC - AE.*

Large, bright rooms have sitting areas and terraces facing the sea. Furnishings are somewhat rustic. Rooms are situated in a pair of two-story buildings, with the beach extending right into the property. There are plenty of shade trees, palapa shades and hammocks, as well as a big sandy terrace. Discounts are offered for long stays in low season.

**CABAÑAS MARÍA DEL MAR**, *Carlos Lazo 1 near Playa Norte, phone (987) 70213 or 70179, fax (987) 70173; 55 rooms, $39 to $88, VI - MC.*

Situated just off the north beach, this hotel has three distinct sections: the cabañas with large, plain rooms with private terraces facing a small pool, the three-story "tower" with tile floor, colored glass and a generally higher standard of decor, and the "castle," which is prettier both on the outside and the inside. Rates vary according to room size, location and season and include a light breakfast. All rooms are air conditioned

**HOTEL PERLA DEL CARIBE I**, *Madero 2, phone (987) 70120, fax (987) 70011; 90 rooms, $66 to $70 single or double, VI - MC - AE.*

Nearly all rooms have air conditioning and private terraces. About three-quarters have dramatic sea views. Below is a newly built esplanade running along a rocky stretch of seafront and a beach. Rooms are fairly ordinary, but service is friendly. The hotel is housed in a pair of pink-and-white three-story buildings and has a pool, restaurant and bar.

**HOTEL PERLA DEL CARIBE II** *(formerly Hotel Rocamar), Guerrero at Nicolás Bravo, phone (987) 70586; 30 rooms, high season $50 single or double, low season $40, VI - MC - AE.*

Unlike its namesake, this hotel cannot be recommended. During our visit, the grounds were unkempt and covered with litter, and the building seemed rundown and poorly maintained. This overpriced spot has a tiny pool, restaurant and bar.

**HOTEL MESÓN DEL BUCANERO**, *Hidalgo 11, phone (987) 70210, fax (987) 70126; 11 rooms, $21 to $45 single or double, VI - MC.*

Rooms vary enormously in size, but all are bright and breezy. There are nice touches such as carved wooden doors and bedsteads, stained glass and decorative handicrafts. Rooms are upstairs from a pleasant restaurant and bar.

**HOTEL BELMAR**, *Hidalgo 110, phone (987) 70430, fax (987) 70429; 12 rooms; high season $32 single, $36 double; low season $29 single, $32 double; VI - MC - AE.*

Rooms are bright and set around a pleasant open courtyard, with bits of artwork. All have air conditioning, TV and phone, but there can be noise from the restaurant below.

**HOTEL XUL-HA**, *Hidalgo 23, phone (987) 20075 or 20039; 11 rooms; high season $15 single, $18 double; low season $11 single, $13 double; no cards.*

Pleasant, simple rooms, some with garden view, are set in a modern building.

**HOTEL EL CARACOL**, *Matamoros 5, phone (987) 70150, fax (987) 70547; 18 rooms, high season $24 single or double, low season $12, air conditioning $12 more, VI - MC - AE.*

Rooms are bright, clean and simple. Two have kitchens, at a higher price.

**HOTEL CARIBE MAYA**, *Madero 9, phone (987) 44917; 25 rooms; high season $14 single, $17 double; low season $11 single, $14 double; VI - MC - AE.*

Rooms are simple but pleasant, with good cross-ventilation.

**HOTEL MARCIANITO**, *Abasolo 10, phone (987) 20111; 8 rooms, $12 single, $15 double, no cards.*

The entrance is unprepossessing, but rooms are bright, clean and cozy.

**CASA POC-NA**, *Matamoros at Carlos Lazo, phone (987) 70090; 85 beds set in 12 dormitories; $5 per night plus one-time deposit.*

This privately-run youth hostel is clean and simple, with a pleasant common area beneath a big palapa roof. Unlike government-run hostels, this has dormitories where heterosexual couples can stay together.

**HOTEL POSADA DEL MAR**, *Rueda Medina 15-A, phone (987) 70044 or 70300, fax (987) 70263; 46 rooms; high season $47 single, $56 double; low season $36 single, $45 double; VI - MC - AE.*

Rooms are large, bright and pleasant with private terraces, but some of the furnishings and the landscaping could use a little work. The hotel is housed in a big, three-story orange building facing a beach. There is a pool with palapa shades and music on weekends.

**HOTEL D'GOMAR**, *Rueda Medina 15, phone (987) 70541; 16 rooms, high season $42 to $45 single or double, low season $27 to $31, no cards.*

Situated near the ferry terminal, the entrance lies down a long corridor. Rooms are furnished in modern style with lots of greys and pinks, but they are dark and not all of them are air conditioned. This place does seem a little overpriced.

**HOTEL FRANCIS ARLENE**, *Guerrero 7, (987) 70312; 12 rooms, high season $23 to $36, low season $18 to $27, no cards.*

Rooms vary considerably. Some are brighter and more pleasantly furnished than others. Some have terraces, other don't. The same applies to air conditioning and kitchenettes.

**HOTEL VISTALMAR**, *Rueda Medina near Matamoros, phone (987) 70209, fax (987) 70096; 36 rooms; high season $14 single, $18 double; low season $11 single, $14 double; VI - MC.*

A few rooms have air conditioning and cost $18 to $27. The hotel is across from a beach. Rooms are big but very plain.

**HOTEL ISLEÑO**, *Madero 8, phone (987) 70302; 20 rooms, $18 single or double with private bath, $14 with shared bath, no cards.*

Rooms are bright, clean and simple.

**HOTEL MARÍA JOSÉ**, *Madero 25, phone (987) 70244 or 70245; 14 rooms, $12 single or double, no cards.*

Rooms are bright but rudimentary. The building has narrow stairs and splattered paint.

### Hotels out of town

**VILLAS HI-NA-HA**, *Fraccionamiento Paraíso Sac Bajo, phone (987) 70615; 6 large villas, high season $220, low season $165, VI - MC - AE.*

Each villa can accommodate up to seven people. Each has a living room and kitchen below, bedrooms upstairs and a sun deck on the roof. They are pinkish beige on the outside, and very comfortably furnished inside in shades of beige and white. They face a splendid beach with palapa shades and views of Cancún in the distance.

**HOTEL MARÍA'S KAN-KIN**, *Fraccionamiento Mar Turquesa toward the southern end of the island, phone (987) 70015, fax (987) 70395; 6 rooms, high season $54 single or double, low season $36, VI - MC - AE.*

Low-slung buildings are set on a lavishly vegetated slope. Rooms are big, and some have sea views from upstairs terraces. Though furnishings are nothing special, this has the feel of an exclusive retreat. The restaurant is one of the best on the island.

**HOTEL CRISTAL MAR**, *Fraccionamiento Paraíso, Laguna Macax, phone (987) 70007 or 70089, fax (987) 70594; 38 suites; high season $105 single or double, two-bedroom suite $116, deluxe suite $127; low season $77 / $88 / $99; VI - MC.*

Suites in this three-story beachfront hotel are furnished conservatively, but the grounds are lavishly landscaped and well kept. The beach is shaded by palms and palapa shades. All suites offer air conditioning and kitchenette. The hotel has a bar, restaurant, pool, dive shop and rentals of bicycles and motor scooters.

**MARINA ISLA MUJERES**, *Fraccionamiento Paraíso Sac Bajo, phone (987) 70594; 11 suites, high season $60 single or double, low season $40, VI - MC.*

Suites at this small beachfront hotel are big and bright, but furnishings are very ordinary.

**HOTEL MARINA PARAÍSO**, *Prolongación Rueda Medina across from the airstrip, phone (987) 70252; 8 rooms, high season $21 to $27 double, low season $15 to $21, no cards.*

Rooms are bright and attractive, some in split-level form with separate sitting areas and kitchenettes, but the grounds are unkempt. Some bungalows sleep up to four. There are slips for yachts and sailboats.

**HOTEL GARRAFÓN DE CASTILLA**, *Carretera Garrafón km 7, no phone; 12 rooms, high season $15 single or double, low season $11, VI - MC.*

Rooms have sea views and air conditioning, but furnishings are garish, the grounds are unkempt, service is sluggish and things get noisy when day-trippers from Cancún arrive by the boatload at the snorkeling park next door. On the other hand, rates are cheap and the snorkeling is good.

## WHERE TO EAT

Not surprisingly, Isla Mujeres is a good place for fish and seafood. There are many restaurants in town, and a few to the south, most notably **MARÍA'S KAN KIN**, *situated in Fraccionamiento Mar Turquesa toward the southern end of the island* and easily reached by taxi. This open-air, palapa-roofed restaurant is set amid exuberant vegetation and offers good views of the sea. It concentrates on French preparations of local fish and seafood and is fairly expensive. Main courses run from $11 to $15. Food and service are excellent.

In town, **CAFÉ CITO** *at the corner of Juárez and Matamoros* is a casual spot with interesting full-course specials. It offers good breakfast and selections of pancakes and fruit drinks at all hours. Its tables each have glass covers, beneath which there are displays of seashells set in white sand. **MESÓN DEL BUCANERO**, *on Hidalgo between Madero and Abasolo*, has a pleasant open-air dining room and moderate prices. It serves a variety of pizzas as well as pasta, meat and seafood dishes. **ROLANDI'S**, *right across the street*, has a similar menu. This stretch of Hidalgo street is lively at night, and there are several other restaurants nearby.

## SEEING THE SIGHTS

Part of the attraction of Isla Mujeres is its fine white sand beaches, the biggest of which is **Playa Norte** (north beach), also known as **Playa Los Cocos**, *at the northern end of the island.* As it drapes around toward the western side, it becomes known as **Nautibeach**. Also on the western side, *about 5 km south*, is **Playa Paraíso** and, a bit further, **Playa Lancheros**.

*Near the southern tip of the island* is **Parque Nacional El Garrafón**, where a reef just a few feet offshore is popular with snorkelers  perhaps too popular. Hordes of day-trippers from Cancún take much of the fun out of it, and the reef is not in very good shape. The park also has an aquarium and a small museum, as well as dressing rooms, showers and restaurants. *Open daily from 8 am to 5 pm, and admission is $3.*

At the very tip of the island is **Ixchel**, a few small mounds that are virtually the only visible reminder of ancient Mayan life on the island. There is a lighthouse nearby. The site is interesting not for the ruins but for dramatic views of the sea from high on a rocky bluff. About 2 km north of here are ruins of a different sort, the **Hacienda Mundaca**, built by a 19th century slave trader and pirate. This once grand estate now lies abandoned, and nobody even bothers collecting admission fees to its extensive but overgrown grounds.

**Isla Contoy** is a bird sanctuary situated near Isla Mujeres. More than 70 species can be spotted there, including pelicans, spoonbills, herons and cormorants. The island is very narrow and has several small lakes surrounded by mangrove or coconut palms. It also has fine beaches, good snorkeling, an observation tower and a small museum. The only local resident is a guard.

One or two companies take small groups to visit the island. One place to get information on tours is **La Isleña** *on Morelos street between Rueda Medina and Juárez, near the ferry pier in Isla Mujeres.*

## SHOPPING

This ain't Cancún, but a handful of shops scattered around town do offer selections of Mexican handicrafts. There are several shops in the streets near the ferry pier.

## ENTERTAINMENT & NIGHTLIFE

A favorite form of early evening entertainment is to head over to the *zócalo*, or central plaza, to watch basketball games between local teams. Occasionally, a concert is held there later on. Apart from that, restaurants and bars account for much of the nightlife, such as it is.

## COZUMEL

*Cozumel is situated 19 km off the Caribbean coast and is the biggest island in Mexico.*

Cozumel, meaning *land of swallows* in Mayan, has long been overshadowed in popularity by Cancún, but in the eyes of many divers and snorkelers it remains unbeatable. This resort island also attracts people who are looking simply for a quiet place to relax by the seaside.

For literally thousands of years Cozumel has drawn traders and navigators, right up to the present moment with its immense popularity as a port of call for Caribbean cruise ships. It was inhabited when the Spanish first arrived in the early 16th century, and it has had many ups and downs. In following centuries it became a lair for pirates. Early in the 20th century it cashed in on the chewing-gum craze by transshipping and growing chicle. It was the site of a US Air Force base in the Second World War, and it found a new vocation in tourism in the 1960s when the outside world discovered the beauty of the coral reefs and the colorful tropical fish that ring much of the island.

**San Miguel de Cozumel**, on the western side of the island, is the only town of any importance. It is an attractive town with a lively central plaza surrounded by pedestrian-only streets. When cruise ships arrive, disgorging their many hundreds of passengers, the streets fill up and taxis, shops, cafés and various tourist attractions suddenly do a roaring business. Few cruise ships dock during the weekend, and this is probably a better time to see Cozumel.

The coral reefs that lie just offshore are the prime attraction for many visitors. Some who weren't snorkelers or divers before visiting Cozumel become converts. There are also good bathing beaches, though these are often smaller than those on the mainland, and scenic drives around the perimeter of the island. Although day visitors abound from Cancún and other mainland resorts, it is just as possible for people staying in Cozumel to use the island as a base for visits to the mainland.

## ARRIVALS & DEPARTURES

### By Air

Continental Airlines flies from Houston to Cozumel (airport code CZM) and Mexicana from Miami. There are also occasional international charter flights. Mexicana provides service from Mexico City and Mérida, while Aerocozumel, a Mexicana affiliate, flies from Cancún at two-hour intervals using propeller planes and also offers a daily flight from Chichén Itzá. Cozumel's international airport lies just 2 km north of the town of San Miguel and is linked by taxi to all parts of the island. Collective vans meet incoming vans and charge $2.50 per passenger to San Miguel, $5 to most of the hotels further south.

### By Ferry

Passenger ferries to Cozumel leave from a big pier near the main plaza in Playa del Carmen and arrive near the center of San Miguel de Cozumel. Two companies compete for your business, one with big, air-conditioned boats at a one-way fare of $6, the other with smaller, open vessels for $4.50. Refreshments are sold aboard most vessels, and the crossing averages about 45 minutes. Before buying a ticket, check the departure times of both companies; you may save yourself a wait. Round-trip tickets often provide no discount and lock you into returning by a vessel of the same company.

There are about 25 crossings a day in each direction, with the first departure from Playa del Carmen at 5 am and the last one at 8:45 pm (but check locally – schedules do change). From Cozumel the first departure is at 4 am and the last one at 8 pm.

For passengers coming from Cancún or other points, the bus-ferry combination is simple. The ferry pier in Playa del Carmen is just a couple of minutes' walk from the bus terminal. Resist the temptation to buy a joint bus-ferry ticket. It will lock you into using a particular company and may entail extra waiting.

Car ferries for Cozumel leave from Puerto Morelos, midway between Playa del Carmen and Cancún. Service is once a day, and schedules change every week. Departure time from Puerto Morelos may be any-where from 5 am to 12 noon, and the return trip from Cozumel leaves between 9 am and 4 pm. For information, phone (987) 10008. The fare is $42 per car plus $7 per passenger.

## ORIENTATION

Cozumel is a big island, 64 km long between its most distant points and 14 km wide. The town of **San Miguel** *is situated on the western coast toward the northern end of the island.* Hotel zones extend both north and south from San Miguel along a narrow coastal highway. Many lower-priced hotels are situated in the center of town.

**Palancar reef**, *toward the southwest corner of the island*, is among the spots most favored by divers. **Chankanaab park**, *a bit further north*, is well suited for snorkeling. There are many other reef formations around the island. The eastern side of Cozumel has been developed very little, in part because of the powerful surf. The perimeter of the southern and central parts of the island is circled by a paved road, and there is another paved road running east from San Miguel across the center of the island. There are poor dirt roads around the northeastern tip. Most sites for diving are situated off the southern part of the island.

San Miguel is laid out in a mostly rectangular grid. **Avenida Rafael Melgar** runs along the waterfront, and the parallel avenues (*avenidas*) have numbers in multiples of five. **Avenida Juárez** runs perpendicular to the other avenues and forms the boundary between north and south for purposes of street addresses. Streets (*calles*) with even numbers lie north of Avenida Juárez and streets with odd number lie south. Calle A.R. Salas street lies between Calle 1 Sur and Calle 3 Sur.

**CARVINGS IN CHANKANAAB PARK, COZUMEL**

The **ferry pier** is almost an extension of Avenida Juárez. Arriving passengers who walk straight up half a block find themselves in the **Plaza del Sol**, San Miguel's central plaza. The streets immediately surrounding the plaza are open to pedestrians only and are lined by many shops.

There are no public bus services in Cozumel except for one route serving residential areas, but the center of town is fairly compact and taxi fares are reasonable, just over $2 for trips of up to 6 km. Fares can sometimes jump when there is a cruise ship in port, however. There are several spots just past the plaza to rent cars, motor scooters or bicycles. The tourism information booth on the ferry pier can provide maps.

## WHERE TO STAY

Lodgings in Cozumel tend to be more expensive than in Playa del Carmen or Isla Mujeres but cheaper than in Cancún. The lower-priced hotels are mostly concentrated in the town of San Miguel. The more expensive hotels are situated outside town along the beaches to the north or south. Virtually all hotels are on the western side of the island. The kilometers in some addresses show the distance from San Miguel. Some hotels are situated across the highway from the beach, while several seaside hotels lack natural beaches altogether. A number of hotels have changed names in recent years; an old friend may have a new moniker.

Camping is possible at two beaches on the eastern coast of Cozumel, **Playa Bonita** and **Playa Río Chen**, but independent transportation is needed to get there.

*Hotels in town*

**HOTEL MAYA COZUMEL**, *Calle 5 Sur 4, phone (987) 20011; fax (987) 20781; 37 rooms, $27 single, $32 double, VI - MC - AE.*

Rooms are quiet and simply but appealingly decorated in shades of blue and green. All have air conditioning and TV. There is a pool with bougainvillea providing plenty of color.

**HOTEL COLONIAL**, *5ª Avenida Sur, corner of A.R. Salas, phone (987) 20211, fax (987) 21387; 28 rooms, high season $50 single or double, low season $38, VI - MC - AE.*

Entry to this handsome, modern four-story building is by a long, tree-shaded passageway. Rooms are comfortably furnished and equipped with air conditioning, TV, phone and kitchenette. Each has a separate sitting area, but these tend to be quite dark, and the hotel's sole elevator does not inspire confidence.

**HOTEL MESÓN SAN MIGUEL**, *Juárez 2-B facing the plaza, phone (987) 20233 or 20323, fax (987) 21820; 97 rooms, high season $56 single or double, low season $33, VI - MC.*

Rooms in this very centrally located hotel are furnished simply and equipped with air conditioning, TV, phone and private terraces. Half face the plaza. Interior corridors are long and gloomy, but work is being put into renovation.

**HOTEL SAFARI INN**, *Calle 7 Sur by the waterfront, phone (987) 20101, fax (987) 20661; 12 rooms, $30 single or double, VI - MC.*

Rooms are bright and simply but comfortably furnished, with air conditioning.

**HOTEL BAHÍA**, *Calle 5 Sur near the waterfront, phone (987) 24034, fax (987) 21387; 28 rooms, high season $45 single, $50 double, low season $4 less, VI - MC - AE.*

Each room has air conditioning, TV, phone, pleasant furnishings including sofas, and private terraces. Some rooms have sea views, while the view from others is unimpressive.

**HOTEL LÓPEZ**, *facing the plaza, phone (987) 20108; 34 rooms; high season $18 single, $23 double; low season $15 single, $18 double; no cards.*

Rooms in this four-story hotel are bright, clean, simple and quiet. Some upstairs rooms have views of the ferry pier.

**HOTEL EL PIRATA**, *5ª Avenida Sur 3-A, phone (987) 20051; 27 rooms, $27 single or double, VI - MC, 10% surcharge on credit cards.*

Rooms have air conditioning, TV, tile floors and very ordinary furnishings. The hotel faces a pedestrian-only street.

**HOTEL SOBERANIS**, *Rafael Melgar between Calles 5 and 7 Sur; 12 rooms, $23 single, $27 double, VI - MC.*

Rooms are big but very plainly furnished. Half have sea views, all have air conditioning. The hotel faces the waterfront near the center of town.

**HOTEL MARY CARMEN**, *5ª Avenida Sur 4, phone (987) 20581; 27 rooms, $23 single or double, VI - MC.*

Bright, air-conditioned, carpeted rooms in this two-story city-center hotel are set around an uninteresting courtyard.

**HOTEL EL MARQUÉS**, *5ª Avenida Sur 180, phone (987) 20677, fax (987) 20537; 47 rooms, $27 single or double, VI - MC - AE.*

Rooms are air-conditioned and bright but have dismal views. Furnishings are tacky but comfortable.

**HOTEL VISTA DEL MAR**, *Rafael Melgar 45, phone (987) 20545, fax (987) 20445; 24 rooms, high season $44 single or double, low season $39, VI - MC.*

Rooms are big and bright, some with private terrace, all with air conditioning, refrigerator and phone, but decor is very plain, service is sluggish, and this five-story building has no elevator. It faces the waterfront near the center of town.

**HOTEL PLAZA COZUMEL**, *Calle 2 Norte 3, phone (987) 22722, fax (987) 20066; 49 rooms, high season $66 single or double, low season $55, VI - MC - AE.*

There's a pool and reasonably furnished rooms with air conditioning and TV, but the entrance is scruffy and rooms seem overpriced.

**HOTEL FLORES**, *A.R. Salas 72, phone (987) 21429; 30 rooms, high season $17 single, $20 double, low season $3 less, air conditioning $3 extra, no cards.*

Furnishings are quite basic, and there is some noise on the street side.

### Hotels south of town

**HOTEL INTER-CONTINENTAL PRESIDENTE**, *Carretera Costera Sur km 6.5, phone (987) 20322, fax (987) 21360, US and Canada reservations (800) 361-3600; 253 rooms; high season, garden view rooms $215 single or double, ocean view rooms $259, beachfront rooms $303, low season $61 less, VI - MC - AE - DC.*

This hotel is the costliest and the best on the island. It faces 1 km of sandy beachfront with a reef nearby and water so clear that visibility routinely exceeds 25 meters. Rooms are decorated in modern Mexican pinks and purples, with plenty of marble, white cedar and painted tile. All have air conditioning, satellite TV, minibar and hair dryer. The hotel has its own water desalination plant that works by reverse osmosis. Amenities include restaurants, bars, pools, a dive shop, and tour agency. The lobby has a high palapa roof and brightly colored sofas. Rooms are approached by garden passageway.

**PLAZA LAS GLORIAS COZUMEL**, *Carretera Costera Sur km 1.5, phone (987) 22588 or 22411, fax (987) 21937; 168 rooms, high season $143 to $165 single or double, low season $116, VI - MC - AE.*

This five-story, salmon-colored building is fancifully designed with plenty of nooks, gables and arches. Amenities include a pool, whirlpool, two artificial beaches at the edge of a reef, and a dive shop. Most guests are divers. Rooms are bright, and all have sea views, separate sitting areas, pastel decor, air conditioning, TV and phone. A few duplex units have private jacuzzis and can accommodate up to six people.

**HOTEL CLUB SOL COZUMEL**, *Carretera Costera Sur km 6.8, phone (987) 23777, fax (987) 22329; 52 rooms, high season $54 to $62 single or double, low season $37 to $47, VI - MC - AE.*

This hotel consists of a series of low-rise buildings set on lushly landscaped grounds. Rooms have air conditioning, tile floors and rustic furnishings. The hotel has two restaurants and presents three special buffet dinners each week. It is across the road from a small, rocky beach and snorkeling platforms.

**HOTEL LA CEIBA**, *Carretera Costera Sur km 4.5, phone (987) 20844, fax (987) 20065, US reservations (800) 877-4383; 113 rooms, high season $121 single or double, low season $88, VI - MC - AE.*

This hotel caters largely to divers. It faces a tiny beach and diving platform. Rooms are decorated in nautical theme and all have sea views, as well as air conditioning, TV, phone and minibar. They are set in buildings of four and seven stories. There are two restaurants and a pool.

**DIAMOND RESORT COZUMEL**, *Carretera Costera Sur km 16.5, phone (987) 23443, US and Canada reservations (800) 858-2258; 300 rooms; high season $242 double, $165 single; low season $182 double, $124 single; VI - MC - AE.*

This is an all-inclusive resort with meals, most drinks and sporting activities such as tennis and snorkeling included in room rates. Most guests arrive on tour packages that provide greatly reduced group rates Rooms are set in two-story thatched villas with eight rooms in each cluster. Decor is modern Mexican style. All have air conditioning and TV. The hotel faces the beach with a reef right in front.

**HOTEL BARRACUDA**, *Rafael Melgar 628, phone (987) 20002 or 21243, fax (987) 23633, VI - MC - AE; 50 rooms; high season $61 single, $72 double; low season, $44 single, $50 double; VI - MC - AE.*

This three-story pink building at the southern edge of town has an artificial beach and dive platform. Rooms are simply decorated, all with sea views and air conditioning.

**HOTEL VILLABLANCA**, *Carretera Costera Sur km 3, phone (987) 20730, fax (987) 20865; 24 rooms, high season $55 single or double, low season $43 to $54, VI - MC - AE, 6% surcharge on credit cards.*

Rooms vary in size and are plain but comfortable, with air conditioning and a rustic ambiance. It is set on large grounds with a small pool and a tennis court. A small beach and snorkeling platform lie across the road.

**SOL CARIBE COZUMEL**, *Carretera Costera Sur km 2.5, phone (987) 20700, fax (987) 21301; 321 rooms, high season $153 single or double, low season $132, VI - MC - AE.*

This sprawling hotel has a pair of nine-story buildings, a big, whimsically shaped pool, waterfalls, and vast tropical gardens. The huge, openair lobby has a conical wooden roof. This really feels like a convention hotel, and service is impersonal. Rooms are comfortable, but the hotel is situated some distance from the beach, which is reached by a tunnel.

**FIESTA AMERICANA COZUMEL REEF**, *Carretera Costera Sur km 7.5, phone (987) 22622, fax (987) 22666, US and Canada reservations (800) 343-7821; 162 rooms, $171 single or double, VI - MC - AE - DC.*

This seven-story hotel has big, comfortable rooms with air conditioning and TV, a lavishly landscaped pool area, three restaurants and two bars. It is across the highway from the seafront, however. It is linked by a pedestrian bridge to the beach and snorkeling area.

**FIESTA INN**, *Carretera Costera Sur km 1.7, phone (987) 22899, fax (987) 22154; 180 rooms, high season $99 single or double, low season $88, VI - MC - AE.*

Three buildings each of three stories are set around an enormous but uninviting pool area. Rooms have air conditioning and carpeting in cool shades of blue and turquoise. Only a few have sea views. The hotel is situated across the highway from the beach.

### Hotels north of town

**MELIÁ MAYAN PARADISOS**, *Carretera Costera Norte km 5.8, phone (987) 20411, fax (987) 21599, US and Canada reservations (800) 336-3542; 167 rooms; high season $206 single, $314 double, including meals, drinks and sporting activities; low season $173 single, $264 double; $6 to $12 extra for rooms with ocean view; VI - MC - AE.*

This five-star hotel has switched to all-inclusive. Guests, most of whom arrive on package tours, pay a fixed rate that includes all meals and most drinks and activities. There are two big pools, two restaurants, two bars and two buildings (one four and 14 stories) with guest rooms.

Decor is similar in both. Rooms are big and comfortably furnished, with air conditioning, TV and phone. The hotel is situated near the northwestern corner of the island and faces a big beach with shallow water.

**HOTEL EL COZUMELEÑO**, *Playa Santa Pilar, phone (987) 20050 or 20344, fax (987) 20381, US reservations (800) 437-3923; 100 rooms; high season $147 single, $155 double; low season $115 single, $121 double; VI - MC - AE.*

This five-story pale orange building faces the beach about 5 km north of town and offers the usual five-star amenities.

**HOTEL PRÍNCIPE**, *Carretera Costera Norte km 3.5, phone (987) 21779, fax (987) 20016; 100 rooms, high season $110 to $121 single or double, low season $62 to $93, VI - MC - AE.*

This beachfront hotel offers a big pool and brightly decorated rooms and junior suites, all with sea views, air conditioning and TV.

**HOTEL CORAL PRINCESS**, *Carretera Costera Norte  km 2.5, phone (987) 23200, fax (987) 22800; 48 rooms, high season $108 single or double, low season $96, rooms with sea view $7 more.*

Rooms in this nine-story building are big, bright and appealing, with white marble floors and air conditioning. In the absence of natural beach, there is an artificial beach with a platform for swimming and snorkeling.

**HOTEL FONTÁN**, *Carretera Costera Norte  km 2.5, phone (987) 20300, fax (987) 20105; 49 rooms, high season $77 single or double, low season $60, VI - MC - AE.*

Rooms in this four-story building all have sea views plus air conditioning and carpeting. There is no beach here, just a tiny inlet.

**SOL CABAÑA CLUB CARIBE**, *Playa Santa Pilar, phone (987) 20161 or 20017, fax (987) 21599, US and Canada reservations (800) 336-3542; 48 rooms, high season $115 single or double, low season $99 single or double, VI - MC - AE.*

This two-story hotel, situated about 5 km north of town, has an appealing palapa-shaded restaurant and bar on the beach, but room decor is garish and somewhat crude. The beach is broad, but large rocks leave only a narrow entry to the sea.

## WHERE TO EAT

The abundance of fresh fish and seafood can make dining out a pleasure in Cozumel, while lovers of meat, pasta, and other types of dishes are also well looked after. Restaurants in the center of town tend to be casual and unpretentious. In the hotel zones to the north and south, sheer distance can make it simpler to "eat in" at hotel restaurants.

Some of the more elegant and refined restaurants are situated inside hotels, for example, **EL ARRECIFE** for Italian dishes and **EL CARIBEÑO**, an outdoor restaurant with seafood specialties and musicians at night. *Both are at the Inter-Continental Presidente and both are expensive.*

In the center of town, **LA CHOZA**, 10ª Avenida Sur at A.R. Salas, is a casual, palapa-roofed spot with home-style Mexican dishes including chicken *mole* and grilled snapper; for desert, the frozen avocado pie comes highly recommended. Prices are moderate. A block away, **SANTIAGO'S GRILL**, *A.R. Salas at 15ª Avenida Sur*, is a small restaurant offering big cuts of beef and grilled shrimps.

**PIZZERÍA ROLANDI**, *Rafael Melgar at Calle 6 Norte*, offers European-style pizzas along with pasta and fish dishes in a garden courtyard.

**PIZZA PRIMA**, *A.R. Salas 109*, offers American versions of pizza and pastas, along with Italian versions of seafood.

**CASA DENIS**, *Calle 1 Sur*, half a block from the plaza on a pedestrian street, is an inexpensive and thoroughly unpretentious place for tasty Mexican specialties such as *enchiladas*. **EL FOCO**, *5ª Avenida Sur at Calle 13*, a bit south of the center, is a classic taco restaurant, also offering grilled meats, sausages, ribs and melted cheese with tortillas, at inexpensive prices. A few blocks east of the center, **LOS MOROS**, *35ª Avenida near Calle 3 Sur*, is favored by Cozumeleños for authentic Yucatán-style dishes, including distinctive preparations of fish, chicken and pork, with big portions and moderate prices.

*North of town, at km 1.5 on the Carretera Costera del Norte,* **LOBSTER HOUSE** is a romantic spot serving guess what. Food and atmosphere are pleasing, and prices are high, varying according to the weight of the lobster. One of the rare restaurants on the eastern side of the island, **MEZCALITO'S**, offers seafood and sandwiches in a beachfront setting at moderate prices. It is situated where the cross-island road meets the eastern coastal road. *Also on the east side and a little further south,* **PLAYA BONITA BEACH CLUB** is a good spot for a swim and Mexican *antojitos* or grilled fish.

## SHOPPING

As a free port, and as an important cruise ship port, Cozumel offers plenty of shopping. Several shops specialize in high-quality silver jewelry (if you want sterling, look for the .925 symbol). Others offer varied Mexican handicrafts, including ceramics, glassware, *papier mâché* animals, wooden masks, assorted textiles, hammocks and many other items. Still others offer selections of clothing or liquors.

Most tourist-oriented shops are clustered along Avenida Rafael Melgar near the Plaza del Sol, around the plaza itself, and in the pedestrian streets immediately behind the plaza. There is a **crafts market** *on Calle 1 Sur just behind the plaza*. Another cluster of shops is situated by the ferry terminal just south of the center of town.

## ENTERTAINMENT & NIGHTLIFE

Nights tend to be quiet in Cozumel. Sunday evening is a very special time at the Plaza del Sol when many local families come simply to stroll. The plaza takes on a festive mood, with musicians and balloon vendors. There are one or two discotheques near the plaza, open late in the evening.

## SEEING THE SIGHTS

In the absence of bus service and with the distances involved, most points of interest in Cozumel can be reached only by taxi, car, or motorcycle. If you are planning to visit only one or two spots on a given day, high car rental rates may make it considerably cheaper to take a taxi and arrange for the driver to come back for you later at a fixed hour. Some of the unpaved roads in remote parts of the island can be treacherous, especially during the rainy season.

In San Miguel, exhibits at the **Museo de la Isla de Cozumel** present local flora, fauna, and ecosystems, including coral formations, as well as artifacts from the Mayan and Spanish eras and works by local painters. Items are well presented and include a reproduction of a Mayan house. *The museum is situated on Avenida Rafael Melgar between Calles 4 and 6 Norte and is open daily from 10 am to 6 pm. Admission is $3.* Upstairs, drinks and snacks are served on a terrace facing the sea.

Cozumel does not have any archaeological sites of particular interest, but a couple of sites nonetheless draw many visitors. If these were in a less heavily touristed area, they probably wouldn't attract much attention. The most important set of ruins are those at **San Gervasio**, situated in the interior of the island toward the north. *To get there, head east along Avenida Juárez and continue for 8 km out of town, then turn north along a well-marked road for a further 7 km. The site is open daily from 8 am to 4:30 pm Admission is $3, and there is also a road toll of $1.*

Archaeologists have surmised that this site was occupied continuously by Mayans from the fourth to the 14th centuries A.D. and was used as a ceremonial center, but all that remains today are some stone mounds and columns scattered over a broad area. Good shoes and mosquito protection are essential. The site is poorly marked, and bilingual guides charge $12 for a tour. Handicrafts and drinks are sold at stalls near the entrance. A visitors' center was under construction.

A visit to San Gervasio is a good excuse for a bicycle ride. Roads are paved, traffic is light and there are no hills, making this one of the few routes in Mexico where cycling can be recommended even for inexperienced riders. Bicycles can be rented at several spots in the center of San Miguel, in the streets just behind the plaza.

**Parque Chankanaab** is a marine park *situated 9 km south of San Miguel.* Although it has a diving area and four dive shops, it is most noted for snorkeling, with a big, fish-filled lagoon and a broad platform for entering the water. Equipment is available for rental. *The park is open daily from 7 am to 5:30 pm. Admission is $4, free for children under 10.* It includes a broad, sandy beach with palapa shades, a swimming area, botanical garden, a small museum displaying seashells and photos of the reefs, and an area with stone paintings intended to resemble ancient Mayan work. There are

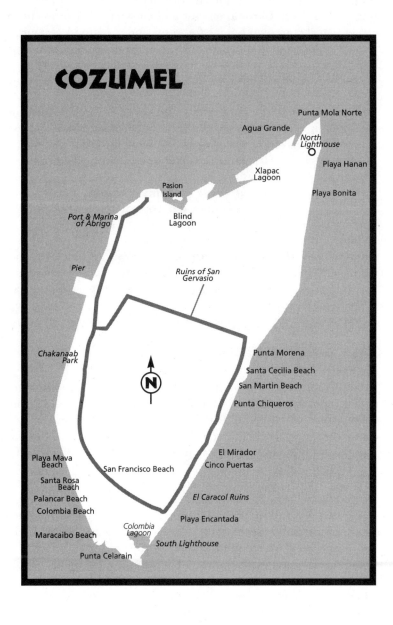

**COZUMEL**

Punta Mola Norte

Agua Grande

*North Lighthouse*

Playa Hanan

Xlapac Lagoon

Pasion Island

Playa Bonita

Port & Marina of Abrigo

Blind Lagoon

Pier

*Ruins of San Gervasio*

Chakanaab Park

Punta Morena

Santa Cecilia Beach

San Martin Beach

Punta Chiqueros

Playa Mava Beach

El Mirador

Cinco Puertas

San Francisco Beach

Santa Rosa Beach

Palancar Beach

*El Caracol Ruins*

Colombia Beach

Playa Encantada

Maracaibo Beach

*Colombia Lagoon*

*South Lighthouse*

Punta Celarain

also numerous gift shops, several snack, bars and a pricey, palapa-roofed restaurant facing the sea and offering fish, seafood and sandwiches.

*Just south* is **Playa Corona**, quieter and cheaper, with access to the same reef, snorkeling equipment for rent, and a seafood restaurant. *Further south*, **Playa San Francisco** actually comprises two beaches known as **Playa Maya** and **Playa Santa Rosa**. This is a long stretch of sandy beach where hotel development has been held back for environmental reasons. Many local people come here on Sundays. There are two or three restaurants, as well as dressing rooms and rental of beach chairs and snorkeling equipment. Divers use this beach to reach the Santa Rosa reef, which is noted for its sharp, wall-like drop. *Continuing south*, visitors reach the **Parque Nacional Submarino de Palancar**, whose offshore reef is rated by diving specialists as one of the best in the world.

*At the southern tip of the island is* **Punta Celaraín**, marked by a lighthouse surrounded by sand dunes and tropical forest, with pounding waves and secluded beaches below. The last several kilometers are along a dirt road.

*On the eastern side of Cozumel* are several coves and long beaches, among them **Playa Bonita**, with fine sand, a good restaurant, moderate surf and the possibility of camping. Camping is also possible at **Playa Chen Río** *just to the north.* At many beaches along the eastern shore, high waves and strong riptides can make swimming dangerous.

## SPORTS & RECREATION
### Snorkeling and Diving

Fabulous coral reefs flush with brilliantly colored tropical fish made Cozumel's reputation. Anyone who can swim can also snorkel. The only equipment required are fins and a tightly fitting mask and pipe. These can be rented at most snorkeling beaches for a few dollars a day. After that, you just swim out a short distance, float on the surface of the water, breathe through the pipe, and peer at the reef below you.

Scuba diving is a far more elaborate exercise and requires tanks with pressurized air. It is utterly essential to take diving lessons before setting out. These can be arranged through the dive shops that have proliferated at hotels, beaches and in town. Instruction is available in English. Diving can be dangerous if you don't know what you're doing. It is also an expensive undertaking. Some hotels offer packages that include rooms and diving.

**Chankanaab Park**, *9 km south of San Miguel*, is one of the most popular spots for snorkeling and an easy place for beginners to learn the ropes. Several hotels can direct guests to small snorkeling areas just offshore. More dramatic but harder-to-reach spots include the Palancar and Colombia reefs toward the southern end of the island.

**Palancar reef** is among the top choices for divers because of its varied coral formations and its dramatic series of underwater peaks and valleys. Because the reef *lies nearly 2 km offshore*, it is necessary to go with a group or charter a boat. The reef is almost 5 km long. At the bottom it has red and black coral and enormous sponges. An area of reef called the Horseshoe is favored by many divers for its sensational ravines and canyons.

**Colombia reef**, *several kilometers south of Palancar*, is a prime area for experienced divers to go deep. It, too, is endowed with a labyrinthine structure of ravines and canyons, and toward the bottom divers may encounter large groupers, as well as the occasional eagle ray or giant turtle.

**Santa Rosa**, *just north of Palancar*, has an abrupt drop just a short distance out that divers call the **Santa Rosa Wall**. Suggested more for experienced divers, it has currents that make it suitable for drift diving, and it extends to a great depth. There are a number of tunnels and caves, and many sponges, groupers and angelfish.

**Tormentos reef**, *near Chankanaab Park*, is a shallower reef favored by underwater photographers for its colorful backdrop of sea cucumber, arrow crab, sponges and coral shrimp.

**Paraíso reef**, *just south of the cruise ship pier*, is used as a practice spot for novice divers and is popular for night diving. It has an impressive array of star coral, brain coral sea fans and sponges.

**Plane Wreck** is a spot *near Hotel La Ceiba 4.5 km south of San Miguel*. In 1977 film producers deliberately crashed a plane in the water here. Shallow and close to shore, it is a training ground for novice divers and has colorful sponges and large coral structures. It also has an underwater "trail" marked with signs indicating different types of marine life.

This is only a partial list of dive sites around Cozumel. Dive shops have proliferated around the island. They can provide all necessary equipment and arrange all manner of excursions using a variety of vessels, some going to lesser known spots. Some dive masters have strong opinions about which spots are most interesting.

## EXCURSIONS

Cozumel's insular location should not stop visitors from doing some exploring on the mainland. Aerocozumel provides daily air service to **Chichén Itzá**, allowing a leisurely visit to the fabulous Mayan ruins there with a return the same day. Closer at hand, the ruins of **Tulum** and **Cobá** can be reached by ferry and bus via Playa del Carmen. Other activities that can be enjoyed with a same-day return include a visit to the **Xcaret** water park, diving at **Akumal**, snorkeling at **Xel-Ha**, or beachcombing at remote spots in between. Details on all these spots appear further on in this chapter.

These places can all be visited on a do-it-yourself basis. Some of them can also be visited, at higher cost but greater ease, through organized tours. Information is available at tour desks at the bigger hotels and tour agencies scattered through the streets near the plaza.

These same tour companies will be happy to provide information on excursions by boat for diving, snorkeling or **deep-sea fishing**. The best season for fishing is from late April to June, when marlin, dory and swordfish abound. As well, **semi-submersible vessels** take visitors on 90-minute underwater excursions to some of the reefs. This probably won't interest divers, who can enjoy the real thing, but not everyone is a diver.

## PRACTICAL INFORMATION
### Airlines
For reservations in Cozumel:
• **Continental**: *(987) 20487*
• **Mexicana**: *(987) 20133*
• **Aerocozumel**: *(987) 20877*

### Car Rentals
Rates tend to be quite high in Cozumel. Rental cars are available at the airport, the cruise ship terminal, in the center of town and at several of the bigger hotels. **Avis**, **Budget**, and **Hertz** are all represented.

The biggest local firm is **Fiesta Cozumel**, *Calle 11 Sur 598 a few blocks from the center, phone (987) 20725 or 21389*. They operate tour desks at many of the resort hotels.

### Currency Exchange
Cash and travelers' checks can be exchanged at several banks around the plaza, but only during regular banking hours: *Monday to Friday, 9 am to 1:30 pm*. There are one or two *casas de cambio* in the streets behind the plaza that stay open longer.

### Laundry
• **Express Lavandaría**, *Calle A.R. Salas between 5ª and 10ª Avenidas*, provides same-day drop-off service and also self-service machines.

### Motor Scooter & Bicycle Rentals
At least a half-dozen spots in the streets behind the plaza just outside the pedestrian zone rent motor scooters, bicycles or both. It is usually necessary to sign a credit card voucher or to leave a large cash deposit.

Daily rental fees for bicycles average between $6 and $10, while motor scooters usually cost $25 to $30 a day.

**Tourist Information**

The **state tourism office** *is located upstairs in the big government building facing the Plaza del Sol,* but the less formal **tourism information booth** *along the ferry pier* can often be more helpful.

# PLAYA DEL CARMEN

*Playa del Carmen lies 66 km south of downtown Cancún and 54 km from Cancún airport. It is situated just off Highway 307.*

**Playa del Carmen** is what some people who wind up in Cancún are really looking for. It is a medium-sized resort with fine beaches, a laid-back atmosphere and decent selections of moderately priced restaurants and hotels. It is also the main terminal for passenger ferries to Cozumel.

Not so long ago, Playa del Carmen (known to locals simpy as Playa) was a vaguely bohemian place, slightly off the beaten track and popular with thrifty European travelers. Fishing boats lined the beach, pigs wandered along the main street and tranquility reigned. Traces of that era persist. There are still fishing boats on the beach, and people on low budgets are still taken care of, but the town has grown, the pigs have been banished, big new resort hotels have sprung up in a zone called Playacar just south of where the town used to end, and a new class of tourists has arrived, blending congruously with the tie-dyed-T-shirt-and-sandals set.

The main street has become a pedestrian mall lined with restaurants and shops. It bustles day and night. Between there and the ferry pier lie a big plaza with a children's playground. Playa del Carmen is definitely a lived-in sort of place, without the stark separation between visitors and locals found in Cancún. At shops along the main street, you are as likely to find a bunch of bananas as a fancy necklace.

North of Playa del Carmen are a couple of isolated and interesting resort hotels in an area known as **Punta Bete**, and halfway to Cancún is the quiet town of **Puerto Morelos**, with small beaches and hotels, modest diving facilities, and the car ferry terminal for Cozumel. More information on these destinations is given after this section.

## ARRIVALS & DEPARTURES

**By Bus & Taxi**

Three bus companies, Playa Express, Interplaya, and Oriente, between them provide service several times an hour between Cancún, Playa del Carmen and Tulum. Oriente uses older but more comfortable vehicles. Other companies also operate on this route, but less frequently. The first southbound departure from Cancún is at 4 am and the last one at 10:30 pm. The trip takes a little over an hour, and the fare is about $2, payable on board. All buses operate from a terminal near the main plaza in Playa del Carmen or from the streets just outside.

By taxi from downtown Cancún or from the hotel zone, the fare is $30. From Cancún airport, fares are exorbitant – around $60. There are several ways around this. The easiest, and slowest, is to take the collective van to the terminal in downtown Cancún and a bus from there. Alternately, you can walk across the airport parking lot past the security booth at the airport perimeter and flag a taxi there. Taxis from Cancún are not allowed to pick up passengers on airport grounds, but outside the perimeter this restriction does not apply. There is a steady flow of taxis, and they charge about $30 to Playa del Carmen. A cheaper way is to have a taxi take you to the highway junction 4 km from the airport ($3 fare) and flag a bus from there (not suggested at night).

Returning from Playa del Carmen to Cancún airport, taxi fare is $27. Alternatives are to go by bus to the Puerto Morelos junction, where taxis are usually waiting and charge $12 to the airport, or to continue by bus to the trickier confines of the clover leaf junction 4 km from the airport, where taxis returning empty from the airport can be flagged ($3 fare).

By bus from Playa del Carmen to Tulum, besides frequent second-class services there are 12 daily first-class departures. To Cobá, and continuing to Valladolid, buses go at 5 am, 10 am, and 5 pm. To Mérida, there are 11 daily departures, including an express bus at 10 am, and to Chetumal, with connections for Belize, there are 12 buses a day. ADO has four daily first-class buses to Villahermosa, two of them continuing overnight to Mexico City ($55) and one to Veracruz. All buses leave from the terminal near the main plaza or from streets a block or so west.

### By Car

Playa del Carmen lies 66 km south of downtown Cancún and 54 km from Cancún airport. It is situated just off Highway 307, which continues to Tulum, 65 km further south, and on to Chetumal near the border with Belize. Highway 307 is mostly flat and straight but has no shoulders over most of its length. It has been widened to four lanes for a short stretch south of Cancún. Plans call for it to be widened as far south as Tulum.

### By Ferry

Passenger ferries to Cozumel leave from a big pier near the main plaza in Playa del Carmen, arriving near the center of San Miguel de Cozumel. Two companies compete for your business, one with big, air-conditioned boats at a one-way fare of $6, the other with smaller, open vessels for $4.50. Refreshments are sold aboard most vessels, and the crossing averages about 45 minutes. Before buying a ticket, check the departure times of both companies; you may save yourself a wait. Roundtrip tickets often provide no discount and lock you into returning by a vessel of the same company.

There are about 25 crossings a day in each direction, with the first departure from Playa del Carmen at 5 am and the last one at 8:45 pm (but check locally; schedules do change). From Cozumel the first departure is at 4 am and the last one at 8 pm.

## ORIENTATION

Streets in Playa del Carmen are laid out in a rectangular grid pattern. **Avenida Juárez** is a boulevard running the nine blocks between the highway and the beach. Streets to the north of Avenida Juárez have even numbers and those to the south have odd numbers, but street numbers are not used very much. **Avenida 5** is the big pedestrian street running parallel to the beach, which lies one block to the east.

At its northern end Avenida 5 is open to motor traffic. The avenues are numbered in multiples of five. There is a big main plaza bound by Avenida Juárez, Avenida 5, and the beach, with a tourism information booth in one corner. To its south are the ferry pier and a walkway skirting the Continental Plaza hotel.

**PLAYA DEL CARMEN**

Most points in Playa del Carmen are within easy walking distance. Taxis are available at all hours along Avenida Juárez between Avenidas 5 and 10, near the bus terminal. Taxi fares tend to be rather high, however, sometimes $4 or so for a short trip. Most of the Playacar resort area, south of town, and hotels beyond the northern edge of town, are taxi distance, especially with baggage or at night. These same areas can be reached by walking a half hour or so along the beach.

The beach extends for many kilometers in both directions from the center of town, but it is broader and more appealing heading north (turn left when facing the sea). Just when it looks like you have run out of beach, you walk around a sandy promontory and another vast stretch of beach lies before you. There is little shade, however. The island of Cozumel acts as a partial breakwater and prevents waves from being very rough.

## NUDE BATHING SPOT

*About 3 km north of the center of town, just beyond **Las Palapas** and **Shangri-La** hotels, there is a small cluster of palm trees marking a stretch of beach where nudity is common.*

## WHERE TO STAY

The less expensive hotels are found mostly in the central part of town or just to the north. Some face the beach, but most are a block or two away. The very cheapest spots are located further from the beach. The most lavish hotels are situated just outside town.

### Hotels in or near the center of town

**CASA DE GOPALA**, *Calle 2 between Avenidas 10 and 15, phone (987) 30054; 16 rooms; high season $24 single, $30 double; low season $15 single, $18 double; no cards.*

The bright, airy rooms here are simple but pleasant, housed in a rustic three-story building with sea views from the top floor. Situated on a quiet back street, this friendly hotel has a pretty garden passageway, but watch for uneven stones.

**POSADA CORTO MALTÉS**, *Calle 10 near the beach, phone (987) 30206; 12 rooms, $23 to $33 single or double, no cards.*

Rates vary according to season and to whether the bath is private or shared. This spot is quite enticing despite its hard-edged French owners. The grounds are shaded by tropical forest, with white sand under foot. Simple, agreeably rustic rooms are set in palapa-roofed huts.

**POSADA LAS FLORES**, *Avenida 5 near Calle 4, phone (987) 30085; 12 rooms, $12 to $18 single or double, no cards.*

This quiet, friendly place is centrally located. It has a sand-covered, tree-shaded garden courtyard with hammocks. Rooms are simple but clean and represent excellent value if you can make do without toilet seats.

**BLUE PARROT INN**, *Calle 12 at the beach, phone (987) 30083, fax (987) 30049; 22 rooms, bungalows and villas, $23 to $58, VI - MC.*

This friendly, bustling, mildly funky establishment has a crazy jumble of low-slung, single- or multi-room buildings sprawling over a broad swath of beachfront. All are simply but brightly furnished, many are palapa-roofed, and some have private terraces with hammocks. The Blue Parrot is known for its lively restaurant and bar, with musicians some evenings.

**HOTEL-RESTAURANT DA GABI**, *Calle 12 between Avenida 5 and the beach, phone (987) 30048; 10 rooms, high season $36 single or double, low season $14 to $18, no cards.*

Set in an attractive burnt-orange building, rooms here vary considerably. Some have sea views, and some have palapa roofs. All are decorated with elegant tiles, but furnishings are very simple. Service is friendly.

**HOTEL MOLCAS**, *next to the main plaza near the ferry pier, phone (987) 30070 or 30136, fax (987) 30138; 35 rooms; high season $65 single, $75 double; low season $60 single, $65 double; VI - MC - AE.*

This strategically situated hotel is one of the oldest in Playa del Carmen. For years it was *the* hotel in town. Though its rooms are big, bright and comfortable, with tile floors, air conditioning and TV, things are starting to look a little worn. The hotel has a pool and an open-air restaurant facing the beach and the ferry pier.

**HOTEL ALBATRÓS** and **HOTEL ALBATRÓS ROYALE**, *Calle 8 at the beach, phone (987) 30001, fax (987) 30002, US reservations (800) 527-0022; 53 rooms and bungalows, high season $42 to $72 single or double, low season $30 to $44, VI - MC, discounts for cash.*

These friendly twin establishments offer a choice between rustic, palapa-roofed cabañas at the Albatrós and nicely furnished, four-unit villas at the Albatrós Royale. The latter has well-tended gardens, terraces with hammocks and thatched ceilings in the upstairs rooms. The Albatrós has several bigger bungalows with refrigerators.

**HOTEL COSTA DEL MAR**, *near the beach between Calles 10 and 12, phone (987) 30058; 37 rooms, high season $24 to $48 single or double, low season $19 to $38, VI - MC - AE.*

There is something for everyone here, ranging from rustic cabañas to simple but pleasant fan-cooled rooms to more snazzily decorated air conditioned rooms. The place has atmosphere, but the grounds are a little dusty. There is a big palapa-shaded restaurant and bar by the beach.

**HOTEL ALEJARI**, *Calle 6 between the beach and Avenida 5, phone (987) 30374; 15 rooms, high season $40 to $60 single or double, low season $27 to $45, VI - MC.*

Prices vary according to whether the room is air conditioned, equipped with kitchenette or by the beach. A tight cluster of two-story red-

and-white buildings are set on exuberantly landscaped grounds. Rooms are big but plain and a little stuffy.

**BUNGALOWS CUEVA PARGO**, *Calle 8 between Avenida 5 and the beach, phone (987) 30351; 8 rooms, high season $30 to $54, low season $24 to $42, VI - MC.*

The biggest bungalows have kitchenettes and can accommodate up to four people, the smallest have shared bath. Rustic, simply furnished, palapa-roofed bungalows are spread over heavily vegetated grounds.

**YAX-HA**, *on the beach between Calles 8 and 10, no phone; 4 cabins, $27 to $36 for up to three people, no cards.*

Each cabin has a kitchen. Service is friendly.

**HOTEL ROSA MIRADOR**, *between Calles 12 and 14, one block from the beach, phone (987) 30567, fax (987) 30537; 10 rooms, high season $27 to $32 single or double, low season $18 to $24, VI - MC with 7% surcharge.*

This four-story, whitewashed building is set on a back street. Rooms on the upper floors have sea views and two beds. All are simply furnished. The owner, Don Beto, is knowledgeable about the surrounding area.

**HOTEL VILLA DEL SOL**, *Avenida 15 between Calles 12 and 14, no phone; 10 rooms, high season $30 single or double, low season $18, no cards.*

Set on an isolated back street, this new hotel has simple but attractive rooms with high thatched ceilings and colorful weavings. The courtyard is covered with gravel, and trees there are just starting to grow.

**QUINTA MIJA**, *Avenida 5 near Calle 14, phone (987) 30111, US reservations (800) 538-6802; 18 rooms and apartments, high season $45 to $85, low season $30 to $60, no cards.*

The apartments at this three-story American-run hotel are big and pleasantly, though not lavishly, furnished in shades of beige and blue. The rooms are much smaller but have some nice decorative touches.

**BANANA CABAÑAS**, *Avenida 5 near Calle 6, phone (987) 30036; 11 rooms, high season $27 single or double, low season $21, VI - MC - AE.*

This rustic spot has cabañas with high roofs and white stucco walls and some low-ceilinged apartments. Decor is simple. Parts of the grounds are beautifully tended while others are painfully bare.

**HOTEL MAYA BRIC**, *Avenida 5 between Calles 8 and 10, phone (987) 30011; 24 rooms; high season $32 single, $40 double; low season, $18 single, $21 double; VI - MC.*

Rooms, simply but comfortably furnished, are set in two-story motel-style buildings. The grounds are landscaped but unkempt, with a pool.

**HOTEL DELFIN**, *Avenida 5 near Calle 6, phone (987) 30176; 14 rooms, high season $24 single, $27 double, $5 less in low season, VI - MC.*

Rooms in this four-story hotel are large but simple, with a jarring pink and green color scheme.

**POSADA SIAN KA'AN**, *Avenida 5 near Calle 2, phone (987) 30202; 17 rooms; high season $30 single or double, low season $23, some rooms with shared bath at half price, no cards.*

Rooms are clean and bright, but the grounds are scruffy and service is sluggish.

**HOTEL AZUL PROFUNDO**, *Calle 14 by the beach, phone (987) 30415; 20 rooms; high season $12 single, $15 double, slightly less in low season; double rooms by the beach $36 high season, $27 low season; no cards.*

Housed in a pair of rather forlorn-looking buildings, rooms here are big but poorly furnished, with terraces facing the beach. New owners are refurbishing this place bit by bit. We wish them well.

**HOTEL ELEFANTE**, *Avenida 10 near Calle 10, phone (987) 30037; 38 rooms; high season $15 single, $21 double; low season $12 single, $18 double; no cards.*

This two-story motel-style structure on a dusty back street has big but dumpy rooms, some with kitchenette.

**HOTEL TRINIDAD FACES**, *Avenida 5 between Calles 10 and 12, phone (987) 30328; 15 rooms; high season $23 single, $27 double; low season $12 single, $15 double; no cards.*

Rooms are simple and cool. The grounds are poorly kept. There is a small pool, but it looks a bit grimy.

**VILLAS DEPORTIVAS JUVENIL**, *Calle 8 at Avenida 30, no phone; 200 dormitory beds at $5 per person, plus 5 cabañas for 2 to 3 people at $14 to $18, no cards.*

This youth hostel is open to all and has ten large dormitories, segregated by sex. It is bright and clean but a bit isolated.

**CABAÑAS NUEVO AMANECER**, *Calle 4 between Avenidas 5 and 10, phone (987) 30030; 14 rooms, low season $18 single or double, high season $23, no cards.*

Palapa-roofed rooms are dark, and the scruffy grounds are used for parking. Some rooms have refrigerators.

**POSADA LILY**, *Juárez at Avenida 10, phone (987) 30116; 25 rooms, $12 to $18, single or double, no cards.*

This big blue and white building has basic, noisy rooms.

**POSADA MARINELLY**, *Juárez between Avenidas 10 and 15, phone (987) 30140; 8 rooms, high season $15 single, $18-$21 double, low season $11 to $15, no cards.*

The attractive tree cover outside is deceptive; this place is grubby and needs refurbishing.

**HOTEL PLAYA DEL CARMEN**, *Juárez at Avenida 15, no phone; 17 rooms, $12 single, $18 double, no cards.*

This two-storey, U-shaped building is along a noisy street. Rooms are very basic and poorly furnished.

### Hotels in Playacar

**CONTINENTAL PLAZA PLAYACAR**, *facing the sea just south of the ferry pier, phone (987) 30100, fax (987) 30105, US reservations (800) 882-6684; 180 rooms, high season $189 single or double, low season $149, VI - MC - AE.*

This elegant new hotel has a wavy exterior sculpted to blend with the shoreline. There are fine stretches of beach and a handsome walkway in front. Although the hotel gives its address as Playacar, it is really well within Playa del Carmen; the main plaza is nearby. The hotel has two restaurants, a big pool with swim-up bar, a lighted tennis court and colorful jungle mural in the lobby. Rooms, a majority with sea views, are comfortably furnished with air conditioning, satellite TV and private terraces or balconies. Suites with kitchenette and dining area are available. Many guests obtain reduced group rates by booking their rooms as part of a tour package.

**DIAMOND RESORT PLAYACAR**, *2 km south of town, phone (987) 30339, US and Canada reservations (800) 858-2258; 300 rooms; high season $242 double, $165 single; low season $182 double, $124 single; VI - MC - AE.*

This is an all-inclusive resort with meals, most drinks and sporting activities such as tennis and boating included in room rates. Most guests arrive with tour packages that provide greatly reduced group rates Rooms are set in two-story thatched villas with eight rooms in each cluster and are decorated in Mexican style, with air conditioning and TV. The hotel faces the beach, but the grounds sprawl and most rooms are several minutes' walk from the beach or pools.

**CARIBBEAN VILLAGE PLAYACAR**, *2.5 km south of town, phone (987) 30506, US and Canada reservations (800) 858-2258; 300 rooms; high season $220 double, $154 single; low season $165 double, $116 single; VI - MC - AE.*

This is another all-inclusive resort with meals, most drinks and sporting activities included in room rates. Again, the vast majority of guests arrive with tour packages which provide greatly reduced group rates. Rooms are clustered in 22 salmon-colored villa-style buildings of one to three stories scattered over grassy grounds with pools. Each room has air conditioning, phone, TV and bathtub.

The hotel is situated near a new 18-hole golf course but about ten minutes' walk from the beach. Transportation is provided to a private beach club. Activities include tennis, cycling, sailing, scuba lessons, snorkeling and volleyball.

### Hotels north of town

**LAS PALAPAS**, *facing the beach 2 km north of Playa del Carmen, phone (987) 22977, fax (987) 30458; 55 rooms, high season $135 single, $162 double* *including two meals a day; $9 to $13 less in low season, $10 to $12 more for units nearest the beach, VI - MC, full payment required for advance reservations.*

This idyllic spot consists of a cluster of whitewashed, thatch-roofed twin-story villas with grassy areas and trees in between, almost a tropical seaside version of an Alpine resort! The clientele is mostly European, and the manager is German. Rooms are cooled by sea breezes and fans, and the upstairs rooms have lofty, thatched ceilings. The restaurant has a good reputation, and there is a big pool.

**SHANGRI-LA CARIBE,** *facing the beach 2 km north of Playa del Carmen, phone (987) 22888, fax (987) 30500, US reservations (800) 538-6802; 70 rooms; high season $105 to $180 single, $135 to $180 double, including two meals a day; low season $75 to $150 single, $90 to $150 double; VI - MC with 6% surcharge.*

Rates vary according to the distance from the beach. The layout and the rooms are very similar to those at Las Palapas, except that there is sand instead of grass. The two are right next to one another, and from the beach they appear to be part of the same hotel.

## WHERE TO EAT

Most restaurants in Playa del Carmen are situated along or near **Avenida 5**, the main pedestrian street, many with tables outdoors. In the evening some restaurants display their offerings on plastic-wrapped dishes and post touts in the street to lure customers inside. Others have musicians who do this same job more effectively. Spots listed below are among the better ones, but there are several more good restaurants along Avenida 5 and on Avenida Juárez facing the plaza. Prices are mostly moderate, and many restaurants offer two-for-one specials on drinks in the early evening. Visitors will find a wide selection of Mexican, Italian and American dishes, with an abundance of fish and seafood.

For big appetites and tight budgets, in the streets just behind the bus terminal are several *rosticerías*, modest restaurants with chickens roasting on spits and tasty, low-cost meals. A couple of small taco restaurants face the municipal market on Avenida 10 near Calle 6.

**LOS LIMONES,** *Avenida 5 and Calle 6*, open evenings only, is one of the more romantic spots around (and one of the more expensive). Set around a jungle-festooned courtyard, it offers nicely prepared Mexican and European dishes. **CHICAGO,** *just across the street*, is recommended for homesick Americans, with trendy decor, American sports on TV, and a variety of Mexican and American dishes.

*A few doors over,* **FLIPPER'S** offers meats, fish and seafood grilled outdoors over charcoal. The **BLUE PARROT INN,** *facing the beach just past Calle 12*, has evening barbecues in a funky, open-air setting. **DA GABI,** *on Calle 12 between Avenida 5 and the beach,* is a romantic spot for pastas and Italian-style seafood beneath the stars.

**MÁSCARAS,** *Avenida Juárez facing the plaza,* has good pastas, pizzas and fish. *Almost next door,* **EL TACOLOTE** offers Mexican dishes, with a selection of tacos with meat, cheese or both. The restaurant of the **HOTEL MOLCAS** has a fairly ordinary Mexican menu, *but it faces the ferry pier* and is a good spot for a meal or drink while awaiting the boat to Cozumel.

## SHOPPING

Playa del Carmen jumped into the fray for visitors' shopping dollars only a few years ago, but **Avenida 5,** the main pedestrian street, is now lined with shops selling assortments of jewelry, clothing and handcrafts. The street has not entirely lost its earlier vocation: there are still several grocery stores and fruit shops.

## ENTERTAINMENT

Musicians perform in the evening at several open-air restaurants along **Avenida 5.** Musical offerings range from marimba duos to Andean ensembles to rock and roll. It's easy to see and hear who's performing where just by walking along the street.

The **Blue Parrot Inn,** *along the beach near the north end of town,* also has musicians some evenings.

## EXCURSIONS

Playa del Carmen is a good base for day excursions to **Cozumel** (by ferry) for diving or snorkeling, to **Tulum** or **Cobá** (by road) to see the ruins, or to any of the spots between Playa and Tulum mentioned a few pages on, including the **Xcaret** water park, **Akumal** for diving, **Xel-Ha** for snorkeling, or beachcombing at remote spots in between. Xcaret is just a few minutes away by taxi or bus.

## PRACTICAL INFORMATION

**Car Rentals**
• **National** *operates from the Hotel Molcas*
• **Budget** *from the Continental Plaza*
• **Elite** *from an office on Avenida 5 near Calle 2*
   Rates tend to be high.

**Currency Exchange**
   **Bancomer,** *Avenida Juárez near Avenida 25,* has tended to offer the best exchange rates and also provides Visa and Mastercard cash advances.

There are a couple of *casas de cambio* on Avenida 5 facing the main plaza. Exchange rates are less favorable than at the banks, but hours are longer.

**Laundry**
• **Maya Laundry**: *Avenida 5 near Calle 2, offers same-day service*

**Tourist Information**
There is a **tourism information booth** *in one corner of the main plaza as you approach from the bus terminal; open late most evenings.* Some staff members are knowledgeable, others much less so. It is possible to purchase prepaid telephone cards there for long-distance calls, accepted by public telephones right next to the booth.

# PUNTA BETE

*Punta Bete lies about midway between Playa del Carmen and Puerto Morelos, about 2 km from Highway 307, to which it is linked by several dirt roads.*

**Punta Bete** is not a town but rather a long, sandy, idyllic stretch of mostly undeveloped beach with gentle waves and a handful of resorts and restaurants. It is easiest to reach by taxi or rental car. Bus users who are prepared to walk from the highway should be certain they know where to disembark.

## WHERE TO STAY

**LA POSADA DEL CAPITAN LAFITTE**, *no phone; reservations via Mérida (99) 239082, fax (99) 237142, US reservations (800) 538-6802; 59 rooms; high season $105 single, $140 double including breakfast and supper; low season $75 single, $93 double; VI - MC - AE.*

This resort, named after a French pirate, consists of bright, cheerful bungalows, many facing the white sand beach, all cooled by sea breezes and fans, with tile floors and bark drawings on the walls. Some rooms are situated in newer, more elegantly decorated two-story cabañas. The hotel offers a big, palapa-shaded open-air restaurant, a pool, a game room with satellite TV, a dive shop with scuba instruction, a gift shop and car rental agency. A reef just 200 meters offshore provides diving and snorkeling.

**KAI LUUM**, *right next to La Posada del Capitán Lafitte, no phone; reservations via Mérida (99) 239082, fax (99) 237142, US reservations (800) 538-6802; 40 tents, high season $80 single, $98 double, including breakfast and supper; low season $66 single, $88 double; no cards.*

This is a deluxe tent resort. That's right, guests sleep in tents, but these aren't just any old tents. They are sheltered by palapa shades, and each has a bed, a carpet, and a small table. Each tent can accommodate up to three people, and half lie directly on a white sand beach. There is no electric power; lighting in the tents and the dining room is by candle or paraffin lamp. The dining room is a long, palapa-shaded shed with a sand floor, cushioned chairs and communal dining. The bar works on the honor system. Kai Luum shares a dive shop with **La Posada del Capitán Lafitte**. There is a reef nearby.

**PLAYA PARAISO** *is a restaurant and beach club located 15 km north of Playa del Carmen and 13 km south of Puerto Morelos.*

There are plans for large-scale hotel development on this site, which faces a broad, sandy, crescent-shaped beach. For the moment, it mostly serves tour bus passengers who come for the luncheon buffet (2 pm to 5 pm, $11 per person) and for a swim.

# PUERTO MORELOS

> *Puerto Morelos lies 2 km off Highway 307.*

**Puerto Morelos** is a sleepy town midway between Cancún and Playa del Carmen with empty expanses of beach nearby and reefs just offshore. Despite its proximity to Cancún, only 36 km to the north, and to Cancún airport, just 25 km away, it has managed to escape massive development. There are several small hotels in town and others just outside, including a luxury resort.

It is served by a handful of buses operating between Cancún and Playa del Carmen. Most visitors who come by bus disembark at the highway junction and use taxis for the remaining hop. There are taxi stands at the junction and at the central plaza.

Puerto Morelos is the terminal for the car ferry to Cozumel. Service is once a day, and schedules change every week. Departure time from Puerto Morelos may be anywhere from 5 am to 12 noon, and the return trip from Cozumel leaves between 9 am and 4 pm. The fare is $42 per car plus $7 per passenger. *For information, phone (987) 10008.*

## WHERE TO STAY

**CARIBBEAN REEF CLUB**, *1 km south of the central plaza, phone (987) 10191, fax (987) 10190; 21 suites, high season $193 for up to four people, low season $143, VI - MC.*

This very comfortable and exclusive American-run resort hotel occupies the site of a former coconut plantation and stretches over a long swath of nearly deserted beachfront. Suites are housed in a group of three-story buildings, all facing the sea and all with big bedrooms and living rooms, full kitchens, central air conditioning, satellite TV, lavish furnishings, marble floors and plenty of painted tile. Grounds are well landscaped. The hotel has a big pool and palapa shades on the beach, which is sandy although in some places there are large rocks in the water. The use of snorkeling equipment, sailboards and sailboats is included in room rates. The restaurant sometimes closes in low season.

**RANCHO LIBERTAD**, *1 km south of the central plaza, phone (987) 10181, US reservations (800) 305-5225; 5 rooms; high season $61 single, $72 double, including a cold breakfast, a few dollars less in low season, no cards.*

Bright, simple fan-cooled rooms at this small American-run hotel have a nautical theme and are quite attractive. A vast palapa-shaded shed with a sand floor is used for meals and various activities.

**HACIENDA MORELOS**, *Avenida Melgar one block from the central plaza, phone (987) 10015; 12 rooms, high season $50 single or double, low season $45, no cards.*

Big, bright rooms all face the beach and have kitchenettes, tile floors and fans. The hotel has a pool, restaurant, and bar. There is a reef right in front for snorkeling.

**POSADA AMOR**, *Avenida Rojo Gómez half a block from the central plaza, phone (987) 10033; 20 rooms, high season $21 to $31, low season $19 to $28, no cards.*

This friendly, sprawling, family-run spot, two blocks from the beach offers several types of rooms, some accommodating up to four people and all big, bright and fresh. A few have shared bath. The restaurant has a high palapa roof and menus in several languages. The hotel offers transportation to a nude beach 3 km away.

**HOTEL OJO DE AGUA**, *Avenida Rojo Gómez three blocks north of the central plaza, phone (987) 10027; 16 rooms, high season $50 single or double, low season $39, no cards.*

This beachfront hotel offers big, bright simple rooms with kitchenette.

## WHERE TO EAT

**RESTAURANT PELICANOS**, *by the central plaza facing the sea*, and **RESTAURANT LAS PALMERAS**, *just half a block south*, are casual spots offering fish, seafood and meat dishes at moderate prices. The latter also operates a dive shop. Meals are available also at the **POSADA AMOR** *just beyond the plaza*.

## BETWEEN PLAYA DEL CARMEN & TULUM

The 65-km (40-mile) stretch of coast between Playa del Carmen and Tulum was mostly undeveloped until just a few years ago. Tourism planners spoke then of something they called the *Cancún-Tulum corridor*, and this is quickly taking shape. The stated intent is to keep projects at fairly low levels of density, but **Puerto Aventuras**, a big integrated resort development, has already swallowed a chunk of coastline, and others may follow. **Xcaret**, just south of Playa del Carmen, has been bulldozed and converted into one of the world's most sophisticated water parks. Several big resort hotels at points further south are either on the drawing board or have already become reality.

This stretch of coast, especially the area around **Akumal**, is favored by many divers and snorkelers. Fish remain abundant around most of the reefs, but true *aficionados* are losing the seclusion they could enjoy until recently. There are still pristine stretches of fine sandy beach which remain undeveloped. Hurry if you want to see them in their natural state.

Highway 307 runs parallel to the coast but follows an inland course averaging about 2 km from the seashore between Cancún and Tulum. The various beaches and developments along the coast are connected to the highway by side roads. This is no problem for those who arrive by car, but bus passengers can face some serious walking unless they chance upon a passing taxi.

Buses run several times an hour along this stretch of highway between early morning and early evening. *See Arrivals & Departures in the Playa del Carmen section above for ways of getting to and from Cancún airport.* Rental cars are available at Puerto Aventuras and Akumal, but rates can be quite high. Taxis are sometimes hard to find. Most of the taxis serving this area are based at Playa del Carmen or Tulum.

## XCARET

> *Xcaret is easy to reach by a well-marked, 2-km side road from Highway 307.*

What was once a spectacular cove 6 km south of Playa del Carmen has been transformed by human energy and imagination, and perhaps also by a touch of human greed, into a better-than-Disney water park, amusement area, botanical garden, and zoo. Publicity material refers to **Xcaret** (pronounced eesh-ka-RETT) as "Nature's sacred paradise." This might be easier to swallow had bulldozers not altered the site quite as radically.

It is easy to be cynical about this type of commercial park, but we admit, grudgingly, that the developers have done a pretty good job of it. Visitors will have to judge for themselves.

## ARRIVALS & DEPARTURES

By bus from Cancún or Playa del Carmen, any second-class bus bound for Tulum will drop passengers at the junction, from where a free shuttle runs to the park entrance (though lapses have been reported). Xcaret is similarly easy to reach from points to the south. By taxi, it is a short (but fairly expensive) trip from Playa del Carmen. Tours including transportation and entrance fees run daily from Cancún, costing $45 for adults and $35 for children, easier than a do-it-yourself tour but double the cost. Some of these tours offer optional visits to Tulum, Xel-Ha or Cobá. *For information in Cancún, phone (98) 830654 or 830743.*

## SEEING THE PARK

The most spectacular and unusual attraction at Xcaret is the **underground river.** A gentle current carries swimmers through a series of caves and open crevasses from the middle of the park to a point near the shore. It is quite an experience, and it is organized efficiently. Swimmers' belongings are transported (free) to the end of the river.

Swimmers and sunbathers also have at their disposal a series of beaches, terraces, pools, lagoons and ocean inlets. The park has an **aviary** with a broad array of birds ranging from peacocks to parrots and short nature trails highlighting jungle vegetation. At the entrance are scale models of important Mayan sites, and there are a couple of tiny ruins inside. Plans call for a giant aquarium and for a mock Mayan village with handicrafts workshops.

*The park is open daily from 8 am to 5 pm, and admission is $15, half price for children under 11, no charge for children under five. Lockers cost an additional $1 and towels can be rented for $3.* Other ways to spend money include horseback rides for $30 an hour, parasailing for $30, or swimming with dolphins for $50.

## WHERE TO EAT

There are three restaurants inside the park: **LA COCINA** for light meals, **LA CALETA** for seafood in a jungle setting at high prices, and a buffet restaurant open only to groups. Another restaurant outside the park *near the highway junction,* **RESTAURANT XCARET,** offers less expensive seafood.

# PAMUL

*This secluded beach is situated about 20 km south of Playa del Carmen.*

**Pamul** is rocky in places, but there are good snorkeling and diving possibilities, and palm trees provide plenty of shade. At night in July and

August giant turtles come here to lay their eggs. If you spot any, keep your distance and turn off your flashlight to avoid frightening them.

## WHERE TO STAY

**PAMUL RV PARK & CABAÑAS**, *reservations (987) 43240, has space for 90 RVs ($12 a night with all services, lower weekly and monthly rates), campsites at $3 per person, and seven bungalows (high season $15 single or double, low season $12) with big but sparsely furnished rooms.*

This establishment has a restaurant (simple menu, reasonable prices), dive shop, palapa shades on the beach, and laundry service.

# PUERTO AVENTURAS

> **Puerto Aventuras is situated 26 km south of Playa del Carmen.**

This is a giant integrated development with hotels, numerous condominium complexes, a marina, an 18-hole golf course, restaurants and even a small museum. It is handsomely laid out, with tones of beige and ochre dominating and canals adding to the allure. There is a suburban lifelessness to the place, however, with the streets nearly deserted.

The beach is attractive but by no means the best on Mexico's Caribbean coast, and **Puerto Aventuras** (literally, Port Adventure) is plagued with time-share salesmen peddling overpriced shares of resort property. This has lead some wags to call it *Puerto Amarguras* (Port Bitterness).

## WHERE TO STAY

**HOTEL CONTINENTAL PLAZA PUERTO AVENTURAS**, *phone (987) 35133, fax (987) 35134, US and Canada reservations (800) 882-6684; 63 rooms, high season $99 single or double, low season $79, VI - MC - AE.*

This hotel is situated a few minutes' walk from the beach. Formerly called Marina San Carlos, it is an attractive beige and terra cotta structure, though some rooms have poor views. Higher-priced studios (with kitchenette) and suites have views of the sea or of the pool and marina. All rooms have air conditioning and TV. Decor includes elements of marble, with white and teal the dominant colors.

**HOTEL OASIS PUERTO AVENTURAS**, *phone (987) 35050, fax (987) 35051; 271 rooms; high season $308 single, $396 double, including meals, drinks and sporting activities; low season $165 single, $220 double; VI - MC - AE.*

This big beachfront hotel has adopted the all-inclusive formula and caters mostly to people on package tours. Rooms, all with air conditioning and TV, have bright blue and white decor. Half face the sea, the other half face the marina. Some have kitchenettes.

## WHERE TO EAT

There are several eating places in Puerto Aventuras, most notably **RESTAURANT PAPAYA REPUBLIC,** *on the far side beyond the golf course,* which draws many people from outside. It is tucked between a stand of tropical forest and a small beach. It is both elegant and rustic at the same time. The broad menu emphasizes fish and seafood, but there are lighter items also. Prices are on the high side of moderate.

## SEEING THE SIGHTS

The **Museo Pablo Bush Romero** displays Mayan pieces and items from Caribbean shipwrecks, in particular from El Matancero, a Spanish galleon that sank in 1741. *The museum is open daily from 10 am to 1 pm and 2 pm to 6 pm. Voluntary contributions are requested.*

**Cenote Azul,** *one km south of Puerto Aventuras, with the entrance by the highway,* is a swimming area created when the ground collapsed from above a big underwater pool. The water is crystal clear and refreshing, and it is deeper than it looks. It is reached by a 200-meter trail through the jungle. This natural pool is a bit muddy around the edges, and there are ropes and ladders to ease entry. There are also some interesting rock formations.

## XPU-HA

*Just south of Puerto Aventuras,* this is another of those idyllic, sparsely developed beaches. Several tiny hotels are scattered along the beach, including **VILLA XPU-HA** *(no phone, 5 rooms, $30 single or double, no cards)* whose simple rooms have tile floors and good cross-ventilation. There are a restaurant and dive shop nearby.

## KANTENAH

This stretch of coast *between Puerto Aventuras and Akumal, about midway between Playa del Carmen and Tulum,* has fine beaches which have proven irresistible to developers of big all-inclusive resorts. Each hotel has a long side road from Highway 307. During our visit there were still no telephones.

## WHERE TO STAY

**EL DORADO RESORT,** *reached by a well marked side road near Kilometer 95, Cancún phone (98) 843242 or 843319, fax (98) 846952, US* *reservations (800) 544-3005; 135 rooms by late 1995; high season $190 single, $284 double including meals, drinks and sporting activities; low season $117 single, $174 double; VI - MC - AE - DC.*

Rooms in this new and growing all-inclusive resort are set in a cluster of two-story pink buildings. All are big, suite-style rooms with bright floral bedspreads, plenty of marble, air conditioning and TV. Only a few have sea views, however. The beach has a rocky surface in some places near the water's edge. The hotel has two pools, two restaurants, three bars and landscaped grounds.

**ROBINSON CLUB TULUM**, *reached by a well marked side road near Kilometer 100, Cancún phone (98) 811010 or 811005; 300 rooms, introductory rate $152 to $180 double, including meals, drinks and sporting activities, VI - MC - AE - DC.*

Despite its name, this all-inclusive resort hotel is situated more than 30 km north of Tulum. It is part of a German hotel group and marks their first venture in the western hemisphere. Clusters of three-story villas, painted pale yellow, blue and terra cotta, are set on vast grounds. Higher rates apply at villas near the beach, although there are no direct sea views. All rooms have two queen-size beds and air conditioning, with beige and teal decor and plenty of marble. Eight tennis courts, a gym, aerobics classes, evening shows and a mini-club for children are included in room rates. Diving courses and a golf driving range are offered at extra cost.

# AKUMAL

> *Akumal is about 35 km south of Playa del Carmen and 2 km from the highway.*

**Akumal** is a favorite spot among divers and snorkelers and also has fine beaches. It includes a central resort zone plus an area just north called **Half Moon Bay**, with houses and condominiums, and another resort zone to the south called **Aventuras Akumal**, reached by a separate road. Some hotels arrange diving or deep-sea fishing excursions.

There is no real village here, but there is a small shopping area. A bit further north is **Yalkú**, an inlet with excellent snorkeling. It is reached by an unmarked road.

**VILLA DE ROSA**, *Aventuras Akumal phone (987) 41271, rates vary, VI - MC.*

Run by three Americans, this is an intimate complex of villas, condominium units and standard hotel rooms. High season rates range anywhere from $55 for a hotel room for two people to $209 for a three-bedroom beachfront villa, with discounts for long stays (all rates higher at Christmas). Low season rates are about 20 per cent less. All rooms are equipped with air conditioning, TV and microwave ovens. Staff and owners are friendly and very helpful. The hotel has a commercial kitchen that delivers meals to guests, a dive shop, and rentals of cars, bicycles, sailboards, kayaks and canoes. It also offers a range of dive packages and can arrange deep-sea fishing and land excursions in the surrounding area.

**HOTEL CLUB AKUMAL CARIBE** and **VILLAS MAYA**, *Akumal, phone (987) 22532, fax (98) 847041, US reservations (800) 351-1622, in Canada (800) 343-1440; 64 rooms, high season $85 single or double in bungalows, $99 in hotel, low season $60 to $85, VI - MC - AE.*

This establishment offers both bungalows, with most set in clusters around a garden and a couple by the beach, and regular hotel rooms in an adjacent three-story building, with all facing the sea. There are a pool, dive shop, restaurant, snack bar and pizzeria on the grounds. Various dive packages and meal plans are available. Rooms are air conditioned, and some have kitchenettes. The bungalows are bigger but more simply furnished than the hotel rooms.

Under the same management, **VILLAS FLAMINGO**, *about 1 km north along Half Moon Bay*, offer four deluxe, split-level condominium units with pink, Moorish-style exteriors and very spacious rooms. A vehicle is a must.

**LAS CASITAS AKUMAL**, *next to Hotel Club Akumal Caribe; 18 two-bedroom villas; high season $193, low season $127, VI - MC - AE.*

These comfortable, air-conditioned units all face the sea.

**AKUMAL CANCÚN HOTEL AND BEACH RESORT**, *Akumal, phone (987) 22453, fax (987) 22567; 92 rooms, high season $110 single or double, low season $83, VI - MC - AE - DC.*

Rooms are divided between four Mediterranean-influenced buildings. Many have sea views, and all have air conditioning, in-room safety deposit boxes, and Mexican rustic decor with painted tiles, carvings and bark paintings. The hotel has an enormous circular restaurant, game and TV rooms, two tennis courts, a big pool and palapa shades on the beach. Small boats take divers and snorkelers to a reef about half a mile away.

**CLUB OASIS AKUMAL**, *Akumal, phone (987) 42303; 120 rooms, $98 per person including meals, drinks and sporting activities, VI - MC.*

This all-inclusive resort provides tennis, bicycles, windsurfing, sailboats, snorkeling, canoes, kayaks, a gym, two pools and evening entertainment. It also has a dive shop (extra charge for scuba equipment). There is a reef close to the beach. Rooms are set in two- and three-story buildings and furnished simply, with air conditioning and TV. Many have sea views.

**AVENTURAS AKUMAL VACATIONS**, *Aventuras Akumal, phone (987) 22804; 14 villas and condominium units; high season $98 for condos, $204 for villas; low season $76 to $165.*

Villas face the sea. Each has two or three bedrooms plus kitchen.

Condominium units are studio style, most with kitchen. Lower rates apply to those without kitchen. Extra discounts apply at certain times of year. Fishing trips and land excursions are available.

## CHEMUYIL

*Chemuyil is located just south of the Akumal area.*

This is a gorgeous, crescent-shaped white sand beach, with young palms planted to replace those destroyed several years ago by a hurricane. There is a $2 admission fee. Among amenities here are a small RV park ($3 per person), a campground (also $3 per person), and a decent-looking government-owned hotel.

During our visit the government was looking for buyers for the hotel, and nobody there knew about room rates or anything else. Facing the beach is an open-air restaurant and bar with good seafood at high prices. Diners have to sit on awful bar stools.

## XCACEL

*Xcacel is south of Chemuyil, about 800 meters from the highway.*

**Xcacel** (pronounced eesh-ka-SELL) is another idyllic, crescent-shaped beach just a little further south. Here, too, admission is $2 and camping and RV facilities are available for $3 a person, with public toilets and showers. The beach is long and dazzling, but there is little shade. There is good snorkeling from a point at one end, and just off the beach is a *cenote*, or fresh-water swimming hole. The sole restaurant here has overpriced food but reasonably priced drinks.

An elderly American woman named Pat (she declined to divulge her family name) lives here in a tiny house trailer and has set for herself the mission of helping save **endangered turtles**. Working with biologists from the state wildlife service, she looks after a group of six tanks in which young turtles are raised, including, recently, a twin-headed green sea turtle.

The nesting season runs from May to September, with July and August the peak months. At that time volunteers patrol the beach every night to stave off human predators who want turtle eggs to sell as an aphrodisiac. Only organized groups are allowed to visit then. She finds tourists a plague, but their cash donations are helpful.

# XEL-HA

> *Xel-ha is situated five minutes' walk from Highway 307.*

This reef-lined cove north of Tulum has been turned into a national park which, under certain conditions, is a snorkelers' paradise. At times, though, the water becomes so thick with humans that many of the fish are scared off. The time to come is early in the morning before the tour buses arrive from Cancún or during the low season.

*The park is open from 8 am to 4:30 pm Admission is $5, children under 12 free.* Visitors are warned not to feed the fish and not to apply suntan oil before entering the water. Lockers and snorkeling equipment can be rented. The park has several handicrafts and clothing shops and a restaurant, **COCO LOCO**, with expensive seafood dishes.

## NEAR XEL-HA

On the other side of the highway and *about 300 meters south* is a minor archaeological site, *open 8 am to 5 pm, admission $3.* Visitors must walk some distance along a bumpy road and rocky trail, with little to see. But further in is an attractive *cenote*, or swimming hole, draped by jungle.

*One kilometer south of Xel-Ha*, with a reception area at the edge of the highway, is **Dos Ojos** (literally, two eyes), a series of caverns offering something very special for divers and snorkelers, run jointly with a local Indian community. For land-lubbers, there is a foot tour through the **Mil Columnas** underground chamber, which is open at both ends and filled with stone columns where stalagmites and stalactites have joined.

Snorkelers are taken deep into the jungle, from where they descend to a subterranean river and caverns illuminated by powerful underwater lights. Certified divers, accompanied by a guide, can penetrate up to 500 meters (the length of five city blocks) through the crystal clear waters of the caverns past fantastic rock formations. Diving tours cost $30 to $75. All tours go at fixed hours. *Phone ahead at (987) 12020 to check on current hours and rates.*

# TULUM & COBÁ

> *Tulum lies along Highway 307; Cobá is situated just off a paved road running northwest from Tulum, a distance of 42 km.*

The ruins of the ancient Mayan cities of **Tulum** and **Cobá** are a scant 42 km apart, but they are as different as can be. Tulum has the distinction of being the only important group of ruins in Mexico that are right by the edge of the sea, but they are not in particularly good shape, and the vast number of visitors who come each day from Cancún, 131 km to the north, is not helping matters. To help conserve the structures scattered about the site, visitors are no longer allowed to climb or enter them. Most of these structures are quite low, and only a handful are really worth seeing. What makes Tulum special is the sight of these grey stone edifices in outline against the turqoise Caribbean. Besides the ruins, there are several beaches and a string of small beach hotels toward the south.

While Tulum exudes a great sense of openness and space, Cobá conveys a mood of seclusion and solitude. Visible structures at Cobá are less numerous (most remain hidden beneath the jungle), and not nearly as many visitors come to see them, but they are far more dramatic. They include two very high pyramids, including one that soars 42 meters, and both of these can be climbed, providing stunning views of the surrounding jungle. Rather than sitting in open grassy areas of the sort found at most archaeological sites in Mexico, the ruins of Cobá are hidden deep in a vast jungle park. Visitors should wear good walking shoes and be prepared to put them to good use.

If you have time to visit only one site and you have to choose between Tulum and Cobá, we would recommend Cobá. Many visitors find it worth the additional 40 minutes or so it takes to get there. As a bonus, you can see it in relative peace. It is not nearly as crowded as Tulum. The village of Cobá is quite tiny, but there are several decent restaurants and a narrow choice of places to stay.

## TULUM

Tulum is more than an archaeological site. It is also a beach resort. A path leads from the ruins to a picturesque beach below. To the south are a string of beaches, some quite idyllic, with many small hotels scattered along a small coastal road over a distance of several kilometers. Further south along this road lie the village of **Boca Paila** and the **Sian Ka'an nature reserve**.

There are also hotels and other services in the town of Tulum (commonly referred to as **Tulum Pueblo**), which lies along the main highway 4 km south of the ruins and a short distance inland. At certain beaches, including the big beach just south of the ruins, nudity seems to be accepted.

## ARRIVALS & DEPARTURES
### By Bus

Buses run from a terminal in town, and most stop also at an intersection several minutes' walk from the ruins. Taxis are available in town and near the ruins. Second-class buses between Tulum, Playa del

Carmen and Cancún run several times an hour from early morning to early evening, and there are also a few first-class services. The second-class fare between Cancún and Tulum is $4, and travel time is 2 1/2 hours each way. For Cobá service, see the Cobá section just below. To or from Chetumal, there are about 12 buses a day, with connections for Belize. There are four direct buses a day from Tulum to Chichén Itzá and Mérida, and many connections in Cancún. ADO has one overnight first-class bus from Tulum to Puebla, with immediate connections for the final hop to Mexico City. There are no buses along the road to Boca Paila and the Sian Ka'an nature reserve.

**By Car**

Tulum lies along Highway 307, which runs from Cancún to Chetumal, near the border with Belize. South of Tulum, the highway runs some distance inland. Other roads run south along the coast to Boca Paila and Punta Allen, and northwest to Cobá and beyond to a junction with the Cancún-Valladolid highway.

## WHERE TO STAY

There are two hotels just five minutes' walk from the ruins and others in Tulum town 4 km away. These are shown here first. Most Tulum hotels are scattered along the beaches, and only those near the northern end are within easy walking distance of the ruins. Others are more remote and require a private vehicle or taxi. Several are quite attractive.

Beach hotels are shown here from north to south. Along the beach electricity is produced by generator, meaning it is usually turned off by late evening; telephones, where they exist, use cellular or radio links.

**HOTEL ACUARIO**, *at the highway intersection for the ruins, no phone; 27 rooms, high season $36 single or double, low season $27, no cards.*

Rooms are housed in a pair of two-story buildings and have TV and marble floors. There is a pool, surrounded by a bare concrete deck. The owner seems rather irascible.

**HOTEL EL CRUCERO**, *at the highway intersection for the ruins, no phone; 16 rooms, $9 single, $12 double, no cards.*

Motel-style rooms here are very basic.

**HOTEL MAYA**, *on the main boulevard in town across from the bus terminal, phone (987) 12034; 16 rooms, $14 single, $21 double, no cards.*

This hotel offers bright, clean, simple rooms.

**POSADA SAN MARCOS**, *on the main boulevard in town near the bus terminal, phone (987) 12016; 6 rooms, $30 single or double, no cards.*

Large, nondescript rooms have air conditioning and TV. There is some road noise.

**CABAÑAS MIRADOR**, *on the beach 700 meters south of the entrance to* *the ruins, no phone, 22 cabañas, $6, no cards.*

Basic thatched huts have sand floors and hammocks but no beds. Toilets are up a long flight of stairs.

**CAMPING SANTE FE,** *on the beach 750 meters south of the entrance to the ruins, no phone, 30 cabañas plus space for 25 tents, cabañas $9 to $18 depending on size and season, dormitory beds $3, camping $2 per person, no cards.*

Thatched huts have concrete floors (a few have sand floors) with beds. Toilets and showers are nearby, as are a restaurant and dive shop.

**CABAÑAS DON ARMANDO,** *on the beach 800 meters south of the entrance to the ruins, no phone; 37 cabañas, $12 to $18, no cards.*

Cabañas here are fresh with sand floors and beds (some also have hammocks). Most have windows. Toilets and showers are shared. The restaurant is inexpensive.

**HOTEL EL PARAÍSO,** *near the beach 1 km south of the ruins, phone (987) 23636, fax (987) 12007; 10 rooms, high season $33 single or double, low season $24, no cards.*

Motel-style rooms are bright, simple and fairly comfortable, with private bath. Electricity is available from 5 pm to 10 pm The reception area, along with the bar and restaurant, are some distance from the rooms.

**CABAÑAS GATOS,** *on the beach 2.2 km south of the ruins, no phone; 20 cabañas, high season $18 to $24, low season $9 to $15, no cards.*

The most eccentric spot in Tulum, dotted with knickkancks and antiques; very casual. It's in a garden setting, shaded by mature palms. Cabañas have stone walls and thatched roofs; some have private bath. The restaurant closes in low season; the bar is open year-round. The beach immediately in front is rocky, but there is a sandy beach nearby.

**NOXOCK TUNICH,** *on the beach 4.5 km south of the ruins, no phone; 15 cabañas, $9 to $15, no cards.*

The cabañas have concrete floors, high roofs and very basic furnishings. Electricity is available from dusk to 10 pm

**CABAÑAS QUE FRESCO,** *on the beach 5 km south of the ruins; 3 cabañas with more on the way, $18 to $23, no cards.*

Cabañas are big, with concrete floors, skylights and mosquito nets. There is a small restaurant here.

**OSHO OASIS,** *on the beach 6.5 km south of the ruins, phone (987) 42772; 29 cabañas, $40 to $80, no cards.*

Round stone buildings have thatched roofs and stone floors, many with private bath. The deluxe cabañs are very big and lavishly furnished. The grounds are carefully landscaped, with passageways of sand. Electricity is available until 11 pm The restaurant offers vegetarian dishes as well as fish and seafood in Mexican, French and Japanese preparations.

**CABAÑAS ANA Y JOSÉ**, *on the beach 7 km south of the ruins, no phone; 16 rooms, high season $36 to $45, low season $30 to $36, no cards.*

This spot is friendly and has some older stone cabañas by the beach, with good cross-ventilation, and some newer two-story stucco-covered structures behind with terraces and palapa ceilings in the upstairs rooms. All accommodations have private bath. Electricity is available from dusk until 10 pm The restaurant is moderately priced and pleasant, with palapa roof and sand floor. Bicycles are available for rent.

**CABAÑAS TULUM**, *on the beach 7 km south of the ruins, no phone; 16 rooms, $30 single or double, no cards.*

All rooms have private bath and large terraces facing the sea, but decor is nondescript and tired-looking. There is a small restaurant.

## WHERE TO EAT

There are several small restaurants near the entrance to the ruins, but the restaurants *at the highway junction,* connected to the **ACUARIO** and **EL CRUCERO** hotels, are better bets. In town, **AMBROCIO'S**, *near the bus terminal,* is always open and offers a good selection of meat and seafood dishes at moderate prices. *In the beach area, toward the southern end,* the **OSHO OASIS** and **ANA Y JOSÉ** hotels both have good restaurants. Some items at the Osho Oasis show French or Japanese influences.

## VISITING THE RUINS

*The archaeological site is open daily from 8 am to 5 pm. Admission is $5, Sundays and holidays free. There is an $8 charge for video cameras.* Handicrafts and refreshments are sold at numerous stalls near the entrance. It is best to arrive early in the morning to avoid being overwhelmed by busloads of day-trippers from Cancún. Bilingual guides cluster near the entrance. Their rates vary according to the number of people in a group.

Tulum dates from the decline of the ancient Maya civilization. It was settled between the 10th and 12th centuries A.D. and was probably still occupied when the Spanish arrived in the early 16th century. Most surviving structures date from the 12th to 15th centuries, showing influences from the Toltecs of central Mexico. It is partly surrounded by thick walls with inner walkways, leaving no doubt that it was designed as a fortress. There are five gates. The wall itself is well preserved, but many of the buildings within have been worn down over the centuries, although interesting details remain visible here and there.

The first building on the right after entering bears the prosaic name **Structure 20**, a former palace with a caved-in roof and fragments of paintings on the walls. Just behind is a funerary platform with a grave in the center. Heading toward the sea, you come to the better preserved **Temple of the Frescoes** with a carved figure of a winged, bird-tailed god and murals (visible through steel bars) depicting the three realms of the Mayan universe, the underworld, the living and the heavens above.

Continuing toward the sea, you reach **El Castillo** (*the castle*), the highest building in Tulum. It stands atop a high limestone cliff overlooking the Caribbean and combines a palace-type base with a temple and watchtower above, with some stucco ornamentation and interior frescoes visible from a distance. To prevent erosion, visitors are no longer allowed to climb the steps to see them up close. Directly adjacent is the biggest structure at Tulum, the **Temple of the Descending God**, with a stucco carving of a winged god and fragments of a religious mural. Again, it can no longer be climbed.

The site extends some distance to the north, but most of the several dozen other structures are less impressive. The proximity of the sea adds hugely to the attraction.

## SIAN KA'AN NATURE RESERVE

*The northern edge of the reserve lies just south of Tulum.*

**Sian Ka'an**, from Mayan words meaning *where the sky is born*, is a biosphere reserve covering nearly 530,000 hectares (1.3 million acres, or more than 2,000 square miles) in the central-eastern part of Quintana Roo state. The reserve, established in 1986, forms part of a complex hydraulic system, encompassing a variety of wetlands. In 1987 it was added to the UNESCO list of world heritage sites

About one-third of the reserve is covered by tropical forest, and another third is composed of savannas and mangrove. The final third contains coastal and marine habitats. Many bird and mammal species are found here, as well as crocodiles and several rare species of sea turtles. Among the 336 bird species identified here are the ocellated turkey, great currasow, parrots, toucans, trogons, white ibis, roseate spoonbill, jabiru stork, wood stork, flamingo and 15 species of herons, egrets and bitterns.

The reserve has been divided into a core zone, limited to conservation and scientific research, and a buffer zone, where low-impact human activities are permitted. These include the traditional activities of small fishing and farming communities and a limited amount of tourism such as bird-watching tours and deep-sea fishing. The village of **Boca Paila** *lies in the northern part of the reserve* and contains a couple of fishing lodges. At **Punta Pelícano**, *65 km south of Tulum*, accommodations and meals are available at the edge of a cove, with excellent snorkeling and good beaches nearby.

A group called **Los Amigos de Sian Ka'an** conducts conservation and research activities and organizes regular visits to the reserve. *Information* *and reservations are available at the group's office in Cancún (3rd floor, Plaza América, Avenida Cobá 5), phone (98) 849583 or 873080.* Day tours cost $48 with departure from Tulum or $115 from Cancún. Groups normally vary between four and nine persons.

Bilingual wildlife biologists escort visitors by road to Boca Paila and by boat from there along lagoons and mangrove-lined canals. Unfortunately, some tours arrive only at mid-day. The early morning hours are better for birding, although the scenery is attractive at any hour. December to February is the best season to see migratory species. Crocodiles normally can be seen only at night. The trip usually includes a swim in a fresh-water lagoon. Visitors should bring swimsuits, sunhats, and sunscreen.

# COBÁ

In addition to the ruins at Cobá, there is also a small lake facing the town and another off to one side of the ruins, but neither is fit for swimming. The town is small, compact, and very peaceful.

## ARRIVALS & DEPARTURES

### By Bus & Taxi

Buses to Cobá leave Playa del Carmen at 5 am, 10 am, and 5 pm, departing from Tulum one hour later. Return trips from Cobá are at 7 am and 3 pm. From Valladolid to Cobá, there are buses at 4:30 am and 1 pm. From Cobá to Valladolid, departures are at 6:50 am, 11:50, am and 6:50 pm These timings are not exact, and it is best to arrive early at departure points to avoid missing the bus. It is a long wait for the next one. A practical but more costly alternative is to hire a taxi at Tulum and negotiate a rate for a two- or three-hour wait at Cobá.

### By Car

Cobá is situated just off a paved road running northwest from Tulum, a distance of 42 km. This same road meets the Cancún-Valladolid highway near the village of X-Can.

## WHERE TO STAY

There are three places to stay. One is pleasant, comfortable and a tad expensive, while the other two are quite rudimentary. There is nothing in between.

**VILLA ARQUEOLÓGICA DE COBÁ**, *phone (987) 42087; 40 rooms, $55 single, $63 double, VI - MC - AE.*

Situated near the lake at the edge of town, this attractive hotel has small, simple, attractive rooms colored white and cerise. It is administered by the Club Méditerranée group. All rooms are air conditioned. Guests have access to a tennis court, swimming pool, billiards room, library, TV room, gift shop and bar. The restaurant is elegant and fairly expensive, offering Mexican and French dishes. This hotel is sometimes overwhelmed by tour groups, but at other times it is nearly empty.

*Along the main street,* **HOTEL-RESTAURANT EL BOCADITO** and **HOTEL-RESTAURANT ISABEL** each offers a handful of bare-bones rooms. *El Bocadito, with private bath and some elementary furnishings for $10, is better value than the Isabel, with shared bath and truly stark rooms for $7.* Both offer good food on pleasant terraces at moderate prices. The full-course meals at El Bocadito are very good value. Both are also good places to have something to drink while waiting for the bus.

## WHERE TO EAT

In addition to the two hotel restaurants listed above, other eating places include the restaurant at the **VILLA ARQUEOLÓGICA** (expensive), the **NICTE-HA** *nearby, facing the lake,* with a selection of Mexican dishes at moderate prices, and three more *near the entrance to the ruins:* **LOS FLAMINGOS**, **EL FAISAN**, and **CARACOL**. The Caracol offers fresh seafood.

Also *near the entrance to the ruins* is **Sterling Shop**, which offers selections of silver jewelry and hand-painted figurines.

## VISITING THE RUINS

*The archaeological site is open daily from 8 am to 5 pm. Admission is $4, Sundays and holidays free.* Stalls by the entrance sell handicrafts and detailed guides to the ruins. To get there from the main street, just head to the lake and turn left. Be prepared for plenty of walking. Good shoes are essential, and insect repellant and sunhats can be useful.

Unlike many other Mayan sites, with their open, grassy expanses, Cobá remains shrouded in jungle. Visitors see not just archaeological splendors but also an enthralling jungle park that exudes an air of solitude and really does feel like a lost city. Broad pathways run beneath high canopies of trees and connect the main groups of ruins. Several narrower, unmarked trails strike off across other portions of jungle.

Cobá flourished from the seventh to the ninth centuries A.D. Evidence suggests it was abandoned after the 11th century. It lay at the center of a great network of stone-paved roads and appears to have had close links with the distant city of Tikal, in what is today northeastern Guatemala. Only a small portion of the ruins have been excavated.

Archaeologists have designated several groups of ruins. Soon after entering the site, visitors come upon the **Cobá group**. At first there are just low mounds, but taking a short path to the right you are suddenly struck by the magnificent sight of an enormous, soaring pyramid called **La Iglesia** (*the church*). You can climb the sides of this pyramid and watch as a splendid view of the surrounding jungle unfold before you. Footings become less secure near the top, and rain can turn the steps slippery.

Further along the main path, to the left, is the **Chumuc Mul group**, whose principal pyramid is topped with brightly colored motifs, but this area is covered by dense bush and can be visited only with special permission.

After a long walk through the jungle, visitors come to the **Nohoch Mul** group, whose great pyramid, of the same name, soars 42 meters, the height of a 12-story building. Although it is higher than La Iglesia, its 120 steps are not as steep, and both the climb and the descent are easier. The view is even more magnificent, with vast and almost unbroken expanses of jungle stretching over great distances. Behind Nohoch Mul is **El Castillo** (*the castle*), whose nine chambers can be reached by a stairway.

Returning from Nohoch Mul, follow the signs to **Las Pinturas** (*the paintings*), where the walls of a temple display polychromatic fragments of once magnificent murals. On the way to Las Pinturas is a narrow, circular trail along the way leading to the more interesting **Macanxoc** group, with a small temple and clusters of intricately carved stelae.

## CHETUMAL

*Chetumal lies off Highway 186 and is the gateway to Belize.*

Few visitors come to **Chetumal** unless they are headed to or from Belize, which is certainly reason enough. The town itself is modern and nondescript, but it has a new archaeological museum, and visitors can go on excursions to the Kohunlich ruins and to Bacalar.

Chetumal was designated a free port long before Mexico signed any free trade agreements, and people from all over the Yucatán came here to shop. With import tariffs now much lower throughout Mexico, this traffic has slowed to a trickle, although many shoppers still come from Belize. This remains a good place to look for imported items.

### A CAPITAL PLACE
*Chetumal is the state capital of Quintana Roo, which occupies the eastern third of the Yucatán peninsula and extends north beyond Cancún.*

## ORIENTATION
The central area of Chetumal is compact. **Álvaro Obregón** is an

important street running through the center, intersecting with **Avenida de los Héroes**, which runs the few blocks to the waterfront and out in the opposite direction toward the main bus terminal.

Taxis around town are very cheap. In contrast, car rental rates in Chetumal are exorbitant. The sole **car rental agency** *is situated in the Hotel Continental Caribe on Avenida de los Héroes.* A **tourism information booth**, *along this same avenue near the municipal market, is open 8 am to 1 pm and 5 pm to 8 pm, Monday to Saturday.* The new **Museo de la Cultura Maya** was set to open in a handsome building *next to the market.*

## ARRIVALS & DEPARTURES

### By Air

Chetumal has a small airport (airport code CTM) close to town with daily service from Mexico City by Aviacsa and from Cancún by TAESA or Bonanza.

### By Bus

The main bus terminal, sometimes called the Caribe terminal, is a lofty, modern structure at the edge of town, next to the San Francisco Asís supermarket. First-class buses to Cancún (5 hours, $12) run eight times a day with limited stops, including overnight services. To Mérida (6 hours, $12-$15) there are five first-class buses and six second-class services. To Mexico City (23 hours, $54) there are three daily first-class buses. There are seven additional buses to Villahermosa (9 hours, $19) with connections to numerous points in eastern and central Mexico. Direct service is also available from Chetumal to Valladolid, Campeche, Palenque, San Cristóbal de las Casas, Tuxtla Gutiérrez and Veracruz.

Pioneros, a small, independent company, has its own terminal a few blocks away. It runs seven second-class buses each day to Cancún and intermediate points.

Buses for Belize operate from the Lázaro Cárdenas market, commonly known as the Mercado Nuevo. Batty Bus and Venus between them run to Belize City and intermediate points hourly from 4 am to 6 pm, plus a final departure at 6:30 pm. Taxis are cheap and will help with connections to or from the other terminals.

### By Car

Chetumal is reached by Highway 186, which crosses the barren and solitary southern part of the Yucatán peninsula from Villahermosa. Highway 307 from Cancún meets Highway 186 just west of Chetumal, as does the main road for Belize. Highway 184 for Mérida meets Highway 307 some distance north. Immigration authorities sometimes conduct spot checks on roads leading from Chetumal.

## WHERE TO STAY

**HOTEL MARLON,** *Juárez 87, phone (983) 29411 or 26555; 50 rooms, $30 single or double, VI - MC - AE.*

This modern and attractive three-story building is well situated and faces a small garden courtyard with a pool. Rooms are decently furnished, with air conditioning, TV and phone, although some are a little dark.

**HOTEL EL CEDRO,** *Héroes 103, phone (983) 26878; 22 rooms, $24 single, $27 double, VI - MC - AE.*

Most rooms are big, bright and nicely furnished, with air conditioning, TV and phone, although there is some noise on the street side.

**HOTEL PRINCIPE,** *Héroes 326; phone (983) 24799 or 25167, fax (983) 25191; 53 rooms, high season $33 single or double, low season $29, VI - MC - AE.*

Situated midway between the city center and the main bus terminal, this modern, three-story building has a pool and restaurant. Rooms are comfortably furnished, with air conditioning, TV and phone. The pool area is sometimes a little noisy.

**HOTEL LOS COCOS,** *Héroes 134, phone (983) 20530, fax (983) 20920; 80 rooms, $50 single or double, VI - MC - AE.*

This city-center hotel was known previously as El Prado and before that as Hotel Presidente. The lobby has a tropical atmosphere with wicker furniture, mirrors and colorful wall panels. This long, two-story building has a pool and garden on one side. Rooms, all with air conditioning, TV and phone, are furnished in modern Mexican style but are not aging well.

**HOTEL CASABLANCA,** *Obregón 312 near the palacio municipal, phone (983) 21248, fax (983) 21676; $18 with fan, $33 with air conditioning and TV, no cards.*

This two-story motel-style building has bright, pleasantly furnished rooms.

**HOTEL CONTINENTAL CARIBE,** *Héroes 171, phone (983) 21100 or 21080, fax (983) 21607; 74 rooms, $37 single, $56 double, VI - MC - AE.*

Rooms, most facing a garden and pool, have air conditioning, TV and phones, but are furnished unappealingly. This Best Western affiliate was considering a switch to Holiday Inn.

**CARIBE PRINCESS,** *Obregón 168, phone (983) 20520 or 20900; 36 rooms, $27 single, $35 double, VI - MC.*

Hallways are dark, but this quiet and reasonably central spot is otherwise pleasant, with air conditioning, TV, tile floors and floral bedspreads.

**POSADA PANTOJA,** *Lucio Blanco 95, phone (983) 21781; 12 rooms, $12 with fan, $19 with air conditioning and TV, no cards.*

This three-story building away from the center has large, bright, simple rooms, most with good cross-ventilation.

**ALBERGUE CREA**, *Veracruz at Obregón, phone (983) 23465; 65 beds, $4 per person, no cards.*
This youth hostel is clean and quiet. It is situated not far from the center.

**HOTEL EL DORADO**, *5 de Mayo 42 at Othón Blanco, phone (983) 20315 or 20316; 25 rooms, $15 with fan, $27 with air conditioning and TV, no cards.*
Room decor is a bit tired, with clashing colors. Some are dark, while others are bright and breezy. Service is friendly.

**HOTEL BIG BEN**, *Héroes 48, phone (983) 20965; 17 rooms, $11 single, $14 double, no cards.*
Rooms in this friendly, family-run spot are fresh but very basic. The reception area, up a narrow stairway, is the family living room.

**HOTEL MARÍA DOLORES**, *Obregón 206, phone (983) 20508; 41 rooms, $10 single, $13 double, no cards.*
Rooms are rudimentary. The entrance lies through an alleyway.

## WHERE TO EAT

Chetumal is not famed for its restaurants, but there is a reasonable variety, and prices are generally moderate. Because the city lies in a free port, imported wines and liquors are cheaper than in most other parts of Mexico.

**SERGIO'S PIZZAS & STEAK HOUSE** and **CACTUS GRILL** *are situated across from each other at the corner of 5 de Mayo and Obregón.* Both are snazzily decorated and moderately priced. **PISCIS**, *at Élias Calles and Avenida de los Héroes,* and **MANDINGA**, *Belice 214,* are pleasant and inexpensive spots for seafood dishes, including fresh cocktails. **RESTAURANT ARCADAS**, *centrally situated at Zaragoza and Avenida de los Héroes,* is open all night.

## EXCURSIONS

The ruins of **Kohunlich** *are situated 58 km west of Chetumal by Highway 186 to the village of Nachicocom and the 9 km south by a paved road from there.* The site is open daily from 8 am to 5 pm; admission is $3, Sunday free. Buses run regularly along the highway, but not south to the ruins. A round trip by taxi from Chetumal, with one hour of waiting time, costs about $45. Bring your own refreshments.

Kohunlich was built between the second and fifth centuries A.D. It is surrounded by heavy forest and only partly excavated. The most important structure is the **Pirámide de los Mascarones** (*pyramid of the masks*), partly protected by a newly built thatch covering. Climbing a central stairway, you can see huge, three-meter-high masks of the sun god, with part of the original red tincture still visible. The first building you see upon entering the site is the **Acrópolis**, with various stairways, temples, towers, patios and interior rooms.

**Bacalar**, *38 km north of Chetumal along Highway 307* and connected by local minibus twice an hour, is an old town perched at the edge of a multi-hued lake, the **Laguna de Bacalar**. *In the center of town, next to the tree-shaded central park*, is the **Fuerte de San Felipe**, built in the 18th century to repel pirate attacks. *Open from 10 am to 6 pm, Tuesday to Sunday (admission 30 cents)*, it has heavy stone walls, several ancient cannon, a small historical museum and vistas over the lake.

Some visitors may choose to stay overnight in Bacalar instead of Chetumal. There are several small hotels by the lakeside about 1 km north of town, as well as **HOTEL LA LAGUNA**, *2 km south of town, no phone; 30 rooms, $39 high season single or double, $33 low season, no cards*. This pleasant, three-story turquoise-and-white building has bright, clean, simple rooms, most with terraces overlooking the lake. The restaurant is decorated with thousands of inlaid shells.

# 11. CENTRAL & WESTERN YUCATÁN

The **Yucatán peninsula** has long been part of Mexico, but it has jealously maintained its own identity. Before the Spanish conquest it was dominated by the **Mayan** culture while central Mexico was in the sway of the Aztecs and Toltecs, and it stayed largely apart during the colonial period as well. Even after independence, local ruling elites plotted to secede from Mexico.

Geographically, the Yucatán lies nearer to Havana than to Mexico City. It sits atop a low limestone shelf which, except in the south, is virtually devoid of rivers and lakes, with water moving underground instead. It is almost entirely flat, apart from the **Puuc hills** near Uxmal. Poor soils kept agriculture from prospering in most parts of the peninsula, with the result that even today large areas are virtually uninhabited.

## HISTORY

Mayan civilization began to emerge several centuries before the birth of Christ and reached its apogee between the fourth and tenth centuries A.D. It was toward the end of this period that the great cities and ceremonial centers of the northern Yucatán achieved their greatest importance, overtaking the development of Central America and Chiapas.

Soon afterward, the **Toltecs** of central Mexico began their invasions of the Yucatán, leading to a renewal at **Chichén Itzá** but to declines in some other places. Mayan leadership suffered one of its periodic splinterings, leading to internecine strife. Population pressures may have put a strain on agriculture, eliminating the surpluses that had sustained the great cities, which were abandoned one by one.

By the time the Spanish arrived in the early 16th century, the Mayans were no longer strongly organized, and local chieftains surrendered in 1542 to forces led by members of the Montejo family, who consolidated

their control of the peninsula in the following years, reducing the once mighty Mayans to peonage.

Harsh treatment of the Mayans, and the establishment of Spanish-run agricultural estates on their lands, led to numerous revolts, the mightiest of which triggered the War of the Castes in the late 1840s, decades after Mexico had become independent of Spain. Local ruling elites, dreaming of secession from Mexico, armed some of the Mayan peasants, who obtained additional arms from the British through Belize.

The Mayans came very close to vanquishing their oppressors, but the tide turned and vengeance was horrible. A large part of the Indian population was massacred. During this uprising, churches throughout the Yucatán, as hated symbols of white oppression, were looted systematically of decorative elements, which is why most of them look so bare today.

In the course of the 20th century, the Mexican Revolution re-established indigenous land rights in the Yucatán. *Henequen (sisal)*, used in making rope, was once an economic mainstay, but has been in decline for many decades. The development of other agro-industrial sectors and the growth of tourism have totally reshaped the economy.

## VISITING THE YUCATÁN

*The Yucatán faces the Caribbean to the east and the Gulf of Mexico to the north and west. To the south lie the northern fringes of Belize and Guatemala, and to the southwest lie the Mexican states of **Tabasco** and **Chiapas**. The peninsula itself is split into three states, with **Quintana Roo** to the east, **Yucatán** state in the center with the northern shore forming the base of an inverted triangle, and **Campeche** state to the west.*

*Cancún and other parts of Quintana Roo is covered in the chapter on the Mexican Caribbean. This chapter deals with areas of Yucatán and Campeche states, moving from east to west. We start with **Valladolid** midway between Cancún and Mérida, moving on to the Mayan ruins of **Chichén Itzá** and thence to **Mérida**, the biggest and in many ways most alluring city on the peninsula, and finally to the formerly walled city of **Campeche**. Along the way, we make side trips to the bird sanctuary of **Río Lagartos**, the time-warp town of **Izamal**, the beach resorts of **Progreso** and **Celestún**, and the Mayan ruins of **Uxmal**, the **Puuc hills** and **Edzná**. It is an enticing voyage.*

# VALLADOLID

*Valladolid lies in the northeastern part of the Yucatán peninsula exactly midway between Cancún and Mérida, each 159 km away.*

For visitors arriving from Cancún or other points along the Caribbean coast, **Valladolid** (pronounced ba-ya-doh-LEED) provides the first taste of colonial Mexico, with some buildings dating back to the 16th century, several hotels housed in colonial-era structures, and a big, traditional *zócalo*, or central plaza. There is little here of intrinsic interest to warrant a long visit, but Valladolid is pleasant and well situated for excursions to other places, particularly the Mayan ruins of Chichén Itzá just 40 km west.

Bird enthusiasts will want to visit Río Lagartos, 110 km north. Local attractions in Valladolid include its many colonial buildings, including several churches, and its *cenotes*, natural below-ground pools suitable for swimming.

## ARRIVALS & DEPARTURES

### By Bus

Valladolid's terminal is shared by several bus lines and lies at the corner of Calles 37 and 54, about ten minutes' walk from the *zócalo*. First-class express buses to Mérida are run by three competing companies, including ADO, with 13 daily departures altogether. They also offer eight daily express services to Cancún. Trip time for either is about two hours. Second-class buses in either direction depart hourly from 5 am to 10 pm, with Mérida-bound buses stopping at Pisté, next to Chichén Itzá, a 40-minute trip. Five additional buses go to Mérida via Izamal.

Second-class buses to Tizimín go hourly from 5 am to 10 pm, with connections for Río Lagartos in the morning and afternoon. Direct buses to Cobá and Tulum go at 4:30 am and 1 pm. There are also three daily departures to Chetumal, with morning departures permitting same-day connections to Belize.

### By Car

Valladolid is linked to Cancún and Mérida by a costly new four-lane toll highway and also by the narrower, more crowded Highway 180. A slower, more northerly route from Mérida goes via Izamal. Highway 295 connects Valladolid with Tizimín and Río Lagartos to the north and with Felipe Carrillo Puerto to the south, where it meets the highway to Chetumal and Belize.

### By Rail

A slow (3 1/2 hours) passenger train links Mérida and Valladolid, but mostly in darkness. Departure from Mérida is at 4:40 pm and from Valladolid at 3:50 am!

## ORIENTATION

The center of Valladolid follows the traditional grid pattern, and streets have numbers rather than names. Even-numbered streets (*calles*) run north and south, odd-numbered streets east and west. The central plaza, or *zócalo*, is bounded by Calles 39, 40, 41 and 42. Using these numbers, it is easy to calculate how many blocks any given intersection is from the plaza. Numbers rise to the south and the west and fall to the north and east.

Taxis in Valladolid are inexpensive, and minibuses serve some outlying neighborhoods. The main bus terminal is at the corner of Calles 37 and 54. Some buses arriving from out of down drop passengers in the *zócalo* on their way to the terminal.

## WHERE TO STAY

Most hotels in Valladolid are situated within a couple of blocks of the *zócalo*.

**HOTEL EL MESÓN DEL MARQUÉS**, *Calle 39 facing the zócalo, phone (985) 62073 or 63042, fax (985) 62280; 38 rooms, $36 single or double, suites $45, VI - MC - AE.*

This is the best hotel in town. It occupies a colonial mansion and a newer three-story building set around two lush courtyards, one with a pool, the other with a very pleasant restaurant. Rooms are nicely decorated, and many are air conditioned. Service is friendly.

**HOTEL SAN CLEMENTE**, *next to the cathedral at the corner of Calles 42 and 41, phone (985) 62208 or 63161; 64 rooms; $18 single, $22 double with fan; $24 single, $27 double with air conditioning; no cards.*

This modern, three-story building is set around a pool and terrace. Rooms are simple but comfortable.

**HOTEL MARÍA DE LA LUZ**, *facing the zócalo at the corner of Calles 42 and 39, phone (985) 62071; 33 rooms, $23 single or double, VI - MC.*

Rooms here have air conditioning and TV and are nondescript but reasonably comfortable. The building is set around a pool. There is a big restaurant in front.

**HOTEL DON LUÍS**, *corner of Calles 39 and 38, phone (985) 62024; 42 rooms, $14 single, $19 double with fan, $3 more with air conditioning, no cards.*

This modern, three-story hotel has a pool and plain but reasonably comfortable rooms.

**HOTEL ZACÍ**, *Calle 44 between Calles 37 and 39, phone (985) 62167; 40 rooms; $14 single, $21 double with fan; $20 single, $24 double with air conditioning, no cards.*

Rooms are simple but comfortable, with tile floors and TV. This modern three-story building has a few colonial decorative touches. There is a small pool.

**HOTEL LILY**, *Calle 44 between Calles 37 and 39, phone (985) 62163; 20 rooms, $8 single, $12 double, cheaper with shared bath, no cards.*
Rooms are clean and quiet but very basic. There is a small terrace.

## WHERE TO EAT

The restaurant of the Hotel **EL MESÓN DEL MARQUÉS**, *Calle 39 facing the zócalo*, is set in a garden courtyard and offers a good selection of meat and seafood dishes, including some Yucatecan specialties, at reasonable prices. It also prepares good breakfasts and excellent fresh fruit salads. *Just around the corner*, **RESTAURANT DEL FRAILE**, *Calle 40 between Calles 37 and 39*, serves regional dishes in a colonial atmosphere, with heavy wooden furniture and an ancient stone wall to one side.

**CASA DE LOS ARCOS**, *on Calle 39 half a block from the zócalo*, offers a wide range of meat and seafood dishes, including seafood cocktails and *ceviches*. The restaurant of the **HOTEL MARÍA DE LA LUZ** presents buffets some of the time. Meals are also served at several stalls *in the small market facing the zócalo at the corner of Calles 39 and 40.*

## SEEING THE SIGHTS

Like churches elsewhere in the Yucatán, those in Valladolid were stripped almost bare of decoration during the 19th century Caste Wars and other uprisings. The austere but very handsome church of **San Bernardino de Siena** and the attached former convent of **El Sisal**, *situated near the western edge of town*, were erected starting in 1552 and are thought to be the oldest colonial structures in the Yucatán. A few original paintings are still visible behind some of the side altars in the church. **San Cervacio cathedral** (alternate spellings are sometimes used) *faces the zócalo* and has an interesting carved façade and a big, strikingly austere interior. The **church of San Roque**, *at the corner of Calles 41 and 38*, houses a tiny museum presenting Mayan handicrafts and photographs.

Valladolid is known for its *cenotes*, pools of ground water exposed by the formation of caves or by the collapse of the ground above. Visitors to the **Cenote Dzitnup**, sometimes called **Cenote X-Keken**, are led down a series of slippery steps to a cave with crystalline waters suitable for swimming and a small whole in the roof allowing natural light to enter. *Situated 7 km west of the center of town, it is open from 7 am to 5 pm. Entry costs $1.20.*

**Cenote Zací**, *in the center of town on Calle 36 between Calles 37 and 39*, is a tree-shaded, open-air pool down a long series of steps and through a small cave. It is not very appealing for swimming since the water is murky and partly covered by a green scum, but it is picturesque nonetheless. Up at ground level is a tiny museum displaying embroideries and photos of Mayan life. *The cenote is open 8 am to 6 pm. Admission is $1.20.*

A minor curiosity, *on Calle 40 between Calles 33 and 35*, is a big, green-and-white four-story private house built in the form of a Chinese temple.

## PRACTICAL INFORMATION

### Bicycle Rental

Antonio "Negro" Aguilar, *Calle 44 between Calles 39 and 41*, rents bicycles at $3 per four-hour period.

### Handicrafts

A small **market** *facing the zócalo at the corner of Calles 39 and 40* offers local and regional crafts, including embroidered cotton blouses and dresses, sandals and basketware.

### Laundry

**Lavandería Automática Teresita**, *at the corner of Calles 33 and 42*, provides inexpensive same-day service.

## EXCURSIONS

Valladolid is an excellent base from which to visit the fabulous Mayan ruins of **Chichén Itzá** *40 km to the west*. You can set out at a reasonable hour and still arrive well ahead of the hordes from Cancún. Details are provided later in this chapter. The fascinating town of **Izamal**, *106 km west of Valladolid*, lies nearer to Mérida (details are shown under "Excursions" in the Mérida section) but can also be visited from here.

## RÍO LAGARTOS

**Río Lagartos**, *110 km north of Valladolid*, is a fishing port and nature reserve at the mouth of a shallow estuary that is home to a rich abundance of birdlife, including thousands of flamingos.

### ARRIVALS & DEPARTURES

To reach Río Lagartos by bus from Valladolid, you have to connect at Tizimín. Service between Valladolid and Tizimín goes hourly: the first departure from Valladolid is at 5 am, the last return at 7 pm. Between Tizimín and Río Lagartos, there are 11 buses in each direction, leaving an hour or two apart, with the last return at 5:30 pm. These two routes are served by different companies; their terminals are next to each other near the public market in Tizimín. Neither scores highly on punctuality or comfort.

### SEEING THE AREA

It is easy to arrange private excursions along the estuary. Boatmen await visitors along the picturesque waterfront here, and some even meet arriving buses to offer their services. For about $40, they will take you out for two hours or more to see colonies of brilliant pink flamingos, as well as pelicans, cormorants and herons.

It is important not to go near the flamingos' nesting grounds, for if they are frightened they may take to flight and their long legs can knock eggs out of their nests. Away from the nesting grounds it is possible, with a little patience, to catch the glorious sight of dozens of flamingos flying in formation. Birds are most abundant early in the day and against toward sunset, but even at mid-day there is plenty to see.

Excursions are also organized by the **HOTEL MARÍA NEFERTITIS** (no phone), housed in a red and white building with big, bare rooms. Downstairs rooms are $12 to $15, the breezier upstairs rooms $18. Two inexpensive seafood restaurants are *situated near the hotel*, **LA CUEVA DE MACUMBA**, with a pleasant, palapa-shaded garden patio, and **ISLA CONTOY**, with a screened terrace facing the waterfront.

## TIZIMÍN

**Tizimín** is one of the biggest towns in the Yucatán, lying in cattle ranching country, but there is little to interest most visitors apart from the pleasant but ordinary central plaza, the public market, and an old church and convent nearby.

Two modest hotels, **HOTEL SAN CARLOS**, *Calle 54 #407, phone (986) 32094*, and **HOTEL SAN JORGE**, *Calle 53 #411, phone (986) 32037, both near the main plaza*, are a notch above the María Nefertitis in Río Lagartos.

## CHICHÉN ITZÁ

The ruins of **Chichén Itzá** display the glory and the majesty of one of the most imposing cities built by the ancient Mayans, showing influences also from the Toltecs who came down from central Mexico. Situated about 120 km east of Mérida, 40 km west of Valladolid and 200 km west of Cancún, this awe-inspiring ensemble of pyramids, temples and court-yards is still in remarkably good shape. It is one of the most heavily visited archaeological sites in the western hemisphere.

*The site is open from 8 am to 5 pm*; if you can, try to arrive early in the morning. That way you can avoid being overwhelmed by the hordes arriving on tour buses from Cancún, and you can also avoid the intense mid-day heat. Alternately, plan to visit toward the end of the day. It lies just east of the scruffy, sprawling, characterless village of Pisté, which has many hotels and restaurants. Several interesting hotels are situated on the other side of the ruins near a secondary entrance. An alternative is to stay in the more attractive city of Valladolid, 40 km to the east, though this is less convenient if you plan to go to the evening sound and light show at the ruins.

## ARRIVALS & DEPARTURES

### By Air

Aerocaribe has a daily flight from Cancún, while Aerocozumel, part of the same company, flies from Cozumel. Both use propeller-driven aircraft. The airstrip is near the ruins, and each flight is met by taxis. Schedules provide for several hours at the ruins.

### By Bus

Countless tour buses bring visitors from Cancún in air-conditioned comfort, and there are also several from Mérida. These trips must be booked through tour companies or hotel tour desks at the point of origin and usually include the entrance fee to the ruins as well as lunch and, in most cases, a guided visit.

Regular public bus services are limited mostly to second-class buses run by Autotransportes de Oriente. Travelers who can tolerate numerous stops and an absence of air conditioning will enjoy substantial savings and greater flexibility. Hourly buses from Cancún, Valladolid and Mérida stop at Pisté, where there is a small terminal. In each case, the first departure is at 5 am, with return trips well into the evening. The Pisté terminal is about 15 minutes by foot or three minutes and $2 by taxi from the main entrance to the ruins. A handful of buses go right to the entrance: inquire at the information desk there to see if any go at a suitable hour. Otherwise, you'll have to go to the terminal in Pisté, from where buses to Mérida leave hourly on the hour, those to Valladolid and Cancún hourly on the half-hour. Timings are approximate, and buses sometimes leave ahead of schedule. First-class buses go to Cancún at 11:15 am and 5:30 pm, and to Mérida at 3 pm.

### By Car

Chichén Itzá lies near the new four-lane toll highway linking Cancún and Mérida. The old Highway 180, which runs parallel, passes through the village of Pisté and bypasses the main entrance to the ruins, situated on a sideroad. Parking costs $3 a day.

### By Taxi

Taxis between Chichén Itzá and Valladolid cost $20 to $25. Most of the vehicles used as taxis in Pisté and Chichén Itzá are at least 20 years old. Fares for some short trips, for example to the Balankanché caves, are exorbitant.

**PYRAMID AT CHICHÉN ITZÁ**

## WHERE TO STAY

Hotels of many descriptions are situated along the highway in the village of Pisté, just west of the ruins, while several others are clustered on a small road on the other side of the ruins near a secondary entrance.

### Hotels east of the ruins

**HOTEL MAYALAND**, *next to the eastern entrance to the ruins, phone (985) 10128 or 10129, fax (985) 10127; 64 rooms; high season $106 single, $122 double; low season $86 single, $97 double; VI - MC - AE.*

Built in 1930, this hotel has a grand main entrance with lofty wooden beams and painted tiles on the stairs. Lavish gardens surround the pool. Rooms are simple and spacious, with solid wooden furniture and broad outdoor terraces and balconies. Most have air conditioning, TV and phones. Rooms in the original three-story section are smaller but more refined than those in a newer section. The hotel has an elegant, high-ceiling dining room, a separate buffet restaurant catering mostly to day visitors, a grill by the pool and a snack bar.

**HOTEL HACIENDA CHICHÉN**, *across from Hotel Mayaland, phone (985) 10045, for reservations call Mérida (99) 248844, fax (99) 245011, US reservations (800) 624-8451; 18 bungalows, $94 single or double, VI - MC - AE - DC.*

Open only from November to April, rooms are set in cottages on lavish grounds amidst mature trees and stone hedges. Decor includes

Spanish colonial furniture. The main building dates from the 17th century. This was once a cattle ranch; later it was a sisal plantation. From the 1920s to the 1940s, it housed the Carnegie Institute's archaeological expedition, and the cottages were built as lodgings for staff members.

**VILLA ARQUEOLÓGICA CHICHÉN ITZÁ**, *300 meters from the eastern entrance to the ruins, phone (985) 10034, fax (985) 10018; 40 rooms, $69 single, $76 double, VI - MC - AE.*

This two-story hotel, managed by the Club Méditerranée group, is set around a pleasant tree-shaded garden and pool. Guests have the use of a tennis court and library. Rooms are simple but comfortable, with air conditioning. Decor is modern Mexican, with whitewashed stucco and pink and mauve fabrics. The restaurant is elegant and expensive, with Mexican and French specialties.

**HOTEL DOLORES ALBA**, *along the main highway 2 km east of the ruins, no phone, reservations in Mérida (99) 285650; 20 rooms, $18 single, $21 double, $6 extra for air conditioning, no cards.*

Rooms, set in bungalows with jungle views, are simple but pleasant. Most have fans and good cross-ventilation. There is a small, reasonably priced restaurant. This hotel is friendly and offers good value but is not well situated for visitors without cars.

*Hotels in Pisté*

**HOTEL MISIÓN PARK INN CHICHÉN ITZÁ**, *along the highway, phone (985) 10022, fax (985) 10023; 42 rooms; high season $77 single, $96 double; low season $50 single, $60 double; VI - MC - AE.*

This two-story, L-shaped building is set around a pool and garden. There is plenty of red tile everywhere. Rooms are air conditioned and comfortable, though decor is rather ordinary. There are two restaurants and a bar.

**STARDUST INN**, *along the highway, phone (985) 10122; 51 rooms, high season $45 single or double, low season $39, VI - MC - AE.*

The building surrounds a large pool. Rooms are decently furnished, with air conditioning, TV and carpets, but some are a bit dark. The hotel has a restaurant and bar. It also has a small and very humble annex called **POSADA NOVELO**, with scruffy rooms facing a barren yard for $18, single or double.

**PIRÁMIDE INN**, *along the highway, new phone number pending; 45 rooms, $36 single, $39 double; VI - MC - AE.*

Rooms are air conditioned and bright but a trifle garish, with royal blue decor. Some face the highway and are noisy. Rooms in back face a garden, a pool and a tiny Mayan ruin! The hotel also offers a trailer park and campground.

**POSADA CHOC-MOL**, *along the highway, no phone; 5 rooms, $16 single, $18 double, no cards.*

Rooms are clean and basic, with tile floors and fans.

**POSADA EL PASO**, *along the highway toward the plaza, no phone; 14 rooms, $12 single, $15 double, no cards.*

Rooms in this two-story building, set around a small garden, are clean but very simple, with fans and good cross-ventilation but some highway noise.

**POSADA POXIL**, *just west of the plaza, phone (985) 10116 or 10123; 7 rooms, $9 single, $15 single, no cards.*

Rooms are bright but bare. There is an insalubrious pool.

## WHERE TO EAT

Chichén Itzá and its surroundings receive far more day visitors than overnighters, with many arriving by the busload. In response to this, several enormous buffet restaurants have sprung up, seating as many as 500 people and often serving lunch only. Among them is **PUEBLO MAYA**, *along the highway across from the Pirámide Inn*, with open-air seating beneath enormous palapa shelters separated by ponds and gardens. The luncheon buffet costs $9, including musical entertainment and the use of a swimming pool. There is a handicrafts shop at the entrance.

Another in this genre is **HACIENDA XAYBE'H D'CÁMARA**, *also along the highway*, with a gigantic air conditioned dining room, a stage for musicians and dancers, waitresses dressed in brightly colored *huipiles*, and a pool for the use of customers. This spot stays open longer hours, with a breakfast buffet for $5, a lunch buffet for $9, and *à la carte* suppers until 9 pm.

The most elegant (and expensive) restaurants in the area are those in the **VILLA ARQUEOLÓGICA** and **MAYALAND** hotels, *accessible from the eastern side of the ruins* but not very convenient as supper spots for visitors who are staying in Pisté.

Fortunately, there are many small if not particularly lavish restaurants in Pisté itself that stay open in the evening. These include **EL VELÓZ**, *next to the Stardust Inn*, offering regional dishes, seafood and pizza. **SAYIL**, *facing the Misión Park Inn*, has a variety of Mexican and Yucatecan specialties. *Nearer the center of town*, **EL POLLO MEXICANO** offers roast chicken at modest prices, **CHICHÉN ITZÁ** specializes in Yucatecan dishes, **MISTER TACOS** offers you-know-what plus pizza, and **LAS REDES** has regional dishes and seafood at inexpensive prices. Several other restaurants are clustered nearby. The restaurant of the **POSADA POXIL**, *just beyond the plaza*, offers decent full-course meals for $5.

## VISITING THE RUINS

There are several different approaches to visiting archaeological ruins. Some enthusiasts buy detailed guidebooks and follow each step religiously, trying to learn the significance of everything they see and hoping not to miss anything, while others are happy simply to stroll and to allow the splendor of the site to sink in. There is certainly no shame in following the latter course unless you are keenly interested in archaeology. Guided tours are available for those who prefer an in-between approach.

*The Chichén Itzá archaeological site is open daily from 8 am to 5 pm Admission is $6, but is free on Sundays and holidays. There is an $8 charge for the use of video cameras.* The site has two entrances. The main entrance is on the western side and offers baggage storage, currency exchange, a bookshop, several handicrafts shops, and an expensive but mediocre restaurant. A smaller entrance on the eastern side is intended mostly for guests at nearby hotels.

Guides are available at the main entrance. For a 90-minute tour in English or Spanish, the fee is $5 per person for groups of four to eight people. For $30 per group, guides speaking English, Spanish or French will provide a 2 1/2-hour tour to groups of one to 25 people. Every evening there are sound and light shows at the ruins. A Spanish show starts at 7 pm and costs $4. For the English show at 9 pm, admission is $6.

Chichén Itzá grew between the seventh and ninth centuries A.D. and then lay abandoned. It was resettled in the 12th century, about the time Toltecs from central Mexico invaded the Yucatán and began to blend their culture with that of the Mayans. Deities and warriors from both cultures are represented in stone carvings that remain visible today. The city was abandoned again in the 14th century but remained a site of pilgrimage long afterward.

A small **museum** at the main entrance to the ruins displays sculptures, bas-reliefs and explanations of Mayan history. One of the first buildings visitors encounter upon entering the site is the stunning pyramid called **El Castillo** (*the castle*), soaring 24 meters. From the top there is a good view over the whole archaeological zone. This pyramid was erected in the eighth century, well before the arrival of the Toltecs, but it was modified to incorporate Toltec themes. It is sometimes called the Pyramid of Kukulcán, the Mayan adaptation of Quetzacóatl. The temple at the top is dedicated to this plumed serpent that was a central deity of the Toltec culture.

Archaeologists and numerologists are intrigued by the notion that the pyramid presents the Mayan calendar carved in stone. Four stairways, one facing each cardinal point of the compass, ascend to the top. Each stairway has 91 steps. Adding the top platform, this comes to 365, one for each day of the solar year. El Castillo is divided into nine levels, each divided in two by a stairway. This makes 18 terraces, one for each month of the Mayan calendar.

Each façade of the pyramid has 52 panels, one for each year in the calendar cycle. In the days immediately surrounding the spring and autumn equinoxes in March and September, sunlight falls in such a way as to create a series of triangles on the north stairway that appear to imitate the movements of a serpent. This is interpreted to mean that Kukulcán is leaving his temple to bless the earth. Inside El Castillo is another pyramid that once held two jade-bedecked statues. Entrance is permitted for several hours each day, but the dark, narrow stairway and fetid air will deter most claustrophobes.

On the western side of El Castillo is the biggest of Chichén Itzá's seven **ball courts**, used for a religiously inspired game that sometimes ended in human sacrifice. Carvings nearby depict decapitated players. Some 135 meters long and 65 meters wide, it is bound by stone walls that exhibit surprising acoustical characteristics, with sounds rebounding from a great distance.

Flanking the ball court, the **Temple of the Bearded Man**, named for a figure that appears on a mural, has several carved pillars and bas-reliefs, and the **Temple of the Jaguars** has columns and tablets with carvings representing serpents and jaguars. Between the Temple of the Jaguars and El Castillo is the **Temple of Skulls**, or *Tzompantli*, a stone platform carved with rows of human skulls and eagles tearing out human hearts. Equally gruesome scenes are depicted at an adjacent platform.

The **Sacred Cenote**, is a broad and deep natural well about 300 meters north, reached by a dirt path. Sacrificial objects, ranging from jade jewelry to human remains, have been found by divers. Returning to the main site, visitors can see the **Platform of Venus**, symbolized in Toltec lore by feathered serpents.

Beyond this is the **Group of the Thousand Columns**, which includes the Toltec-designed **Temple of the Warriors**. Numerous pillars in front give this complex its name and once supported the roof of the temple, which caved in some time ago. Nearby are the remains of a sweat lodge, which had an underground oven and drains for the water, and what are thought to be remnants of enclosed market stalls. Toward the southern part of the ruins are several badly decayed structures showing more Mayan and less Toltec influence.

A little beyond is **El Caracol** (*the snail*), named for an interior spiral staircase in this circular building. Windows near the top are aligned with certain celestial bodies and were probably used for astronomical observations to set the times for important rituals and for crop planting. Further toward the edge of the site is the **Casa de las Monjas** (*nunnery*), which may have been a royal palace. Its many rooms reminded Spanish visitors of a convent, hence the name. This building is quite massive, and along with its annex it has panels carved with animals, flowers and masks. Turning left, visitors reach **La Iglesia** (*the church*), with animal carvings in the upper part of the façade, and **Akab-Dzib** (*obscure writing*), though to be the oldest structure excavated on the site. Hieroglyphs found on a carving here have never been decoded.

Each evening sound and light shows lasting 35 minutes are presented in front of El Castillo (7 pm in Spanish, 9 pm in English). Colored lights highlight some of the carvings, and there is a solemn, mock-dramatic narration. The effect is decidedly corny and may horrify purists, but evening entertainment does not exactly abound around here.

### Grutas de Balankanché Caves

The **Grutas de Balankanché** are a series of caves *situated 6 km east of Pisté, 1 km from the highway.* Taxis from Pisté may be expensive: check the fare before embarking. Buses between Pisté and Valladolid will drop passengers 1 km from the caves. *Admission is $5 most days, $2 on Sundays. Visitors are escorted into the caves in groups hourly from 9 am to 4 pm Tours in English are at 11 am, 1 pm and 3 pm. A French tour is given at 10 am, and the other tours are in Spanish.* Each tour lasts 30 minutes, penetrating 1 km into the caves, with lighting focused on the myriad formations created by stalagmites and stalactites.

Near the entrance are a botanical garden emphasizing plant species known to the ancient Mayas and a tiny museum presenting several aspects of Mayan culture, notably ceramics and religious observances.

# MÉRIDA

> *Mérida lies in the northwestern part of the Yucatán peninsula, with highways radiating in several directions.*

**Mérida** is everything Cancún isn't. Cancún is young, brash, hedonistic and flashy. Mérida is gracious, venerable, sedate and full of history and culture. The Yucatán has long liked to think of itself as slightly different from the rest of Mexico, and this tradition endures in Mérida, which manages somehow to retain an independent air. Visitors enjoy strolling through its streets and plazas despite the infuriating narrowness of the sidewalks in some places, and they take pleasure from the city's wealth of colonial architecture. It also has a good collection of museums and an intellectual tradition that results, for instance, in local newspapers that are a cut above the provincial average.

This is a big city, with about a million inhabitants, although it certainly doesn't feel that big. The city is at its best on Sundays, when several streets in the center are closed to motor traffic and the calm is broken mostly by the sounds of bands playing in the *plaza grande*, as the Meridanos called their central plaza. On other days, the noise from vehicle motors reverberates through the narrow streets, creating a fearful din.

Mérida is a place where visitors are well looked after. Hotels and restaurants are varied and priced much lower than those on the Caribbean coast of Mexico. Mérida is a good base from which to visit many of the Yucatán's archaeological sites as well as the beaches of Progreso, the beaches and bird sanctuary of Celestún, and the fascinating time-warp town of Izamal. Come and enjoy it.

## ARRIVALS & DEPARTURES

### By Air

Mérida's international airport (airport code MID) lies 7 km southwest of the city center. It was once the Yucatán's busiest point of entry, but that was before the explosive growth of Cancún. Aeroméxico has daily nonstop service to Mérida from Miami and two or three flights a week from New Orleans. Mexican flies from Miami with a stop in Cozumel and also has twice-weekly flights to and from Havana. Guatemalan airline Aviateca links Mérida with Houston and Guatemala City.

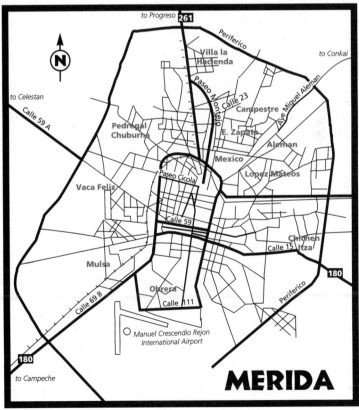

MERIDA

Domestic service is more ample. Aeroméxico and Mexicana each fly several times daily from Mexico City. Aviacsa and Aerocaribe, a Mexicana affiliate, compete on routes linking Mérida with Cancún, Villahermosa, Tuxtla Gutiérrez and Oaxaca. Mexicana flies from Cozumel.

## By Bus

Mérida has several bus terminals. The main terminal, shared by many bus lines, is situated on Calle 69 between Calles 68 and 70, a few blocks from the heart of the city. Most long-haul services, and nearly all first-class services, operate from here, as do some second-class services.

Deluxe services operate from a small, air-conditioned terminal half a block away, on Calle 69 between Calles 70 and 72. UNO has super-deluxe service to Cancún (3 1/2 hours, $18) twice daily and to Villahermosa (10 hours, $44) once daily. ADO GL has regular deluxe service to Cancún ($12) five times a day and to Villahermosa ($29) twice, with one continuing to Mexico City (24 hours, $60) and the other to Veracruz (19 hours, $46). Cristóbal Colón Plus has overnight service to San Cristóbal de las Casas ($30) and Tuxtla Gutiérrez ($34).

From the main terminal, ADO has first-class buses to Campeche (2 1/2 hours, $7) every half hour from 6 am to 3 pm and then at irregular intervals until 11:30 pm, including frequent early-evening departures. This same company has 10 trips a day to Cancún (4 hours, $11), nine to Valladolid (2 hours, $6), 14 to Villahermosa (10 hours, $22-$29), daytime and overnight services to Palenque (9 hours, $19-$22), five to Mexico City (24 hours, $49-$60) and three to Veracruz (19 hours, $38-$46).

Expreso de Oriente has hourly first-class express service to Cancún (3 1/2 hours, $11) from 6 am to midnight plus four a day to Valladolid and six a day to Playa del Carmen. Further service to Cancún is provided by Autotransportes del Caribe, with 15 first-class trips a day ($11-$15) plus 13 second-class trips ($9).

To Chichén Itzá ($3), Autotransportes de Oriente has second-class service hourly from 5 am to midnight. These buses continue to Valladolid ($4) and Cancún ($7). Several continue to Playa del Carmen, and at 11 am there is a direct bus to Cobá (4 hours, $6).

To Uxmal, Autotransportes del Sur has seven buses a day. At 8 am, there is also an archaeology buff's special, stopping at several sites in the Puuc Hills for a half-hour each and at Uxmal for 90 minutes, returning to Mérida at 4 pm For the full excursion, the fare is a bargain at $10. Check the day before to make sure it is operating.

To Chetumal (8 hours, $12-$18), with connections for Belize, Autotransportes Peninsulares and Autotransportes del Caribe have a total of about a dozen daily departures, some first-class and some second-class, many going via Ticul. As well, there are additional services to Ticul.

Autotransportes del Sureste offers second-class service on routes to Campeche ($5) nine times a day and to Palenque ($13), Villahermosa ($16), San Cristóbal de las Casas ($19) and Tuxtla Gutiérrez ($23) once or twice a day.

Buses to Progreso (40 minutes, $1.20) run from a separate, more central terminal on Calle 62 between Calles 65 and 67. Express buses run at least four times an hour between 5 am and 9 pm. They can also be flagged along Calle 60.

Second-class buses to Izamal (1 1/2 hours, $2) run from this terminal about 20 times a day. Additional departures to Izamal operate at least once an hour from a primitive terminal at Calle 50 and Calle 67. Buses to Celestún (2 hours, $4) leave just across from here at intervals of one to two hours.

## By Car

A new four-lane toll highway runs east from Mérida to Chichén Itzá, Valladolid and Cancún, with the trip time to Cancún now shortened to a little over three hours. Tolls are exorbitant, however, and most traffic continues to move over the old two-lane Highway 180, which is slower and more crowded. Highway 180 also runs southwest from Mérida to Campeche and beyond, with links to central Mexico.

Highway 261 originates at Progreso on the Gulf coast just north of Mérida and continues south, providing a slower alternate route to Campeche via Uxmal and other archaeological sites. Among other routes radiating from Mérida is Highway 184, running southeast through the lonely center of the peninsula on the way to Chetumal.

## By Rail

Yucatán's formerly narrow-gauge network used to attract rail fans with its antique coaches and open platforms, but years ago it was converted to standard gauge and it now uses conventional passenger equipment. Dual-gauge trackage is still visible at the Mérida station, a handsome yellow and white building with a majestic clock tower at the corner of Calle 55 and Calle 48. Trains run daily to Tizimín, Valladolid, Peto and Sotuta. Current schedules allow a same-day return trip to Tizimín with an early-morning departure from Mérida. Departures to other points are in late afternoon, with pre-dawn returns.

Through service between Mexico City and Mérida no longer operates. A daily train does connect Mérida with Campeche, Palenque, Coatzacoalcos and Córdoba, but service is so slow, uncomfortable and robbery-prone that it can be suggested only for true fanatics.

## ORIENTATION

The center of Mérida follows the rectangular grid pattern established by the Spanish, with most streets numbered rather than named. Even-numbered streets run north and south, odd-numbered streets go east and west. The central plaza, or *plaza grande*, is bounded by Calles 60, 61, 62, and 63. Numbers rise to the north and to the west.

The northern part of the city has long been more fashionable than the rest, and its most fashionable thoroughfare is the **Paseo de Montejo**, which starts nine blocks north of the *plaza grande* and extends to the outskirts of the city. There are several hotels and restaurants along here.

The **tourism information booths** at the airport and the main bus terminal are next to useless. Go instead to the **tourism office** at the corner of Calles 60 and 57, across from the Peón Contreras theater, which is more helpful.

## WHERE TO STAY

Mérida has a broad range of hotels, including a good selection in the middle and lower ranges and growing competition in the upper range. Anyone arriving from Cancún will be pleasantly surprised at the prices. The great majority of hotels in Mérida are clustered in or near the city center within a few blocks of the *plaza grande*, or central plaza. Most of the upper-range hotels are situated near the Paseo de Montejo to the north.

### Hotels near the Paseo de Montejo

**HYATT REGENCY MÉRIDA**, *Avenida Colón at Calle 60, phone (99) 420202, fax (99) 257002, US and Canada reservations (800) 233-1234; 300 rooms, $88 single or double for superior rooms up to $204 for Regency Club rooms including breakfast, VI - MC - AE - DC.*

This 17-story building (the tallest in Mérida) has richly appointed, air conditioned rooms, including a two-floor Regency Club. Amenities include a gym, pool, tennis, and jogging track. The elegant triangular lobby is clad in marble and wall sculptures. The hotel opened in 1994, and the lower-priced rooms offer exceptional value for money.

**HOLIDAY INN MÉRIDA**, *Avenida Colón between Calle 60 and Paseo de Montejo, phone (99) 256877, fax (99) 257755; 213 rooms, $154 single or double for standard rooms, $275 for junior suites, VI - MC - AE - DC.*

Rooms in this four-story hotel are nicely decorated but less lavish than at the Hyatt. Amenities include a gym, pool and tennis.

**HOTEL FIESTA AMERICANA**, *Avenida Colón at Calle 60.*

This 350-room luxury hotel was set to open in early 1995.

**HOTEL EL CONQUISTADOR**, *Paseo de Montejo at Calle 35, phone (99) 262155 or 269199, fax (99) 268829; 161 rooms, $95 single or double, VI - MC - AE - DC.*

A pool and bar are perched atop this eight-story building. Rooms are air conditioned, with pale blue decor. There are two restaurants, one offering a breakfast buffet.

**HOTEL MONTEJO PALACE**, *Paseo de Montejo at Calle 41, phone (99) 247644, reservations (99) 246046, fax (99) 280388, US reservations (800) 437-9607; 90 rooms, $85 single or double, VI - MC - AE - DC.*

Under the same management as the Hotel Paseo de Montejo, this hotel has an interesting lobby with appealing tile work, but rooms are musty and very ordinary in decor. Guests may use the bigger pool at the other hotel.

**HOTEL PASEO DE MONTEJO**, *Paseo de Montejo at Calle 41, phone (99) 239033, reservations (99) 246046, fax (99) 280388, US reservations (800) 437-9607; 92 rooms, $54 single or double, VI - MC - AE - DC.*

Rooms here are characterized by plastic furniture and aging carpet. There is a big pool.

### City center hotels: upper range

**HOTEL CASA DEL BALAM**, *Calle 60 #495 at Calle 57, phone (99) 248844 or 248130, fax (99) 245011, US reservations (800) 624-8451; 54 rooms, $121 single or double in high season, slightly less in low season, VI - MC - AE - DC.*

Rooms in this seven-story building are large and bright, with double-glazed windows to reduce street noise. Furnishings are simple, with some colonial touches. Rooms have air conditioning, TV, phones and tile floors. There are a small courtyard and a pleasant pool area.

**HOTEL LOS ALUXES**, *Calle 60 #444 near Calle 49, phone (99) 242199, fax (99) 233858, US reservations (800) 782-8395; 152 rooms, $69 single or double, VI - MC - AE.*

This seven-story building offers standard modern hotel decor, with carpeting, air conditioning, TV and phones. A few larger rooms, at $95, have jacuzzis.

**HOTEL D'CHAMPS**, *Calle 70 #543 at Calle 67, phone (99) 248655, fax (99) 236024; 90 rooms, $73 single or double, VI - MC - AE.*

Situated 1 1/2 blocks from the bus terminal, this hotel consists of two buildings, a big garden, and a pool area. Rooms are small but pleasantly furnished in shades of pink and grey, with air conditioning, TV and phones.

**HOTEL RESIDENCIAL**, *Calle 59 between Calles 76 and 78, phone (99) 244844, fax (99) 240266; 66 rooms, $73 single or double, VI - MC - AE.*

This six-story pink-and-white building has chandeliers in the lobby and appealingly decorated blue-and-white rooms, with air conditioning, TV and phone. The hotel has an elegant (and rather expensive) dining room and a tiny pool. It is a bit away from the center.

**HOTEL DEL GOBERNADOR**, *Calle 59 #535 at Calle 66, phone (99) 237133 or 237001, fax (99) 281590; 60 rooms, high season $62 single or double, low season $55, VI - MC - AE - DC.*

Most rooms in this modern three-story building face a small pool and are pleasantly decorated. All have air conditioning, TV and phones. The hotel is modern and efficient but lacks charm.

**HOTEL MÉRIDA MISIÓN PARK PLAZA**, *Calle 60 #491 at Calle 57, phone (99) 239500, fax (99) 237765, US reservations (800) 752-3596; 145 rooms, high season $78 single or double, low season $74, VI - MC - AE - DC.*

Rooms are large and bright, with simple furnishings, tile floors, air conditioning, TV and phone, but this 10-story building has slow elevator service, and the pool area is barren.

**HOTEL AMBASSADOR MÉRIDA**, *Calle 59 #546 at Calle 68, phone (99) 242100, fax (99) 242701; 98 rooms, $69 single or double, VI - MC - AE - DC.*

Rooms are small and pleasantly furnished, but the hotel has a tired, rather dated look. Each room has air conditioning, TV and phone, and there is a tiny pool.

**HOTEL CALINDA PANAMERICANA**, *Calle 59 #455 between Calles 52 and 54, phone (99) 239111 or 239444, fax (99) 248090, US and Canada reservations (800) 228-5151; 110 rooms, $79 single or double, VI - MC - AE - DC.*

The entrance to this hotel lies through what was an elegant colonial mansion onto which has been grafted a big and rather ugly seven-story building. Rooms are big but very ordinary, with air conditioning, TV and phones. The hotel has a pool, restaurant and bar.

**HOTEL EL CASTELLANO**, *Calle 57 #513 between Calles 62 and 64, phone (99) 230100, fax (99) 230110; 170 rooms, high season $69 single or double, low season $50, VI - MC - AE.*

This is a great, cavernous, soulless place, 11 stories high. Rooms are big and bright, with air conditioning, TV and phone, but are gaudily furnished.

### City center hotels: middle range

**HOTEL TZIRANDA**, *Calle 57 #474 between Calles 52 and 54, phone (99) 240341 or 240242; 18 rooms, high season $30 single or double, low season $24, VI - MC - AE.*

This small, pretty, family-run hotel occupies a 19th-century house and a three-story annex. Rooms are quiet and pleasant, with fresh tile work, air conditioning, TV and phones. The reception area is located in a cheerful salon.

**HOTEL COLONIAL**, *Calle 62 #475 at Calle 57, phone (99) 236444 or 248108, fax (99) 283961; 73 rooms, $54 single or double, VI - MC - AE - DC.*

This misnamed hotel occupies a modern five-story building. Rooms are small and pleasantly furnished, with air conditioning, TV and phone, though they are less elegant than the lobby would suggest. There is a small pool.

**HOTEL POSADA TOLEDO**, *Calle 58 #487 near Calle 57, phone (99) 231690, fax (99) 232256; 23 rooms, $30 single, $33 double, $4 more for air conditioning, VI - MC.*

Rooms vary greatly. Downstairs rooms with fans are big, with high ceilings and attractive floor tiles. Air conditioned rooms are smaller, noisier and less pleasant. There are comfortable seating areas on terraces outside the rooms.

**HOTEL COLÓN**, *Calle 62 #483 at Calle 57, phone (99) 234355, fax (99) 244919; 53 rooms, $33 single, $38 double, VI - MC.*

This hotel has a beautifully tiled lobby and main stairway, but furnishings in the rooms are decidedly tired. The hotel offers a pool and steam bath, and rooms come with carpeting, air conditioning, TV and phone.

**HOTEL DEL PARQUE**, *Calle 60 #495 between Calles 57 and 59, phone (99) 247844, fax (99) 281429; 20 rooms, $30 single, $33 double, VI - MC.*

Rooms here have air conditioning, TV and phone but are small and rather unappealing. Rooms facing the street are noisy, while the others are dark.

**HOTEL REFORMA**, *Calle 59 #508 at Calle 62, phone (99) 247922, fax (99) 247223; 45 rooms, $26 single, $32 double, VI - MC.*

Set in a poorly adapted colonial building, rooms are small and plain, with fans. Some are dark and windowless, others face the street and are noisy. There is a small pool.

**HOTEL MAYA YUCATÁN**, *Calle 58 #483 between Calles 55 and 57, phone (99) 235395, fax (99) 234642; 80 rooms, $50 single or double, VI - MC - AE.*

This seven-story slab building has slow elevators and cheaply furnished rooms. It conveys a general ugliness. Rooms are air conditioned, with TV and phones, and there is a pool.

### City center hotels: lower range

**HOTEL SANTA LUCÍA**, *Calle 55 #508 between Calles 60 and 62, phone (99) 282662 or 282672; 51 rooms, $26 single, $29 double, VI.*

This quiet, three-story hotel has friendly staff and pleasant, modern rooms set around a narrow courtyard. Most are air conditioned, with TV and phone. A few have fans and are slightly cheaper.

**HOTEL TRINIDAD**, *Calle 62 #464 between Calles 55 and 57, phone (99) 213029 or 232033; 19 rooms, $12 to $27 for up to four persons, no cards.*

This delightful and decidedly eccentric hotel has the feel of a 19th-century auberge in southern France. It will appeal to people of an artistic temperament, but it is not for everyone. Antique furniture and modern art are scattered about the myriad gardens and salons. Set in a colonial mansion, each of its rooms is different. All have high ceilings and fans, varying in size as well as in price, and some are quite dark. Ask to see several rooms before checking in.

**HOTEL TRINIDAD GALERÍA**, *Calle 60 #456 at Calle 51, phone (99) 232463, fax (99) 242319; 31 rooms, $18 single, $21 double, VI - MC - AE - DC.*

This hotel is under the same ownership at the Hotel Trinidad, and it shows. The entrance lies through what looks like an art gallery, with modern paintings and sculptures. Deeper inside are an exuberant garden with bits of pottery, old furniture and modern art scattered about, as well as a small pool. Rooms, however, are somewhat dark and poorly furnished.

**HOTEL CASA BOWEN**, *Calle #521-B near Calle 65, phone (99) 286109; 28 rooms, high season $14 single, $16 double, $2 less in low season, no cards.*

Among the best of the budget hotels in Mérida. Rooms are big, bright and airy, with decent furnishings, a few with kitchenette. There is a small garden courtyard and a sitting area downstairs with wicker furniture.

**HOTEL MUCUY**, *Calle 57 #481 between Calles 56 and 58, phone (99) 237801 or 285193, fax (9) 237801; 24 rooms, $12 single, $15 double, no cards.*

This hotel is a good budget choice. Rooms are simply but decently furnished, although floor tiles are aging poorly. The hotel has an attractive lobby and a small garden facing an ancient stone wall.

**HOTEL LAS MONJAS**, *Calle 66A #509 near Calle 63, phone (99) 286632; 30 rooms, $12 single, $14 double, no cards.*

Situated on a quiet side street, this friendly spot has clean and very simple rooms that vary in size. Two have air conditioning, with a supplement.

**HOTEL MONTEJO**, *Calle 57 #507 between Calles 62 and 64, phone (99) 280277; 22 rooms, $23 single, $25 double, $3 more with air conditioning, VI - MC - AE.*

Rooms in this two-story hotel are set around a pleasant courtyard but are somewhat dark, with worn furnishings.

**HOTEL FLAMINGO**, *Calle 57 #485 between Calles 56 and 58, phone (99) 247755, fax (99) 247070; 31 rooms, $23 single, $27 double, $4 more for air conditioning, VI - MC - AE.*

Rooms in this rather ugly three-story building are simply but decently furnished, with TV. Some of the tile work needs replacing. There is a pool.

**HOTEL JANEIRO**, *Calle 57 #435 between Calles 48 and 50, phone (99) 233602; 20 rooms, $15 single or double with fan, $3 more with air conditioning, no cards.*

Rooms are bright and simple. The hotel has a pool, and there are plenty of rocking-chairs in the lobby.

**HOTEL DOLORES ALBA**, *Calle 63 #464 between Calles 52 and 54, phone (99) 285650, fax (99) 283163; 42 rooms, $18 single, $21 double, $6 more for air conditioning, no cards.*

Rooms are small and simply but pleasantly furnished and face the pool or a paved-over courtyard used for parking.

**HOTEL MARGARITA**, *Calle 66 #506 between Calles 61 and 63, phone (99) 237236; 26 rooms, $9 single, $11 to $13 double, no cards.*

Rooms are simple, most of them rather dark.

**GRAN POSADA**, *Calle 65 #529 between Calles 64 and 66; phone (99) 240551; 10 rooms, $6 single, $9 double, no cards.*

Rooms are big and face a pleasant garden but are really quite rudimentary.

**HOTEL MARÍA TERESA**, *Calle 64 #529 between Calles 65 and 67, phone (99) 285194; 27 rooms, $10 single, $14 double, no cards.*

Rooms are small and quite basic.

**HOTEL OVIEDO**, *Calle 62 #515 between Calles 65 and 67, phone (99) 286711; 33 rooms, $15 single or double, no cards.*

This hotel occupies an impressive colonial building, but rooms are really quite bare.

**HOTEL BECIL**, *Calle 67 #550-C between Calles 66 and 68, phone (99) 246764; 12 rooms, $15 single, $18 double, no cards.*

Rooms are clean, bright and quiet but rather basic. Better value can be found elsewhere.

**HOTEL POSADA DEL ÁNGEL**, *Calle 67 #535 between Calles 66 and 68, phone (99) 232754; 30 rooms, $20 single, $23 double, no cards.*

Rooms are simple, and most are rather dark. Again, better value can be found elsewhere.

## WHERE TO EAT

Restaurants in Mérida are varied and generally not very expensive. **PORTICO DEL PEREGRINO**, *Calle 57 between Calles 60 and 62*, offers regional and international dishes. It has an air-conditioned dining room and an open terrace in back. **LOS ALMENDROS**, *Calle 50 between Calles 57 and 59*, offers Yucatecan dishes such as pok chuck and cochinita pibil. **EL MESÓN** has a varied menu and a terrace *facing Parque Hidalgo*.

**CAFÉ PEÓN CONTRERAS**, with a dining room and terrace *facing the small plaza of the same name*, is similar to a French bistro in decor. The menu centers on meats and pizza, and prices are moderate. **ALBERTO'S CONTINENTAL**, *at the corner of Calles 64 and 57*, has a Lebanese menu and series of dining rooms in a splendid 17th century mansion. **LA BELLA ÉPOCA**, *upstairs in the Hotel del Parque on Calle 60 between Calles*

*57 and 59*, offers a mixture of Lebanese, French and Yucatecan dishes, including some vegetarian items. The old-fashioned dining room overlooks a small park.

*Along the Paseo de Montejo*, **SOBERANIS**, *between Calles 37 and 39*, offers seafood dishes at moderate prices. **RINCÓN ORIENTAL**, *near Calle 37*, offers 1950s-style Sino-American cuisine. **DULCERÍA Y SORBETERÍA COLÓN**, *near Calle 39*, is a good spot for deserts. *Between Calles 43 and 45*, **SAN VALENTÍN**, with meats, seafood and tacos, and **PIZZERÍA LAS YARDAS**, both have splendid outdoor terraces.

## ENTERTAINMENT & NIGHTLIFE

On Sundays there are free band concerts and presentations of regional music in the **plaza grande** at several hours throughout the day.

The **Casa de la Cultura Maya**, *Calle 63 between Calles 64 and 66*, presents free concerts of regional music Tuesdays at 8 pm

**Cine Plaza Internacional**, *Calle 58 at Calle 59*, presents foreign films, usually with subtitles. Programs change every couple of days.

## SHOPPING

Among items to buy in Mérida are embroidered cotton dresses and blouses called *huipiles*, men's tropical dress shirts called *guayaberas*, straw hats of the type often called Panama hats, and hammocks. A large selection can be found in a section of the **municipal market** *at Calles 56A and 67* and the nearby **Bazar de Artesanías**.

The **Casa de la Cultura Maya**, *Calle 63 between Calles 64 and 66*, has a good selection of regional handicrafts, as does the gift shop of the **Museo Nacional de Arte Popular**, *Calle 59 between Calles 48 and 50*.

## SEEING THE SIGHTS

A good place to start is the tree-shaded **central plaza**, called the *plaza grande* rather than the *zócalo* as in most other parts of Mexico. *On the east side of the plaza, separated from it by Calle 60*, is the 16th century **cathedral**, big, bare and stark, with very little of its original decoration still intact. To the left of the main altar is the **Cristo de las Ampollas**, a black statue of Christ, the most important ornament in the cathedral.

*On the south side of the plaza* is the very ornate **Casa de Montejo**, a private mansion built originally in the 16th century and subsequently rebuilt. It stayed in family hands for more than four centuries until the 1970s, when it was converted to a banking center. It can be visited during banking hours. *On the west side* is the 16th-century **Palacio Municipal**, painted yellow and white and topped by a clock tower. Finally, *on the north side*, the **Palacio de Gobierno** is noteworthy by the murals by local artist Francisco Castro Pacheco.

*Heading north along Calle 60,* there are several small plazas, starting with the **Parque Hidalgo** *near Calle 59* facing the 17th century **Iglesia de Jesús**, a Jesuit church. *Just north of the church* is the **Parque de la Madre**, facing the Italianate **Teatro Peón Contreras**. Beyond this is the central courtyard of the **Universidad Autónoma de Yucatán**. Finally, there is the **Parque Santa Lucía** *near Calle 55.*

If you prefer to sit back and let someone else show you around, **Transportación Turística Carnaval**, *Calle 55 between Calles 60 and 62, phone (99) 272476 or 276119,* offers bus tours of the city.

---

### LEARN ABOUT MEXICAN HANDICRAFTS

*The **Museo Nacional de Arte Popular**, a few blocks from the center on Calle 59 between Calles 48 and 50, presents fine samples of weaving, pottery, ceramics and the implements used in their production. It also exhibits masks, hand-painted wooden objects, glassware and copperware items. The ground floor is dedicated to objects from the Yucatán, while the upper floor presents a survey of items from across Mexico. There is a handicrafts shop in back. The museum is open Tuesday to Saturday from 8 am to 8 pm and Sunday from 9 am to 2 pm. Admission is free.*

---

The **Museo de Arte Contemporáneo Ateneo de Yucatán** is a new museum of modern art *situated in the Pasaje de la Revolución next to the cathedral.* It presents a selection of paintings, lithographs, weavings and ceramics. *It is open daily except Tuesday from 9 am to 5 pm Admission is $3.*

The **Museo de la Ciudad**, *Calle 61 between Calles 58 and 60,* has a small display of maquettes and other objects depicting the history of the city. *It is open Monday 9 am to 2:30 pm, Tuesday to Friday 9 am to 6 pm, and Saturday 9 am to 1 pm. Admission is free.*

The **Pinoteca Juan Gamboa Guzmán**, *Calle 59 between Calles 58 and 60,* presents a small collection of paintings and sculptures, some on historical themes. *It is open Tuesday to Saturday, 8 am to 8 pm, and Sunday 8 am to 2 pm. Admission is free.*

The **Museo Regional de Antropología**, *on Paseo de Montejo at Calle 43,* presents a collection of Mayan pieces including some original murals. It also offers explanations (in Spanish only) of Mayan history and customs. *The museum is open Tuesday to Saturday from 8 am to 8 pm, admission $4, and Sunday from 8 am to 2 pm. Admission free.*

**Casa de la Cultura Maya**, *Calle 63 between Calles 64 and 66,* has a small museum depicting the region's tradition of song. *It is open Monday to Saturday from 9 am to 2 pm Admission is free.* There is also a large handicrafts shop here.

The **Antigua Hacienda y Museo de Yaxcopoil**, *in the town of Yaxcopoil 28 km south of Mérida on the highway to Uxmal,* provides a taste of 19th century life in the Yucatán. This former henequen (*sisal*) plantation actually dates from the 17th century, but the surviving buildings are more recent and include the lodgings of the plantation owner and sheds used in farming operations. Leaflets are offered in several languages, and there are good displays of 19th century furniture and utensils.

Additional restoration work seems to be required, however, and we found the staff to be of limited helpfulness. *It opens Monday to Saturday 8 am to 6 pm and Sunday 9 am to 1 pm. Admission is $4. For information in Mérida, phone (99) 264311 or 272602.*

## EXCURSIONS

Mérida can be used as a base for visits to the ruins of Chichén Itzá, Uxmal, and Kabah, Sayil, and Labná in the Puuc hills. It is also within easy striking distance of Progreso and of Celestún. These points are all covered separately in this book. They can be visited by car, by bus, or by organized tour. **Mayaland Tours**, *Calle 60 between Calles 55 and 57*, offers a number of excursions.

In this section, we'll describe **Izamal** – one of the more interesting excursions available from Mérida.

## IZAMAL

**Izamal**, *72 km east of Mérida*, is a step back in time, really a most unusual town. It calls itself *la ciudad de las tres culturas*, the city of the three cultures, referring to the ancient Mayan, the Spanish colonial, and the modern Mexican. It is the first two that are more in evidence.

### ARRIVALS & DEPARTURES

Izamal is linked by a secondary highway connecting Mérida and Valladolid running north of the main highways. It can be visited as an excursion from either place or as a stopover in between. The trip from Mérida is about one hour by car or 1 1/2 hours by bus.

There are several interesting towns along the way, including **Hoctún** with its enormous church. Mérida service is provided by two competing bus companies (separate terminals in Mérida but a shared terminal in Izamal) with departures about twice an hour. The last bus back to Mérida goes at 8:30 pm (see page 187). Only a few buses go to Valladolid, with the last departure at 5 pm. As well, there are through services to Cancún.

### SEEING THE SIGHTS

If you arrive by bus, one of the first things you'll notice is the taxi stand outside the terminal: all taxis here are horse-drawn carriages! Wander over to the *plaza grande*, or main plaza, and you'll see another taxi stand

**A TRADITIONAL HOUSE IN IZAMAL**

with a row of horse-drawn carriages. There is very little motor traffic in town. Something else you'll notice is the remarkable visual integrity of Izamal: virtually every building in the center of town is painted an identical shade of dark yellow with white trim.

There are two big plazas in the center of town, both facing the enormous 16th century Franciscan **convent of San Antonio de Pádua** with its church, the **Santuario de la Virgen de Izamal**. The main plaza is tree-shaded and arcaded on each side. One of these groups of arches leads to the big grassy courtyard in front of the convent and church, built on the base of an ancient pyramid. The church shows yellow stucco in front and ancient stone behind: it was built using stone from the temple it replaced. It is more ornate than most churches in the Yucatán, with gold paintings above the main altar.

There are several other pyramids nearby, all now just heaps of rubble. The biggest of them, **Kinich Kakmó**, occupies a large city block *to the left of the convent.* By climbing it you can get good views of the town and the surrounding countryside.

There are two tiny hotels facing the *plaza grande*, both with dark, bare rooms, shared bath and a very rustic feel. **HOTEL CANTO** is the less unappealing of the two. Several restaurants have tried their luck but seem to have failed. If you can find nothing else, there is a small restaurant in the bus terminal.

## PRACTICAL INFORMATION

### Airlines
• **Aeromexico**: *(99) 279566 or 279000*
• **Mexicana**: *(99) 246754 or 231292*
• **Aerocaribe**: *(99) 286786*
• **Aviacsa**: *(99) 269087*
• **Aviateca**: *(99) 461296*

### Bicycle & Motorcycle Rental
• **Moto Rent and Bicycle**: *Calle 54 #364 between Calles 35 and 37, phone (99) 261568*

### Bookshops
• **Librerías Dante**: with branches in several locations, *including the corner of Calles 59 and 68 and the corner of Calles 60 and 57*, offers detailed guidebooks to the archaeological sites in several languages as well as art books and dictionaries.

### Car Rentals
Rates are more reasonable than in Cancún, and there is keen competition. A big cluster of car rental agencies, including international names and the often cheaper local firms, *is situated along Calle 60 between Calles 55 and 59*. It is simple to compare rates.

### Consulates
• **Britain**: *Calle 58 #498, phone (99) 286152*
• **United States**: *Paseo de Montejo #453, phone (99) 255011 or 255554*

### Currency Exchange
Mérida is the best place in southeastern Mexico to change US dollars, whether in cash or travelers' checks, with the most favorable exchange rates. Good rates can be found at **Euromex**, part of the Banamex complex *in the Casa de Montejo facing the plaza grande*, open banking hours only. There are several other *casas de cambio* around the central area with longer hours.

### Laundry
• **Lavandería Automática Anny's**: *Calle 64 #470 at Calle 55*, provides inexpensive, same-day service.

### Tourist Information
There is a **tourism information booth** *at the corner of Calles 60 and 57, two blocks north of the central plaza*.

# PROGRESO

> **Progreso lies just 32 km north of Mérida.**

This seaside resort presents a generally scruffy appearance once you get away from the beach. The main beach is long and sandy, with gentle waves, and the seafront *malecón* has been attractively renovated with a broad, brick-paved walkway. A very lengthy new pier, extending several kilometers out to sea, has failed to draw the anticipated cruise ship traffic. There is a small but picturesque lighthouse opposite the public market. Progreso is popular among inhabitants of Mérida for family excursions on Sundays and holidays. Although there are a few hotels, these tend to be fairly modest.

Just to the east is the suburb of **Chicxulub** (linked by frequent local buses), with quiet and inviting stretches of beach, a barren concrete *zócalo*, and a couple of very simple hotels and restaurants. Most of the beachfront between Progreso and Chicxulub is occupied by clusters of private condominium units, a few available for short-term rental.

West of Progreso, at **Yucalpetén**, there were ambitious plans to develop a substantial resort area, but things have fallen through. A lavish hotel, the Fiesta Inn, has closed, and the only hotel in operation is a private resort for government workers. Some condominium projects have gone ahead, however.

## ARRIVALS & DEPARTURES

The bus terminal is situated on Calle 29 between Calles 30 and 32. Express buses to and from Mérida (40 minutes, $1.20) run at least four times an hour between 5 am and 9 pm and can be flagged along Calle 60 in Mérida.

## ORIENTATION

Progreso itself is laid out in a rectangular grid pattern with streets numbered rather than named. The street numbering system changed recently: subtract 50 from even-numbered streets to get the new numbers.

## WHERE TO STAY

**HOTEL PLAYA LINDA,** *facing the beach at Calle 26, no phone; 8 rooms, $15 single or double, $30 during busy periods, no cards.*

Rooms are big, bright and simple.

**HOTEL REAL DEL MAR,** *facing the beach at Calle 20, phone (993) 50798; 15 rooms, $17 single or double, $26 for up to four people.*

Rooms are bright and simple, but the hotel is showing its age. It has a good restaurant.

**HOTEL PROGRESO**, *Calle 28 at Calle 29, phone (993) 50039; 13 rooms, $15 single, $18 double, $8 more for air conditioning.*

Bright, carpeted rooms are simply furnished and make good use of decorative tiles.

**HOTEL SAN MIGUEL**, *Calle 28 between Calles 29 and 31, phone (993) 51357; 20 rooms, $12 single, $14 double, no cards.*

Rooms are clean and simple, with fans.

**HOTEL TROPICAL SUITES**, *facing the beach at Calle 20, phone (993) 51263; 16 rooms, $15 single or double.*

Rooms vary. Some have kitchenettes and some face the sea, while others are dark and windowless. All are simple. The narrow entrance is uninviting.

## WHERE TO EAT

The *malecón*, running along the seafront, is lined with simple but appealing restaurants serving fresh fish and seafood at moderate prices. Suggested restaurants along the *malecón* include **REAL DEL MAR** *at Calle 20*, **MARINOS** *at Calle 24*, **SOL Y MAR** *at Calle 30*, and **FRAGATTA** *on Calle 30 one block from the malecón*.

In **Chicxulub**, there are several restaurants *near the main pier*, including **LA MARISQUERÍA DEL MUELLE** and **LOS TIBURONES**.

# CELESTÚN

> *Celestún is 92 km west of Mérida.*

The town of **Celestún** is a minor beach resort that also happens to lie within a bird sanctuary. It is a friendly, casual, and decidedly unglamorous spot with a handful of simple hotels and several good seafood restaurants.

The best bathing beach lies about 1 km north of town (turn right facing the sea); it is cleaner, and there are not as many fishing boats. Boatmen at the main beach in town can take visitors along the coast and up the nearby, mangrove-lined estuary to see colonies of brilliant pink flamingos as well as pelicans, cormorants, egrets, herons and ducks. The cost is about $40 for a two-hour trip. It is crucial not to frighten flamingos in their nesting grounds, for they may take to flight and their long legs can knock eggs from their nests.

## ARRIVALS & DEPARTURES

Celestún lies almost due west of Mérida. There are 13 buses a day in either direction (2 hours, $4), with departures one to two hours apart between 5 am and 8:30 pm.

## WHERE TO STAY

**HOTEL MARÍA DEL CARMEN**, *Calle 12 between Calles 13 and 15, phone (99) 280419 or 280152; 14 rooms, $12 single, $18 double, no cards.*
Clean, bright rooms all have balconies facing the sea.

**HOTEL SAN JULIO**, *Calle 12 between Calles 9 and 11, no phone; 9 rooms, $8-$9 single, $11-$12 double, no cards.*
Big, clean, simple rooms are set around a sandy courtyard facing the beach.

**HOTEL GUTIÉRREZ**, *Calle 12 between Calles 13 and 15, phone (99) 280160 or 280313; 14 rooms, $15 single, $18 double, no cards.*
This three-story hotel has simple rooms, some a little dark. A few have sea views. The entrance is on the beach. Long-distance telephone service is available here.

## WHERE TO EAT

*The corner of Calles 12 and 11* is restaurant central. A cluster of simple but appealing eating spots offers fresh fish and seafood at low prices, among them **LA PLAYITA**, **CHIVIRICO**, **ÁVILA** and **CELESTÚN**. There are more along the beach, including **LOS CARACOLES** *near Calle 7.*

# UXMAL & THE PUUC HILLS

*Uxmal lies along Highway 261, 80 km south of Mérida.*

The **ruins of Uxmal** are not as impressive as those of Chichén Itzá, but in some respects they are more beautiful, pure Mayan in style without the Toltec overlays. Uxmal is really out in the countryside. It consists of an archaeological site, a small cluster of hotels, and not much else. There is no town.

Most visitors come on day excursions from Mérida, although there are two very pleasant hotels near the entrance to the ruins. The only hotel suitable for budget travelers is 4 km away and awkward to reach without a car. An alternative is to stay in the town of Ticul, an option that, again, is more practical for those with cars.

Uxmal lies at the edge of the only hilly part of the Yucatán, an area known as the Puuc hills. It forms part of a circuit that includes several smaller and more isolated archaeological sites in the Puuc hills, notably Kabah, Sayil and Labná. Nearby are the caves of Loltún. The town of Ticul is interesting for its handicrafts and for its extensive use of bicycles.

## ARRIVALS & DEPARTURES

Uxmal lies along Highway 261, which provides an alternate route between Mérida and Campeche. There are seven buses a day from Mérida and five from Campeche, stopping near the Hotel Hacienda Uxmal. The last bus back to Mérida leaves at 7 pm, and the last departure to Campeche is at 6:30 pm. It is a good idea to double-check with the ticket seller at the archaeological site. Some of these buses also stop near the ruins of Kabah and Sayil, but service is too infrequent for this to be a practical option.

**Autotransportes del Sur** runs an archaeology buff's special, leaving Mérida at 8 am, stopping at several sites in the Puuc hills for a half-hour each and at Uxmal for 90 minutes, returning to Mérida at 4 pm. For the full excursion, the fare is a bargain at $10. Check the day before to make sure it is operating. If this doesn't work out, renting a car in Mérida may be the best option for visiting sites beyond Uxmal, as well as Loltún and Ticul.

## WHERE TO STAY

**HOTEL HACIENDA UXMAL**, *300 meters from the ruins, phone Mérida (99) 252122 or 252133, fax (99) 257022; 78 rooms, $86 single, $97 double, VI - MC - AE.*

Rooms in this spacious and traditional hotel, open since 1954, are simple and pleasantly appointed, with wooden ceiling beams, wooden louvers on the windows, and TV. Air conditioning is available for a supplement. Broad terraces outside the rooms have chairs and coffee tables. The grounds are well landscaped and shaded, with a pool, restaurant and bar.

**VILLA ARCHEOLÓGICA UXMAL**, *300 meters from the eastern entrance to the ruins, phone Mérida (99) 247053; 40 rooms, $55 single, $63 double, $3 less in low season, VI - MC - AE.*

This two-story hotel, managed by the Club Méditerranée group, is set around a pleasant garden and pool. Rooms are simple but comfortable, with air conditioning. Decor is modern Mexican, with whitewashed stucco and pink and mauve fabrics. The restaurant is elegant and expensive, with Mexican and French specialties. Guests have the use of a tennis court, library and video room. Long-distance telephone calls can be made from here but are very costly.

**HOTEL MISIÓN UXMAL PARK INN**, *2 km north of the ruins, phone Mérida (99) 247308; 59 rooms, $87 single or double, VI - MC - AE - DC.*

This three-story, crescent-shaped building has a big pool, restaurant and bar. The ruins are visible in the distance from the middle and upper floors. Rooms, all with balconies and fans, are big but rather spartan for a hotel of this category. This spot is not convenient for those without vehicles.

**RANCHO UXMAL**, *4 km north of the ruins, no phone; 16 rooms, $23 single or double, no cards.*

Motel-style rooms are simple but enlivened by paintings with Mayan motifs. There are a pool, restaurant and bar. Trailer parking is available for $3 per vehicle, camping for $2 per person. This spot is awkward without a private vehicle.

## WHERE TO EAT

Hotel restaurants provide the main options at Uxmal. Meals are good but a bit expensive. Breakfast and lunch are available in the mediocre restaurant at the entrance to the ruins. Light refreshments are sold at the entrances to the sites in the Puuc hills.

For those headed to or from Mérida by car, **RESTAURANT LOL PICH**, *just north of the town of Muna 16 km north of Uxmal*, is a pleasant spot with palapa shades, trees and lots of plants. It offers nicely prepared regional dishes at low prices, including an excellent *poc chuk*, a type of grilled pork. The town of **Ticul** also has good restaurants; these are mentioned below.

## VISITING THE RUINS

*The site is open daily from 8 am to 5 pm. Admission is $7, free on Sundays. Parking is $1, and there is an $8 fee for the use of video cameras.* At the entrance to the site are a restaurant, gift shop, bookshop, and baggage storage.

Uxmal was an important city between the seventh and ninth centuries A.D. and was contemporary with Palenque and Tikal. The image of the rain god Chac appears frequently in masks and carvings, a reflection, no doubt, of the scarcity of water in this region. The site is noted for its intricate stone mosaics, the ornate friezes on its upper walls and its rows of columns and vaulted arches.

*Situated near the entrance*, the 35-meter-high **Pyramid of the Magician** is built on an oval base. On the western side is a handrail to help in the steep ascent. From the top there are excellent views over the rest of the site. *To its west* is the **Nunnery Quadrangle**, a series of four temples facing a central patio and decorated above with masks, images of snakes and geometric patterns.

*Past a ball court to the south* is the vast but graceful **Governor's Palace**, nearly 100 meters long and decorated with geometric patterns requiring more than 20,000 individually cut stones. These are overlaid with images of serpents and human faces. *To one side of the palace* is the **House of the Turtles**, named for carvings on its cornice, *and to another* is the 30-meter-high **Great Pyramid**, which is only partly restored.

Evening sound and light shows recount Mayan legends and help bring out some details of the Governor's Palace that are less evident in natural light.

## Near Uxmal
## KABAH

Situated 23 km south of Uxmal along Highway 261, **Kabah** is the most impressive of the minor sites in the Puuc hills. **Kodz Poop**, or the *Palace of Masks*, is set on a high terrace and has nearly 300 masks carved in its façade. A small pyramid is set on the same platform. The **Palace** has a broad façade with several doorways and columns in the center of each doorway.

A jungle path leads to the **Temple of Columns**, named for the rows of columns on the upper part of its façade. Across the highway is a heap of rubble that was once the Great Temple, and beyond that is a finely restore **monumental arch**. *The site is open daily from 8 am to 5 pm, and admission is $3, free on Sundays.*

## SAYIL

Situated 5 km south of Kabah, or 28 km south of Uxmal, along a secondary road cutting through the Puuc hills, **Sayil** is interesting for its jungle setting and its three-tiered, multi-room, multi-columned **Palace**. From the top can be seen the enormous stone-lined cisterns used to conserve water. Another building, **El Mirador**, is scarcely worth the 400-meter walk. *The site is open daily from 8 am to 5 pm, and admission is $3, free on Sundays.*

## LABNÁ

There is little of interest here apart from a monumental arch adorned with latticework and masks. *The site, 9 km east of Sayil, is open daily from 8 am to 5 pm, and admission is $3, free on Sundays.*

## LOLTÚN CAVES

Situated between the archæological sites and the town of Oxkutzcab, the **Loltún caves** are noted for their elaborate stone columns and chambers. Wall paintings and other evidence suggest that these caves have been is use for at least 2,500 years, and several important archaeological pieces have been discovered here. *Guides accompany visitors on hour-long tours of the caves at 9:30 am, 11 am, 12:30 pm, 2 pm and 3 pm. Admission is $5, Sundays $2.*

There are no buses. The caves can be reached by taxi from Oxkutzcab.

# TICUL

**Ticul** *is situated 86 km south of Mérida near the Puuc hills area.* From Mérida it can be reached by Highway 261 to Muna and Highway 184 from there. It is served by buses. One immediately evident characteristic is the paucity of motor traffic and the widespread use of bicycles. Even the taxis are pedal-powered. Families go about in three-wheelers with large platforms in front. Ticul is noted also for its embroidered cotton blouses and dresses. A selection can be found in the public market area.

**RESTAURANT LOS ALMENDROS,** *on Calle 23 near Calle 28,* is nothing fancy but is famous throughout the Yucatán as the originator of *pok chuk,* a tasty grilled pork dish. There are two small hotels in the center of town, both rather dismal. **HOTEL SIERRA SOSA,** *on Calle 26 near the zócalo,* is not quite as bad as the other.

Toward the outskirts is **HOTEL-RESTAURANT CERRO INN,** *Calle 23 between Calles 44 and 46, phone (997) 20260; 14 rooms, $12 single, $15 double, VI - MC.* Rooms are dark and plain, but the grounds have plenty of trees and shrubs. There is a pleasant palapa-shaded restaurant. Across the street is **HOTEL BUGAMBILIAS,** *phone (997) 20761; 20 rooms, $15 single, $21 double, VI-MC.* Here, too, the rooms are dark and rather simple, but the grounds are pleasant, with lots of flowering shrubs.

# CAMPECHE

> **Campeche lies along Highway 180.**

The city of **Campeche** (pronounced cam-PAY-chay), the capital and biggest population center in the state of the same name, feels today like something of a backwater. In the 17th century it was busy enough and prosperous enough to attract the attention of pirates, and in response it became one of the few walled cities in the western hemisphere. Today remnants of the three-century-old series of walls, bastions and gates that kept the pirates out are still extant, and two of the bastions, or *baluartes,* house small museums.

Campeche has been eclipsed by other seaports on the Gulf of Mexico, and it does not have a populous hinterland to develop its commerce. Nor has much attention been devoted to building its tourism potential, with the result that the city is bypassed by many travelers on their way between Mérida and points to the south and west. While Campeche may not merit a long visit, it is certainly worth a brief stopover.

The heart of the city is the area nine blocks wide and five blocks deep that once lay within the walls. While there are few outstanding examples of architecture, the general effect of the tightly packed, brightly painted three-story buildings along these narrow streets is quite pleasing. It bears a certainly resemblance to the colonial districts of Santo Domingo or Carthagena across the Caribbean, and in some ways it looks like a mini-Havana.

Some decades ago, landfill was poured into the sea to extend the city. The area that now sits between the old city and the waterfront consists largely of semi-abandoned parking lots, although two of the bigger hotels are also situated there. Still, Campeche's pervasive sense of history can make for a delightful short visit, and the ruins of Edzná lie nearby.

## ARRIVALS & DEPARTURES

### By Air

Campeche airport (airport code CPE) is situated 4 km from the city center. Aeroméxico operates a daily flight from Mexico City. There is no other regular service.

### By Bus

The ADO first-class terminal lies away from the city center along Avenida de los Gobernadores. Buses to Mérida (2 1/2 hours, $7) leave at half-hour intervals from 5:30 am to 7:30 pm There are three daily departures to Mexico City (21 hours, $47-$56), three to Villahermosa (7 hours, $16), two to Chetumal and one to Veracruz. To Palenque (6 hours, $13), there are direct buses at 10:45 am and 12:30 at night. Caribe Express, operating from the same terminal, goes directly to Cancún (6 hours, $15) twice a day.

From the second-class terminal directly behind, Autrotransportes del Sur has two night-time departures to Palenque ($11) plus five trips to Villahermosa and overnight service to San Cristóbal de las Casas and Tuxtla Gutiérrez. Another company, Camioneros de Campeche, has five daily buses to Uxmal.

### By Car

Campeche lies along Highway 180, which runs northeast to Mérida and Cancún and southwest to Ciudad del Carmen and Villahermosa. The first stretch is four lanes wide. Highway 261 offers a slower alternate route to Mérida via Uxmal and other archaeological sites. It also runs south to Escárcega, where it meets Highway 186, which provides a more westward direct link to Villahermosa and an eastward link to Chetumal.

### By Rail

The daily passenger train linking Mérida, Campeche, Palenque, Coatzacoalcos and Córdoba cannot be recommended. It is slow, uncomfortable and prone to robberies. It no longer runs through to Mexico City.

## ORIENTATION

Most points of interest are located in the old part of the city, surrounded by a series of *baluartes*, or bastions, that formed part of the fortifications built in the late 17th century. Scarcely anything is left of the original walls that surrounded the city, but there remain two grand gates, the **Puerta de Mar** facing the sea and the **Puerta de Tierra** facing inland, at opposite ends of Calle 59. Streets (*calles*) running east and west in the old city have odd numbers running from 51 to 65, while north-south streets are even-numbered, from 8 to 16. Avenida Ruiz Cortines is the seafront boulevard two blocks west of Calle 8. Remember that the seafront is on the west side of the city.

The **tourism office** is situated beneath a palapa shelter plunked on a parking lot between the Hotel Baluartes and the **Baluarte de San Carlos**, near the southwestern corner of the old city. Hours are irregular, but there is usually someone there in the morning and in the late afternoon. Staff are helpful, but they have little printed information, not even local maps.

## WHERE TO STAY

Good hotels exist but do not abound in Campeche. Hotels which were once good choices have decayed because of poor maintenance, while others were never very good to begin with. Visitors seeking lower-end lodgings may have to settle for something quite gloomy.

**HOTEL DEL PASEO**, *Calle 8 #215 just south of the city center, phone (981) 10100 or 10077, fax (981) 10097; 48 rooms, $48 single, $58 double, VI - MC.*

This new hotel is a welcome addition to the dismal local scene. Set in a modern building with a small shopping arcade, rooms are fresh and pleasant, with central air conditioning, TV and phone.

**RAMADA HOTEL CAMPECHE**, *Avenida Ruiz Cortines facing the sea, phone (981) 62233, fax (981) 11618; 148 rooms, $83-$95 single, $90-$104 double, VI - MC - AE - DC.*

The higher prices are for rooms with sea views. Rooms are bright and attractively furnished in shades of beige and pale blue, with tile floors, air conditioning, TV and phone. The lobby is rather ordinary. The hotel has a pool, restaurant, bar and discotheque.

**HOTEL BALUARTES**, *Avenida Ruiz Cortines facing the sea, phone (981) 63911, fax (981) 62410; 104 rooms, $55 single, $58 double, VI - MC - AE.*

It is hard to believe this was once Campeche's top hotel. Set in a boxy, five-story building, rooms are carpeted and air conditioned with bright but poorly arranged furnishings. A big pool is surrounded by a barren terrace. This place exudes an air of shoddiness. Service is sluggish.

**HOTEL DEBLIZ**, *Avenida Las Palmas, 2 km north of the city center, phone (981) 10111, fax (981) 61611; 120 rooms, $58 single, $70 double, VI - MC.*

Rooms in this modern, four-story, mirror-finish suburban hotel have views of the pool and very ordinary decor. Service is slow, and physical decay appears to be setting in.

**HOTEL ALHAMBRA**, *Avenida Resurgimiento, 2 km east of the city center, phone (981) 66800 or 66822, fax (981) 66132; 94 rooms, $44 single, $48 double, VI - MC - AE.*

Rooms in this three-story motel-style structure are bright but furnished in tawdry style.

**HOTEL POSADA SAN ÁNGEL INN**, *Calle 10 #307 between Calles 53 and 55, phone (981) 67718; 15 rooms, $20 single, $23 double, $5 more with air conditioning, no cards.*

Rooms are carpeted but otherwise simply furnished and somewhat dark.

**HOTEL COLONIAL**, *Calle 14 #122 between Calles 55 and 57; phone (981) 62222 or 62630; 30 rooms, $18 single, $20 double, $5 more with air conditioning, no cards.*

Rooms in this two-story building are set around a covered courtyard. They vary in size and look rather bare. Some are quite dark.

**VILLA JUVENIL CREA**, *on the university campus, 3.5 km east of the city center, phone (981) 61802; 70 beds, $3 per person.*

This youth hostel provides dormitory lodgings. It is situated within a sports complex, and there is a cafeteria nearby.

**HOTEL CASTELMAR**, *Calle 61 #2 between Calles 8 and 10, phone (981) 62886; 19 rooms, $13 single or double.*

This place has a certain seedy charm to it, although rooms are bare and uncomfortable.

**HOTEL LÓPEZ**, *Calle 12 #189 between Calles 61 and 63, phone (981) 63344; 39 rooms, $23 single with fan, $30 double with air conditioning, VI - MC - AE.*

Dark, prison-like rooms have ugly furnishings and cost too much.

**HOTEL AMÉRICA**, *Calle 10 #252, phone (981) 64588; 52 rooms, $27 single, $33 double, VI - MC.*

This overpriced place is falling apart and should be avoided. The colonial-style building and its rooms badly need renovation. Staff are not helpful.

## WHERE TO EAT

The hotel scene in Campeche may be rather dismal, but this gloom does not extend to the local restaurant scene. With an abundance of fresh fish and seafood, including pompano, red snapper and crab, it is possible to eat both cheaply and well.

Several restaurants line Calle 8, the street in the old city lying nearest the sea. **MIRAMAR**, *Calle 8 at Calle 61*, is pleasant and elegant, with prices that are high by Campeche standards but moderate almost anywhere else. The menu provides a long list of fish and seafood dishes, including some wonderful stews and soups. **MARGANZO**, *Calle 8 between Calles 57 and 59*, has an arched dining room and moderate prices. Specialties include *pan de cazón*, which is baby shark wrapped in tortillas. **LA PUERTA DEL MAR**, *almost next door*, has cheaper prices and tasty dishes, including a variety of seafood cocktails.

**DEL PARQUE**, *Calle 8 at Calle 57*, is a more modest spot that stays open 24 hours. Two more all-night restaurants, **LA PARROQUIA** and **LOS PORTALES**, *both on Calle 55 between Calles 10 and 12*, are big, bright simple places with big menus.

## SEEING THE SIGHTS

A good place to begin a visit, after gleaning what information you can from the tourism office, is the neighboring **Baluarte de San Carlos**, *near the seafront toward the southern end of the old city, by the corner of Calles 8 and 65*. This handsome, circular stone bastion houses a museum displaying a collection of photos and drawings from the city's past, along with a few artifacts. The building itself is perhaps more interesting than its contents, including its dungeon and outdoor observation post. *The museum is open 8 am to 8 pm. Tuesday to Saturday, and admission is free.*

*Three blocks north, near the corner of Calle 59*, the **Baluarte de la Soledad** houses an interesting collection of carved stelae from archaeological sites around Campeche state. *This collection is on display 8 am to 8 pm Tuesday to Saturday and 8 am to 1 pm Sunday. Admission is free.*

*Continuing north to Calle 51*, and with similar opening hours, the grounds of the **Baluarte de Santiago** contain a tiny but lush botanical garden with more than 250 plant species.

Rounding out the museum scene, the **Museo Regional**, *on Calle 59 between Calles 14 and 16* has Mayan artifacts including some fine jade pieces downstairs, along with depictions of Mayan history. The upstairs exhibits are devoted to the colonial period, including reminders of pirate attacks and religious art and manuscripts. *It is open 8 am to 8 pm, Tuesday to Sunday, and admission is $4.*

The saucer-shaped building near the Baluarte de San Carlos houses the state congress. *At the southern end of Calle 10 is the* 16th century **Iglesia de San Román**, built for Indians living outside the old city and graced with a famous black statue of Christ. *Near the Baluarte de la Soledad is the* austere, twin-spired **Catedral de la Concepción**, facing the pleasant, tree-shaded **parque principal**, where band concerts are sometimes held on Sunday afternoons. The **Mansión Carvajal**, *on Calle 10 near Calle 53*, taken over for use as a government building and now open to the public, recalls the opulent life of an earlier period and is an example of the stately houses built by merchants in Campeche's heyday.

Of the four original gates to the city, two have disappeared, while the **Puerta de Mar** (sea gate), *facing the sea at one end of Calle 59*, is a reconstruction standing in isolation. Far more impressive is the **Puerta de Tierra** (land gate), *at the other end of Calle 59*, with its original stone structure intact and sections of the wall still in place to give it some context. On Friday evenings at 8 pm, a sound-and-light show is presented at the Puerta de Tierra. There is a $3 charge.

## EXCURSIONS

The **ruins of Edzná**, *on a secondary road 65 km southeast of Campeche*, are not easy to reach independently without a car, but a company called Picazh operates daily tours, with departures from the *Puerta de Tierra* and from the ADO terminal at 9 am and 2 pm, subject to a minimum group size. The cost is $15 per person for transportation plus $12 for guide services. *For information, call Picazh at (981) 64426.* The state tourism office, situated between the *Baluarte de San Carlos* and the Hotel Baluartes, can arrange transportation and guide services for $24 per person for a minimum of two persons. Taxis charge $60 to $75 for the round trip, including waiting time.

Because of its isolation and undeserved lack of fame, this Mayan site receives relatively few visitors. *It is open daily from 8 am to 5 pm with a $4 admission fee, free on Sundays and holidays.* Refreshments are available at the entrance. Large areas remain unexcavated because of a shortage of funds. The site was inhabited for 12 centuries ending around 900 A.D., with the final three centuries being the most important period of development. Prior to that, inhabitants had built an elaborate system of canals, cisterns, lagoons and artificial wells to channel rain water for use during the dry season and to prevent flooding.

The spacious main plaza at Edzná, called the **Great Acropolis**, is surrounded by temples and enormous limestone terraces. The most impressive building is the 31-meter-high **Five-Level Pyramid**, with the roof of each platform serving as a terrace for the level above and a tiny temple at the top, which can be reached by a broad central stairway. Wall carvings and stelae at each level depict members of the ruling elite in opulent attire and also contain hieroglyphs describing aspects of astronomy and history. Other structures facing this plaza include the **Temple of the Moon** and what was a sweat lodge.

*On the east side* of a smaller plaza called the **Small Acropolis** is a structure with carved representations of human heads, jaguars and various geometric elements. *To the southwest* is the pedantically named **Structure 414**, noted for a series of carved masks with grotesquely protruding eye sockets and huge teeth and tongues. This may have given Edzná its name, which means *House of Grimaces*.

# 12. TABASCO & SOUTHERN VERACRUZ

The region comprising the state of **Tabasco** and the **southern part of Veracruz** state lies along the main land routes between the Yucatán peninsula and central Mexico. It was home to the ancient **Olmecs**, who built the first of Mexico's great pre-Hispanic civilizations some 3,000 years ago. The most striking Olmec remnants are the enormous carved heads to be found in several museums and public places.

The region includes rainy lowlands facing the southern shore of the Gulf of Mexico and a higher interior ridge. Big areas are drained by great rivers including the Usumacinta, Grijalva, Tonalá, Coatzacoalcos, Papaloapan, and their many tributaries, passing in some places through dense rain forest. Other areas are quite swampy.

The oil industry has given the region a big economic boost, although much of southern Veracruz has been bypassed. Tabasco state, apart from the city of Villahermosa, is sparsely populated. (The famous hot pepper is named for the state, not the other way around.) Bananas and cocoa are its most important farm commodities, and the state government has been promoting tourism.

**Villahermosa** boasts several museums and parks, notably the fabulous **La Venta museum-park**, with large Olmec carvings scattered over a wooded area. Further west, the cities of **Coatzacoalcos** and neighboring **Minatitlán**, over the state boundary in Veracruz, are hot, expensive and singularly unattractive centers of oil, petrochemical and shipping activity, to be avoided if possible.

But in the hills to the northwest, and living in a whole different world, is a cluster of three towns: **San Andrés Tuxtla**, **Santiago Tuxtla**, and **Catemaco**, known collectively as *Los Tuxtlas* and each with its own special charms. A short way beyond lies the picturesque riverside town of **Tlacotalpan**.

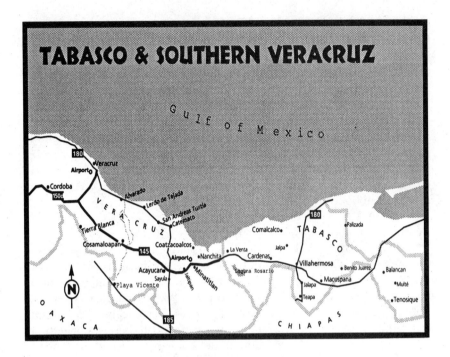

**TABASCO & SOUTHERN VERACRUZ**

| Tabasco |
|---|

# VILLAHERMOSA

> *Villahermosa is located off Highway 180.*

**Villahermosa**, the main link between central Mexico and the Yucatán, once had the reputation of being hot, sprawling and ugly, totally belying its name (*hermosa* is Spanish for beautiful). The first two adjectives still apply, but the conversion of several downtown streets to lively and attractive pedestrian malls has blunted the third. By and large, the city has a modern feel to it, and nowhere more so than in the **Tabasco 2000** complex of government buildings and hotels, northwest of the city center.

The foremost attraction for most tourists is the **Parque-Museo La Venta**, which combines parkland with splendid archaeological pieces. Next door are a natural history museum and a children's park with playgrounds and a small zoo. Elsewhere in the city, the museums of anthropology and of popular culture are both worth visiting.

This city, with its air connections and wide range of hotels, can also be used as a base to visit the fabled ruins of **Palenque** in Chiapas state, two hours away by road.

## ARRIVALS & DEPARTURES

### By Air

Aeroméxico, Mexicana, and Aviacsa all provide daily nonstop flights between Villahermosa and Mexico City. Aviacsa and Aerocaribe (a Mexicana affiliate) also connect Villahermosa with Oaxaca, Tuxtla Gutiérrez, Mérida and Cancún. Aerolitoral (an Aeroméxico affiliate) flies to Veracruz and Monterrey, but fares are high.

The airport is situated 13 km east of the city just off Highway 186 and just past the toll bridge over the Grijalva river. Shared vans provide economical transportation to the city. Taxis from the city to the airport charge about $9. The airport code is VSA, and there is a tourism information booth in the terminal building.

### By Bus

Villahermosa is a busy hub for bus travel through most of southeastern Mexico. ADO, the dominant first-class bus line here, has its terminal along Paseo Javier Mina several blocks from an elevated highway, also known as Boulevard Grijalva, and about 1 1/2 km from the city center. The terminal has a tourism information office (open irregular hours) and baggage storage at an hourly rate. Taxis are the usually best way of getting to or from the terminal even though the wait can sometimes be long.

ADO has a total of 28 daily departures in each direction between Mexico City and Villahermosa (14 hours, $33-$40, mostly overnight but with a few daytime services, early morning departures), 18 to Mérida (10 hours, $22-$28), most stopping at Campeche (7 hours, $16-$20), six to Cancún (14 hours, $32-$37), eight to Chetumal (9 hours, $19), 27 to Veracruz (8 hours, $17-$21), 20 to San Andrés Tuxtla (6 hours, $11-$13), 27 to Veracruz (8 hours, $17-$21), 10 to Palenque (2 hours, $5-$6), and one to Oaxaca (13 hours, $25, overnight). Some of these are operated by the ADO GL luxury division. UNO, the super-luxury division, has begun limited service here. Cristóbal Colón operates from the same terminal and offers seven daily departures to Tuxtla Gutiérrez (6 hours, $9-$11).

The second-class terminal is a few blocks away on the other side of the elevated highway (Boulevard Grijalva). This is where you'll find most buses for shorter trips within the region.

### By Car

Villahermosa is an important highway junction. Highway 180, portions of it widened to four lanes, provides the main link from Mexico City and Veracruz state. From Villahermosa, this highway turns north and then east again to the Yucatán peninsula.

Highway 186 goes to the Yucatán by a more southerly route, ending at Chetumal and passing near the border with Belize. This is also the road to take for Palenque. Highway 195 runs south from Villahermosa to Tuxtla Gutiérrez.

## ORIENTATION

Villahermosa lies at the confluence of several rivers, but you really don't notice them much. The **Río Grijalva** flows right past the center of the city, separated from it, however, by a busy roadway. There are also several lakes in the area. The **Parque-Museo La Venta** faces a long and narrow bay of the **Laguna de las Ilusiones**, within easy walking distance of several top-end hotels.

Street layout breaks away from the rectangular grid pattern common in so much of Mexico, and some streets meet at odd angles. **Boulevard Grijalva**, an elevated highway that is also called **Avenida Ruiz Cortines**, crosses the city from east to west. Some streets in the city center are closed to motor traffic. These streets and the surrounding area are sometimes called the *Zona Luz* or *zona remodelada*.

Parks and museums are scattered around several parts of the city. The **CICOM** complex, which includes the anthropology museum, is located along the bank of the Río Grijalva a short distance south of the city center. Most medium- and low-priced hotels are situated in or near the center, while the top-end hotels are mostly clustered near the vast **Tabasco 2000** complex to the northwest, which includes government offices, a convention center and a shopping mall.

The **main tourism information office** is also located in Tabasco 2000 and is a helpful source of information and maps once you manage to find it. *It is upstairs in an office building at Paseo Tabasco 1504, not far from a big floral clock (reloj floral)*, which people use when giving directions within the complex.

Buses can get you many places, but taxis are really a much easier way to get around and are fairly cheap. They operate on a shared basis and will take several passengers who are headed in the same general direction. Fares for short trips rarely exceed $1.50. There are sometimes long lines for taxis in front of the ADO terminal.

The weather in Villahermosa is almost always hot and sticky, and annual rainfall is heavy. April is the driest month, September and October the rainiest.

## WHERE TO STAY

Villahermosa has a broad range of accommodations, although gaps exist in the lower part of the middle price range or the upper part of the budget range. Most medium- and low-priced hotels are located in or near the city center, the top-end places further out, mostly in a cluster near the Tabasco 2000 complex.

**HOLIDAY INN VILLAHERMOSA PLAZA**, *Paseo Tabasco 1407, phone (93) 164400, fax (93) 164446; US or Canada toll-free 800-465-4329; 190 rooms, $121 single or double, VI - MC - AE - DC.*

Located in the heart of the Tabasco 2000 complex, this tall hotel offers large, comfortable, air-conditioned rooms and the usual first-class amenities including in-room bars, a posh restaurant, tennis courts, and big fantasy-shaped pool.

**HYATT REGENCY VILLAHERMOSA**, *Juárez 106, phone (93) 134444, fax (93) 151235; US toll-free 800-228-9000, Canada 800-268-7530; 211 rooms, $135 single or double, VI - MC - AE.*

Located at the edge of the Tabasco 2000 complex and near the Parque-Museo La Venta, this hotel greets guests with a big marble lobby, spacious grounds, comfortable air-conditioned rooms with blue and green decor, a choice of bars and restaurants, and a big pool.

**HOTEL CENCALI**, *Juárez near Paseo Tabasco, phone (93) 151999, fax (93) 156600; 120 rooms, $83 single or double, VI - MC - AE - DC.*

This three-story air-conditioned hotel, next to Hyatt Regency, has an interesting lobby with colorful murals and a poolside restaurant but rather ordinary rooms.

**CALINDA VIVA VILLAHERMOSA**, *Paseo Tabasco and Boulevard Grijalva, phone (93) 150000, fax (93) 153073; US toll-free 800-228-5151; 241 rooms, $80 single or double, VI - MC - AE.*

Near Tabasco 2000 and Parque-Museo La Venta, this hotel has a big pool and a small, noisy lobby. Rooms are big, with air-conditioning, white tile floors, and blue decor. There are a restaurant and bar.

**HOWARD JOHNSON HOTEL**, *Aldama 404 near 27 de Febrero, phone (93) 144645; 84 rooms, $46 single or double, VI - MC - AE - DC.*

This city-center hotel is fresh and new with comfortably furnished, air-conditioned rooms. It opened in 1994 but has a strangely dated look.

**HOTEL PLAZA INDEPENDENCIA**, *Independencia 123 near Plaza de Armas, phone (93) 121299, fax (93) 144724; 88 rooms, $41 single, $44 double, VI - MC - AE - DC.*

Rooms in this cheerful place are comfortable but a bit ordinary. Some are a little dark, and in a few the furniture has a battered appearance. The hotel offers air conditioning, a small pool and a pleasant location.

**HOTEL MADAN**, *Pino Suárez 105 near Reforma, phone (93) 121650; 20 rooms, $33 single, $36 double.*

Rooms are small but modern and comfortably furnished, with carpeting, air conditioning and television.

**HOTEL DON CARLOS**, *Madero 418 near Lerdo, phone (93) 122499, fax (93) 124622; 116 rooms, $43 single or double, VI - MC - AE.*

This is a big and rather ordinary place. Rooms have marble floors, air conditioning and television.

**HOTEL MIRAFLORES**, *Reforma 304 near Madero, phone (93) 120022 or 120054, fax (93) 120486; 68 rooms, $40 single, $43 double, VI - MC - AE.*
Rooms in this six-story hotel are small, bright, air conditioned and very ordinarily furnished. It is located on a pedestrian street.

**HOTEL OVIEDO**, *Lerdo 303 between Madero and Juárez, phone (93) 121455; 46 rooms, $9 single, $10 double, no cards.*
Rooms are simple and somewhat dark but have pretty tile floors and fans. Decent for the price.

**HOTEL TABASCO**, *Lerdo 317 between Madero and Juárez, phone (93) 120077, 120564; 31 rooms, $9 single, $12 double, no cards.*
Rooms are bright and basic, with fan.

**HOTEL RITZ DE TABASCO**, *Madero 1009 near Carranza, phone (93) 121611, fax (93) 121092; 71 rooms, $30 single, $33 double, VI - MC - AE.*
Rooms are small and comfortably furnished, with air conditioning, but the location is not central.

**HOTEL PALOMINO PALACE**, *Mina 222 across from the ADO terminal, phone (93) 148431; 45 rooms, $21 single or double, no cards.*
This building has six floors and no elevator. Most rooms have an abundance of street noise, although a few in back are quieter. All have fans. Several have air conditioning, for a supplement. Furnishings are basic and a bit battered. This place cannot be recommended, but if you arrive by bus late at night, it may have to do. Other hotels near the terminal are even worse.

## WHERE TO EAT

Tabasco is noted for the quality and freshness of its fish and seafood, and also for certain regional delicacies such as iguana, lizard and smoked oysters. Shrimp fresh from the nearby Gulf of Mexico are prepared in a variety of fashions, and there is a profusion of fresh fruit.

But for a city of its size and apparent prosperity, Villahermosa has surprisingly few good restaurants, and not many in the central part of the city. A number of spots scattered around the center offer Mexican favorites done acceptably well, but often that's about the best that can be said. Hotel restaurants can help fill the gap.

**EL GUARAGUAO**, *27 de Febrero at the corner of Mina*, offers a selection of regional dishes as well as Mexican *antojitos* in a small but pleasant dining room. **EL MESÓN DEL DUENDE**, *Méndez 1703 west of the city center*, is a more elegant and more expensive spot with interesting variations on common meat and seafood dishes and jazz on weekends. Open late, closed Wednesdays. A block away, **EL MESÓN DEL ÁNGEL**, *Méndez 1604*, specializes in Spanish dishes, including *paella* and *fabada*, an Asturian pork and bean stew. Open late, closed Sundays.

**CAPITÁN BEULO** is a cruise boat that offers meals on board, featuring fresh fish and shrimp. Prices are higher than you might pay on shore but include scenery along the Río Grijalva. *The boat docks at the end of Zaragoza street near the city center and sails at 1:30 pm and 3:30 pm daily except Monday. There's also an evening sailing at 9:30 pm Tuesday to Saturday, but it's dark and you miss the scenery. Phone (93) 181658 for information.*

Among hotel restaurants, **BOUGAINVILLEA** *at the Hyatt Regency* has a reputation for good food, a romantic atmosphere, and stiff prices.

## SHOPPING

Regional handicrafts include a broad variety of basketware items as well as leather goods and wooden drums. Several shops in the downtown pedestrian zone offer these and other goods. Shops include **Mis Recuerdos**, **Villa Arte**, and **Artesanías Tabasco**, *all situated in the area bounded by Juárez, Reforma, Gil y Saenz, and Lerdo de Tejada streets.*

## ENTERTAINMENT & NIGHTLIFE

The downtown pedestrian zone is pleasant for an early evening stroll. You can check local newspapers for film listings; American films are usually shown in English with Spanish subtitles. There is a **planetarium** in the Tabasco 2000 complex with three showings each evening. Several of the big hotels have discotheques.

## SEEING THE SIGHTS

**Parque-Museo La Venta** is a museum without walls, a park that also happens to be a museum, holding colossal stone sculptures carved in an ancient Olmec city that flourished 2,500 years ago. Pieces include five enormous carved heads, some weighing more than 20 tons and their features still very much intact. Their large lips have led some archeologists to surmise African influence.

These and other pieces were brought from the archaeological site of **La Venta**, about 125 km west near the border with Veracruz state. The site was first excavated in 1925, and work was accelerated after oil exploration crews moved into the area. Tabascan historian and statesman Carlos Pellicer Cámara intervened to have the pieces moved to where they are now, in many cases following the configuration of the original site. Some of the other carvings portray animals, jaguars in particular, and there are several stone altars. There are 30 large pieces altogether. They are linked by a maze of paths going through the tropical foliage of the park, which can be followed on a map available at the entrance.

La Venta park-museum lies within the larger **Tomás Garrido Canabal park**, *situated 2 km northwest of the city center toward the Tabasco 2000 complex.*

*The entrance is not always easy to spot. It lies along Boulevard Grijalva a short distance east of Paseo Tabasco. It is open 10 am to 4 pm, Tuesday to Sunday, and admission is $1.50.* (The sound and light shows have been discontinued.) On one side is an inlet of the Laguna de las Ilusiones.

*Next door* is the **Centro de Convivencia Infantil**, a children's park containing playgrounds and a small zoo. Nearby is a small museum of natural history. *Both are open 10 am to 4 pm, Tuesday to Sunday, and admission is free.*

The **Centro de Investigaciones de las Culturas Olmeca y Maya**, easy to translate and commonly abbreviated to **CICOM**, *wedged between the Río Grijalva and the Pereférico Carlos Pellicer Cámara roadway (the museum is also named after him), west of the intersection with Paseo Tabasco.* CICOM is a cluster of buildings including the **Museo Regional de Antropología**. Exhibits outline the various ancient cultures of Mesoamerica, with an emphasis on the Olmec and Maya civilizations. One display presents Comalcalco, an ancient city whose ruins lie near Villahermosa. *The museum is open 10 am to 4 pm, Tuesday to Sunday, and admission is $1.50;* CICOM also includes a research center, a sculpture garden, a restaurant and a few shops.

The **Museo de Arte Popular** depicts aspects of Tabascan life since the arrival of the Spanish. One room displays Indian masks and musical instruments, and in another a rural thatched hut has been recreated. Other exhibits show clothing and utensils from various eras. There also are temporary exhibits. *This small museum is located on Zaragoza near Rayón, just a few minutes' walk from the city center. It is open, like so much else here, from 10 am to 4 pm, Tuesday to Sunday. Admission is free.*

**La Casa de los Azulejos** is a historical building that was once the house of Carlos Pellicer Cámara, the aforementioned historian, archaeologist, statesman, and poet. *Located near the corner of Juárez and 27 de Febrero in the city center,* it has exhibits portraying the history of the city. *The building is open 10 am to 6 pm, Tuesday to Sunday, and admission is free.*

The **Zona Luz**, sometimes called the *zona remodelada*, is the traditional city center, some of its streets now closed to motor traffic to create attractive pedestrian malls. A short distance outside the pedestrian zone is the **Plaza de Armas**, a pleasant, tree-shaded park with several monuments. It also faces the ornate **Palacio de Gobierno**.

## EXCURSIONS

The ruins of **Palenque** lie just two hours from Villahermosa by road. Palenque is covered in the Chiapas chapter of this book. Most visitors choose to stay there overnight (among other reasons, hotels there are cheaper), but it certainly is close enough to visit in a single day from Villahermosa, especially if time is tight. It's easy to reach by car, and ADO has first-class buses going there and back every couple of hours. If you prefer an organized tour, this can be arranged by any of several travel agencies in Villahermosa (among them the travel desks at the bigger hotels or **Viajes Villahermosa**, *27 de Febrero 207, phone (93) 125456*). This is an expensive way of doing it, however. The typical charge for a full-day tour including guide and lunch runs to about $60 per person.

The Mayan ruins of **Comalcalco** are less impressive than Palenque but are closer and interesting in their own right. This was one of the earliest cities built from brick rather than stone, which was in short supply. Mortar was produced from the lime content of oyster shells. Comalcalco is thought to have reached its peak between the 6th and 8th centuries A.D. The site contains ornate stucco façades with colored bas-reliefs portraying humans and animals as well as masks and glyphs. Some of the more interesting sculptures are protected by thatched shelters. One structure called the Palace lies atop a breezy hill. Structures at this site are fragile, and climbing on them is not allowed.

*The ruins lie 55 km northwest of Villahermosa* and are easy to reach by car. Buses run several times an hour from the second-class terminal in Villahermosa to the town of Comalcalco; to get from the town to the ruins, taxis go all the way, while local minibuses leave you about 1 km away.

*South of Villahermosa*, the small towns of **Tacotalpa**, **Tapijulapa**, and **Oxolotán** are clustered in the hilly countryside east of Teapa. **Oxolotán**, the most distant, *lies 100 km from Villahermosa*. They don't offer any extraordinary sights, but they exhibit a special colonial charm, with cobbled streets and red-tile roofs. Oxolotán has a 17th-century Dominican convent and is the site of a peasant-run theater workshop, which gives open-air performances (but schedules are hard to obtain). Buses run from the second-class terminal in Villahermosa.The surrounding countryside is very pretty, with its dramatic hillsides and exuberant vegetation.

**Tacotalpa** has an interesting pre-colonial history and later was used by the Spanish as a refuge from coastal pirate attacks, but now it is primarily an agricultural center. **Tapijulapa** has an old church from whose site there are extraordinary views of surrounding valleys and hills. The town is also noted for the skills of its basket-weavers.

## PRACTICAL INFORMATION
**Airlines**
• **Aeroméxico**: *Periférico Carlos Pellicer 511, phone (93) 126991*
• **Mexicana**: *Madero 109, phone (93) 163132*
• **Aerocaribe**: *Mina 901, phone (93) 143202*

**Car rentals**
Available at the airport and at major hotels. **Avis, Dollar, National,** and several local companies are represented in Villahermosa.

**Currency Exchange**
*Banks are open weekdays from 9 am to 1:30 pm* and will be your main alternative to the often poor exchange rates offered by hotels.

**Tourist Information**
The **main tourism information office** is located in an office building *at Paseo Tabasco 1504 in the Tabasco 2000 complex. Open weekdays, 8 am to 4 pm; phone (93) 162889 or 163633,* it is not easy to find, but staff are helpful and provide good maps. There are tourism information booths at the airport and the ADO bus terminal, but hours are somewhat irregular.

> ### Southern Veracruz

Three towns clustered close to one another in pleasant, verdant valleys are known collectively as *Los Tuxtlas.* Each has its special allure. **Catemaco** is the best known of the three, with its lakeside setting, its traditions of witchcraft, and the nearby **Nanciyaga** forest preserve and mineral baths. **San Andrés Tuxtla** is the largest of the three, noted among other things for its cigar factories. **Santiago Tuxtla** is perhaps the most picturesque of the three with its narrow, cobbled streets and enormous Olmec head in its main square.

San Andrés Tuxtla lies between the other two towns. Catemaco is 12 km east and Santiago Tuxtla 14 km west. Buses provide frequent connections. This region is situated along a busy route between the Yucatán peninsula and central Mexico, but economic development has largely bypassed it in recent times. It maintains a curiously old-fashioned atmosphere and draws few foreign visitors, although Catemaco is popular with Mexican tourists. Accommodations are adequate but not lavish.

Northwest toward the Gulf coast and then a short hop up the Papaloapan valley lies **Tlacotalpan**, a sedate riverside town with well preserved colonial streets and plazas.

# CATEMACO

> *Catemaco is situated along Highway 180.*

# ARRIVALS & DEPARTURES
Highway 180 is a main route between the Yucatán and central

Mexico. A handful of long-distance buses stop here, including overnight service to or from Mexico City by ADO, but most stop instead at San Andrés Tuxtla, 14 km to the west and connected by frequent regional buses. To reach the lake, walk down the steep, narrow street from where the bus leaves you. The road running next to the lake is the Paseo del Malecón.

## WHERE TO STAY

**HOTEL LA FINCA**, *Highway 180, Kilometer 147, phone (294) 30084; 36 rooms, $66 high season, $58 low season, single or double, VI - MC - AE.*

Situated at the edge of the lake several kilometers south of town, this is the fanciest hotel in the area, with a pool, grassy lawn, and a narrow beach, rendered noisy by water scooters rented by some of the guests. Rooms are big, pleasant and air conditioned, with terraces facing the lake. The hotel also has a restaurant and discotheque.

**HOTEL PLAYA AZUL**, *2 km east of town, phone (294) 30001 or 30042; 80 rooms, $36 single, $42 double, VI - MC - AE - DC.*

Set on spacious grounds, with a pool and restaurant, this older lakefront hotel became rather run down, but new owners are renovating it bit by bit. Rooms are in two sections of the hotel, one with cottages set amid tropical vegetation, the other with much less appealing rows of motel-style units. The hotel arranges nature tours in the region.

**HOTEL DEL LAGO**, *Paseo del Malecón, phone (294) 30160 or 30431; 39 rooms, $24 single, $36 double, VI - MC - AE.*

Under the same management as the Hotel Playa Azul, this friendly, in-town hotel, near the lake, has small but well arranged rooms set around a tree-shaded pool.

**HOTEL BERTHANGEL**, *Francisco Madero 1, phone (294) 30007 or 30009; 22 rooms, $30 single, $39 double, VI - MC.*

Situated near the basilica, one block from the lake, this hotel has pleasant, air-conditioned rooms, many with interesting views.

**HOTEL LOS ARCOS**, *Madero 7, phone (294) 30003, fax (294) 30250; $21 single, $24 double, with fan; $6 more with air conditioning; VI - MC.*

This friendly, central hotel has a pool, parking area, and large but plain rooms.

**HOTEL JULITA**, *corner of Degollado and Playa, phone (294) 30008; 4 rooms, $9 single or double.*

Run as an appendage to the more elegant restaurant downstairs, this funky place has simple rooms with fan and hot water, plants everywhere, armchairs on a terrace in front of the rooms, and polished concrete floors. An interesting budget choice.

**HOTEL LAS BRISAS**, *Venustiano Carranza 3, phone (294) 30057; 20 rooms, $11 single, $14 double, VI - MC.*

Some rooms here are pleasant, others are small and dark. The hotel faces the central plaza.

## WHERE TO EAT

Catemaco is a good and inexpensive place for fresh fish and seafood, both from the lake and from the nearby Gulf of Mexico. A row of restaurants with similar menus and prices *line the Paseo del Malecón near the lake*. Among them are the **TROPICAL, ALOHA, LA OLA, CARMELITA** and **EL PESCADOR**. The **7 BRUJOS** is a pretty wooden restaurant along this row. *Nearby* is **JULITA**, *one block up at the corner of Playa and Degollado*, more elegant with white tablecloths; its excellent fish and shrimp dishes cost $5 to $7. The **BARULLOS** restaurant, *across from the basilica near the central plaza*, is housed in an intriguing three-story wooden structure.

## SEEING THE SIGHTS

**Laguna Catemaco**, 12 km long and 9 km wide, dominates the town that shares its name. The town lies at the northwestern corner of the lake. The shore is lined by several restaurants and small hotels, with a couple of bigger hotels outside town at either end. At several piers, boatmen offer tours of the lake, including an island with a large monkey colony. Prices depend on the length of the tour. (Don't worry about finding the boatmen: their touts will find *you*.) Fishing and swimming are possible.

In town, up a short hill, is a large plaza facing the domed, twin-steepled **Basílica de Nuestra Señora del Carmen** with its walls and arched ceiling painted in an attractive white and gold pattern. But Catemaco is noted for a different type of religious experience. The area surrounding the town was the scene of ancient Indian **witchcraft** rituals, which today have lost most of their authenticity. A few freelance sorcerers (*brujos*) offer their services to visitors. A hill just outside Catemaco is the site of an annual convention of *brujos*, who come from around Mexico and several foreign countries.

The **Nanciyaga** nature reserve, *facing the north side of the lake 7 km east of Catemaco on the road to Coyame*, offers tours of a small rain forest with varied flora and fauna including toucans and parrots (there's no guarantee you'll see these birds). It also has mineral water baths and mud baths, with optional massage, and by prior arrangement can offer the traditional Indian sweat lodge (*temazcal*) ritual, aimed at spiritual cleansing in a sauna-type setting. It is reachable by car, taxi or boat, but not by bus. *For information, phone (294) 30199 or 30666.*

Catemaco is starting to become a base for so-called ecotourism, with forest treks, excursions to bird-rich parts of the Gulf of Mexico, and river rafting. The Hotel Playa Azul (see above) is arranging some of these tours.

# SAN ANDRÉS TUXTLA

> **San Andrés lies along Highway 180.**

## ARRIVALS & DEPARTURES

Highway 180 runs between the Yucatán and central Mexico. Many long-distance buses stop here, and it is a connecting point for passengers bound for Catemaco or Santiago Tuxtla. There are four terminals, clustered near each other along the highway above town, about 1 km from the center. ADO is the main first-class bus company here, with 28 daily departures to or from Veracruz (2 1/2 hours away and site of the nearest airport), several overnight services to Mexico City, and many departures to Villahermosa and beyond.

Across the road, AU and Cuenco provide second-class services to various points in Veracruz state and on to Mexico City as well as to Tlacotalpan and Tuxtepec, with connections (slow and unreliable) to Oaxaca. AU also runs frequently to Catemaco and Santiago with a more modern fleet than its main competitor, Transportes Los Tuxtlas, whose terminal is further along the road. Rápidos de Papaloapan runs to Tlacotalpan and Cosmoalapan; many of its buses are uncomfortable.

## WHERE TO STAY

**HOTEL DE LOS PÉREZ**, *Rascón 2, near the zócalo, phone (294) 20777 or 20512, fax (294) 23646; 35 rooms, $24 single, $30 double, VI - MC - AE.*

Rooms are comfortable but uninspired, with air conditioning, television and telephone. Service is good, probably making this the best hotel in San Andrés.

**HOTEL DEL PARQUE**, *Madero 5, facing the zócalo, phone (294) 20198 or 20146; 39 rooms, $34 single, $43 double, VI - MC - AE - DC.*

Rooms are dingy and have a very 1950s feel to them. All have air conditioning, television and telephone.

**HOTEL CATEDRAL**, P*ino Suárez, corner of Bocanegra, behind the cathedral, phone (294) 20237; 33 rooms, $6 single, $10 double, no cards.*

This friendly place offers very good value. Simple, tile-lined rooms have fans and hot water.

**HOTEL ISABEL**, *Madero 13, near the zócalo, phone (294) 20923; 8 rooms, $18 single, $24 double, no cards.*

Large, bright rooms are simply furnished, with fan and television, but hallways are dark.

**HOTEL SAN ANDRÉS**, *Madero 6, near the zócalo, phone (294) 20604; 31 rooms, $17 single, $21 double, with fan; $3 more with air conditioning; VI - MC.*

Rooms are small and nondescript, with television and telephone. The entrance is through a café.

## WHERE TO EAT

San Andrés has several simple and pleasant places to eat. **MARISCOS CHAZARO**, *on Fernando Peña street just behind the Hotel Isabel*, has very good seafood cocktails. It closes early. *Around the corner on Allende street* is **MONTEPÍO**, a regular steakhouse.

**LOS CAPERUCITOS**, *on Avenida Juárez down from the cathedral*, has an open terrace and a selection of tacos, enchiladas and other *antojitos*. **GUADALAJARA DE NOCHE**, *further down Juárez just before the small bridge*, is bigger than it looks from outside. It, too, specializes in *antojitos*. The **HOTEL DEL PARQUE** has an outdoor terrace *facing the park*, pleasant for drinks or light meals, and a bigger restaurant inside.

## SEEING THE SIGHTS

San Andrés is not as picturesque as its two neighbors, but it is pleasant all the same. It has changed little in recent years and allows visitors to step back to the simpler Mexico of a generation or so ago. The **central plaza**, or *zócalo*, facing the large **Cathedral of San José and San Andrés**, remains the center of public life.

The nearby countryside produces tobacco of excellent quality, and San Andrés has several **cigar factories**, most of which welcome visitors. Among them is **Puros Ejecutivos**, *along the highway near the ADO terminal, open weekdays 8 am to 6 pm, Saturdays 8 am to 10 am*. Here you can see cigars being rolled by hand in resolutely low-tech fashion. Workers sit at long wooden tables. Boxes are printed on an original 19th-century press, still in use. At the front, a variety of cigars and smoking implements are offered for sale.

Outside town, *12 km south along a dirt road*, the 50-meter-broad **Salto de Eyipantla** (*salto* means waterfall) plunges 40 meters, flanked by tropical vegetation.

# SANTIAGO TUXTLA

> *Santiago Tuxtla lies along Highway 180 some 14 km west of San Andrés Tuxtla.*

## ARRIVALS & DEPARTURES

Many second-class buses stop here, but most first-class buses stop instead at San Andrés, from where there are frequent connections.

**SANTIAGO TUXTLA**

## WHERE TO STAY

**HOTEL CASTELLANOS**, *corner of 5 de Mayo and Comonfor, facing the zócalo, phone (294) 70200 or 70300; 53 rooms, $24 single, $30 double, VI - MC.*

This circular, six-story building is hard to miss. Rooms on the upper floors are better furnished and have good views of the town and the surrounding hills. All have air conditioning and television. Service is friendly. The hotel, which has a pool and a decent restaurant, is surprisingly good for a town this size.

There are a couple of smaller, cheaper places in town, but they are quite dismal.

## SEEING THE SIGHTS

Before doing anything else, you may want simply to stroll along some of the town's narrow, cobbled streets, flanked by low buildings with traditional red-tile roofs and verdant hillsides looming in the distance. A small river runs through one part of town.

In the **central plaza**, or *zócalo*, is an enormous **Olmec head**, thought to be the biggest in existence and unusual in that its eyes are closed. Facing the *zócalo* is the **Museo Tuxteco**, *open Monday to Saturday 9 am to 6 pm, Sunday 9 am to 3 pm, admission $3.* It includes several more Olmec carvings as well as items from the region's more recent history, including an antique sugar press and implements used in witchcraft rites.

Outside town, *7 km along a paved road and then 16 km along a rough dirt road,* is the **Tres Zapotes** archaeological site. These Olmec ruins, thought to be at least 2,000 years old, have been worn down to little more than a series of stone mounds, but the site includes a small museum that exhibits some important carvings, including a large head and a stele depicting human figures in the mouth of a jaguar. Bus service there is infrequent and unreliable. *Further information is available from the Museo Tuxteco.*

# TLACOTALPAN

*Tlacotalpan lies along Highway 175 just 13 km south of the junction with Highway 180 near the Gulf of Mexico.*

## ARRIVALS & DEPARTURES

Highway 175 continues south up the Papaloapan valley and then over a majestic mountain range to Oaxaca and onward to the Pacific coast at Puerto Ángel. The contrast at the continental divide is quite striking. The Gulf of Mexico side is lush and green, the Pacific side much more arid.

ADO provides first-class bus service between Veracruz and Tlacotalpan twice hourly, continuing to Cosamaloapan. Direct buses to Mexico City run twice daily. Cuenco, with a terminal right across from ADO, provides second-class service to or from San Andrés Tuxtla seven times daily and runs six times daily to Tuxtepec, where there are connections to Oaxaca (slow and unreliable).

Rápidos de Papaloapan runs more frequently to San Andrés but its vehicles are less comfortable. AU and TRV leave from near the market with frequent service to Veracruz, Tuxtepec and other points.

## WHERE TO STAY

**POSADA DOÑA LALA**, *Carranza 11, phone (288) 42580, fax (288) 42581; 40 rooms, $33 single, $45 double, VI - MC - AE.*

Located 1 1/2 blocks from Tlacotalpan's twin plazas, this three-story building has pleasant but nondescript rooms with air conditioning and television. Some interior rooms are a little dark.

**HOTEL REFORMA**, *Carranza 2, phone (288) 42022; 21 rooms, $12 single, $18 double, with fan; $21 single, $27 double, with air conditioning and television; no cards.*

This hotel has a bright, pleasant lobby. Rooms are simple and rather ordinary.

Two cheaper places in town are rundown and very basic.

## WHERE TO EAT

You can find ordinary fare in comfortable surroundings at the **POSADA DOÑA LALA**, but for something more interesting (and less comfortable), head for the shore of the river, where several makeshift restaurants offer fresh and tasty seafood dishes. **LA PASADITA** has a superb *caldo de camarones* (a rich broth with plump jumbo shrimps still in their shells) for just $4.

## SEEING THE SIGHTS

Tlacotalpan is interesting both for its serene setting along the broad **Río Papaloapan** and for its colonial plazas and neighboring streets, several of them very well preserved. Low-slung buildings lining cobbled streets are painted in appealing pastel hues. There are two plazas in the center of town, each with its church.

**Plaza Zaragoza** is clad in marble with a Moorish-inspired kiosk in the middle. **Plaza Hidalgo** faces **Candelaria church**, with its very elaborate painted interior. *Also facing Plaza Hidalgo* is the small **Museo Salvador Ferrandó**, which displays 19th century Veracruzan paintings, clothing and furniture as well as some pottery and a few small Olmec pieces. *The museum is open daily except Monday, 10 am to 3 pm and 5 pm to 7 pm. Admission is $1.*

## PRACTICAL INFORMATION

**Tourist Information**

There is a small **tourism office** *on Carranza street next to the Posada Doña Lala*, but hours are irregular.

# 13. CHIAPAS

**Chiapas** is Mexico's southernmost state. It has a long boundary with Guatemala. For years it was easy to remain unaware of Chiapas's very existence. Then on New Year's Day in 1994 guerrilla forces of the previously concealed **Zapatista National Liberation Army** seized four towns (including San Cristóbal de las Casas) and captured headlines around the world. Government forces rushed in.

After ten days of fighting, an uneasy truce took hold. Guerrilla forces vanished from open view, but they remained ensconced in their hideouts in the Lacandón jungle, from where they ran a brilliant propaganda campaign against social and political injustice. Peasants who took advantage of the disorder to seize cattle ranches (which in many cases were established on lands stolen from their forbears) occupied and began to farm these lands. Government mediators and foreign observers swarmed through the area, but many months later there was still no firm settlement.

Centuries before Spanish colonization, Chiapas had been the site of grand Mayan city-states, notably **Palenque** and **Yaxchilán**. During colonial times Chiapas was ruled from Guatemala, and authorities did little to halt suppression of the Indian population that was being conducted through massacres, epidemics and enslavement.

Chiapas did not become part of Mexico until the 1820s. Even today it is more Guatemalan than Mexican in terms of its highland Mayan culture, some speech patterns, and many aspects of its social development, with greater concentrations of poverty and more heavily authoritarian rule than in the rest of Mexico. In the early 1980s, Chiapas became home temporarily to tens of thousands of Indian refugees fleeing the scorched-earth policies of the Guatemalan army. Many have remained.

Chiapas has a coastal plain known as the **Soconusco**, bordering on a broad inland ridge of mountains forming an extensive and heavily Indian highland region, with lowlands again further north and east. The economy remains dependent primarily upon agriculture, with coffee, cattle and bananas the main staples. Chiapas also accounts for more than half of Mexico's hydroelectric production, which sits in odd contrast with its many hundreds of villages that are still not connected to the national electricity grid.

The Chiapas highlands also boasted a vibrant tourism industry, centered in the delightful colonial town of San Cristóbal de las Casas. Followed the uprising by the Zapatistas (named in honor of Emiliano Zapata, a hero of the Mexican Revolution of the 1910s), tourism all but dried up. As 1994 wore on, tourists began to trickle back but in nowhere close to their previous numbers. This is a pity. Except during those few days of fighting, the area has been safe for travel. The army set up roadblocks where passengers are sometimes asked to show documents – more an annoyance than a serious hindrance to travel. At the time of writing a resumption in fighting appeared unlikely, but until things are fully settled you may want to pay attention to the newspapers before going there.

Palenque, the site of a fabulous set of ancient Mayan ruins in the northern part of Chiapas, lies outside the area affected by the uprising, as does **Tapachula** in the south, an important transit point for travelers to and from Guatemala.

## CHIAPAS HIGHLIGHTS

*If you do go to Chiapas, **San Cristóbal de las Casas** should be at the top of your list. This is an old colonial town with traditional low-slung buildings, cobbled streets, a fresh mountain climate, and an engaging contemporary Mayan presence. **Palenque**, in the north of the state, is renowned for its splendid ancient Mayan ruins with hilltop temples and a marvelous jungle setting. **Tuxtla Gutiérrez**, the state capital and biggest city in Chiapas, is rather unattractive but has a wonderful zoo and, from neighboring **Chiapa de Corzo**, boat trips through the spectacular **Sumidero canyon**. **Comitán**, nearer the Guatemalan border, is a base for visits to the **Montebello lakes**. And for adventurers, there are the hard-to-reach ruins of **Bonampak** and **Yaxchilán**.*

*This is an order of priorities and not, as a glance at the map will tell you, the order in which to conduct your visit. That will be determined by where you are arriving from and where you plan to go afterwards. Getting to Chiapas takes extra effort, but it's well worth it. No international flights go there, but connecting domestic flights serve Tuxtla Gutiérrez, near San Cristóbal de las Casas, as well as Villahermosa in Tabasco state, not far from Palenque. Those who travel by road are rewarded by fine mountain scenery in many parts of the state.*

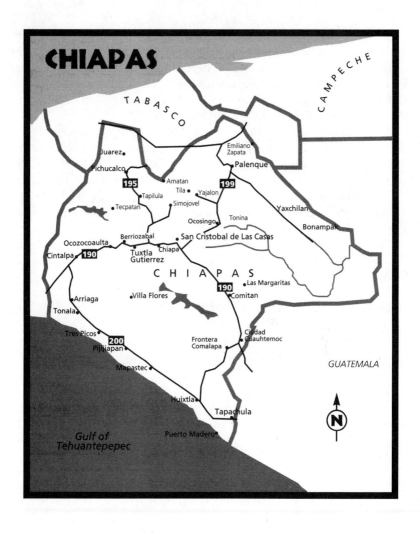

# PALENQUE

> *Palenque lies 186 km northeast of San Cristóbal de las Casas and 142 km southeast of Villahermosa. Highway 186, running between Villahermosa and the Yucatán peninsula, meets the main road to Palenque near Catazajá. From there it is 26 km south.*

The ruins of **Palenque** are among the most beautiful in Mexico, with a big array of hilltop temples, bas-reliefs with distinctive, and an unparalleled jungle setting. The site remains in remarkably good condition. Unless ancient ruins leave you totally cold, you can spend many worthwhile hours there and at the nearby museum.

But this may not be your only reason for visiting. Palenque is a good base from which to visit the splendid series of waterfalls at **Agua Azul** and the simple but impressive jungle waterfall at **Misol-Ha**. Tours are also arranged to the distant and remote ruins at **Bonampak** and **Yaxchilán**.

The town of Palenque lies 8 km from the ruins. A small backwater until recently, it has grown quickly since the highway was paved in the late 1970s. Today it is a bigger and still decidedly uninteresting place.

Those with limited time can easily visit the ruins of Palenque on a day excursion from Villahermosa, two hours away by car or bus and served by many flights.

## ARRIVALS & DEPARTURES

### By Air

Palenque has a small airstrip, but the nearest airport with regular service is at Villahermosa, two hours away by road.

### By Bus

Several bus companies serve Palenque, each with its own terminal. Most of the terminals are clustered along Avenida Juárez just west of the central area. The Cristóbal Colón terminal lies outside town on the road to the ruins.

ADO has eight daily first-class departures to Villahermosa (2 hours, $5), three to Campeche (6 hours, $13) and Mérida (9 hours, $20), and one each, overnight, to Mexico City (16 hours, $39), Cancún (13 hours, $36) and Chetumal (7 hours, $18).

Cristóbal Colón competes on most of these routes, at marginally higher fares, with three daily departures to Villahermosa, one each to Mexico City, Mérida, and Cancún via Chetumal. It also runs three times daily to San Cristóbal de las Casas and Tuxtla Gutiérrez.

Autotransportes Tuxtla Gutiérrez has the most frequent service to Ocosingo (3 hours, $3-$4), San Cristóbal (5 hours, $5-$6) and Tuxtla (7 hours, $8-$9), with both first-and second-class buses and departures every couple of hours. Additional first-class service on this route is provided by Pullman de Chiapas and TRF.

Frequent minibuses run north to the highway junction at Catazajá, with connections to Villahermosa and other points, and south past the cutoffs for Misol-Ha and Agua Azul.

**By Train**

Palenque is still served by passenger train. Until the highway was paved in the late 1970s, this was the most comfortable way to arrive. Nowadays the train is slow, uncomfortable, unreliabl,e and prone to robberies – definitely not recommended.

## ORIENTATION

The town of Palenque and the ruins of Palenque lie 8 km apart. Most hotels and other services are in town, but several hotels are situated along the road between them. Others are elsewhere in the area. Minibuses connect the town and the ruins several times an hour throughout the day, leaving from the corner of Hidalgo and Allende. The museum at the archaeological site is closed. A new, bigger museum is situated along the road 2 km before you reach the entrance.

Streets in the center of Palenque town follow the familiar grid pattern and have names rather than numbers. The central plaza is often referred to simply as the *parque* and lies toward the eastern part of the center. One of the more attractive spots in town, it faces Santo Domingo church and the *Casa de la Cultura*, which houses the tourism office.

Avenida Juárez is the most important street in town, running west from the *zócalo* past many hotels, shops and restaurants. At the western end are a big monument depicting a Maya chieftain's head and a traffic circle, with one road going southwest to the ruins.

Palenque lies at a low altitude, and the climate is hot and humid. It is also one of the rainiest places in Mexico.

## WHERE TO STAY

Hotels are available in most price ranges, and several offer rustic settings.

### Hotels In or Near Town

**HOTEL MISIÓN PALENQUE PARK PLAZA**, *eastern edge of town, phone (934) 50241, fax (934) 50300; 160 rooms, $97 high season; $78 low season, single or double, VI - MC - AE - DC.*

Set on a sprawling estate on the fringe of town, this hotel has a high pyramid-shaped lobby, with rooms set in a pair of two-story wings. Many have views of rolling hills nearby. Upstairs rooms have better views and high, slanted ceilings. Decor is modern Mexican, with mottled concrete and bold colors. Rooms have air conditioning and television, and you'll find a big pool and restaurant.

**HOTEL CHAN-KAH CENTRO**, *Juárez 2, corner of Independencia, near the parque, phone (934) 50318, fax (934) 50489; 17 rooms, rates from $28 single with fan to $41 double with air conditioning, VI - MC.*

This five-story hotel (with elevator) has good views of the countryside from the upper floors, especially from the rooftop bar. Rooms are bright, but decor and layout may seem somewhat crude or eccentric. Some rooms have interesting paintings. All have television. There is a restaurant on the ground floor.

**HOTEL CASA DE PAKAL**, *Avenida Juárez, half a block from the parque, phone (934) 50393; 15 rooms, $26 single, $30 double, VI - MC - AE.*

Beds have cedar headboards, but rooms are otherwise plain. Air conditioning, television.

**HOTEL PALENQUE**, *Avenida 5 de Mayo facing the parque, phone (934) 50188 or 50189, fax (934) 50039; 36 rooms, $36 high season, $24 low season, single or double, VI - MC.*

This once grand hotel has gone to seed. The big, three-story L-shaped building has suffered the ravages of time, and some rooms are out of use. Remaining rooms were once smartly decorated but now look shabby. A big tropical garden is ill kept. Rooms have air conditioning and television. The hotel has a pool, parking area and restaurant.

**HOTEL PLAZA PALENQUE**, *northern edge of town on the road to Catazajá, phone (934) 50555, fax (934) 50395; 100 rooms, $69 single or double, VI - MC - AE.*

Big, modern and nondescript, on an isolated site, this Best Western affiliate has a gym and a pleasant pool area with a palapa-shaded bar. Air conditioning, television, restaurant.

**HOTEL KASHLAN**, *corner of 5 de Mayo and Allende, phone (934) 50297; 59 rooms with fan, $15 single, $18 double, VI - MC.*

This friendly hotel next to the ADO terminal (look for the big yellow exterior) is one of the better lower-priced choices. Rooms are small and simple but bright and clean.

**HOTEL VACA VIEJA**, *5 de Mayo 42, corner of Chiapas, central, phone (934) 50377 or 50388; 28 rooms with fan, $12 single, $18 double, VI - MC - AE.*

Rooms are simple and somewhat shabby.

**HOTEL REGIONAL**, *Juárez 119 near Aldama, central, phone (934) 50183; 30 rooms with fan, $10-$14 single, $15-$20 double, depending on season, no cards.*

This hotel has a terrace with trees and plants but rooms are basic and gaudily decorated.

**HOTEL MISOL-HA** (*not to be confused with Cabañas Misol-Ha outside town*), *Juárez 14, one block from the parque, phone (934) 50092; 28 rooms with fan, $12-$20 single, $15-$23 double, depending on season, VI - MC.*

Tile walls, but plain, stuffy rooms.

Several other hotels are clustered along a short, quiet street variously called La Cañada, Calle Merle Green or Prolongación Hidalgo. This street lies near the traffic circle with the big Maya monument. Addresses below are those provided by each hotel.

**HOTEL LA CAÑADA**, *Prologación Hidalgo, no number, phone (934) 50102; 7 rooms, $12 single, $18 double, VI - MC.*

Bungalows containing simple rooms with fans and wood ceilings are set deep in tree-shaded grounds. A big palapa-shaded restaurant is at the entrance.

**HOTEL CHABLIS**, *Merle Green 7, phone (934) 50870; 20 rooms, $29 single, $35 double, VI - MC.*

Modern, air-conditioned, pleasant rooms, with tiles and bright colors.

**HOTEL XIBALBA**, *Merle Green 9, phone (934) 50411, fax (934) 50392; 8 rooms, $20 single, $25 double, VI - MC - AE.*

Rooms are big and bright but rather plain, with air conditioning. There is a travel agency on the premises.

**HOTEL MAYA TULIPANES**, *La Cañada 6, phone (934) 50201; 36 rooms, $31 single or double, VI - MC - AE.*

Rooms are modern, nondescript and somewhat dark, with air conditioning. There is a small pool.

### Hotels Outside Town

**HOTEL CHAN-KAH RUINAS**, *Kilometer 3 on the road to the ruins, phone (934) 50318, fax (934) 50489; 60 cabins, $58 single, $69 double, VI - MC.*

Set in the jungle and linked by stone pathways, the cabins here are big, with stone floors, wood trim, brightly colored bedspreads, big windows, and terraces with rocking chairs. Some have fans, other have air conditioning. This very distinctive hotel has a spring-fed pool and palapa-shaded restaurant and bar.

**HOTEL VILLAS KIN-HA**, *Kilometer 2.7 on the road to the ruins, phone (934) 50533 or 51112, fax (934) 50544; 40 rooms and 40 more planned, $35 single or double, $5 extra for air conditioning, VI - MC - AE.*

Bungalows here have palapa roofs, tile floors, stucco walls and bright bedspreads. They stay fresh even without air conditioning. The grounds have expanses of plain grass, a pool, palapa-covered restaurant and bar, a trailer park charging $10 per vehicle, and camping for $3 per person.

**HOTEL EL PARAÍSO**, *Kilometer 2.5 on the road to the ruins, phone (934) 51110, fax (934) 51140; 8 rooms, $29 single, $35 double, VI - MC.*

The large, plain rooms in this misnamed hotel are situated behind the huge tour-group-oriented Restaurant Los Leones. There were plans to provide a trailer park and camping facilities.

**MAYABELL**, *inside the national park near the museum*, provides facilities for trailers and for camping. Rates vary.

**HOTEL CALINDA NUTUTÚN PALENQUE**, *3 1/2 km south of town on the road to Ocosingo, phone (934) 50161, fax (934) 50620; 60 rooms, $53 single, $65 double, VI - MC - AE - DC.*

Consisting on a large two-story building and several smaller ones, this hotel is set next to a well known river swimming area. The large, bright rooms have orange and white decor, tile floors and air conditioning. Grounds are extensive but not very well kept. Camping facilities are $6 per person, with toilets and showers provided.

**CABAÑAS MISOL-HA** *(not to be confused with Hotel Misol-Ha in town), 18 km south of Palenque, 1 1/2 km off the road to Ocosingo, phone (934) 50274; 17 cabins; $27 high season, $18 low season, single or double, no cards.*

Wooden cabins, simply but delightfully decorated and spaced well apart, are surrounded by jungle and situated near the Misol-Ha falls. They are built and run by a local Indian cooperative. Three bigger cabins each accommodate two couples and provide full kitchens and separate dining areas ($54 high season, $36 low season). Light meals are available nearby.

## WHERE TO EAT

There's not much happening in the restaurant scene here. Hotel restaurants are often your best bet, especially if you're staying somewhere out of town. Menu choices tend to be fairly standard even at the better spots. Apart from hotel restaurants, you'll mostly find simple meals served in modest surroundings.

One notable exception is **LA SELVA**, *near the Maya monument at the beginning of the road to the ruins*, with a bigger menu, more polished service and, needless to say, higher prices. Nearby, the restaurant at **HOTEL LA CAÑADA** is special not so much for its food but for its big palapa shade and relaxing atmosphere.

Among other hotel restaurants in town, the **CHAN-KAH CENTRO**, *near the parque*, has a sort of jungle atmosphere and a good variety of Mexican dishes, and the **KASHLAN**, *near the ADO terminal*, includes several vegetarian dishes on its menu. For something cheaper, **RESTAURANT MAYA**, *facing the parque*, is a popular spot for standard Mexican fare. Many simpler places are scattered about town, including a cluster on Avenida 5 de Mayo near Mina street and one or two spots next to the ADO terminal.

## SEEING THE SIGHTS

You came to see the archaeological site, but first here is a brief mention of the tree-shaded **parque**, the liveliest and most attractive spot *in the center of Palenque*, pleasant for an early evening stroll. It is bounded by the simple Santo Domingo church, the *palacio municipal*, the *Casa de la Cultura* with its occasional art displays and concerts, and a number of hotels and restaurants.

The **Balneario Nututún** is a swimming area *3 1/2 km south of town* where the Rio Chacamax forms a refreshing natural pool. The Hotel Calinda Nututún Palenque provides dressing rooms and and towels for $1.50. Another idea is to go horseback riding in the jungle; this can be arranged by local travel agencies.

The **Palenque archaeological zone** *lies 8 km southwest of town and is served by frequent minibuses, and is open daily from 8 am to 5 pm.* By visiting early, you avoid both the crowds and the midday heat. If you choose, you may hire a guide at the entrance to show you around. English-speaking guides are usually available. A joint ticket for the ruins and the nearby museum is $5 (a guide is extra).

The new **museum**, *which was set to open daily except Mondays from 8 am to 5 pm, is situated 2 km before the entrance to the ruins.* It is housed in an imposing group of three modern buildings that include a restaurant and gift shop and replace a smaller structure at the entrance to the ruins. On display are many pieces excavated from the ruins, including stone carvings, ceramic bowls and vases, jade items, and countless figurines. Some of the most important pieces were taken to the National Museum of Anthropology in Mexico City, but the government announced in 1994 that the impressive contents of newly discovered royal tombs would remain in Palenque.

*The museum and the entrance to the ruins are connected by a winding road and by a shorter footpath.*

### The Ruins of Palenque

Palenque is a Spanish name: there is no clear idea what Indian names it might have had. The earliest items found at the site date from about 300 B.C. This ancient city appears to have reached its height around 700 A.D. and to have been abandoned by 1000 A.D.

The builders of Palenque situated the city near the foothills of the Tumbalá mountains to offer protection against attack from the rear. It had a view over the Gulf of Mexico across the plains in front, which at the time remained covered in jungle. The magnificence of the setting remains evident today. Originally many of the buildings were coated with stucco and painted with brightly colored pigments, but today only vague glimmers of this remain. There are an estimated 500 structures in the area, of which fewer than 40 have been excavated. Work continues on several others.

The first building on the right as you enter is the **Temple of the Skull**, built atop a tall pyramid. Like many of the other temples, it has one large room flanked by two smaller ones with square entrances in front and high ceilings formed by ingenious arches. Nearby is the **Temple of Inscriptions**, the tallest pyramid at Palenque, which can be mounted by a series of very steep steps. It contains several large bas-reliefs and three large stone panels carved with 620 hieroglyphics.

In 1952, deep inside the pyramid, archeologists discovered a crypt containing a large sarcophagus, inside which was found a now famous jade mask and many other ornaments. The adjacent **Temple of the Jaguars**, and several other temples, contained bas-reliefs with themes that seem almost Asian, depicting lotus flowers, not then known in this part of the world, and displaying similarities to Hindu motifs. Some rooflines resemble the shape of an Oriental pagoda. This enigma remains unexplained.

The **Palace**, the biggest group of structures at Palenque, is set on a long platform and contains a maze of patios, corridors, stairways and rooms. Various bas-reliefs depict sacred quetzal birds, priests, *Cha'ac* (the god of water), and the 13 Mayan heavens interspersed with serpents and eagles. On the eastern side of the site, the **Temple of the Sun**, named for a carved panel showing priests holding up offerings to the sun. The **Temple of the Cross of Palenque** has panels showing a youth in a quetzal headdress facing an old man dressed in a jaguar skin. Many additional structures dot the site. *For further information, look for **The Easy Guide to Palenque** by Richard Bloomgarden.*

## SHOPPING

Several shops along **Avenida Juárez** offer brightly colored weavings, traditional clothing, leather goods, ceramics and other handicrafts items from Chiapas and Guatemala. A few Indian women sell weavings at the bus stop near the entrance to the ruins. There is also a gift shop at the museum.

## ENTERTAINMENT & NIGHTLIFE

Entertainment possibilities are limited. In the early evening, the **rooftop bar of the Hotel Chan-Kah Centro**, near the *parque*, is a good spot to watch the sun set over the nearby hills. You can see if anything is doing at the *Casa de la Cultura*, which sometimes presents art exhibitions or marimba recitals. After that, it's up to your imagination.

## EXCURSIONS

*Going 18 km south of Palenque on the road to Ocosingo and then 1 1/2 km along a well marked cutoff,* you come to **Misol-Ha**, with a high waterfall in a dramatic jungle setting. Below the waterfall is a large natural pool suitable for swimming. The scene is quite idyllic. The area is controlled by a local Indian cooperative, and admission is $0.75. Near the entrance are a small restaurant and the delightful Cabañas Misol-Ha for overnight stays (*see Where to Stay, above*).

**Agua Azul** *is reached by heading about 60 km south of Palenque along the same road and then 4 km along a cutoff.* This is a 7 km stretch of dazzling waterfalls and fast-flowing river, with several calm areas suitable for bathing. But be very careful: some stretches of water are deceptive, and many bathers have drowned. It is better to avoid visiting here after heavy rains: the current becomes stronger, and the water loses the blue color the area is named for. Some visitors are content just to walk along the pathways parallel to the river and the falls. It can become crowded during holiday periods. Areas further upstream are quieter, but beware of swaying foot-bridges. The entry fee is $0.75. Both near the entrance and further up there are stalls selling refreshments and light meals. You can also find a campground and very basic accommodations consisting of tiny cabins with hammock hooks or a larger space with dormitory beds.

If you don't have a car, the best way to get to Misol-Ha and Agua Azul is by group tour from Palenque, which can be arranged through local travel agencies and some hotels. The full circuit lasts five or six hours with visits to both places, and the cost is about $8 per person. There also may be public buses going in once or twice a day: check with the tourism office in Palenque to see if they are running. Otherwise, you can take a second-class bus south from Palenque (or north from San Cristóbal or Ocosingo) and, from the appropriate junction, make the short hike to Misol-Ha or the long hike to Agua Azul

Palenque is also the base for most visits to the remote ruins of **Bonampak** and **Yaxchilán** near the border with Guatemala:

### Bonampak

The ruins of Bonampak are noted for the murals depicting aspects of ancient Maya life, complete with warriors, priests, kings and musicians in elaborate costumes. Many centuries of deterioration, and clumsy attempts at cleaning the murals, have dimmed the original colors, but reproductions are displayed.

### Yaxchilán

**Yaxchilán**, by the edge of Usumacinta river, is a bigger site, considered to be of greater archaeological importance. Several of the buildings and stelae display exceptionally fine carvings. The jaguar motif favored by an 8th century king is prominent. In the central plaza are statues of crocodiles and jaguars, and from atop the taller buildings, some covered with trees, are magnificent views of the site and the surrounding jungle and river.

### Getting to Bonampak & Yaxchilán

Part of the attraction of these two sites is their very remoteness. Bonampak, 155 km southeast of Palenque, can be reached by private vehicle, but the latter half of the route is very rough. Four-wheel drive is advisable during rainy periods, and there are no gasoline stations along the way. Yaxchilán is even more remote and involves a 20 km boat trip from Frontera Echeverría, easy going downriver but up to two hours for the return.

A sensible alternative is to seek an organized tour from Palenque. These go whenever a minimum group of four can be assembled. The tours last two days and one night, with accommodations in tents or simple dormitories. All land and river transportation and all meals are looked after, and the total cost is about $90 per person. A more expensive option is to go by light aircraft. Both sites have airstrips, and both can easily be visited in a few hours.

Several travel agencies in Palenque can handle arrangements for the land or air option. *Among these is Viajes Pakal-Kin, Avenida 5 de Mayo near the parque, phone (934) 51180.*

## PRACTICAL INFORMATION

### Currency Exchange

There are a couple of banks along Avenida Juárez, but you face the usual problems of short hours, long lines and poor rates. Change money before arriving in Palenque if you can.

### Tourist Information

The **tourism office** is situated *around the corner from the Casa de la Cultura, off to one side of the parque near the corner of Jiménez and 5 de Mayo. It is open Monday to Saturday from 8 am to 9 pm, with an afternoon break at unannounced hours.* Staff are helpful, but the maps they provide are next to useless.

# TUXTLA GUTIÉRREZ

> *Tuxtla Gutiérrez lies at the junction of several highways, including routes 190 and 195.*

Tuxtla Gutiérrez (pronounced just as it looks) is the state capital and biggest city in Chiapas, with an estimated population of about 400,000. A modern city with a hot, sticky climate, it can well be described as aggressively ugly. Why, then, would we suggest anybody go there?

First, if you're going to or from **San Cristóbal de las Casas**, there's a good chance you'll be passing through Tuxtla (most people call it simply that). Second, as unattractive as Tuxtla may be at first glance, it does have its points of interest.

These include the finest zoo in Mexico and a respectable regional museum. The neighboring town of **Chiapa de Corzo** is the base for boat excursions through the Sumidero canyon. Some visitors may prefer to stay in quiet, intimate Chiapa de Corzo and hop over to Tuxtla from there. Local buses connect them every three minutes. Unless you're going on business, you probably won't need more than a day or so in the Tuxtla area. You may even be able to see most of what you want on a day excursion from San Cristóbal.

## ARRIVALS & DEPARTURES

### By Air

Tuxtla Gutiérrez has two airports, the close-in **Terán airport**, about six km west of the city, and the newer, less convenient **Llano San Juan airport**, about 35 km west of the city, whose longer runway can handle the Boeing 727 aircraft used by Mexicana on some of its Mexico City flights. The other airlines use Terán airport.

Smaller aircraft, such as the Fokker 100 jets used by Aviacsa, can land safely there. Aviacsa (which has its headquarters in Tuxtla Gutiérrez) serves Mexico City and Tapachula as well as Oaxaca, Villahermosa, Mérida and Cancún. Aerocaribe, a Mexicana affiliate, competes on these latter routes, also from Terán airport.

Taxis between there and the city cost about $5. From Llano San Juan airport, taxis charge $15 and collective vans $5, with return service provided from the Mexicana ticket office on Avenida Central. The code for both airports is TGZ. Neither sees any regular international flights.

### By Bus

Each bus company has its own terminal in Tuxtla Gutiérrez, all in or near the city center. Plans to build a shared central terminal keep getting postponed.

Omnibus Cristóbal Colón is the dominant first-class bus company serving Tuxtla from a scruffy terminal at the corner of 2a Avenida Norte Poniente and 2a Calle Poniente Norte. Service to San Cristóbal de las Casas (1 1/2 hours, $3) goes twice hourly from 5 am to 9 pm (some of them run by the Sur second-class division). About half these buses continue to Comitán, and several run to the Guatemalan border at Ciudad Cuauhtémoc. Buses to Arriaga, Tapachula and intermediate points go every hour or two from 7 am to midnight. There are five daily departures to Palenque (eight hours, $11) and seven to Villahermosa (seven hours, $10), several of them going overnight.

There are also three daily departures to Oaxaca (two overnight, 10 hours, $18), four to Salina Cruz, continuing or connecting to Huatulco (nine hours, $14) and Puerto Escondido (11 hours, $17), two to Campeche and Mérida, one each to Cancún and Chetumal, and two to Veracruz. Buses to Mexico City (19 hours, $40-$49), all go overnight, with eight departures between mid-afternoon and mid-evening.

Pullman de Chiapas, a new company, planned to run competing services on several of these routes. ADO, with a terminal at 5a Avenida Sur Poniente and 9a Calle Poniente Sur, runs twice daily to Mexico City, also serving Coatzacoalcos, Veracruz and Puebla.

Autotransportes Tuxtla Gutiérrez (ATG) is the dominant second-class bus company in the region and also runs a handful of first-class services. Its terminal is on 3a Avenida Sur Oriente between 5a and 7a Calles Oriente Sur. ATG goes hourly to San Cristóbal de las Casas from 4 am to midnight, with many continuing to Comitán and the Guatemalan border at Ciudad Cuauhtémoc. To Palenque via Ocosingo and the Agua Azul cutoff, ATG has departures every couple of hours from 5 am to midnight, including several first-class services. It also runs to Villahermosa, Arriaga and Tapachula.

Local service to Chiapa de Corzo runs at three-minute intervals from 5 am to 7 pm and less frequently after that. The departure point is at 2a Avenida Sur Oriente and 2a Calle Oriente Sur.

**By Road**

Tuxtla Gutiérrez lies at the junction of several highways. All are two-lane roads. Highway 190, the most important, forms part of the Pan-American highway and connects Tuxtla with Oaxaca state, where it meets other highways running northwest to Mexico City. East of Tuxtla, Highway 190 goes to San Cristóbal de las Casas and then turns south toward the Guatemalan border at Ciudad Cuauhtémoc, running parallel to the border and meeting the coastal highway near Tapachula.

Highway 195 runs north from Tuxtla to Villahermosa, where it meets Highway 186 east to the Yucatán and northwest toward Mexico City.

## ORIENTATION

Tuxtla Gutiérrez is laid out mostly in a rectangular grid pattern. Most streets and avenues have numbers rather than names. The city is divided into quadrants, with numbers rising according to the distance from the central plaza (*zócalo*). Avenues (*avenidas*) run east and west, streets (*calles*) run north and south.

To avoid confusion (or perhaps to create it), each street designation or address is accompanied not by one but by two cardinal points of the compass, North (*Norte*, abbreviated *Nte*), South (*Sur*), East (*Oriente*, abbreviated *Ote*), or West (*Poniente*, abbreviated *Pte*). You're not likely to be in Tuxtla long enough to want to bother figuring out how this system works. The letter "a" following the number of a street or avenue fills the same function as the "th" in English, as in 5th Avenue, for instance.

**Avenida Central** is one of the two axes that divides the city into quadrants and is the most important local artery. In the eastern part of the city it changes names to **Boulevard Ángel Albino Corzo**, and in the more fashionable western part of the city it changes names to **Boulevard Doctor Belisario Domínguez**. Needless to say, the *zócalo* lies at the corner of Avenida Central and Calle Central. The central part of the city holds little of interest for most visitors. Many of the better hotels, restaurants and shops lie further west.

The smaller and older town of **Chiapa de Corzo** lies about 15 km east of Tuxtla, just beyond the Rio Grijalva, which runs through the Sumidero canyon.

## GETTING AROUND

Taxis are cheap in Tuxtla Gutiérrez and will probably be your most useful means of getting around. Most trips within town cost less than $2. Local buses run frequently along many routes. One useful local bus service goes to and from Chiapa de Corzo at very frequent intervals, departing from the corner of 2a Avenida Sur Oriente and 2a Calle Oriente Sur.

Taxis to Chiapa de Corzo cost about $12.

## WHERE TO STAY

As already mentioned, the center of Tuxtla Gutiérrez has only limited appeal, and little is missed by seeking lodgings toward the outskirts or, indeed, in smaller, quieter Chiapa de Corzo. Upper-category hotels lie in the west end along Boulevard Belisario Domínguez, including the new Hotel Camino Real, which was not yet completed when we visited. We'll give a rundown here by district.

### Central Hotels

**HOTEL REGIONAL SAN MARCOS**, *1a Avenida Sur Oriente near 2a Calle Oriente Sur, phone (961) 31940; 40 rooms, $18 single, $21 double, VI - MC - AE.*

This big blue building near the cathedral has four stories and no elevator. Rooms are clean, bright and air conditioned but fairly ordinary.

**HOTEL SAFARI**, *2a Avenida Norte Oriente between 5a and 6a Calles Oriente Norte, phone (961) 27452 or 27472, fax (961) 27563; 104 rooms, $35 single, $43 double, VI - MC - AE.*

Rooms are decorated in shades of pale orange and brown, with worn carpeting, air conditioning and television. The parking area faces the rooms.

**HOTEL MARIA EUGENIA**, *Avenida Central near 4a Calle Oriente, phone (961) 33767 to 33771, fax (961) 32860; 74 rooms, $46 single, $57 double, VI - MC - AE.*

Each room has carpeting, wood paneling and a desk, as well as air conditioning, television and telephone. Views from the windows are dismal, and there is some traffic noise.

**GRAN HOTEL HUMBERTO**, *Avenida Central near 1a Calle Poniente, phone (961) 22044, fax (961) 29771; 111 rooms, $40 single, $50 double, VI - MC - AE - DC.*

Rooms are big, bright, air conditioned and carpeted, but musty and worn. There is noise from traffic and, on weekends, from dances on the top floor.

**HOTEL AVENIDA**, *Avenida Central Poniente #224, phone (961) 20807; 28 rooms, $14 single, $18 double, no credit cards.*

This simple establishment provides bright rooms with fan, hot water and old wooden furniture. Rooms facing the street are noisy.

**HOTEL POSADA DEL REY**, *1a Calle Oriente Norte #310, phone (961) 27871, 27924 or 27911, fax (961) 27563; 40 rooms, $30 single, $35 double, VI - MC - AE.*

Rooms have ugly brick walls but pleasant tiles. Those facing the street are reasonably quiet; interior rooms are dark and claustrophobic.

Several hotels in the $10 to $15 price range lie in the streets immediately to the north and east of the *zócalo*. Perhaps the best of these is the modern **HOTEL PLAZA CHIAPAS** at *2a Avenida Norte Oriente and 2a Calle Oriente Norte, four blocks east of the Cristóbal Colón terminal.*

A 90-bed youth hostel, **VILLA JUVENIL CREA**, with dormitory beds for $4, *lies east of the center at Boulevard Ángel Albino Corzo 1800.* Men and women are segregated.

### Hotels West of the Center

**HOTEL BONAMPAK TUXTLA**, *Belisario Domínguez 180, phone (961) 32050, 32047 or 32048, fax (961) 27737; 70 rooms, $57 single, $65 double, VI - MC - AE.*

This Best Western affiliate is one of the city's older hotels. It has a spacious lobby and big, bright rooms decorated with drawings inspired by ancient codices. All rooms have air conditioning and television. The hotel also has a restaurant, discotheque, swimming pool, tennis court, and garden, but its single elevator is a little creaky.

**HOTEL FLAMBOYANT**, *Belisario Domínguez, 4 km west of the center, near Las Galas shopping center, phone (961) 50888 or 50999, fax (961) 50087; 120 rooms, $118 single or double, VI - MC - AE.*

There are great expanses of marble in this beige, Moorish-inspired establishment. Three wings form a U shape around a large pool. Air conditioned rooms, with television, are decorated in beige and pale green. A restaurant, tennis courts and other services are available. The hotel's discotheque, El Sheik, is housed, sensibly, in a separate building.

**HOTEL ARECAS**, *Belisario Domínguez, 5 km west of the center, phone (961) 51122, 51128 or 51129, fax (961) 51121; 60 rooms, $51 single, $63 double, VI - MC- AE.*

This friendly establishment has a large circular lobby and spacious rooms that make good use of painted tiles. Rooms have air conditioning and television, and there is a small pool, but the grounds can use some work.

**HOTEL PALACE INN**, *Belisario Domínguez, 4 km west of the center, phone (961) 50574, fax (961) 51042; 24 rooms, $24 single, $28 double, VI - MC.*

Rooms here are quite ordinary but decent enough for the price. Each has air conditioning, television and telephones. There is a small pool.

### Hotels in Chiapa de Corzo

**HOTEL LA CEIBA**, *Avenida Domingo Ruiz, two blocks west of the zócalo, phone (961) 60389; 37 rooms, $27 to $30 single, $30 to $40 double, VI - MC - AE - DC.*

This pretty, three-story, whitewashed building sits on a quiet street, with a bright, inviting lobby and a pool and garden in back. Rooms are a little dark but have some nice touches of color and tile floors. Only a few are air conditioned; the rest have fans

**HOTEL LOS ANGELES**, *southeast corner of the zócalo, no phone; 11 rooms, $9 single, $15 double, no credit cards.*

This place has seen better days. Rooms are big and high-ceilinged but rather shabby and bare.

## WHERE TO EAT

Tuxtla Gutiérrez is not a diner's paradise, but it does have some decent restaurants, often with an emphasis on steaks. Among these are **LA CARRETA**, a steakhouse *at Belisario Domínguez 681*, and **EL GANADERO**, *near the Hotel Bonampak*. Further east, *at Avenida Central Oriente #837*, is **LAS PINCHANCHAS**, set in an open courtyard and noted for its marimba performances. The menu includes a number of regional specialties, but there are mixed reports on the quality of the food.

**TRATTORIA SAN MARCO**, *facing the zócalo behind the cathedral*, is a busy place with tables both outdoors and indoors and a broad menu including pizzas.

Nearby, the cheerful **MESÓN MANOLO** *at Avenida Central Poniente #238* has a big menu and cheap prices. *Along Boulevard Belisario Domínguez near 15a Calle Poniente*, **RESTAURANT BÁVARO** offers German specialties. Further west, *near the Hotel Arecas*, is the **SPAGHETTERIA VALLE D'AOSTA** (closed Thursday), with an appealing outdoor terrace and pizza and pastas on the menu. There are many other restaurants along this same thoroughfare.

For Japanese dishes, try **RESTAURANT SAKURA**, *located in the seedy Hotel Real de Tuxtla on Boulevard Ángel Albino Corzo*. Tuxtla has several big Chinese restaurants with menus comparable to what you might have expected in the US 30 years ago.

### In Chiapa de Corzo

There is some good eating amid interesting surroundings in Chiapa de Corzo. Many small restaurants line the *embarcadero*, or wharf, where boats leave for the Sumidero canyon. On Sundays there are marimba performances. For something more elegant, try the **JARDINES DE CHIAPA**, *one block west of the zócalo*, with tables facing an interior garden courtyard. The menu includes meats, seafood and local specialties. Similar is **EL CAMPANARIO**, *half a block east of the zócalo*. **LOS CORREDORES**, *just off the zócalo*, has a simpler Mexican menu.

## SEEING THE SIGHTS

Tuxtla's **zoo**, or *jardín zoológico*, known officially as the **Zoológico Miguel Álvarez Del Toro**, is widely considered to be the best in Mexico. *Set in a big hillside forest at the edge of town (easily reached by taxi or by buses marked Cerro Hueco)*, the zoo remains cool and breezy even at mid-day, in sharp contrast to the city below. Visits are set out in a long clockwise circuit and take at least 90 minutes even at a fairly brisk pace. Most areas are accessible to wheelchairs, something not to be taken for granted in Mexico, although there are some sharp rises and descents.

The zoo devotes itself exclusively to the fauna of Chiapas, which happen to be quite varied and include many species on the verge of extinction, some jaguars and other large cats among them. Birds on view include the nearly extinct quetzal, with its long tail and brilliant plumage. Messages in the zoo attempt to drive home the conservation message.

Most animals are kept in large enclosures. Cages, where they exist, are spacious. The animals, if anything, blend in *too* well with their surroundings: it can sometimes take sharp eyes to spot them. The zoo includes a reptile house, aviary, insectarium, and night house with nocturnal species. There are snack bars at the entrance and inside the zoo. There is also a tourism office at the entrance. *Zoo hours are 8:30 am to 5:30 pm daily except Monday. Admission is free.*

The Chiapas **regional museum** is housed in a cluster of buildings that includes the impressive 1,200-seat **Teatro de la Ciudad** in **Parque Madero** – *a short distance northeast of the city center.* The **anthropology section** of the museum, *open from 9 am to 4 pm, daily except Monday, free admission,* is bright and spacious, with many stone carvings and pottery objects representing the state's rich heritage. Another section of the museum, devoted mostly to the colonial and early post-independence periods in Chiapas, was closed for renovation; the reopening date was uncertain.

Nearby is the **botanical museum**, *open Monday to Friday 9 am to 3 pm, Saturday 9 am to 1 pm.* And just across a broad walkway is the **botanical garden**, with its large stand of tropical forest, *open 9 am to 6 pm, daily except Monday.* Unfortunately, few of the trees or plant species are marked, limiting the garden's pedagogical function, and there is a smelly stream at one end.

The **Sumidero Canyon** is a long, deep gorge carved by the **Rio Grijalva** (pronounced gree-KHAL-ba) through a grand series of rock formations with sheer walls of stone reaching as high as 1,200 meters (nearly 4,000 feet) above water level. Flooded to allow for hydroelectric generation, the gorge is easily accessible to motorboats, which take groups of passengers on a fast, and occasionally bumpy, 76 km trip to the dam and back in a little over two hours, slowing down sometimes to observe the canyon's abundant bird life as well as a large rock structure near the far end that resembles a giant Christmas tree.

*To get to Sumidero, take one of the boats from the embarcadero, or wharf, just below the zócalo at Chiapa de Corzo. The price for an entire boat is $55. Individual passengers pay $6 each when there are groups of ten or more. NOTE: The problem is, there is sometimes a long wait to assemble a large enough group. Your best chance is on a weekend afternoon.*

Also in Chiapa de Corzo is the **Museo De La Laca**, or lacquerware museum with, what else, a broad display of hand-painted wooden objects, many with very intricate designs. The museum, *located across from the* *municipal market, a block-and-a-half below the zócalo, on the upper floor of the partly ruined building that once housed the convent of Santo Domingo, is open 10 am to 4 pm, daily except Monday, admission free,* and includes a workshop and gift shop.

Nearby, the church of **Santo Domingo** still stands: it is simple and immense, with whitewashed walls and a wood-beamed ceiling. It faces the big and not very attractive *zócalo*, whose most notable feature is a clock tower from the ruins of a former church. On one side of the *zócalo* is a row of handicrafts shops.

In Tuxtla itself, the *zócalo*, also known as the **Plaza Cívica**, sprawls over two blocks divided by Avenida Central. It is a lively place, but it has little of the charm associated with *zócalos* in many other Mexican cities. Its most striking feature is the modern, whitewashed **San Marcos cathedral**, notable for its unusual clock tower.

## ENTERTAINMENT & NIGHTLIFE

A stroll around the *zócalo*, dinner at a restaurant, or possibly a visit to the cinema are among evening pastimes in Tuxtla Gutiérrez. Several of the larger hotels in the west end have discotheques.

## PRACTICAL INFORMATION

### Airline Offices

- **Aviacsa**: *Avenida Central Poniente #1144, phone (961) 37812*
- **Mexicana**: *Avenida Central Poniente #206, phone (961) 25402*
- **Aerocaribe**: *Belisario Domínguez 1934, phone (961) 22032*

### Car Rentals

There are several car rental agencies in Tuxtla:
- **Dollar**: *at both airports and at 5a Avenida Norte Poniente #2260, phone (961) 28932*
- **Gabriel Rent-A-Car**: *at both airports and at Belisario Domínguez 780, phone (961) 20757*
- **Budget**: *Belisario Domínguez 2510, phone (961) 50672.*

### Currency Exchange

Tuxtla Gutiérrez is not a good place to change dollars. Try to get any pesos you need before arriving. Service at most banks is exceedingly slow, and exchange rates tend to be poor. Getting a cash advance on a Visa or Mastercard can be a better bet. At last report, there were no *casas de cambio*.

**Tourist Information**

There are **tourism information booths** at both airports and at the entrance to the zoo. The **main office** is at *Boulevard Belisario Domínguez 950 near 15a Calle Poniente, west of the city center, phone (961) 25509.* The staff, few of whom speak English, can provide simple maps and leaflets on several towns in Chiapas.

# SAN CRISTÓBAL DE LAS CASAS

> *San Cristóbal lies along Highway 190, which forms part of the Pan-American Highway.*

Something special here seems to take visitors in its grip. Perhaps it is the clear mountain air, or the cobbled streets and low tile-roofed buildings, or the sight of Indian villagers in their traditional garb. Whatever it is, few people are left untouched.

The city takes part of its name from **Fray Bartólome de las Casas**, the 16th century Spanish cleric who protected Indians against some of the very harsh depradations inflicted by his countrymen. The name of the city is often shortened to San Cristóbal or, occasionally, to Las Casas. Cristóbal is Spanish for Christopher. An alternate name, popular among some Indians, is **Jovel**, sometimes spelled Jobel. During several periods in its history the city was capital of Chiapas. Indians in the region are Mayans, mostly of the Tzotzil and Tzeltal groups.

The pace here is relaxed. Few people seem to be in a hurry. Many visitors enjoy simply strolling along the city's many old streets. The *zócalo*, or central plaza, is quiet and sedate. The area around the central market and Santo Domingo church is livelier, and here you will see many Indian people from the surrounding villages. There are museums and churches to see, and handicrafts markets to view even if you're just looking.

The Chiapas highlands are noted for colorful weavings which take the form of blankets, shawls, blouses, sashes and bags. You can also find quality leather goods as well as ceramics and jewelry. There is a small but noticeable colony of foreign expatriates here.

Excursions can be made to several of the outlying villages as well as further afield to the ruins of Toniná, near Ocosingo. San Cristóbal can also be used as a base for visits to Tuxtla Gutiérrez or to the Montebello lakes.

Be sure to bring sweaters or other warm clothing. San Cristobal sits at an altitude of 2,110 meters (6,920 feet), and evenings are cool, especially from December to February.

## ARRIVALS & DEPARTURES

**By Air**

The nearest airport with regular flights is at Tuxtla Gutiérrez, 85 km west.

**By Bus**

Buses run frequently along the scenic mountain highway linking San Cristóbal and Tuxtla Gutiérrez. Two important bus companies serve San Cristóbal. Omnibus Cristóbal Colón operates first-class buses under its own name and second-class services under the Sur name. Autotransportes Tuxtla Gutiérrez has many second-class and a few first-class services. Both have terminals along the highway. Several smaller second-class companies also serve San Cristóbal.

Cristóbal Colón and Sur between them run at half-hour intervals between Tuxtla and San Cristóbal (1 1/2 hours, $3) from early morning to mid-evening. They also go hourly between San Cristóbal and Comitán (1 1/2 hours, $3). Several continue to the Guatemalan border at Ciudad Cuauhtémoc, and two go all the way to Tapachula.

To Palenque there are six daily departures (five hours, $7, some go overnight), two continuing to Villahermosa (eight hours, $11). One overnight bus goes to Oaxaca (12 hours, $19), and there are daytime and overnight services to Huatulco (11 hours, $17) and Puerto Escondido (13 hours, $20). Three go overnight to Mexico City (21 hours, $42 to $52), and one each to Mérida, Cancún and Chetumal.

Autotransportes Tuxtla Gutiérrez has the most frequent buses to Palenque with 11 daily departures, some of them air-conditioned first-class services. It also operates hourly to Tuxtla Gutiérrez and every hour or two to Comitán and Ciudad Cuauhtémoc. Additional second-class service on these routes is offered on the shabbier vehicles of Lacandonia, Autotransportes de Pasaje, and Rápidos de San Cristóbal.

Local minibuses to many of the outlying villages leave from near the market.

## ORIENTATION

Unlike many places in Chiapas, streets in San Cristóbal have names rather than numbers. Some streets change names as they pass through the center; different portions of the same street may have different names. The Pan-American highway passes east and west across the southern part of the city, where most of the bus terminals are found.

The *zócalo* lies in the heart of the city and is one of two main focal points, the other being the area a few blocks further north around the market and Santo Domingo church. The *zócalo* is more Spanish, the market more Indian.

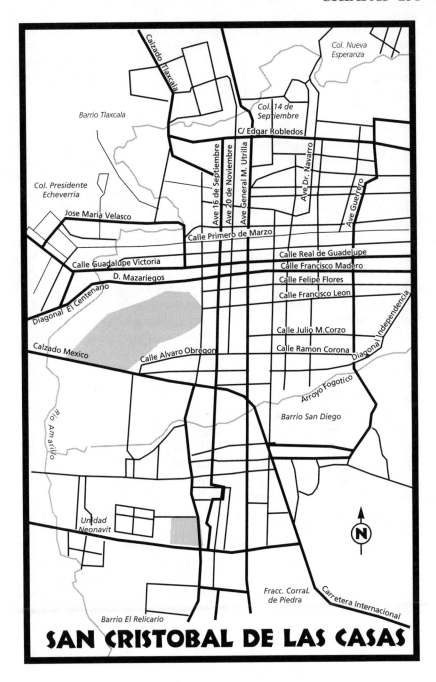

SAN CRISTOBAL DE LAS CASAS

Most points of interest in the city are within easy walking distance of each other. Taxis will be useful if you're tired or have baggage. Minibuses operate within town and to most of the outlying villages, leaving from a rather disorderly terminal near the market. Some tours operate to these villages, and taxis can be hired by the hour.

## WHERE TO STAY

San Cristóbal has a good selection of hotels, most in the central part of the city and really all in the middle and lower ranges, as befits a place that took longer to be discovered by the well-heeled. Many hotels are housed in buildings from the colonial era, and a few are real delights. Scarcely any hotels in San Cristóbal have air conditioning, which is no drawback since temperatures rarely go very high. Many budget hotels are concentrated toward the south end of Insurgentes and neighboring streets, while others may be found along Real de Guadalupe street, which is somewhat more central.

Prices shown here were those in effect during 1994. Because of a sharp drop in the number of visitors following the New Year's Day uprising, many hotels lowered their rates in efforts to lure more customers. If tourism does rebound to something approaching its previous levels, this may be reflected in substantially higher rates at certain hotels, so please treat rates shown here with caution.

### Middle Price Range

**HOTEL CASAVIEJA**, M.A. Flores 27, phone (967) 80385, fax (967) 85223; 37 rooms, $40 single, $50 double, VI - MC - AE.

The name means old house, and it does incorporate a pair of 18th century houses, but this hotel opened only recently. Rooms are set on two levels, most around a small patio with plants and pottery. The restaurant and some rooms face a small garden. Rooms, all with wood ceilings, are simply but tastefully decorated in shades of blue, purple and pale orange. There are two suites with jacuzzis.

**HOTEL CASA MEXICANA**, 28 de Agosto 1, phone (967) 80683 or 81348, fax (967) 82627; 30 rooms, $59 single, $63 double, VI - MC - AE.

Most rooms in this well situated hotel are set around an attractive covered courtyard with luxuriant vegetation. The restaurant faces another covered courtyard, full of painted tile and pieces of artwork and pottery. Rooms are small but comfortable, decorated in white with embroidered purple bedspreads.

**NA-BOLOM**, Vicente Guerrero 33, phone (967) 81418; 12 rooms, $32 single, $41 double, VI - MC - AE - DC (10% surcharge on credit cards).

Situated a short distance from the city center, this is no ordinary hotel but part of a research center and museum. (See more on Na-Bolom in

"Seeing the Sights," below.) Most rooms are set in a sprawling 19th-century mansion with a big garden and extensive wooded grounds; other rooms are in cabins at the far end of the grounds. Each room has a fireplace. Furnishings, including artwork and knickknacks, provide a cozy and very old-fashioned atmosphere. Buffet meals, $6 to $8, are served at fixed hours, providing a chance to meet researchers and volunteers.

**HOTEL D'MONICA I**, *Insurgentes 33, phone (967) 80732; 70 rooms, $39 single, $48 double, VI - MC.*

This handsome, three-story, U-shaped building is set around a garden courtyard. Rooms are carpeted, with wood ceilings, dark furniture and television. The restaurant sometimes has marimba performances, and there is a separate breakfast room. This centrally located hotel is often used by tour groups.

**HOTEL D'MONICA II**, *5 de Febrero 18, phone (967) 81363; 30 rooms, $24 single, $27 double, VI - MC.*

This hotel is run by the same people as its namesake, but all resemblance ends there. The D'Monica II has small, ordinary rooms with industrial carpeting, facing an uninviting covered courtyard.

**HOTEL CIUDAD REAL CENTRO HISTÓRICO**, *Plaza 31 de Marzo 10 (on the zócalo), phone (967) 80187; 31 rooms, $36 single, $45 double, VI - MC - AE.*

Rooms are small but pleasant with wood paneling, stucco and tiles. Many rooms are a bit dark, but a few have views of the *zócalo*. The hotel has a café set in a covered courtyard

**HOTEL SANTA CLARA**, *Insurgentes 1 on the zócalo, phone (967) 81140 or 80871; 40 rooms, $31 single, $39 double, VI - MC.*

Rooms are fairly ordinary and some are a little dark, but they make good use of tiles and have phones and televisions. Housed in a converted 16th century mansion, this hotel has a pleasant, plant-filled courtyard and a less agreeable area around the pool.

**HOTEL POSADA DE LOS ANGELES**, *Francisco Madero 17, near the zócalo, phone (967) 81173, fax (967) 82581; 20 rooms, $40 single, $50 double, VI - MC - AE.*

Rooms are simply but comfortably furnished, with television and phone. This three-story building is set around two courtyards, one of them housing a restaurant.

**HOTEL FLAMBOYANT ESPAÑOL**, *1º de Marzo 15, phone (967) 80045 or 80412, fax (967) 80514; 51 rooms, $64 single, $76 double, VI - MC - AE.*

This appears to be the most expensive hotel in town. Rooms are set around two bright, flowery patios, and there are a rooftop gym and lounge. Furnishings include embroidered bedspreads and lots of painted tile. Some rooms facing the street may be noisy.

**HOTEL DIEGO DE MAZARIEGOS**, *5 de Febrero 1, corner of General Utrilla, phone (967) 80621, fax (967) 80827; 77 rooms, $47 single, $56 double, VI - MC - AE - DC.*

This hotel once enjoyed an almost mythical reputation among regular visitors to San Cristóbal, but it has been resting on its laurels. It consists of two building on opposite sides of General Utrilla Avenue, one block north of the *zócalo*. Rooms in the original building, on the east side, are better. Each has a fireplace and heavy wooden furniture, but there is plenty of tired industrial carpeting and an inappropriate pink-and-white color scheme in the patio areas. Rooms in the west building, where the reception area is situated, have rather ordinary furnishings. They are set around a covered courtyard with lots of vegetation.

**HOTEL FRAY BARTÓLOME DE LAS CASAS**, *Niños Héroes 2, corner of Insurgentes, phone (967) 80932; 26 rooms, $23 single, $27 double, no cards.*

The high-ceilinged rooms here are decorated in tones of brown and beige with wooden furniture. The hotel has a big but not very attractive courtyard.

**HOTEL PALACIO MOCTEZUMA**, *Benito Juárez, 16 phone (967) 81142, fax (967) 81536; 42 rooms, $31 single, $39 double, VI - MC.*

The courtyard here is flowery and appealing. Big, carpeted rooms have lots of wood and tiles.

**HOTEL DON QUIJOTE**, *Cristóbal Colón 7, phone (967) 80920 or 80346; 24 rooms, $18 single, $23 double, VI - MC - AE.*

Rooms are small but attractively furnished. The upstairs rooms have more light. Situated on a quiet side street.

**HOTEL PLAZA SANTO DOMINGO**, *General Utrilla 35, phone (967) 81927; 23 rooms, $29 single or double, VI - MC.*

Rooms in this centrally situated hotel are quiet and pleasantly furnished but a little dark.

**HOTEL PARADOR MEXICANOS**, *5 de Mayo 38, phone (967) 81515, fax (967) 80055; 24 rooms, $23-$27 single, $26-$30 double, VI - MC.*

Two buildings face each other across a stone-paved parking area and a small garden. Rooms are big but ordinary. Tennis is available.

**HOTEL ARRECIFE DE CORAL**, *Crescencio Rosas 29, phone (967) 82125, fax (967) 82098; 46 rooms, $40 single, $50 double, VI - MC.*

A series of two-story pink buildings is set around a big, empty lawn. Rooms have very ordinary furnishings, and those near the street may be noisy. A bit away from the center.

**HOTEL CIUDAD REAL TEATRO**, *Diagonal Central 32, just off the highway near the western edge of town, phone (967) 81886, fax (967) 82853; 65 rooms, $58 single, $69 double, VI - MC - AE.*

Rooms in this U-shaped, two-story building face a series of three lawns, some stalked by large tropical birds.

**HOTEL BONAMPAK**, *Calzada Mexico 5, along the highway near the western edge of town, phone (967) 81622 or 84310, fax (967) 81621; 50 rooms, $50 single, $60 double, VI - MC - AE.*

This Best Western affiliate is comfortable but thoroughly ordinary. On the grounds are a trailer park and campsite, $5 per person, vehicles free; light, water, toilets and showers are provided.

### Lower Price Range

**HOTEL POSADA SAN CRISTÓBAL**, *Insurgentes 3 near the zócalo, no phone; 10 rooms, $12 single, $15 double, no cards.*

Simple, attractive rooms have wood ceilings, wood furniture and polished concrete floors. Entry is through a stone-paved patio. Very good for the price.

**HOTEL REAL DEL VALLE**, *Real de Guadalupe 14, phone (967) 80680; 36 rooms, $14 single, $17 double, VI - MC.*

Simple rooms with wood ceilings set around a big stone-paved patio.

**HOTEL SAN MARTÍN**, *Real de Guadalupe 16, phone (967) 80533; 26 rooms, $11 single, $14 double, no cards.*

Clean, simple rooms. Both live and stuffed birds decorate a small patio.

**POSADA SANTIAGO**, *Real de Guadalupe 32, phone (967) 80024; 9 rooms, $12 single or double, VI - MC.*

Rooms are carpeted but rather small and dark.

**CASA MARGARITA**, *Real de Guadalupe 34, phone (967) 80957; 26 rooms, $8 single, $11 double, VI.*

Rooms are large and somewhat shabby, with shared bath. But there is an attractive terrace, which is now a gathering spot for young travelers.

**HOTEL POSADA JOVEL**, *Flavio Panigua 28, phone (967) 81724; 20 rooms, $8 single, $11 double, no cards.*

Rooms are small and simple but clean and fresh. Some are without private bath.

**HOTEL POSADA GLADYS**, *Real de Mexicanos 16, no phone; 4 rooms, $11; dormitory beds, $5; all with shared bath, no cards.*

Rooms here are quite basic, but there is a special atmosphere to the place with its garden courtyard and orange trees. Free coffee in the morning. Situated on a quiet colonial street.

**POSADA ADRIANITA**, *1º de Marzo, corner of 5 de Mayo, phone (967) 81283; 20 rooms, $15 with private bath, $10-$12 with shared bath, no cards.*

This otherwise modest place has a big flowery patio. The rooms without bath are actually more attractive. The common bathrooms are bright and clean.

**POSADA DEL SOL**, *1º de Marzo, corner of 5 de Mayo, phone (967) 80495; 13 rooms, $15 with private bath, $9 with shared bath, no cards.*

Rooms are basic, but the common areas are bright and pleasant, with hand-painted codices.

**HOTEL POSADA VALLARTA**, *Hermanos Pineda 10, phone (967) 80465; 20 rooms, $14 single, $17 double, VI -MC.*

Motel-style arrangement. Simple, comfortable rooms, with television.

**HOTEL CAPRI**, *Insurgentes 54, phone (967) 83018 or 83118, fax (967) 80015; 60 rooms, $15 single, $18 double, VI - MC.*

Situated 1 1/2 blocks from the Cristóbal Colón terminal (and not to be confused with the dismal Posada Capri nearby), this hotel is prettier on the outside than on the inside. Rooms are presentable, but noise can reverberate through the narrow three-story atrium.

**POSADA LUCELLA**, *Insurgentes 55, phone (967) 80956; 10 rooms, $9 single, $15 double, no cards.*

Rooms are small and simply furnished; some have private bath.

**POSADA LUPITA**, *Insurgentes 46, phone (967) 86130; 17 rooms, $5 single, $9 double, no cards.*

A pleasant courtyard, but this is a no-frills hotel with shared bath.

**POSADA INSURGENTES**, *Insurgentes 73, phone (967) 82433; 28 rooms, $6 single, $9 double, no cards.*

Marginally better, also with a pleasant courtyard and also with shared bath.

## WHERE TO EAT

The restaurant scene in San Cristóbal has evolved considerably, and offerings have become more varied. It is among the few places in Mexico where vegetarians are well looked after. Also, pizza and pasta dishes have caught on in a big way. Prices are mostly in the low to moderate range.

Several restaurants line Francisco Madero street in the two-block stretch just east of the *zócalo*. Among them are **LA LANGOSTA**, *Madero 9A*, with an interesting selection of seafood and traditional Mexican dishes. It is a bright, cheery, art-lined restaurant with reasonable prices. **PARIS-MEXICO**, *at Madero 20*, specializes in pizza, spaghetti and pancakes. **LOS MAGUEYES**, *28 de Agosto 1*, is a more elegant spot, with a choice of meat and seafood dishes.

**EL TEATRO**, *Primero de Marzo 8*, is a comfortable upstairs restaurant with Italian and Mexican dishes. **LA PARRILLA**, *Belisario Domínguez 32*, has cowboy decor and very good grilled meats and cheese dishes. **CAMINO REAL**, *on Benito Juárez near the highway and the Cristóbal Colón terminal*, and **LOS GALLITOS** nearby *at Calzada de las Américas 8*, both offer traditional Mexican dishes. **LAS BRISAS**, *west of town along the highway*, is big and more expensive, specializing in seafood.

**MADRE TIERRA**, *Insurgentes 19*, has a mostly vegetarian menu. It has an outdoor terrace, a cosy indoor dining room, and a bulletin board with news of cultural activities, rooms to let, special tours, and Spanish language classes. Next door is a bakery with a good choice of breads and cakes. **TULUC**, *up the street at Insurgentes 5*, has a handicrafts display at the entrance and a choice of inexpensive soups, salads, sandwiches, chicken, and pasta dishes. **TIKAL**, *at the far end of Insurgentes near the Cristóbal Colón terminal*, is bright, artsy and friendly. It's a good spot for breakfast and also has good pizzas, pancakes and tamales.

**CAFÉ-BAR LOS AMOROSOS**, *at the corner of Benito Juárez and J.F. Flores*, offers light meals and a good choice of juices, coffees and liquors. Bright and cheerful, with art-lined walls, it is an enjoyable place to linger. **LA GALERÍA**, *on Miguel Hidalgo half a block from the zócalo*, has a pleasant café tucked behind an art gallery and gift shop.

## SEEING THE SIGHTS

The *zócalo*, officially called **Plaza 31 de Marzo**, is a stately central plaza where you can relax and watch life go on around you. On one side is San Cristóbal's massive baroque **Cathedral**, with some gold leaf in the interior but otherwise unremarkable. It achieved fame in 1994 as the meeting-place for peace talks between Zapatista rebels and government officials.

More interesting is the 16th century **church of Santo Domingo** *a few blocks north*. Its ornate pink façade is impressive at any time, but especially when floodlit at night. It has a rococo interior with an abundance of gold leaf and a carved wooden altar, and is surely one of Mexico's most magnificent churches.

Along General Utrilla Avenue as you approach Santo Domingo church are shops and stalls selling regional handicrafts, and each day many other vendors set up a makeshift market in the courtyard of the church and also next to the neighboring (and much simpler) **Caridad church**. If you are going to photograph any of the vendors, you should ask permission first. The **main market**, where a vast and colorful profusion of fresh food is sold, lies just a little further north. It performs a social as well as a commercial role. See "Shopping" below.

A former 16th century convent *next to Santo Domingo church* houses the **Sna Jolobil museum**. Downstairs the museum displays artefacts and historical information from the pre-Columbian and colonial periods. Upstairs are examples of colonial art and the real highlight, a display of traditional clothing showing the centuries-old weaving skills still practised today in many highland villages. *The museum is open daily except Monday from 9 am to 2 pm and 3 pm to 6:30 pm Admission is $4.* The museum shares quarters with a cooperative of Indian weavers, which offers high-quality items for sale.

**Na-Bolom** (meaning *House of the Jaguar* in the Tzotzil Maya language) is more a phenomenon than merely a museum and research institute. *Situated at Vicente Guerrero 33 on the eastern side of town between Comitán and Chiapa de Corzo streets*, Na-Bolom was founded by Danish archeologist Frans Blom and was run for three decades after his death by his energetic widow, Trudi Blom (who died in 1993 at age 92).

The Bloms set as their mission the protection of the dwindling band of Lacandón Indians and preservation of the beleaguered rain forest they inhabit in eastern Chiapas. Researchers, mostly volunteers from different countries, participate in a variety of projects ranging from the care of a tree nursery to exploration of the pre-Mayan Olmec presence in Chiapas. Set on very spacious grounds, Na-Bolom also houses a small hotel and restaurant (see "Where to Stay" above).

The museum displays pre-Columbian objects from the collection of Frans Blom as well as assorted items depicting Indian culture, photos of Lacandones and other groups, and an unconsecrated chapel with religious art. Visitors may also see the extensive library and wander around the grounds. *Opening hours for unaccompanied visits (admission fee $1.50) are 9 am to 1 pm daily except Monday. Those who arrive between 4 pm and 4:45 pm are given a guided tour for a $3 charge and may stay until 7 pm.*

**Museo del Ambar** (**Amber Museum**) is *situated at the entrance to Plaza Siván, a shop selling amber objects and silverware at General Utrilla 10, just south of 28 de Agosto; open 9 am to 7 pm, daily except Saturday, and admission is free.* This small museum displays clothing, household items and money from earlier periods, as well as many amber items.

Those who are very interested in traditional Indian clothing may visit the private collection of **Sergio Castro**. *He lives in the red and white house at Guadalupe Victoria 47*, and most days (except Sunday), shortly after 6 pm, he invites small groups of visitors to see the collection of garments he has amassed during decades of work in Chiapas villages. These now fill several rooms of his house. It is better to reserve a day ahead. Contributions are accepted and are applied toward medical work in the villages.

Other points of interest in San Cristóbal include **Colonia El Cerillo**, *immediately east of Santo Domingo church*, whose streets contain many houses that are more than three centuries old; **Cerro De San Cristóbal** (*Cerro* means hill), topped by San Cristóbal church and providing very good views over the city (it is reached by a long stairway from the end of Hermanos Domínguez street at the corner of Ignacio Allende); and the church of **El Carmen**, *a couple of blocks east along Hermanos Domínguez near the corner of Miguel Hidalgo*, with its tower resting on an unusual arch and facing the Casa de la Cultura, housing a small art gallery, library and auditorium.

## SHOPPING

Mayan Indians of the Chiapas highlands, like their Guatemalan cousins, are famed for their intricate and brilliantly colored weavings. Each village has its own variations on colors or style of dress. In places where people from different villages meet, the trained eye can discern at a glance which village a wearer of traditional dress comes from.

Items that can be purchased include embroidered blouses called *huipiles* (pronounced wee-PEE-lays), shawls, sashes, jackets, caps, handbags, blankets, table covers, placemats and napkins. Other items to purchase include leather goods (such as purses, wallets, belts and boots, some of them embroidered with cloth), ceramic items (small painted animals have become quite popular), and jewelry (especially amber).

The biggest concentrations of **handicrafts shops** are found *along Real de Guadalupe street east of the zócalo or north along General Utrilla avenue near Santo Domingo church.* Some items may be cheaper in the makeshift market that appears each day in the courtyard of the church, spilling over to neighboring Caridad church. The **Sna Jolobil weavers' cooperative** sells top-end items in the former convent next to Santo Domingo. Handicrafts are also sold in several of the outlying villages.

Many of the shops have fixed prices, but elsewhere you can expect to bargain. Do not mistake the bashfulness of many Indian vendors for an absence of commercial acumen. They can bargain quite toughly. You will often get better discounts if you buy several items at the same place, but you may want to shop around first and compare prices.

## ENTERTAINMENT & NIGHTLIFE

San Cristóbal is definitely not the spot to disco till dawn, but it is a pleasant place for a cool evening stroll or for a langurous couple of hours over tea or something stronger in any of several charming cafés. Things tend to wind down quite early.

Occasionally there are concerts or film showings at the **Casa de la Cultura**, *near the corner of Miguel Hidalgo and Hermanos Domínguez.* You will see posters there and at some hotels. You can also inquire at the tourism office in the *Palacio Municipal.*

## EXCURSIONS FROM SAN CRISTÓBAL

Some villages near San Cristóbal have retained many of their ancient traditions and are well worth visiting. They can be reached by car, by taxi, by minibuses (which leave when full from a disorderly terminal near the central market), or by organized tour. Several travel agencies around town offer tours (providing they get enough people to sign up). Two local guides, known simply as Raúl and Alex, await visitors on the north side of the *zócalo* (facing the cathedral) each morning at 9:30 am and offer tours of San Juan Chamula and Zinacantán. Other points can be added upon request. As tourism picks up, other freelance guides will no doubt appear.

**Note:** When going to the villages, it is important to dress conservatively. Also, you should seek permission before photographing anybody. Some people believe cameras can steal the soul. Under no circumstances should you use a camera inside the church at San Juan Chamula. This is heartily shunned and has led in the past to beatings.

## SAN JUAN CHAMULA

*Ten km northwest of San Cristóbal*, **San Juan Chamula**, is famous for its small whitewashed church, facing a large plaza. On Sundays the plaza becomes a public market. The interior of the church is simple but really quite stunning. There are no pews. Rather, worshippers kneel on the floor individually or is small groups, often with rows of candles and burning incense in front of them, and their evident fervor is something to behold. Images of certain saints are dressed in holy garments.

This is a Catholic church but with a difference, showing how some highland Maya have adopted their own style of worship, retaining elements of their pre-conquest beliefs. In recent times some families have been expelled from San Juan Chamula because they joined Evangelical churches and refused to take part in the village's traditional ceremonies, thus disrupting social harmony, or so it was felt. *Visitors are asked to pay of fee of $0.60 at a booth near the church.*

## ZINACANTÁN

**Zinacantán**, *12 km northwest of San Cristóbal in a valley at the end of a fork on the Chamula road*, is noted, among other things, for the embroidered white and pinkish-red tunics worn by some of the men. The **church of San Lorenzo** has profusions of flowers and bright decorations. It also has pews, unlike the church at San Juan Chamula. *Visitors should pay a $0.60 fee at a booth nearby.*

On either side are small handicrafts markets selling brightly colored woven items. If you go with a guide, it should be possible to visit traditional homes where some of these items are produced on hand looms. *Four blocks from the church*, with signs to indicate the way, is the **Museo Tradicional Ik'al Ojov**, displaying traditional dress as well as gourds used for food storage and ceremonial drums. Written explanations are given in Spanish and English. *The museum is open daily 8 am to 6 pm, and contributions are voluntary.*

## AMATENANGO DEL VALLE & TENEJAPA

**Amatenango del Valle**, *37 km southeast of San Cristóbal just off the Pan-American highway*, is noted for its pottery. Besides the traditional pots and bowls, there are also small painted ceramic animals. **Tenejapa**, 28 km northeast of San Cristóbal, has become known for its big Sunday market, mostly food items but some handicrafts also.

**Las Grutas de San Cristóbal** are a series of caves *10 km southeast of the city, admission $4.50*, reachable by minibus, but poorly marked. The caves have huge stalagmites and are illuminated for the first 800 meters. Horses and guides can be hired nearby for trips through the neighboring hills.

## OTHER EXCURSIONS

**Horseback riding** in the hills outside San Cristóbal is said to be excellent, with fine natural scenery and glimpses of rural life. If you are interested, some travel agencies in San Cristóbal can make arrangements. Or ask at your hotel.

If you are headed toward Palenque, five hours by road to the northeast, worthwhile stops along the way include the Mayan ruins of **Toniná** (easily done as a day excursion from San Cristóbal; see the short Ocosingo and Toniná section just below) and the waterfalls and river at **Agua Azul**, covered in the Palenque section. The **Montebello lakes**, *southeast of San Cristóbal beyond Comitán*, can be visited on a day excursion with an early start. They also are covered in a section below.

Organized excursions are offered to most of the places mentioned above and to points further afield. To the remote ruins of **Bonampak** and **Yaxchilán** there are quick (and expensive) one-day trips by light aircraft, or cheaper (and rougher) four-day trips by land and river. Most of these trips are run from Palenque (subject to demand), but they can be booked through certain travel agencies in San Cristóbal (including Viajes Pedro Villanueva, in the Santa Clara Hotel, facing the *zócalo*; they also run some local excursions).

## PRACTICAL INFORMATION
### Car Rentals
• **Budget**: *Diego de Mazariegos 36, phone (967) 81871*
One or two local firms also have offices in town.

### Currency Exchange
Banks in San Cristóbal tend to provide slow service, poor exchange rates and short hours. Not all banks change travelers' checks. There are one or two *casas de cambio* along Real de Guadalupe street half a block from the *zócalo*. Their rates are also poor, but they offer faster service and longer hours, including evenings and weekends. Change money before arriving in San Cristóbal if you can.

**Language Classes**

Information on Spanish language classes is available at the **Centro Cultural El Puente**, *Real de Guadalupe 55, phone (967) 83723*. You can also check posters at Madre Tierra restaurant and at Hotel Real del Valle.

**Laundry**

Several laundries provide inexpensive same-day service, among them **Lavorama**, *Guadalupe Victoria 20A*, and **Lavandaría Mixtli**, *Real de Mexicanos 10*.

**Tourist Information**

The **tourism office**, temporarily disloged from the *Palacio Municipal* (facing the *zócalo*) because of damage wrought during the brief rebel capture of the city early in 1994, was set to move back in and expected to operate daily from 9 am to 2 pm and 5 pm to 8 pm. Staff seemed pleasant but not very knowledgeable.

# OCOSINGO & TONINÁ

*Ocosingo is 68 km northeast of San Cristóbal and 118 km south of Palenque along a winding mountain highway.*

**Ocosingo** (sometimes spelled Ococingo) is a big, hilly, nondescript town in cattle ranching country. It was one of the towns captured by Zapatista rebels on New Year's Day in 1994, and it lies just west of the Lacandón region, where the rebels continued to control some territory. Well into 1994 there was a large and visible military presence in Ocosingo and several roadblocks nearby where travelers were asked to show documents. There was nothing dangerous or threatening about this, but it conveyed an air of foreboding.

## ARRIVALS & DEPARTURES

**By Bus**

Ocosingo is served by many buses passing between Tuxtla Gutiérrez and Palenque via San Cristóbal de las Casas. Autotransportes Tuxtla Gutiérrez offers both first-class and second-class service, with departures in each direction every couple of hours throughout the day. The terminal is situated along the highway uphill from the center of town and will store baggage.

**By Taxi**

If you're traveling on your own and don't have a car, the only practical way to reach Toniná is by taxi from Ocosingo. The fare, with the taxi waiting one hour at the site, is about $25. Passenger-carrying farm trucks pass occasionally along the road to the ruins, but this is not a reliable way of getting around.

## SEEING THE SIGHTS

### The Ruins of Toniná

Some 14 km east of Ocosingo, mostly along dirt road, lie the Mayan ruins of **Toniná**. These ruins are little visited, which makes their dramatic appearance all the more thrilling. Crossing an open field, you suddenly encounter the main structure with its vast series of stone terraces rising up a hillside, with two towers at the top. About two-thirds of the way to the top are a group of ninth-century codices, protected by a shed. These are stone tablets inscribed with pictorial texts.

Toniná achieved its greatest splendor between the sixth and ninth centuries A.D. It survived the collapse of the old Mayan empire and revived in the tenth century, when a new, towering temple temple was built. Soon afterwards a period of destruction set in as new inhabitants moved into the area. Two **ball courts** have been excavated, the bigger of which has an altar at one corner and serves now as the entrance to the site after you follow a short wooded path from the ticket booth.

The vast **pyramid complex**, to the right after you enter, has a series of platforms, some of them topped by temples or palaces. On the fourth platform is a palace notable for its ornamental patterns and for a glyph showing a ferocious jaguar with the symbol of Venus in its eyes. An internal stairway leads to rooms decorated with crossbones and feathered rattlesnakes. On the sixth platform is a mural depicting, in the form of decapitated heads, the myth of the four suns or eras the world goes through with the passing of the seasons. Among the several temples on this platform is one with a carved figure of the earth monster devouring a stone solar sphere.

*The site is open daily from 9 am to 4 pm Admission is $3.* A tiny museum at the entrance displays several codices and some human skulls. Public washrooms are available, but there are no refreshments.

## WHERE TO STAY & EAT

Should you decide to stay overnight in Ocosingo, **HOTEL CENTRAL**, *facing the rather barren zócalo, phone (967) 30024, $13 single, $20 double, no cards*, has 12 small, bright, simple rooms.

**HOTEL AGUA AZUL**, *two blocks down from the zócalo, phone (967) 30302, $9 single, $12 double, no cards*, has a garden courtyard with a pool and 20 small, unattractive rooms.

Several **restaurants** line the *zócalo*, emphasizing beef. This, after all, is cattle country. The most appealing is the restaurant of the **Hotel Central**.

# COMITÁN & THE LAGUNAS DE MONTEBELLO

*Comitán lies along Highway 190 about midway between San Cristóbal de las Casas and the Guatemalan border crossing at Ciudad Cuauhtémoc.*

**Comitán** is a pleasant, hilly town. Besides its own modest attractions, Comitán is a base for visits to the **Lagunas de Montebello**, a group of 68 lakes set in a heavily wooded park. Several of the lakes are noted for their bright green or blue hues imparted by a high mineral content.

## ARRIVALS & DEPARTURES

**By Bus**

Comitán is served by first-class buses of Omnibus Cristóbal Colón (11 buses daily to or from San Cristóbal de las Casas and Tuxtla Gutiérrez, six to the Guatemalan border at Ciudad Cuauhtémoc, two to Tapachula, two to Mexico City) and the second-class buses of Autotransportes Tuxtla Gutiérrez (San Cristóbal or Tuxtla hourly, Ciudad Cuauhtémoc hourly, Tapachula twice daily).

Additional second-class service is provided by Transportes Cuxtepeques. All three terminals are located along the highway. Buses and minibuses to the Lagunas de Montebello and other points in that direction leave from a small terminal on 2a Avenida Poniente Sur half a block downhill from 2a Calle Sur Poniente.

## ORIENTATION

Comitán's rectangular street grid takes little account of the hilly topography, with the result that some streets are very steep. The system of street and avenue numbers is similar to that in Tuxtla Gutiérrez. The climate is fresh.

## SEEING THE SIGHTS

The *zócalo*, or **central plaza**, is big, lively and pleasant. Facing it is the *palacio municipal*, which houses a very helpful **tourism office**, *open Monday to Saturday 9 am to 9 pm, Sunday 9 am to 2 pm,* and an interesting series of murals, including one by painter Manuel Suasnávar depicting the Mayan vision of maize and human genesis. The ancient Maya believed that humans were created from corn, which to them was a sacred plant and the fount of life. Also facing the *zócalo* is the sober four-century-old **Santo Domingo church**.

Next to the church is a small **archaeological museum**, *open 9 am to 6:45 pm daily except Monday.* The house of **Belisario Domínguez**, the doctor and pharmacist who helped bring Chiapas into Mexico, is located *one block south of the zócalo along Avenida Central.* Now converted to a museum (same opening hours), its displays include a typical 19th-century pharmacy. *One block further south* is the **Hermila Domínguez de Castellanos art museum**, which has temporary exhibitions only.

There is a **Guatemalan consulate** *at 2a Avenida Poniente Norte #28, phone (963) 22669, open weekdays 9 am to 2 pm.*

## WHERE TO STAY

**HOTEL LAGOS DE MONTEBELLO**, *along the highway, phone (963) 21092 or 21108; 52 rooms, $35 single, $41 double, VI - MC - AE.*

This big, rambling place has an attractive garden and courtyard and a big pool. Upkeep has been slack, though. Rooms are big but tired. Try for a room near the back, which is quieter.

**HOTEL INTERNACIONAL**, *Avenida Central Sur one block from the zócalo, phone (963) 20110 or 20112; 28 rooms, $20 single, $23 double, VI - MC.*

Rooms are carpeted and reasonably comfortable. Those facing the street can be noisy. Friendly.

**HOTEL REAL BALÚN CANÁN**, *1a Avenida Poniente Sur 7, phone (963) 21094; 40 rooms, $36 single, $42 double, VI - MC - AE.*

The official four-star rating held by this overpriced place serves merely to discredit the rating system. Service is dismal, and room decor is bizarre. Located on a side street near the *zócalo.*

Several smaller, cheaper hotels and *hospedajes* can be found near the *zócalo.* Most are rather unpleasant. **HOSPEDAJE MONTEBELLO** *on 1a Calle Norte Poniente one block west of the zócalo* is one of the better ones.

## WHERE TO EAT

Most restaurants in Comitán concentrate heavily on beef. Among the better ones are **BUFFALO**, with a cowboy motif, and **HELEN'S**, *both near the zócalo.*

## EXCURSION TO LAGUNAS DE MONTEBELLO

To someone arriving from northerly climes, the **Lagunas de Montebello** (also called the Lagos de Montebello) may seem merely ho-hum, but taken in a tropical context they are really quite delightful. There are 22 fair-sized lakes and dozens of smaller ones dotted over a heavily wooded national park. Some are referred to as the *lagos de colores* because of the bright green or blue hues resulting from metallic ores. Five of these – Agua Tinta, Esmeralda, Ensueño, Encantada and Bosque Azul – are easily visible from the main road, which runs 3 km into the park. Others are accessible by dirt roads.

The Lagunas de Montebello are easy to visit as a day excursion from Comitán. *From Highway 190 take the cutoff at La Trinitaria village and continue 32 km to the park entrance.* Part way along, and two km off this road, are the **Chinkultic ruins**, of only minor interest except to real archaeology buffs. The area did have frequent minibus service, but the 1994 uprising hit tourism hard, and service was reduced accordingly.

At **Bosque Azul** you can find a lookout, restaurant, picnic grounds, swimming and horseback riding. Nearby, from the lookout at Laguna Esmeralda, guides can escort you along a forest trail to a series of caves and a big stone arch with a river flowing beneath. The main cave is rather mucky inside.

### Nearby Villages

Turning south near the park entrance and continuing 12 km, you come to the village of **Tziscao** (occasional buses). A short walk takes you to one of the biggest and prettiest lakes in the region. Turning left and continuing another few hundred meters, you reach the **ALBERGUE DE TZISCAO**, which provides clean, simple dormitory lodgings for $4 and very plain meals. Boats and horses can be hired. The lake is very peaceful and extends into Guatemala.

# TAPACHULA & THE CHIAPAS COAST

*Tapachula lies along Highway 200 near the Guatemalan border.*

**Tapachula** is a steamy, undistinguished and rather expensive town near the southern tip of Mexico. It is the unofficial capital of the **Soconusco**, as Chiapas's broad coastal plain is known. There is little reason to pass through Tapachula unless you are on your way to or from Guatemala, which is certainly reason enough. The Guatemalan consulate may well be the spot in Tapachula that is most visited by foreign tourists, and with the easing of visa regulations even that flow has slowed to a trickle. El Salvador also has a consulate here. There are two important **border crossings** nearby, known on the Mexican side as **Talismán** and **Ciudad Hidalgo**.

Tapachula does not lie directly on the Pacific coast, and the "coastal" highway that runs northwest from Tapachula is really an inland highway with a few spurs going to the coast. Beaches in Chiapas are generally unattractive, of dark sand, ill kept, and mostly bereft of services. The state tourism board has talked of developing Barra San José about 40 km northwest of Tapachula, which would also be a jumping-off point for nature tours of nearby estuaries and forests, but so far nobody with money is stepping forward.

The closest Chiapas comes to a beach resort is **Puerto Arista** near the city of Tonalá and close to the boundary with Oaxaca state, but it's not a place to go out of your way to visit.

## ARRIVALS & DEPARTURES: TAPACHULA

### By Air

Aeroméxico, Aviacsa and TAESA all fly daily from Mexico City. Aviacsa also goes to Tuxtla Gutiérrez, with connections to or from Oaxaca, Villahermosa, Mérida and Cancún. The airport lies 17 km southwest of the city on the road to Puerto Madero. You can use local buses if you haven't much baggage. Collective vans charge $5 for door-to-door service. Call (962) 51287 for pick-up in the city. Taxis charge about $11. The airport code is TAP.

### By Bus

Each bus company has its own terminal in Tapachula. For first-class buses, the Cristóbal Colón terminal is at 17 Calle Oriente and 3a Avenida Norte, a short distance from the city center. Sur second-class buses use this same terminal. First-class overnight service to Mexico City (20 hours, $41-$50) runs nine times daily, with departures between early afternoon and late evening. There is one overnight bus to Oaxaca (11 hours, $21). Other buses serve Salina Cruz, with connections to the Oaxaca coast. Two daytime buses go to San Cristóbal de las Casas (7 hours, $11) via Comitán. There are many buses to Arriaga, Tuxtla Gutiérrez and intermediate points between 7 am and midnight. The Cristóbal Colón terminal does not store baggage, but Restaurant Viajero across the street offers this service. Fletes y Pasajes and Autotransportes Tuxtla Gutiérrez provide long-haul second-class services from other terminals.

For connections to Guatemala, Pullman de Chiapas runs four times an hour to Ciudad Hidalgo. Its terminal is one block from the Cristóbal Colón terminal (turn left as you leave the latter). Unión y Progreso has frequent minibus service between Talismán and 5a Calle Poniente in Tapachula. From both border points, many buses go to Guatemala City. With an early start, it is possible to reach San Salvador in a single day.

### By Car

Highway 200 is Tapachula's main lifeline to the rest of the Mexico and was in the process of being widened to four lanes over part of its length.

Highway 195 meets Highway 200 near Tapachula, running to Comitán, San Cristóbal de las Casas and beyond. There are two highways to the Guatemalan border a short distance east or south.

**By Rail**

A daily passenger train inches its way between Tapachula and Veracruz via Juchitán and Tuxtepec. Service is so slow, uncomfortable and unreliable that it cannot be recommended even for railway buffs.

## ORIENTATION

Tapachula is mostly flat and is laid out on the familiar rectangular grid pattern, with most streets and avenues numbered rather than named. The lower the number, the closer you are to the center. Taxis and local buses serve all parts of the city. Getting to and from the border crossings at Ciudad Hidalgo or Talismán, there are many buses and collective taxis leaving from several places in the city. Shared vans can take you from the airport to the border (but not in the opposite direction).

## WHERE TO STAY

The more comfortable hotels are mostly situated outside the city center. Hotels in all categories tend to be more expensive in Tapachula than elsewhere in southern Mexico. The selection of budget hotels is rather poor, but we have a few suggestions anyway.

**HOTEL KAMICO**, *Calle Central Oriente, on the highway toward the border, phone (962) 62640, fax (962) 61878; 92 rooms, $77 single, $89 double, VI - MC - AE - DC.*

Two long two-story buildings are separated by a garden and pool. Rooms are large, with air conditioning and television, and have white-washed stucco walls. Rooms away from the highway are quieter. Pleasant restaurant.

**HOTEL LOMA REAL**, *Carretera Costera km 244, phone (962) 61440, fax (962) 64817; 96 rooms, $99 single, $104 double, VI - MC - AE - DC.*

This hotel is situated on a remote hilltop at the western edge of town. Rooms are large and fairly ordinary. Air conditioning, television, pool, restaurant.

**HOTEL CABILDO'S**, *2a Avenida Norte #17 between 1a and 3a Calles Poniente, phone (962) 66606, fax (962) 66611; 29 rooms, $58 single, $69 double, VI - MC - AE.*

This is a modern, quiet, three-story city-center hotel. All rooms face the pool and have air conditioning and television.

**HOTEL DON MIGUEL**, *1a Calle Poniente #18 between 4a and 6a Avenidas Norte, phone (962) 61143, fax (962) 61059; 39 rooms, $48 single, $59 double, VI - MC - AE.*

Rooms are large and quiet but rather ugly. Air conditioning, television.

**HOTEL SANTA JULIA**, *17 Calle Oriente next to the Cristóbal Colón terminal, phone (962) 63140; 21 rooms, $26 single, $28 double, no credit cards.*
This hotel offers bright, simple, air-conditioned rooms. Those on the street side are noisy.

**HOSPEDAJE CHELITO**, *1a Avenida Oriente #107, around the corner from the Cristóbal Colón terminal; 13 rooms, $15 single, $19 double with fan; $23 single, $28 double with air conditioning; no credit cards.*
Rooms are quiet and reasonably furnished, but most are dark and some have no outside window.

**HOTEL FÉNIX**, *4a Avenida Norte #19 between 1a and 3a Calles Poniente, phone (962) 50755, fax (962) 64747; 47 rooms; $19 single, $22 double with fan; $24 single, $28 double with air conditioning; VI - MC.*
Rooms are quiet and fairly basic. They vary considerably. Some face a garden, others face parking areas or corridors. Some rooms with air conditioning are less appealing than some without.

## WHERE TO EAT

**QUINTA CARMELITO**, *on the highway east of town near the Hotel Kamico*, has a pleasant garden terrace and a broad choice of Mexican dishes. **VILLA JARDIN**, *on the highway just west of town*, specializes in seafood.

In the city center, two Chinese restaurants, **MENG CHENG** (the better of the two) and **CHUNG SEAK** stare at each other across *1a Calle Poniente between 2a and 4a Avenidas Norte.* **HOSTAL DEL REY**, *on 4a Avenida Norte near 1a Calle Poniente,* has an attractive dining room with Mexican dishes and moderate prices. **LOS COMALES**, *facing the zócalo,* is open all night.

## SEEING THE SIGHTS

The *zócalo*, or **central plaza**, is notable mainly for the rectangular shapes into which its trees and shrubs have been trimmed. Facing it is the **Museo Regional del Soconusco** with archaeological and historical displays, *open 10 am to 5 pm daily except Monday, admission $3, free on Sunday.*

The museum is housed in the handsome *palacio municipal*, with its distinctive clock. Next door is the small and undistinguished cathedral. In between is a monument to 19th century reformist president Benito Juárez.

## EXCURSIONS

Outside Tapachula, *12 km to the southeast,* lie the **Izapa ruins**, reached by the Talismán branch of the highway to Guatemala, just beyond where the road forks. Walking or driving 1 km along a poorly marked dirt road to the right, you reach two small groups of stelae and mounds. About 500 meters further along the highway, on the left, are other small stone formations. At each of the three groups someone will ask you to sign a book and "donate" $2. Izapa is thought to mark a link between the ancient Olmecs and Mayas. It will be of interest mostly to true archaeology buffs.

**Puerto Madero**, *27 km southwest of Tapachula,* is a seedy port and beach resort with a handful of small restaurants and a dirty, unpleasant beach.

## PRACTICAL INFORMATION

**Airline Offices**
• **Aeroméxico**: *2a Avenida Norte #6, phone (962) 62050*
• **Aviacsa**: *Avenida Central Norte #52-B, phone (962) 63147*
• **TAESA**: *1a Calle Poniente #8, phone (962) 63732*

**Car Rentals**
Available at the airport and at several of the bigger hotels.

**Consulates**
• **Guatemala**: *2a Calle Oriente #33 between 7a and 9a Avenidas Sur, phone (962) 61252. Open weekdays 9 am to 2 pm*
• **El Salvador**: *Prologación Avenida de Las Palmas, Manzana 35, Casa No. L 8-C, Fraccionamiento Los Laureles, phone (962) 64822*

**Currency Exchange**
Banks in Tapachula provide slow service and poor rates. **Cambios Tapachula** *at the corner of 4a Avenida Norte and 3a Calle Poniente* also offers poor rates, but service is fast and opening hours are long, including weekends. Tapachula is the only city in Mexico where it is easy to exchange Guatemalan quetzals. Many money changers work at the border crossings, but the only way to know if you are getting a decent rate is to ask for both their buying and selling rates and see how wide apart they are.

**Tourist Information**
There are **tourism information booths** at the airport and, in the city center, *at 4a Avenida Norte #35.*

# PUERTO ARISTA

> *Puerto Arista lies 18 km southwest of the city of Tonalá, near the western edge of the Soconusco plain.*

**Puerto Arista** features a long gray sand beach and a very relaxed pace. Few people from outside Chiapas venture here. It's not somewhere you would go out of your way to reach, but if you're in the middle of a long trip by road it may be a suitable place to rest. It is served by frequent minibuses from **Tonalá**, which lies along Highway 200 and is served in turn by many long-distance buses. (Tonalá has a tiny archaeological museum and a carved stele in its *zócalo*, but is otherwise of limited interest to visitors.)

Two things to watch out for at Puerto Arista are the strong riptides and the three-wheeled motorcycles that go whizzing along the beach. Local authorities might also do more to clear the beach of litter. You can make a short excursion to Boca del Cielo to enjoy its estuary and safer swimming.

## WHERE TO STAY

**HOTEL ARISTA BUGAMBILIAS**, *near the west edge of town, has 25 rooms at $60 a night, VI - MC*, with air conditioning, television, pool and an open-air restaurant. It tends to fill up on weekends. **HOTEL LA PUESTA**, *in the center of town, 11 rooms at $21 to $30 a night, depending on season*, is a simple, family-run place. There are also several cheaper spots. **AGUA MARINA**, *nearby*, is among the better ones.

## WHERE TO EAT

The many palapa-shaded restaurants along the beach serve fresh fish. The one at **Hotel La Puesta** is good.

# 14. OAXACA

The state of **Oaxaca** (pronounced wa-KHA-ca) has sometimes been called Mexico's spiritual reserve, and it's not hard to see why. Here, more than almost anywhere else, Mexico's Spanish colonial past and its Indian past – and present – come together in a way that, without shutting out the modern world, keeps it at a respectable distance.

In the Oaxaca heartland, the traditional cultural values of Mexico stand front and center. The city of Oaxaca and many smaller towns are places where people of all ages still gather for evening strolls in lively *zócalos* (central plazas). Old-fashioned public markets are hives of commercial activity and also fill an important social role. Modern ideas of progress and contemporary values of consumerism seem to take a back seat here.

Handsome stone buildings and cobbled streets bear witness to a colonial past stretching back to the sixteenth century, and the faces and clothing to be seen in streets and markets let alone the ancient ruins are clear reminders that civilization here reaches back very much further than that. More than any physical trait, though, there is a special feeling in the air that is difficult to describe but comes across unmistakably once you arrive.

## OAXACA'S BEGINNINGS

Even today Oaxaca is heavily influenced by the Zapotec Indian culture. In ancient times the city of **Monte Albán** became the center of Zapotec life. Construction began about 2,500 years ago. The Zapotecs gradually extended their control over the central valleys and beyond. Their culture reached its peak between the third and eighth centuries A.D. Toward the end of this period there was a sudden and unexplained collapse.

Mixtecs who migrated from the west and north came to dominate much of the area in the 13th century, and they in turn were overwhelmed

# OAXACA AREA

TO TUXTEPEC

146 km TO TEHUACAN

Guelatao de Juarez
Ixtlan
Capulaplan de Menedez

Telixlahuaca

San Pablo Huitzo

El Punto

San Jose El Mogote

Atzompa

OAXACA

Santa Maria El Tule

Teotitlandel Valle

Monte Alban

Tlacoghahuaya

Cuilapan

Dianzu

Yagul

Villa de Mitla

Zaachila

San Bartolo
Coyotepec

Tlacolula

Xaaga

Santo Tomas Jalieza

San Antonio Castillo Velasco

209 km TO
TEHUANTEPEC
& CHIAPAS

Ocotlan

N

217 km TO PUNTO ANGEL
& PUNTO ESCONDIDO

by Aztecs from central Mexico in the mid-15th century. Less than a century later it was the turn of the Spanish to conquer the central valleys.

In the 19th century Oaxaca produced two leaders who were to have a profound impact on all of Mexico. **Benito Juárez**, a Zapotec from the north of the state, became state governor and later president of Mexico, establishing liberal reforms in the domains of education, civil rights and the separation of church and state. Elected president in 1857, he was ousted by European intervention in 1863. **Porfirio Díaz**, who had succeeded Juárez as governor of Oaxaca, controlled Mexico with an iron first from 1876 to 1910, doing much to promote the country's economic development but also leading a despotic and repressive regime, which ended with the outbreak of the Mexican Revolution.

Oaxaca today is one of the poorest states in Mexico, and the question of land ownership is still far from settled. There is little manufacturing, and agriculture is hindered by poor soils, inadequate water supply, and deforestation.

## OAXACA HIGHLIGHTS

*The Pacific coast of Oaxaca provides a stunning contrast. Its offerings range from the chic, newly created resort town of **Huatulco** to the more laid-back **Puerto Escondido** and the even more casual beachside villages of **Puerto Angel** and **Zipolite**. Although still part of Oaxaca, the coastal area presents a very different face.*

*Two mountain ranges sweep across Oaxaca state. Between them lie the central valleys, where the city of Oaxaca is situated. There are lowland areas in the east toward the isthmus of **Tehuantepec** and in the north near the boundary with Veracruz state. There is a narrow plain along part of the Pacific coast. The low-lying zones tend to be hotter and wetter than the mountain areas and the central valleys, parts of which are fairly arid.*

### Planning Your Stay in Oaxaca

Europeans come to Mexico to see the ruins and museums, while Americans head straight for the beaches, or so we sometimes hear. While there is a grain of truth to this, the reality is rather less simple. Many Americans visit the ruins, and there is no scarcity of Europeans on the beaches.

People interested in ancient culture or modern hedonism (or both) will be well looked after in Oaxaca state whichever continent they happen to come from. It is a little harder to reach than parts of Mexico that have better international airline connections, but the rewards are many.

The **city of Oaxaca**, smack in the middle of the state, is well endowed with markets, museums and colonial architecture. Its leafy, car-free central plaza simply happens to be one of the most wonderful places on earth, with its quiet bustle, its great splashes of human color, its sidewalk cafés, and the feeling it conveys of being in the center of things.

Oaxaca is also a base for excursions throughout the central valleys of the state. Popular among visitors are the elaborate Zapotec ruins at **Monte Albán** on a hilltop just outside the city. Also popular are the ruins at **Mitla**, 70 km east of the city, smaller but noteworthy for the fine detail of their carvings. Many points of interest lie along that route, including the giant tree at **El Tule** and towns known for their markets, traditional weaving activities and churches.

Speaking of markets, several towns near Oaxaca have splendid weekly gatherings of Indians from neighboring villages. These weekly markets are held on different days of the week in different towns so that you can see at least one during your stay. If you decide to visit the mountain village of **Guelatao**, the birthplace of Benito Juárez, there is wonderful scenery along the route.

As for the beach resorts, **Huatulco** provides opulent accommodations nestled into a series of nine bays. It is newer and more intimate than Cancún or Acapulco. **Puerto Escondido**, which literally means *hidden port*, is an older spot with a laid-back atmosphere, gorgeous sunsets, many small, moderately-priced hotels, and a good surfing beach. It feels more genuinely Mexican than the bigger resorts, and it lies near the lagoons of **Manialtepec** and **Chacahua**, of special interest to bird-watchers.

Cosier still is **Puerto Angel**, which lies between Huatulco and Puerto Escondido. And just a few kilometers away is **Zipolite**, where most visitors sleep in hammocks and many dispense with swimsuits.

Most other parts of Oaxaca offer little that will interest many visitors. This is especially true of the eastern part of the state, where three sizable towns – **Salina Cruz**, **Tehuantepec**, and **Juchitán** – are huddled near the **Gulf of Tehuantepec**. Visitors traveling overland to or from Chiapas will have occasion to pass through this area, and the best advice is to stay on the move.

If you must stop along the way, Tehuantepec is not quite as grotesquely unattractive as its two neighbors. **Salina Cruz** is a singularly unpleasant industrial port and oil refining center; **Juchitán** is a bedraggled place much studied by sociologists because of its female-dominated social structures and its left-wing voting patterns, but casual visitors are unlikely to want to linger even out of feminist conviction.

# OAXACA CITY & VALLEYS

> *Oaxaca lies at the junction of Routes 190 (connection to Mexico City) and Route 175 (connection with the Gulf of Mexico and the Pacific coast.*

It won't be long after you arrive in Oaxaca before you've caught a sense of this city's subtle magic. The past is alive and well in its stately colonial streets, some bounded by somber stone structures, others lined by stucco-covered buildings painted in lively pastel hues. The Indian traditions of Oaxaca also live on, in the faces of many of its people, in the languages they speak, in the dishes that influence local eating habits and, for visitors who want to carry home a reminder, in a rich variety of quality handicrafts.

The population of Oaxaca is thought to be well above 300,000, although this is disputed. The official 1990 census gave what many think is an unrealistically low figure. The city lies at an altitude of 1,550 meters (5,100 feet) above sea level, assuring a pleasant, spring-like climate most of the year. Days are warm, but temperatures rarely rise to extreme levels. Evenings are sometimes a bit cool, especially from December to February. The center of the city is mostly flat, but there are hills toward the northwest.

No visit to Oaxaca is complete without spending at least a couple of hours in the *zócalo*, the magical and magnetic **central plaza** where families gather for evening strolls, where balloon vendors, shoeshine men and serenading musicians ply their trades, and where life unfolds in all sorts of little ways much as it has for centuries. Whether your time at the *zócalo* is spent watching a bandstand concert, imbibing something at one of many outdoor cafés, or simply witnessing the passing scene, it is not something to be missed.

Oaxaca is a city of museums and old churches and markets, and it lies at the center of a valley full of towns renowned for their ancient ruins or their contemporary weavings or their vibrant weekly fairs. Even the quickest of visits requires at least a day and a half, with a full day to capture some of the highlights of the city plus another several hours for an excursion to the ruins at **Monte Albán**. But that's not really the way to do it. You'll want to allow yourself time to soak up the special atmosphere of the city and to visit a couple of the outlying towns.

If you decide, say, to spend three or four days in Oaxaca, you'll want to get an idea of the general layout of the place. You could start with a visit to the tourism office to get maps and other bits of information. If you're uneasy about doing excursions on your own, you'll also want to stop in at one or two travel agencies or hotel tour desks to see what organized tours

**OAXACA STREET SCENE**

are available. There are several travel agencies around the *zócalo*. Prices and offerings tend to be similar. You are certain to find trips to the archaeological sites at Monte Albán and Mitla. Then after making your arrangements, just head off on foot and start to explore the city.

You'll want to allow yourself some flexibility, but do try to set aside a half-day to see the ruins at Monte Albán. You'll also want to leave a morning free to visit one of the weekly Indian markets in the outlying towns (the biggest and easiest to reach are at **Etla** on Wednesdays, **Zaachila** on Thursdays, **Ocotlán** on Fridays and **Tlacolula** on Sundays), as well as a half-day back in Oaxaca to visit **Santo Domingo church**, the **Regional Museum of Anthropology and History**, and the **Rufino Tamayo Museum of Prehispanic Art**. An additional half-day, or more, can be devoted to other museums and churches in Oaxaca.

The ruins at **Mitla** are further away and less spectacular than Monte Albán but still make for a worthwhile trip. If you want to make a full day of it, you can combine it with a visit to the Sunday market at **Tlacolula**, which is on the way. You can add a brief stop to see the giant tree at **El Tule** and a visit to **Teotitlán del Valle** or **Santa Ana del Valle**, towns near Tlacolula that are noted for their weavings.

Finally, you may want to set some time aside to shop for handicrafts or just to unwind. Even on your busy days, you may find yourself spending your late afternoons and early evenings relaxing at a café by the *zócalo*.

## ARRIVALS & DEPARTURES

**By Air**

Oaxaca's airport (airport code OAX) lies 8 km south of the city. It has not been designated for international service, meaning that all passengers arriving from abroad must first complete immigration and customs formalities in Mexico City or some other transit point. Mexicana, Aeroméxico, and Aviacsa together provide six to eight daily flights between Oaxaca and Mexico City. Daily jet service is available on Aviacsa and Aerocaribe (a Mexicana affiliate) to Tuxtla Gutiérrez, Villahermosa, Mérida and Cancún. Aeromorelos flies turboprop aircraft to Huatulco and Puerto Escondido at high fares. An air charter service called Aerovega was offering cheaper fares; enquire at the Hotel Monte Albán.

Getting to and from the airport, you can choose between an $11 taxi ride or a $3-per-passenger charge for door-to-door service by collective van. Vans are operated by Transportación Terrestre Aeropuerto and leave the airport shortly after the arrival of each flight. Tickets may be purchased at the airport or in town from a small office facing the Alameda de León, open 10 am to 2 pm and 5 pm to 8 pm Monday to Saturday. To arrange a pickup call (951) 44350. There is no public bus service to the airport, and the terminal building is too far from the highway for most people to want to walk it.

**By Bus**

ADO and Cristóbal Colón together account for most first-class services to and from Oaxaca. They share a terminal on Avenida Chapultepec, about 1.5 km north of the city center. Buses to and from Mexico City's TAPO (Eastern) Terminal leave at least once an hour from 6 am until early afternoon, and there are many overnight services. There are also a handful of services to and from Mexico City's Tasqueña (Southern) Terminal. Fares between Mexico City and Oaxaca range mostly from $20 to $23. On deluxe services with extra-large seats the fare is $36. Travel time is nine to ten hours. With the opening of the new highway travel time will be shortened considerably, and there will probably be new mid-afternoon and late-afternoon departures.

*Other first-class services:* There are morning and evening departures to Veracruz ($19, eight hours), overnight services to Villahermosa ($22, ten hours) with connections to the Yucatán, a morning departure to San Cristóbal de Las Casas ($19, nine hours), morning and evening departures to Tuxtla Gutiérrez ($16, seven hours) with connections to San Cristóbal, overnight to Tapachula ($21, ten hours) near the Guatemalan border, and many departures to Tehuantepec and Salina Cruz.

There are also morning and evening departures to Huatulco and Puerto Escondido, but these take the long route via Salina Cruz. This is all right for Huatulco ($13, six hours), but for Puerto Escondido or Puerto Angel the trip is very long and you may do better to take a second-class bus on the short route via Miahuatlán and Pochutla.

If you have time to kill while waiting for your bus, the restaurant of the Hotel Veracruz, almost next door to the first-class terminal, is a bit pricey but is certainly more comfortable than the terminal itself.

*Second-class services:* The second-class terminal is a huge semi-circular building one km west of the city center. Each bus company has its own ticket counter, and finding the right one can be bewildering. Fletes y Pasajes has the biggest operation here, and some taxi drivers, when you ask for this terminal, will ask if you mean the Fletes terminal.

Most services to Puerto Escondido and other points on the Pacific coast of Oaxaca leave from here, and they go mostly in the early morning or at night, with fares set at about $7. Several companies compete on the Puerto Escondido route, including Autotransportes de la Solteca, Autotransportes Oaxaca-Pacífico and Autobuses Estrella del Valle.

Fletes y Pasajes, Transportes Oaxaca-Istmo and some smaller bus lines offer frequent departures to points throughout the central valleys of Oaxaca. Most of these leave from the area toward the right of the terminal as you enter. Buses to Mitla and intermediate points leave several times an hour. Fletes y Pasajes ranges as far as Mexico City, with second-class services several times during the day plus frequently overnight for a fare of $17. Transportes Oaxaca-Istmo has the most frequent service to Tehuantepec, with connections or continuations to Juchitán, Salina Cruz and points in Chiapas; departures are every 60 to 90 minutes from early morning to mid-evening.

### By Car

Oaxaca lies at the junction of two main highways. Route 190 provides the main link from Mexico City and points in Puebla state, continuing southeast to the Gulf of Tehuantepec and on into Chiapas, while Route 175 runs from the Gulf of Mexico in the north to the Pacific coast at Puerto Ángel to the south.

Other highways provide links to many points in Oaxaca, Puebla, and Veracruz states. A new toll highway, completing a fast link from Mexico City via the cities of Puebla and Tehuacán, was scheduled to open at the end of 1994. This was expected to lop about three hours off the travel time from Mexico City, bringing it to under six hours.

### By Rail

Passenger train service to Oaxaca has fallen into a sad state of decay, but there are still opportunities for the dedicated rail fan. The station is situated about 1.5 km northwest of the city center. Overnight trains to and from Mexico City are scheduled to take 14 hours but often take much longer. Sleeping cars and dining cars have vanished from this route. Scheduled departure time at each end is 7 pm. Fares are cheaper than by bus and there is more baggage space. For most passengers these are the main attractions.

There is fine mountain scenery along the rail line running northwest from Oaxaca. One way to enjoy it is by taking the even slower day train to Puebla, which leaves Oaxaca daily at 7:35 am (check at the station the day before to be sure). Only a true fanatic should choose to ride the train the whole way. The alternative is to check a good map for suitable intermediate points and to continue or double back by bus (nearly always faster and more reliable). You can take the train for the short hop from Oaxaca to Zaachila and Ocotlán (7:40 am departure, but check ahead).

## ORIENTATION

The **main tourism information office**, *corner of 5 de Mayo and Morelos, three blocks from the zócalo; open from 8 am to 8 pm Monday to Friday, 9 am to 8 pm Saturday and Sunday; phone (951) 64828,* has helpful staff and long opening hours, something of a rarity. Some of the staff speak English, and free maps are available. This office also helps with complaints and with problems such as lost documents. A **branch office** *nearby on Alcalá street between Morelos and Matamoros is open daily 10 am to 2 pm and 4 pm to 8 pm.* The **airport tourism office** *is open Monday to Friday 7 am to 2 pm and 4 pm to 7 pm, and on Saturday and Sunday 9 am to 2 pm.* Finally, there is a tourism office at the **Monte Albán archaeological site**, *open daily 9 am to 3 pm.*

If this is your first visit to Oaxaca, you'll quickly discover that most of what you're coming to see in the city is planted firmly in the central area. Museums, old churches, handicrafts markets, most hotels and many restaurants are squeezed into a fairly compact area with streets laid out in a rectangular grid pattern in the Spanish colonial style.

At the center of the mini-universe that is Oaxaca lies the *zócalo*, the majestic, tree-shaded **central plaza**. Both the *zócalo* and the adjacent **Alameda de León**, facing the cathedral, are pedestrian-only zones. The *zócalo* is lined on three sides with cafés, restaurants, and hotels; on the fourth side is the **Palacio de Gobierno**, the seat of the state government.

A second pole of interest is the area around **Santo Domingo church** *five blocks to the north*, linked most of the way by pedestrian-only Alcalá street. Many shops, handicrafts stalls and restaurants line the plaza and the streets nearby, particularly to the east and south of the church. The area between Santo Domingo and the *zócalo* constitutes the more fashionable part of central Oaxaca. Here you will find most of the museums and much of the interesting architecture, as well as many hotels, restaurants and shops.

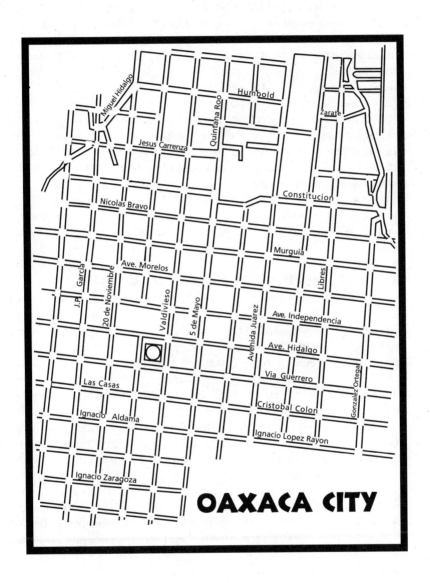

OAXACA CITY

The area south of the *zócalo* is somewhat seedier. Apart from the big handicrafts and clothing market, you'll find relatively little of interest here. This area can be a bit rough after dark.

Many streets change names as they pass through the center of the city, in some instances more than once. Thus Alcalá street, to take one example, becomes Valdivieso street south of Morelos avenue and Bustamante street south of the *zócalo* one street but three different names, depending how far north or south you are. To take another example, Guerrero street east of the *zócalo* becomes Trujano street west of the *zócalo*. Looking at a map, you'll see many other such examples.

If you arrive by air, you'll be approaching the city from the south and will get an idea of the general unattractiveness of the outskirts. For motorists, Pereférico boulevard skirts the center of the city on the south and east, changing names further north to Calzada Vasconcelos. This road intersects with Calzada de Chapultepec, which skirts the city center on the north. These roads, in turn, lead to the main highways.

Monte Albán and the other archaeological sites are located some distance outside the city. Further information appears below in the Excursions section.

## GETTING AROUND OAXACA & ENVIRONS

In most circumstances, your own feet will be the most useful way of getting around the center of Oaxaca. As we mentioned before, the *zócalo* and the adjacent Alameda de León are closed to motor traffic, as are the five-block stretch of Alcalá street heading up to Santo Domingo church and a shorter stretch of 5 de Mayo street. Most points you'll want to visit in the center of town are within easy walking distance of each other. Streets are narrow, speeds are slow, and parking is scarce, which does not exactly add up to a motorists' paradise.

Taxis, of course, will be useful for getting to and from hotels if you have lots of baggage. If you're staying in the area south of the market you may want to consider taxis for reasons of security when going back late at night. Although neither bus terminal is very far from the center of town, the walk is not very pleasant and taxis make things a lot easier. Unless you're going to an outlying area, fares will be under $3. Be aware that taxis are not metered. If you're going more than a short distance, agree first on the fare to avoid any nasty arguments later. City buses operate mostly on routes between the city center or the second-class bus terminal and suburban areas of little interest to most visitors.

For information on getting to and from Monte Albán, see the Excursions section below. For most other excursions outside Oaxaca, you have several options. You can take an organized tour, you can go by public bus (there are frequent departures from the second-class terminal to most places you will want to see), you can rent a car, or you can hire a taxi at a negotiated hourly or daily rate. Given the expense of the last two options, they will be more palatable for groups of three to five people.

If you decide on a taxi, try to select a vehicle that seems to be in reasonable shape and make very certain that you and the driver have a firm understanding of the time and the itinerary involved. Choose one person from your group to do the negotiating, or ask a hotel clerk to negotiate on your behalf.

## WHERE TO STAY

Oaxaca is a pleasant city for walking but rather less good for driving or parking. A good choice of hotels in many price ranges lies within easy walking distance of the *zócalo*, the focal point of the city. Museums, shopping, and restaurants are close by. All this is by way of saying that it will make sense for most visitors to seek lodgings in the center of town.

There are some good hotels toward the outskirts that we mention further down, but the spaciousness, the athletic facilities, and the peace and quiet some of them provide are offset by the inconvenience of getting there and back.

In general, the streets to the north of the *zócalo* are more attractive than those to the south and lie closer to many points of interest. You will find a bigger concentration of budget hotels toward the south, particularly along or near Avenida 20 de Noviembre, but there are some inexpensive choices to the north also. In many hotels you may have to choose between quiet but dark rooms facing the interior of the hotel or brighter but noisier rooms facing the street.

Not every hotel can provide rooms that are both bright and quiet. We point out some that do. Air conditioning is a rarity in Oaxaca but, because of the altitude, temperatures are seldom uncomfortable

### Hotels North of the Zócalo

**HOTEL CAMINO REAL OAXACA** *(formerly the Hotel Presidente), 5 de Mayo 300, phone (951) 60611, fax (951) 60732, US and Canada reservations 800-996-7325; 91 rooms, rates for single or double occupancy: $143 for ordinary rooms, $159 for superior rooms, $176 for deluxe rooms, $220 for suites; VI - MC - AE - DC.*

This is *the* place to stay if you've got the money. Situated on a quiet side street south of Santo Domingo church, this hotel occupies a magnificently adapted sixteenth-century convent with five interior courtyards. The rooms, restaurant and pool are set around the various courtyards, most of them fragrant with tropical vegetation. The street outside is closed to motor traffic so that even the rooms facing the street are quiet.

Rooms are beautifully decorated in shades of dark red, ochre, beige and mauve, with wooden beams, stone arches and plenty of painted tiles. Service is reputed to be very good, as befits the price. The restaurant, El Refectorio, is moderately priced and has a varied menu with Mexican and international specialties. A folkloric show is presented Saturday evenings.

**HOTEL LAS GOLONDRINAS**, *Tinoco y Palacios 411, phone (951) 68726, fax (951) 42126; 27 rooms, $20 single, $26 double, cash only.*

This newish and economical hotel, set in a cluster of low-slung buildings, provides excellent value for money even though it's a good six blocks from the *zócalo* and three blocks from the Alcalá pedestrian street. Rooms are set around three patios with exuberant but carefully tended vegetation. The rooms themselves are furnished very simply, accented with regional handicrafts to lend some color. There are no phones or TV in the rooms, although the lounge in front has a TV. Staff are friendly, and all rooms are set well back from the street, assuring a quiet atmosphere. Very good breakfasts are served in one of the patios. Las Golondrinas means, literally, the swallows.

**HOTEL PARADOR PLAZA**, *Murguía 104 among 5 de Mayo and Alcalá, phone (951) 41977, 42027, fax (951) 42037; 59 rooms, $42 single, $50 double, VI - MC - AE.*

Strategically situated midway between the *zócalo* and Santo Domingo, this hotel offers rooms set around a modern courtyard and attractively furnished in shades of grey, blue and pale orange. Service is friendly, but you face that annoying tradeoff between bright but noisy rooms facing the street and quiet but dark rooms on the far side. The restaurant, El Andador, is good and reasonably priced.

**HOTEL CALESA REAL**, *García Vigil 306 between Matamoros and N. Bravo, phone (951) 65544; 77 rooms, $50 single or double, $59 triple, VI - MC - AE.*

The location is good, service is attentive, and there is plenty of broadloom and tile here, but long hallways lead to rather dark if pleasantly furnished rooms. Restaurant, small pool.

**HOTEL PRINCIPAL**, *5 de Mayo 208 between Murguía and Morelos, phone (951) 62535; 16 rooms, $20 single, $25 double, cash only.*

Big rooms, simply but pleasantly furnished, are set around a bright courtyard.

**POSADA MARGARITA**, *Labástida 115, phone (951) 62802; 14 rooms, $12 single, $15 double, cash only.*

This quiet, humble hotel is well situated, facing an attractive *plazuela*, or small plaza. Its interior patio provides an interesting view of Santo Domingo church. Rooms are simple and a little on the scruffy side.

### Hotels Around the Zócalo and to the East

**HOTEL MARQUÉS DEL VALLE,** *entrance on the Alameda de León, next to the cathedral, phone (951) 63677, 63198, 63295, fax (951) 69961; 95 rooms, $42 single, $45 double, VI - MC - AE.*

This hotel is an old favorite among some seasoned visitors to Oaxaca. Facing the Alameda de León on one side and the *zócalo* on the other, it lies in a car-free zone, which means taxis can't drop you right at the door but also means you can step outside without the annoyance of traffic. Rooms are spacious if rather ordinary in their furnishings and are set around a sort of curving atrium. A number of rooms have good views of the *zócalo* and are bright and cheery, although at night, especially on weekends, there can be noise from serenading mariachis and other musicians – not a drawback for everyone. On the other hand, you can take in the bandstand concerts without even leaving your room. Rooms on the interior side of the hotel are quieter but darker.

**HOTEL SEÑORIAL,** *on the west side of the zócalo, phone (951) 63933; 105 rooms, $32 single, $40 double, cash only.*

Although cheaper than the Hotel Marques del Valle, the Señorial is poorer value. Most rooms are quite dark, and even those at the front of the hotel are separated from the *zócalo* by narrow terraces. On the other hand, it's quiet, and the restaurant is reasonably good.

**HOTEL MONTE ALBÁN,** *on the Alameda de León, phone (951) 62777; 20 rooms, $27 single, $33 double for bright rooms facing the plaza, $20 single, $25 double for windowless rooms on the interior side, cash only.*

Housed in a colonial building with a big covered courtyard, this hotel fills up early. Although rooms are small and simple, the location and the price are right. Folkloric shows are presented here each evening.

**HOSTAL DE LA NORIA,** *Hidalgo 918, phone (951) 47844, fax (951) 63992; 54 rooms, $54 single, $63 double, $72 triple; VI - MC - AE - DC.*

This Best Western affiliate (not to be confused with the Hotel Hacienda La Noria that is away from the center though under the same management), is situated just a block east of the *zócalo*. The building looks as if it has been around for centuries, but in fact it was erected only in the early 1990s using colonial architecture as a model. The rooms and the interior courtyard in this pretty new hotel are lovingly decorated in shades of brown, pale orange and dark mauve with lavish furnishings including some very substantial wooden furniture. Although there can be some street noise, rooms facing the street are fitted with heavy wooden shutters to muffle the sound. Rooms are equipped with TV, phones and ceiling fans, and there is a small restaurant. This hotel represents very good value.

**HOTEL GALA,** *Bustamante 103 just off the southeast corner of the zócalo, phone (951) 42251, 41305, fax (951) 63660; 36 rooms, $50 single, $58 double, VI - MC - AE.*

Lovely furniture and art fill the public areas and hallways, and rooms are nicely decorated in different shades of blue, with phone and TV. Again, rooms facing the street are brighter and a little less quiet, but there is not much street noise here.

**HOTEL LAS ROSAS**, *Trujano 112 near the zócalo, phone (951) 42217; 19 rooms, $20 single, $26 double, VI - MC.*

The entrance here is upstairs from the street, and there is a small, bright courtyard. Rooms are simple but pleasant, and most are quiet.

**HOTEL REAL DE ANTEQUERA**, *Hidalgo 807 near the zócalo, phone (951) 64020, 64635; 25 rooms, $23 single, $27 double, VI - MC - AE - DC.*

Rooms vary in size and brightness, with most set around a covered courtyard and some with balconies. All have phones, TV and fan, but there is a general scruffiness to the place.

**POSADA SAN PABLO**, *Fiallo 102 between Independencia and Hidalgo, phone (951) 64914; 20 rooms, $32 single, $40 double, cash only.*

A pity about the poor state of cleanliness, for the big suite-style units in this venerable building not far from the *zócalo* could be quite a bargain. Sitting areas face the street, while bedrooms are further inside and escape most of the noise. Each unit also has cooking facilities.

### Hotels South and West of the Zócalo

**HOSTAL SANTA ROSA**, *Trujano 201 at the corner of 20 de Noviembre, phone (951) 46714, 46715; 17 rooms, $23 single, $30 double, cash only but was applying to accept Visa and Mastercard.*

Near the market, this small hotel is newly renovated, bright and sparkling, but rooms facing the street are noisy.

**HOTEL MESÓN DEL REY**, *Trujano 212 between 20 de Noviembre and Juárez, phone (951) 60033, 60181, fax (951) 61434; 27 rooms, $20 single, $26 double, cash only.*

Some rooms are dark but others are quite pleasant. Friendly atmosphere.

**HOTEL POSADA DEL CARMEN**, *20 de Noviembre 712 between Zaragoza and Arista, phone (951) 61779; 27 rooms, $11 single, $14-17 double, cash only.*

Among the better of the cheap hotels, with friendly staff. Rooms are small and dark but quiet. Set around a narrow covered courtyard, the doors to all rooms are visible from the reception desk, making for greater security. Hot water in the morning and late evening only.

**HOTEL TÍPICO**, *20 de Noviembre 612 at the corner of Mina, phone (951) 64111; 25 rooms, $12 single, $15 double, cash only.*

A two-story motel-style building. Friendly but rather scruffy.

**HOTEL TREBOL**, *Las Casas 201 at the corner of Miguel Cabrera near the zócalo, phone (951) 61256, fax (951) 40342; 21 rooms, $45 single or double.*

This hotel has a big, bright covered courtyard, but rooms are dark and somewhat eccentrically furnished, and the staff are not helpful. You can do much better for the price elsewhere.

**HOTEL JUÁREZ**, *20 de Noviembre 208 between Hidago and Trujano, phone (951) 64616; 31 rooms, $17 single, $21 double, VI - MC.*

Entry is through a covered courtyard. Rooms are somewhat basic but are freshly painted and have phones. There is the usual tradeoff between bright and noisy rooms or dark and quiet ones.

**HOTEL FRANCIA**, *20 de Noviembre 212, phone (951) 64811; 46 rooms, $17 single, $21 double, 5% supplement for Visa or Mastercard.*

Rooms are big with painted tiles, but the place is rather rundown.

**HOTEL CENTRAL**, *20 de Noviembre 104, phone (951) 65971; 26 rooms, $11 single, $13 double, cash only.*

Quite grubby, rooms are dark or noisy or both.

**HOTEL VALLE DE OAXACA**, *Díaz Ordaz 208, phone (951) 69500, 63707; 36 rooms, $14 single, $17 double, cash only.*

A bit run-down; look for rooms well away from the street.

**HOTEL ANTONIO'S**, *Independencia 601, phone (951) 67227; 16 rooms, $23 single, $27 double, cash only.*

With its dark, covered courtyard and dark, windowless rooms, this is no great find. On the plus side, it is just a block west of the *zócalo* and rooms are quiet and decently furnished.

**HOTEL MESÓN DEL ÁNGEL**, *Mina 518 near Díaz Ordaz, phone (951) 66666; 34 rooms, $45 single or double, cash only.*

Rooms are large and bright if rather plain, and many face a big pool, but the neighborhood is a bit rough, and room rates seem far too high. One claim to fame is that buses to Monte Albán depart from here.

### Hotels Away from the Center

**HOTEL VICTORIA**, *Lomas de Fortín 1, phone (951) 52633, fax (951) 52411; standard rooms $99 single or double, villas $125 double plus $23 for each additional guest, junior suites $142 plus $23 for each additional guest, VI - MC - AE - DC.*

Rooms and suites are scattered across a main pavilion and several smaller structures separated by lavish gardens, all high on a hillside northwest of the city. Standard rooms feature modern Mexican decor in blue and green, villas are modern Mexican in red, and suites are decorated in orange and yellow. All rooms have garden views, and some also provide glimpses of the city below. Ceiling fans provide ventilation. Service is quiet and efficient, and free minibus service is provided to and from the city center. Restaurant and bar.

**HOTEL SAN FELIPE,** *Jalisco 15, San Felipe del Agua, phone (951) 35050, 35090, fax (951) 35755; 160 rooms and suites; $64 single, $80 double, $95 triple, $149 junior suite, VI - MC - AE - DC.*

Gardens, pools, a quiet atmosphere and helpful staff make this big, low-slung hotel rather pleasant, but it is in an isolated spot 5 km from the city center, which costs time in taxis or the free hourly shuttle. Standard rooms have dark tile floors, orange bedspreads and garden views. Restaurant, bar and gift shop on site.

**HOTEL MISIÓN DE LOS ANGELES,** *Calzada Porfirio Díaz 102, phone (951) 51500, fax (951) 51680; 152 rooms and 21 suites, $78 single, $98 double, $117 triple, junior suite $154 single or double; VI - MC - AE - DC.*

Rooms are in a series of two-story buildings scattered over very extensive grounds amidst gardens, a large pool, and tennis courts. Most rooms are newly renovated in shades of ultramarine and pale orange, and furnishings are quite pleasant. Restaurant, bar and disco.

**HOTEL HACIENDA LA NORIA,** *La Costa 100 at the corner of Pereférico, phone (951) 67555, fax (951) 65347; 81 rooms, $36-42 single, $45-53 double, $54-63 triple; rates vary according to season; VI - MC - AE - DC.*

This sprawling suburban hotel is under the same management as the Hostal de la Noria in the city center and is also a Best Western affiliate. It consists of a series of low-rise buildings interspersed by gardens, a pool and a village-style walkway. Noise can sometimes penetrate from a nearby highway. Rooms are pleasant with floral bedspreads, ochre tile floors and whitewashed walls.

**HOTEL FORTIN PLAZA,** *Venus 118, Colonia Estrella, phone (951) 57777, fax (951) 51328; 93 rooms, $74 single, $93 double, slightly less in May and June; VI - MC - AE - DC.*

This hotel is situated on a hillside near a busy roadway. There are good views of the city in the distance, especially at night. Some rooms face away, toward the mountains, and are quieter. Decor is nondescript and what you might expect in a lesser chain hotel. Restaurant and bar.

**HOTEL VERACRUZ,** *Chapultepec 1020, phone (951) 50511; 55 rooms, $24 single, $29 double, VI - MC.*

This hotel is almost next door to the first-class bus terminal. If you're arriving at night by ADO or Cristóbal Colón bus and lack the energy for a hotel search, this may be the answer for your first night's stay. Turn left leaving the terminal and you can't miss it. Rooms are simple but reasonably comfortable. Those at the front and on the left side of the building are noisier because of their proximity to the terminal. The hotel restaurant is a bit pricey but is all right for a meal or snack while waiting for a bus.

**HOTEL REGIONAL DE ANTEQUERA,** *Las Casas 901, phone (951) 60118, 66952; 20 rooms, $15 single, $18 double, VI - MC - AE.*

Those arriving by second-class bus and looking for a room close by are out of luck. This is the nearest hotel to the second-class terminal, but still it lies two blocks and a precarious intersection away, and the area is not all that safe at night. Moreover, rooms are scruffy, and there's lots of noise from the street and from the bar downstairs. Not recommended.

**HOTEL FIESTA INN,** *Avenida Universidad 140, former Hacienda de Candiani, phone (951) 61122; 120 rooms, $75 single or double, VI - MC - AE - DC.*

This new hotel is situated near the airport, which will make it inconvenient for many visitors, even with its free transportation to the city center. Nonetheless, it offers large, well appointed rooms and a full range of services, with a gymnasium, pool, business center, laundry, air conditioning and cable TV. You get good value for money but, again, location is a problem.

## WHERE TO EAT

Oaxaca is not a wealthy city, and the number of local people who can afford to eat at the better restaurants is limited. Many restaurants cater largely to visitors, with the result that menus may be rather tame and regional specialties that are cherished in family kitchens may be hard to find.

Nonetheless, there are several restaurants that can do a respectable chicken *mole* or any of several other traditional dishes. Because Oaxaca is not near any large body of water, fish and seafood selections can be slim. So-called international specialties and generic Mexican dishes tend to dominate most menus, with an emphasis on beef and chicken.

Still, that should not stop you from eating well. Dining tends to be fairly casual in Oaxaca, and reservations are rarely necessary. Most medium- and upper-priced restaurants accept credit cards.

If you have a hankering for authenticity and aren't too fussy about the surroundings or the hygienic conditions, there are a number of food stalls with seating at long tables or counters in the market just south of the *zócalo*, with service from early morning to late afternoon. You won't find printed menus, but in some instances you'll see food cooking in large pots and can simply point to what you want. Prices are generally cheap, and the food is guaranteed to be tasty. You'll also find some of the world's best hot chocolate.

Now for some other restaurants:

### Near the zócalo
**EL ASADOR VASCO** *is upstairs on the west side of the zócalo*, and tables near the big, open windows have very good views. The menu concentrates on grilled meats Mexican or Basque style, along with fish, seafood and

salad dishes and an enticing selection of deserts. Service is efficient though a little cool. Prices are in the middle to upper range.

**RESTAURANT LA CATEDRAL**, *on García Vigil street near Morelos one block north of the cathedral*, has tables around a bright, pleasant courtyard. It is a good place for a leisurely breakfast. For lunch and supper, the menu tends toward steaks, and some lighter dishes are also offered. Friendly service. Musicians most evenings. Moderate prices.

**EL SAGRARIO**, *on Valdivieso street behind the cathedral a half-block north of the zócalo*, has a hip and trendy atmosphere, serving pizza downstairs and steak upstairs, with musicians some nights. Moderate prices. **LA CASA DE LA ABUELA** and **LA CASITA** are two small upstairs restaurants overlooking the Alameda de León *just around the corner from the zócalo*. Both have Mexican menus with some regional dishes. Moderate prices.

**RESTAURANT DEL VITRAL**, *on Guerrero at the corner of Armenta y López one block east of the zócalo*, is *the* spot for elegant dining in a pre-revolutionary ambience. European-accented Mexican specialties. Prices are expensive.

**EL MESÓN**, *on Hidalgo just east of the zócalo*, is a Mexico City-style *taquería*. A good variety of, guess what, tacos. Also, good breakfasts, with big fruit salads an option. Moderate. **GINO'S PIZZAS** and **SANTA FÉ**, a steakhouse, *are situated almost next to each other on 5 de Mayo between Independencia and Morelos*. Prices are moderate.

There are many cafés directly on the *zócalo*. One favorite is the **CAFÉ DEL JARDIN** *near the southwest corner*, popular both with locals and visitors. Good for drinks, snacks, sandwiches and light meals. Efficient service. Low to moderate prices. **RESTAURANT EL SEÑORIAL**, *inside the hotel of the same name*, is located indoors in a pleasant dining room away from the plaza. A big menu and good value. There are three cafés *on the opposite side of the zócalo*, including **TERRANOVA**, where the free *botanas* (light snacks) that accompany drinks are above average. *On the north side of the zócalo, beneath the Hotel Marqués del Valle*, are the **CAFÉ DEL MARQUÉS** and, *next door*, **PIZZA, PASTA Y MÁS**, both overpriced.

### North of the zócalo

**HOSTERÍA DE ALCALÁ**, *Alcalá near Labástida*, is fairly formal by Oaxaca standards. Tables are set around a colonial courtyard with a fountain. A selection of Mexican and international specialties fill the menu, with prices in the middle to upper range. Musicians perform some evenings. **CAFÉ DEL ANDADOR**, *Murguía between Alcalá and 5 de Mayo in the Parador Plaza Hotel*, has an interesting menu with creative variations on common Mexican dishes. It has a pleasant dining room and reasonable prices.

**MORGAN,** *Morelos between Porfirio Díaz and García Vigil,* is an inexpensive, hole-in-the-wall restaurant with excellent pasta dishes and coffee, and good breakfasts also. The owner is from Verona. It is open mornings and evenings only. **FLOR DE LOTO** and **LA MANSION DEL FRAILE,** *a few doors apart on Morelos between Porfirio Díaz and Tinoco y Palacios,* offer inexpensive selections of vegetarian dishes, along with full-course specials. Each also offers a selection of Oaxacan regional dishes, some containing meat.

**CAFÉ HIPÓTESIS,** *Morelos near Porfirio Díaz,* an old-fashioned, book-lined coffee house with a broad choice of coffees and teas and light meals. Busy in the evening, with a bohemian atmosphere. Moderate.

**EL REFECTORIO,** *in the Hotel Camino Real,* offers Mexican and European dishes in a pleasant garden courtyard setting. Moderate to expensive. **RANCHO'S GRILL,** *Porfirio Díaz at the corner of Allende near Santo Domingo church,* is a straightforward, inexpensive steakhouse. **PIZZERIA ALFREDO DA ROMA,** *Alcalá street near Santo Domingo church,* has good pizzas, a cosy atmosphere and moderate prices. **CAFÉ PITA-PE,** *at the corner of Nicolás Bravo García Vigil in the same general neighborhood,* is a small restaurant with a menu including regional specialties. **RESTAURANT-BAR EL DECANO,** *5 de Mayo near Murguía,* offers Mexican specialties at moderate prices.

## SEEING THE SIGHTS

Yes, we've been harping about the *zócalo* quite a bit, but this **central plaza** really is very central to the life of the city. Tree-shaded and closed to motor traffic, it is a gathering spot for people of all ages and social classes. In the center sits an ornate 19th century bandstand, and concerts are given here some evenings. Cafés, hotels, shops, and churches provide the main backdrop.

*On the south side of the zócalo is the* **Palacio de Gobierno,** the seat of the state government, with a big mural in its main stairway depicting several aspects of local history. *Directly adjacent to the zócalo is the* **Alameda de León,** a smaller plaza dominated on one side by the cathedral, with fine baroque carving on its façade.

*Walking one block north from the zócalo* we come to **Macedonio Alcalá street,** sometimes referred to as the Andador Alcalá. Andador means walkway, and this street is reserved for pedestrians along most of its length, including the five blocks leading north to Santo Domingo church, the most magnificent structure in Oaxaca. The street is paved with stone, and many of the buildings along here are covered in stucco and painted in brilliant shades. Many handicrafts shops are located along here.

Other streets in the city center, although not quite as hospitable to pedestrians, offer good examples of architecture from the colonial and early post-independence periods. Few of these buildings are in any way spectacular, but in their integrated setting they provide a harmonious and pleasing effect. The late 19th century **Teatro Macedonio Alcalá**, *at the corner of 5 de Mayo and Independencia*, is noteworthy for its ornate façade and plush interior, but the public is admitted only to see performances, which are rare.

## Museums

**Museo Regional de Antropología e Historia**, *in the former 16th-century convent of Santo Domingo, Alcalá between Constitución and Humboldt, next to Santo Domingo church; open Tuesday to Friday from 10 am to 6 pm, Saturday and Sunday from 10 am to 5 pm, closed Monday; admission $4 but free on weekends and holidays.* Apart from the loveliness of the green stone cloister housing this museum, a key attraction is the splendid collection of regional dress from different parts of Oaxaca state.

The museum also includes sections devoted to archaeological finds, including a very fine collection of Mixtec jewelry and carvings. Several rooms provide portrayals of Oaxaca under Spanish rule, including household and ecclesiastical objects. Written explanations are given in Spanish only.

**Museo de Arte Hispánico Rufino Tamayo**, *Morelos between Porfirio Díaz and Tinoco y Palacios; open Monday and from Wednesday to Saturday, 10 am to 2 pm and 4 pm to 7 pm, Sunday from 10 am to 3 pm, closed Tuesday; admission $3.* The 18th-century house which houses this museum, along with most of the 1,059 archaeological pieces in its collection, were donated by Rufino Tamayo, the renowned Oaxaca-born artist who died in 1990. The five display rooms cover different periods and regions. Some of the objects come from lesser-known civilizations. Classical oncerts are sometimes held here: check at the museum for details.

**Instituto de Artes Gráficas de Oaxaca**, *Alcalá 507 between Constitución and Humboldt; open 10:30 am to 8 pm daily except Tuesday; admission free.* The collection on display here consists mostly of engravings by Mexican and foreign artists. Plans call for the addition of a photo gallery.

**Museo de Arte Contemporáneo de Oaxaca**, *Alcalá 202 between Morelos and Matamoros; open 10:30 am to 8 pm daily except Tuesday; voluntary contribution.* Paintings, sculptures and photos by artists from Oaxaca and other parts of Mexico. The museum has a library and an active program of theatre performances, film showings and academic conferences.

**Casa Museo Rodolfo Morales**, *Murguía between Alcalá and 5 de Mayo*, expected to be open by late 1994 and to feature paintings by local artists.

**Museo Casa de Juárez**, *García Vigil 609 near Allende*, closed for restoration, reopening date uncertain. Situated in a house where future president Benito Juárez spent several years of his childhood early in the

19th century, this museum displays household furnishing from that period as well as documents and personal objects belonging to Juárez.

## Churches

**Santo Domingo,** *five blocks north of the zócalo, usually closed between 1 pm and 4 pm,* is undoubtedly one of the most beautiful churches in Mexico. With its extensive gold leaf, its polychrome stucco, and its massive cupola it is a sight to behold. Built in stages in the 16th and 17th centuries with the help of artisans who converged from other regions, and with enormously thick walls to guard againt earthquakes, it has finely carved features both in its interior and on its massive façade. At dusk candles inside the church create a magical glow, and at night the exterior is floodlit and looks almost like a fairy-tale castle when viewed from certain angles.

**Oaxaca Cathedral,** *whose front entrance faces the Alameda de León adjacent to the zócalo,* has an ornately carved Baroque façade, but the interior, despite its massive size, is not especially noteworthy.

*Just beyond the southwest corner of the zócalo* is **La Compañía** church with its ornately carved façade. *Just beyond the market, at the corner of Aldama and 20 de Noviembre,* is **San Juan de Dios,** also with a carved façade and with important murals inside depicting the conquest. Dating from 1526, this is the oldest church in Oaxaca, and it has a small museum of religious art in back, open irregular hours.

Another fine façade, this one with a bas-relief showing its namesake saint and his adoring monks, fronts **San Agustín** church *on Guerrero street one block east of the zócalo.* **San Felipe Neri** *on Independencia near J.P. García* is noted for its elaborate altars, while **La Soledad** *on Morelos west of Unión* has impressive ironwork and sculpture.

---

### "MONDAYS ON THE HILL" FESTIVAL

*La Guelaguetza (pronounced gay-la-GAY-tza), also known as **los lunes del cerro** (Mondays on the Hill), is an elaborate spectacle of regional dance presented each year on the first two Mondays after July 16. The show is staged in a big amphitheater on the Cerro del Fortín, a hill just northwest of the city center, starting at 10 am and lasting about three hours. Tickets for seating near the stage, available from the tourism office, are expensive and even so can sell out quickly. Groups of ornately costumed dancers represent the seven regions of Oaxaca state, and the event is very popular, causing most hotels to fill up.*

---

## SHOPPING

Handicrafts in Oaxaca are among the most creative and most varied in Mexico. Painted wooden objects (often with animal themes), small pottery items in distinctive black and dark green shades with intricate inlays, blankets and other woven objects sometimes still made using ancient backstrap looms and natural dyes, brightly embroidered *huipiles* (traditional Indian blouses), gold jewelry, leather bags and belts, basketware items, hammocks, and yet more the temptations are many and varied. By the way, the Spanish for handicrafts is *artesanía* (pronounced ar-tay-sa-NEE-a).

Some of the better items may be found in the many handicrafts shops along the **Alcalá pedestrian mall** and some neighboring streets. Several shops along **García Vigil street**, *one block to the west*, are a little less fancy and stock some cheaper items. Serious shoppers will have little trouble zeroing in on the shops with the best selections. Prices are set at fixed levels in most shops, but if you are buying several items together you may be able to bargain, and you may get a slightly lower price if you agree to pay in cash.

**Markets**

Markets provide a cheaper alternative, but you may have to sift through many items to find the better ones, and you must be prepared to bargain. The **Mercado 20 de Noviembre market**, sometimes called **La Merced**, *is situated one block south of the zócalo*. It underwent a big transformation a number of years ago, with most of the stalls selling food items being moved out to the wholesale market near the second-class bus terminal. The place got a much needed facelift, losing much of its character in the process, but it is now an easier – and more sanitary – place to shop. A few food stalls remain, but the market is dominated now by clothing mostly mass produced industrial goods and by a generous selection of handicrafts of all sorts, both local and from other regions.

The **mercado de abastos** (wholesale market), *one km west of the zócalo*, has the colorful array of food stalls you expect to see in a market, and it also has handicrafts stalls. It is especially busy on Saturdays, when a larger than usual number of vendors converge from nearby towns and villages. As well, a small makeshift handicrafts market has sprung up across the plaza from Santo Domingo church. In character it is a cross between the bigger markets and some of the more exclusive shops.

Finally there are the weekly small-town markets listed below under Excursions. Even in towns noted for a particular type of *artesanía* you will not necessarily get the best items or prices. Some vendors travel from market to market, and you will find items from as far afield as Guatemala or western Mexico. Also, don't imagine for a moment that, just because of the rustic setting, vendors don't know the value of their merchandise.

If you are looking for art, two of the leading galleries are **La Mano Mágica** *at Alcalá 203* and **Arte de Oaxaca** *at Trujano 112*. For off-beat exhibitions visit **Arte y Diseño** *at Trujano 423, several blocks west of the zócalo*.

# ENTERTAINMENT & NIGHTLIFE

Oaxaca is not a flashy, knock-them-down sort of place, and its low-key atmosphere is reflected in the entertainment scene. This is no place to vacation if you want to disco till dawn, although you can find ho-hum discotheques at the **Victoria**, **San Felipe**, and **Misión de Los Angeles** hotels toward the edge of town. But leave that for later. Unless you have a very short attention span, you are unlikely to be bored in a truer Oaxacan setting.

Yet again we return to the *zócalo*, whose ornate 19th century bandstand is the setting for regular evening concerts. On Moday and Saturday evenings the state marimba ensemble performs at 7 pm. On Tuesdays and Thursdays it is the turn of the state brass band, also at 7 pm. Occasionally there may be other performaces as well. You can come and go as you please, and there is never any charge.

Even without a concert, the *zócalo* is a lively place in the evening. Merely sitting at a café and watching the passing scene can form an evening's entertainment. Beware of the mariachis and other serenading musicians. You may be tempted to engage their services, but the meter can tick pretty quickly.

Folkloric dances are another part of the evening scene in Oaxaca. **Guelaguetza** (pronounced gay-la-GAY-tsa) is a Mixtec Indian word meaning to give a gift without expecting anything in return, and it is the name given to traditional dance ceremonies. Although performers do expect something in return now, tickets are only $5 to see the dancers and their elaborate costumes each evening at 7:30 pm at the **Hotel Monte Albán** *across the Alameda de León from the cathedral.* Capacity is limited, and you may want to book ahead. The **Hotel Camino Real** presents a more lavish *guelaguetza* spectacle Saturdays at 7 pm. Entry is $30 and includes dinner.

Several restaurants mentioned above provide musical entertainment in the evening. For coffee and chatter in a bohemian atmosphere, try the **Café Hipótesis** *on Morelos near Porfirio Díaz.*

# EXCURSIONS
## MONTE ALBÁN

**Monte Albán**, an ancient Zapotec capital, stands proudly on a hilltop *9 km west* (and mostly uphill) from Oaxaca with a stunning view of the surrounding countryside. Here you can see pyramids, terraces, tombs and sculptures in an area whose oldest traces date back 27 centuries, when civilization is thought to have arrived in the Oaxaca Valley.

Over the centuries most buildings were destroyed and their stones used to erect newer structures, but some architectural traces remain from this early period. Many urns and jade objects have been recovered, and some are displayed at the regional museum in Oaxaca.

Population shifts and migrations brought various cultural influences to bear, and the area under the control of Monte Albán continued to grow. A distinctly Zapotec culture emerged much later, and Monte Albán as we see it today shows the reconstruction that took place during its apogee from the 4th to the 7th centuries A.D. During this time it lay at the center of a highly organized society extending through the central valleys of Oaxaca, but its population and influence began to decline in the 8th century, and from the middle of the 10th century onward, it lay largely abandoned.

Most of the architecture visible today has sloping walls with broad stairways, monolithic columns decorated with bas-reliefs, *tablero* panels with animal motifs, and the use of small, well cut stones used almost as bricks. Vertical stelae are perched in front of buildings or stairways and, as far as archeologists can tell, most buildings were coated with stucco and painted red. The ball courts, used for intense ceremonial contests in which the loser usually had to relinquish his life, date from an earlier period.

### Hours & Fees

The Monte Albán site is open daily from 8:30 am to 5:30 pm. Admission is $4 but is free on Sunday.

### Arrivals & Departures

To get there one easy option is to take a group tour, which can be booked at most travel agencies in Oaxaca. If you prefer going on your own, remember that there are no regular public buses passing nearby. Taxis cost $10-$12 one way, or more than double for the round trip after paying for waiting time.

A company called Autobuses Turísticos offers a roundtrip fare of $2.50, but service is infrequent, with departures from Oaxaca at 8:30 am and then at two-hour intervals from 9:30 am to 3:30 pm (additional trips on Sunday). Return trips leave two hours after arrival, allowing little flexibility, and you must pay a supplement if you want to return at a different time. The departure point in Oaxaca is Mina 518 next to the Hotel Mesón del Angel, already a fair slog from wherever you are likely to be. *Phone (951) 65327 for information.*

### At the Site

At the entrance you'll find a parking area, restaurant, and small museum which serves as an introduction. Pamphlets with detailed information are on sale, or you may hire an English-speaking guide. The site extends over a vast area, but most visitors stick to the core area around the **main plaza**. This rectangular plaza is enormous, roughly 300 meters by

200 meters (about 1,000 feet by 700 feet), and displays a fascinating interplay of light and shadow. Of the temples that were built atop the pyramids facing the plaza, only the supporting walls remain; their flat roofs were supported by wooden beams that could not withstand the ravages of time.

Turning left, you reach the well preserved **Ball Court** with its steep sides and double-T shape. Further along is **Building II**, a small open-air temple with two series of pillars and a strange tunnel (now illuminated by skylights) leading to a small courtyard. **Building P** is of little interest, but on the way is a large house with 13 rooms grouped around a central patio.

Beyond the southern boundary of the main plaza is the **south platform**, which is only partly explored, but there are excellent views from atop its wide central stairway and a large stele along with several sculpture at the bottom. Walking about 250 meters (800 feet) along the top of a hill around the south platform you reach a group of ruins known as **Seven Deer**, where a patio is surrounded by four buildings, one at each of the cardinal points of the compass..

Back in the main plaza, **Building L**, superimposed on the **Dancers Building** from an earlier period, displays stone slabs representing human figures in strange positions and an engraving which gives the building its name. On the way to the next building (**System IV**) you can appreciate the harmony of the main pyramid and the surrounding platforms. Further on are several smaller buildings which are connected structurally into one enormous mound, among them **Building J** clad with stone slabs covered with ancient hieroglyphics. In several places archeologists have dug tunnels displaying the remains of buildings from various earlier periods.

On the northern platform you come to **Tomb 104**, with an ornate façade and a chamber with frescos whose colors and motifs are still visible. One figure is seen wearing an enormous headdress displaying a serpent and feather. In **Tomb 172** nearby, skeletons and offerings have been left intact, while inside **Tomb 105** are some of the finest murals found in Monte Albán. We end the description here, but true archaeology buffs will find plenty more to pique their interest.

## MITLA

**Mitla** *is situated about 45 km east of Oaxaca; the archaeological site is open daily from 8 am to 5 pm. Admission is $3 but is free on Sundays* with second-class buses running several times an hour and taking 70 minutes for the trip. The ruins are about 2 km from the highway, a pleasant walk through the town. Along the way are many shops selling mezcal, a tequila-like liquor made from the juice of a local cactus, and nearer the ruins are several handicrafts shops. There is also a handicrafts market near the entrance.

**Restaurant Mama Teresa**, a short way downhill from the entrance, offers tasty regional dishes. If you plan to stay in Mitla, **Hotel** and **Restaurant La Zapoteca** is a clean, simple place between the town and the ruins; **Hotel** and **Restaurant Mitla**, in the center of town, is more basic.

English-speaking guides may be hired at the entrance. The main interest in a visit here lies in the intricate stone carvings and in the views of barren mountainsides in the distance. Just north of the main site there is a church built on a foundation of earlier ruins. The original settlement at Mitla was inhabited until well after the Spanish conquest in the 16th century.

The main group of ruins is called the **Group of the Columns**, with a long quadrangular structure whose exterior walls and interior patios are covered with mosaic designs created by small cut stones fitted to form a variety of motifs. This building is more of decorative than of architectural interest, and one estimate suggests that it required more than 100,000 cut stones!

## YAGUL & DAINZÚ

**Yagul** is nearer to Oaxaca but harder to reach, *3 km north of the highway,* and not served by public transport. Taxis from Mitla or Tlacolula provide an option. *The site is open daily from 8 am to 5 pm; admission is $2 but free on Sundays.* Less refined and much less visited than Mitla, this site is distinguished by its long terraces and by the enormous size and agreeable proportions of its ceremonial **ball court**. Here too there are impressive views of mountains in the distance. Next to the ball court is the labyrinthine **Palace of Six Patios**, which included apartments for the nobility.

The ruins of **Dainzú**, further west and just south of the highway, are better left to true archaeology buffs.

## TLACOLULA

**Tlacolula**, 30 km east of Oaxaca, served frequently by second-class bus, is the site of the busiest of the weekly markets in the Central Valleys, drawing vendors and customers from many surrounding towns and villages. Sunday is market day in Tlacolula, and a trip here can be combined with visits to Mitla and other archaeological sites in the region.

Tlacolula is also noted for its ornate 16th-century church, which still contains a large part of its original decorative elements, including a statue of Christ said to possess miraculous qualities. The market spills all over the central part of town and displays a colorful profusion of fruits, vegetables, spices and cheap industrial goods of all sorts, but you will also find handicraft items here, including cotton clothing and hand-woven rugs.

## TEOTITLÁN DEL VALLE & SANTA ANA DEL VALLE

Two small towns just a few kilometers north are important centers of weaving. **Teotitlán del Valle**, easily reached from Tlacolula by bus or taxi, has several workshops and showrooms and a good selection of hand-woven rugs in its small open-air handicrafts market. **Santa Ana del Valle**, served less frequently by bus and not as often visited, is the prettier of the two villages, with a picture-postcard church and a cosy central plaza. It also has workshops and a handicrafts market, and boasts a small museum with items portraying local history. The Shan-Dany (meaning "below the hills") museum is open daily from 10 am to 2 pm and 3 pm to 6 pm, $1.50 admission.

## EL TULE

On your way to or from Mitla or Tlacolula, you may wish to pause for a few minutes at **El Tule** about 12 km east of Oaxaca. This is the site of perhaps the world's most gigantic tree, about 42 meters (138 feet) in girth at its trunk and possibly more than 2,000 years old. With the enormous spread of its branches it is easy to see why spiritual qualities have been attributed to this savino tree, whose root system is now fed by a system of pipes to assure its survival. It is located right next to the highway and is surrounded by a fence. If you are traveling by bus it probably makes more sense to make your stop here on your way back to Oaxaca, snap your pictures, and then catch the next bus. They run by here frequently.

## ZAACHILA, OCOTLÁN, GUELATAO

**Zaachila**, about 20 km south of Oaxaca, has its market day on Thursday and also has a small archaeological site up the hill near the church. In **Ocotlán**, a bigger town a bit further south, market day is Friday. Both these places really bustle on their market days with thousands converging from outside. This can make for a fun trip even if you're not interesting in buying anything. Other market days are Monday in Miahuatlán (a considerable distance south), Tuesday in Atzompa and Ayoquezco, Wednesday in Etla and Zimatlán, Thursday in Ejutla, Friday in Atzompa again, Saturday at the wholesale market in Oaxaca and, as mentioned above, Sunday in Tlacolula.

**Guelatao** (pronounced gay-la-TA'O, rhyming with cow) is the birth-place of **Benito Juárez**, Mexican president in the mid-nineteenth century and, as an Indian and the author of a series of important reforms, one of the most revered figures in Mexican history. The town lies about 60 km north of Oaxaca along Highway 175 and can be reached by any bus bound for Ixtlán or Tuxtepec. At the refreshment stalls near the highway they can tell you when to expect buses back. Guelatao is noted for its steep cobbled streets, a modern ceremonial center dedicated to Juárez, with a tiny museum, and a small lake with many ducks, but the real interest of this excursion lies in the mountain scenery along the way.

## PRACTICAL INFORMATION

### Airlines
• **Mexicana**: *Independencia at the corner of Fiallo, phone 65796, 67352, 68414*
• **Aeroméxico**: *Hidalgo 513, phone 61066, 63229, 63765*
• **Aviacsa**: *Porfirio Díaz 102, phone 31809, 31793*
• **Aerocaribe**: *Independencia at the corner of Fiallo, phone 56373, 59324*
• **Aeromorelos**: *Alcalá 501-B, phone 60974, 60975, 61002*

### Airport Van
• **Transportación Terrestre Aeropuerto**, *Alameda de León 1-G, phone 44350*

### Books
  **Librería Universitaria** *on Guerrero street a half-block east of the zócalo* has a selection of books in Spanish and English.

### Bicycle Rentals
• **Bicicletas Martínez**, *J.P. García 509, phone 43144*

### Car Rentals
• **Budget**: *phone 57777, 50330, at the airport 15252*
• **Hertz**: *phone 62434, at the airport 15478*
• **Dollar**: *phone 45332, 43737*
• **Mini Rent**: *phone 51500*

### Consulates
• **US consulate**: *Alcalá 201, phone 43054, open weekdays 9 am to 2 pm; emergency phone 41404*
• **Canadian honorary consulate**: *Doctor Liceaga 119, phone 33777, 52147, open weekdays 9 am to 2 pm*

### Currency Exchange
  Exchange rates tend to be poor in Oaxaca, and service at banks is decidedly sluggish. The best rates we found for cash or travelers' checks were at **Bancomer** *on García Vigil street one block north of the zócalo*. Other banks were paying substantially lower rates.
  *Banks are open only from 9 am to 1:30 pm, weekdays only, and some change money only until 11 am.* Several *casas de cambio*, or exchange dealers, may be found in the streets immediately north of the *zócalo*. While rates are poor, service is faster and hours of operation are much longer, but beware

of shortchanging. If you can obtain pesos before arriving in Oaxaca, that will often be a better bet. Rates for currencies other than the US dollar are especially poor.

## Language Schools
- **Instituto de Comunicación y Cultura**: *Alcalá 307, phone 63443*
- **Instituto Cultural de Oaxaca**: *Juárez 909, phone 53404, 51323*
- **Universidad Autónoma Benito Juárez de Oaxaca**: *postal address: Apdo. 519, Oaxaca, Oax.; phone 65922*, offers language courses with university credits.

## Laundry
Several laundries in the center of Oaxaca provide same-day service at moderate rates. Among them is **Lavandaría Hidalgo** *at the corner of Hidalgo and J.P. López streets*. Ask at your hotel for the nearest *lavandaría*.

## Telephone Code
All telephone numbers shown here have a **951** city code

## Tourist Information & Complaints
*Corner of 5 de Mayo and Morelos, phone 64828, open Monday to Friday 8 am to 8 pm, Saturday and Sunday 9 am to 8 pm.* See the Orientation section for information on other tourism offices.

# HUATULCO

> *Huatulco, a growing resort area, lies off Highway 200.*

**Huatulco** did not happen by accident. It is very much an artificial creation. The planners who put it together had good raw material to work with and grandiose visions of what it would look like in future decades. It encompasses nine bays covering nearly 35 km of coastline surrounded by verdant hills. The area comprised in the master development includes three dozen beaches and extends 5 km back to the main highway.

When Fonatur, the government agency in charge, first moved into the area in 1983, they found communal lands that were only sparsely populated. They faced bitter allegations that long-time residents were shortchanged when their land was taken to build what was hailed as a resort for the 21st century. Things got off to a sluggish start. Investors were more hesitant than they had been at Cancún to plow money into hotel development in a place where few visitors had ever set foot, but one by one they came on board. The first of the big resort hotels opened in 1988.

## THE OAXACA COAST

*So you're headed for the beach. Will it be five-star comfort, or something a little more casual and affordable? On the Pacific coast of Oaxaca state, you have the choice.*

*Huatulco is a glitzy new resort set along a gorgeous series of nine bays occupied, until the early 1980s, only by a few fishermen's huts. It looks a little like a mini-Cancún, and indeed the development process was similar. Both were created by Fonatur, a Mexican government agency whose job is to develop resort towns and to coordinate planning and public infrastructure. Huatulco is sometimes called by the name Bahías de Huatulco (bahía means bay). Three of the bays have been developed so far. Hotels are mostly in the upper price range, although the adjacent townsite has some lower-priced lodgings.*

*Puerto Escondido, two hours west by road, is older, more relaxed and more Mexican. It doesn't have the manicured look of Huatulco or a stark separation between beach and town. With prices fitting a wider variety of pockets, it tends to draw a different crowd. It has beaches where you can walk for miles, and it retains something of the bohemian mood that visitors from an earlier era may recall. Its sunsets are as spectacular as ever. It is also a paradise for surfers. Moreover, there are good bird-watching sites nearby.*

*What Huatulco is to Puerto Escondido, the latter is to Puerto Ángel, which is smaller, more isolated and more intimate, although its beaches are relatively small. Geographically, Puerto Ángel lies between its two bigger neighbors. If you're ready to throw inhibition to the wind, the nude beach of Zipolite is just a few kilometers away. A short distance beyond Zipolite is Mazunte, formerly abjured for the slaughter of turtles but now the site of a turtle research center and museum.*

*These beaches are broad and sandy. The sand isn't quite as white and powdery and the water isn't quite as turquoise as on the Caribbean side, but the Pacific coast has real scenery, with majestic green hills and proud mountains, in contrast to the very flat terrain of the Yucatán peninsula. The food is just as good, and the fish is every bit as fresh.*

Things remain on a smaller scale than in Cancún, with only a fraction the number of hotels, but Fonatur has fond hopes that this will change. For the moment, only three of the nine bays have been developed. These are **Tangolunda**, which houses the biggest and most lavish hotels and a golf course, **Santa Cruz**, with smaller-scale hotel development and a commercial strip, and, between the two, **Chahué**, with no beachfront hotels but with a beach club and marina. A separate townsite, commonly called **La Crucecita**, still has an unfinished look to it, but it is starting to come to life. It has grown with an influx of job-seekers and beginning to feel more like a real city.

**Bahía de Conejos**, just over from Tangolunda, is the most easterly of the bays and the next one slated for development. For the moment it consists of virgin beach. The five bays to the west of Santa Cruz are, in order, **El Órgano**, **El Maguey**, **Cacaluta**, **Chachacual** and **San Agustín**. All are accessible by boat, and all but Chachacual and Cacaluta can also be reached by road.

## ARRIVALS & DEPARTURES

### By Air

Mexicana and Aeroméxico both run daily flights between Mexico City and Huatulco (code HUX). Some are continuations of international flights, but no scheduled carrier runs nonstop flights from abroad. Most travelers must connect in Mexico City, one hour away by air. Charter flights operate from a few cities in the US and Canada on a seasonal basis. As well, Aeromorelos flies between Oaxaca and Huatulco with turboprop aircraft. In some timetables, Huatulco is listed as Bahías de Huatulco, so check both.

The terminal building is of distinctive design, covered by an enormous palapa roof. It is situated 19 km northwest of the town of Santa Cruz Huatulco. Collective vans provide door-to-door service for about $7 per passenger. *To arrange a return to the airport, call (958) 10055, extension 835.* Taxis charge about $14 per car. Penny-pinchers can take advantage of the frequent local bus service between Huatulco and Pochutla. The airport terminal lies only about 300 meters from the highway between these two towns, and buses are easy to flag.

### By Bus

Each bus company has a separate terminal in La Crucecita, as the downtown area of Huatulco is known. Estrella Blanca (which operates under several different names) and Cristóbal Colón are both located along Calle Gardenia (near the corners of Palma Real and Ocotillo respectively).

Several second-class bus lines operate from shelters near where Gardenia meets the main road leading to the highway. Second-class buses or minibuses (some with very little space for baggage) operate west from Huatulco several times an hour throughout the day, serving the airport cutoff, Pochutla and Puerto Escondido. Others head east, less frequently, to Salina Cruz through sparsely populated countryside (meaning they make few stops). Buses to Huatulco are sometimes marked Santa Cruz to avoid confusion with Santa María Huatulco, a village 35 km northwest.

If you are coming from Mexico City, direct overnight service is provided by Estrella Blanca (from the southern terminal, via Acapulco) and Cristóbal Colón (from the eastern terminal, via Salina Cruz) at fares ranging from $36 to $42. Ditto for the return. Between Huatulco and Oaxaca, Cristóbal Colón has daytime and overnight services via Salina Cruz for $16. Estrella del Valle offers second-class service to and from Oaxaca on the more direct route via Pochutla. Additional connections are available at Pochutla.

Cristóbal Colón has daytime and overnight services to Tuxtla Gutiérrez (9 hours, $14) and San Cristóbal de las Casas (11 hours, $16). Estrella Blanca has nine daily departures to Acapulco (9 hours, $22) and hourly service to Puerto Escondido (2 hours, $5).

**By Car**

Huatulco lies off Highway 200, which runs parallel to the Pacific coast from the Guatemalan border to Acapulco and beyond. From Oaxaca there is a scenic mountain highway that meets Highway 200 near Pochutla, west of Huatulco, or a longer, gentler route via Salina Cruz to the east.

## ORIENTATION

The layout of Huatulco can seem confusing with its nine bays and separate townsite. If you are arriving from the airport or from other points to the west, the first part of Huatulco you're likely to see is the town of Santa Cruz Huatulco, commonly called **La Crucecita**, *5 km south of the highway*. **Calle Gardenia**, one of the main streets, runs past restaurants, bus terminals, and the *zócalo*, also known as the *plaza principal*. Many of the other streets are also named after flowers. This is the area where many of the local people live and shop, and it has a number of hotels.

*A short hop south of La Crucecita* is **Bahía de Santa Cruz** (*bahía* means bay and is pronounced ba-EE-a), with beaches, hotels, and a commercial strip that includes three banks. The next bay to the east is **Chahué** (pronounced cha-WAY), *3 km from La Crucecita*. It has a marina and a beach club for the use of guests at certain hotels. It also has parcels of land set aside for future development, but so far no hotels have been built near the beach. *Further east, and connected by a road directly from the highway,* is **Tangolunda**, the most developed of the nine bays with broad expanses of beach, an 18-hole golf course, and most of the bigger, more lavish hotels in the region.

Minibuses provide service between La Crucecita and Tangolunda, with stops in between. Taxis go just about everywhere. The **airport** *lies near the main highway, 19 km northwest of La Crucecita*, and the village of **Santa María Huatulco** is a little further beyond..

# WHERE TO STAY

Nearly all hotels are clustered in three areas. **Bahía de Tangolunda** accounts for most of the big, top-end hotels and a couple of smaller ones; **Bahía de Santa Cruz** is a notch or two below; and **La Crucecita**, an urbanized area away from the beaches, has hotels in several categories, with some at more modest prices. Travelers who arrive on prebooked air-and-hotel packages normally get cheaper rates at the bigger hotels than individuals who book directly with the hotels are able to arrange. The undiscounted rates are shown here.

### Bahía de Tangolunda

**OMNI ZAASHILA RESORT**, *Bahía de Tangolunda, phone (958) 10460, fax (958) 10461; 120 rooms, $208 single or double, $248 with private pool, VI - MC - AE.*

This place has drawn plenty of attention. It consists of a series of low-slung buildings with whimsical roof lines and small arches, all painted a brilliant white with color accents. The lobby has a high palapa roof and a big mural. Rooms all have sea views, marble floors, all-marble bathrooms, and multi-hued decor with greens and purples dominating. Outside are a big fantasy pool, a smaller pool with swim-up bar, and a broad expanse of beach with palapa shades. You'll find air conditioning, restaurants, and other amenities.

**HOTEL CASA DEL MAR**, *Balcones de Tangolunda, phone (958) 10102 or 10104, fax (958) 10202; 25 suites, $152 single or double, VI - MC - AE.*

This small, exclusive hotel is perched on a hilltop with splendid views of Tangolunda bay and a gentle sea breeze. A long series of steps leads to the beach; a pool overlooks the sea. Rooms have air conditioning, superb views and understated pastel decor. The two master suites ($175) have outdoor jacuzzis. The dining room is small, elegant and expensive.

**HOLIDAY INN CROWNE PLAZA RESORT HUATULCO**, *Bahía de Tangolunda, phone (958) 10044, fax (958) 10221; 136 suites, $153 high season, $121 low season, 1 to 3 people, VI - MC - AE - DC.*

This multi-level pink and mauve apparition is terraced snugly into a hillside. All rooms have sea views and separate sitting areas. They are reached by electric cart, elevator or funicular railway. Pools, tennis courts and a restaurant are set on different levels. The hotel lies away from the beach but has a beach club nearby.

**SHERATON HUATULCO RESORT**, *Bahía de Tangolunda, phone (958) 10055, fax (958) 10113; 356 rooms; high season: $138 pool view, $170 ocean front; low season: $110 pool view, $149 ocean front; VI - MC - AE - DC.*

Everything here is big. This six-story orange-beige building has two wings with big rooms decorated in blue and white with beige tile floors.

There is a big multiple-pool area, as well as tennis courts and rather expensive restaurants. Many rooms have good ocean views.

**CLUB MÉDITERRANÉE**, *Bahía de Tangolunda, phone (958) 10033 or 10081, fax (958) 10101; 554 rooms, $117-$126 single, $195-$210 double, meals and activities included, cheaper rates for weekly packages, VI - MC - AE.*

This was the biggest Club Med in the world when it opened in 1988. A cluster of terraced buildings with terra cotta façades is situated on an isolated promontory at the edge of Tangolunda Bay. Below are an expanse of beach studded with palapa shades, a pool and nearly a dozen tennis courts. Other activities include sailing, windsurfing, snorkeling, squash and billiards. The five restaurants offer Mexican, French, Italian and Moroccan dishes. All meals, regular evening entertainment and most sporting activities are included in the price.

**ROYAL MAEVA HUATULCO**, *Bahía de Tangolunda, phone (958) 10000 or 10048, fax (958) 10220; 310 rooms; high season: $245 single, $314 double; low season: $205 single, $291 double; includes meals and activities; VI - MC - AE.*

This is another all-inclusive resort, with meals and many activities included in the room rates. Architecture and decor are fairly ordinary. Facilities include three restaurants, four bars, tennis courts, volleyball courts, and a gymnasium.

**HOTEL CLUB PLAZA HUATULCO**, *Bahía de Tangolunda, phone (958) 10051, fax (958) 10035; 19 rooms and suites; high season: rooms $83 single or double, suites $116; low season: rooms $60, suites $83; VI - MC - AE.*

Modest by Tangolunda standards, this hotel has comfortably furnished rooms, with air conditioning. Suites include jacuzzis and fully equipped kitchens. It is situated across from the Sheraton hotel, several minutes' walk from the beach.

### Bahía de Santa Cruz

**HOTEL BINNIGUENDA**, *Boulevard Santa Cruz, phone (958) 70077, fax (958) 70284; 75 rooms; high season: $75, single or double; low season: $60; VI - MC - AE.*

This hotel is not near the beach, but it is attractive nonetheless. Rooms are well appointed, and the grounds are nicely landscaped, with a big pool. Most rooms face the garden; all are air conditioned. There is a small beach a few minutes' walk from the hotel. Free transportation is provided to the more attractive beach club at Bahía de Chahué.

**HOTEL CASTILLO HUATULCO**, *Boulevard Santa Cruz, phone (958) 70051 or 70171, fax (958) 70131; 107 rooms, high season $86 single or double, low season $76, VI - MC - AE - DC.*

This three-story hotel is across the road from a small beach and also provides transportation to the beach club at Bahía de Chahué. Rooms are pleasant but ordinary, with air conditioning. It has a pool and restaurant.

**MARINA RESORT**, *Boulevard Santa Cruz, phone (958) 70963, fax (958) 70830; 45 suites in the first phase, 130 additional suites under construction; high season $162 single or double, low season $116; VI - MC - AE.*

This new hotel, part of it still under construction, faces an inlet of the sea, with a small beach at one end. A nearby pier accommodates yachts. Each suite has a jacuzzi and kitchenette, including microwave oven. The hotel is built in modular fashion, centered around a large courtyard.

### La Crucecita

**HOTEL FLAMBOYANT**, *Calle Gardenia, facing the zócalo, phone (958) 70105 or 70113, fax (958) 70121; 70 rooms, high season $75 single or double, low season $50, VI - MC - AE - DC.*

Located in the heart of town, this three-story colonial-style hotel has its rooms set around a garden courtyard. Rooms are air conditioned and decorated simply but tastefully. Free transportation is provided to the beach club at Bahía de Chahué.

**HOTEL BEGONIAS**, *Bugambilias and Flamboyán, near the zócalo, phone (958) 70018; 13 suites, high season $45 single or double, low season $30, VI - MC - AE.*

Bright, appealing suites are furnished in peach and white, with fan and television. Each has a sitting area and either two small bedrooms or one big bedroom. Some can accommodate up to four people.

**GRAN HOTEL HUATULCO**, *Calle Carrizal near Palo Verde, phone (958) 70115, fax (958) 70083; 32 rooms, $50 single or double, VI - MC - AE.*

This friendly place is favored by commercial travelers. Rooms are pleasantly furnished, with big desks, air conditioning and television. There are a pool and restaurant.

**HOTEL GRIFER**, *Guamuchil and Carrizal, one block from the zócalo, phone (958) 70048; 13 rooms, $24 single or double.*

This modest hotel has friendly staff and bright, simple rooms, with fan. It is a good budget choice.

**HOTEL BUSANVI 1**, *Carrizal and Flamboyán, one block from the zócalo,* and **HOTEL BUSANVI 2**, *Macuil between Carrizal and Bugambilias, each have rooms for $15-$23 single and $26-$32 double, depending on season.*

Busanvi 1 has air conditioning but no hot water and is unappealingly furnished. Busanvi 2 has fans, hot water and better furnishings, but it is dark and somewhat noisy. Neither is a very good choice.

**POSADA CHAHUÉ**, *Calle Mixie L-75, Bahía de Chahué, phone (958) 70945; 14 rooms, high season $45 single or double, low season $36, VI - MC.*

Located in what, for the moment, is the middle of nowhere, this small, family-run spot has big, bright rooms with air conditioning, comfortable furnishings and attentive service. It lies behind Bahía de Chahué and is about midway between the beach and La Crucecita.

## WHERE TO EAT

When staying at one of the bigger hotels, there is a strong temptation to eat at a hotel restaurant, especially if you have an all-inclusive package and your meals are already paid for. Some of the hotel restaurants are very good, but most are rather pricey. Several of the better (and more expensive) restaurants are located in the Centro Comercial Punta Tangolunda across from the golf course.

A bigger cluster of restaurants, most of them more moderately priced, is situated in La Crucecita near the *zócalo* (central plaza). There are many small restaurants around the beach at Bahía de Santa Cruz emphasizing fish and seafood, some quite inexpensive.

**LA PAMPA ARGENTINA** specializes in steak and pasta and **MISIÓN FA SOL** in Spanish dishes including *paella* and *fabada* (a stew of pork and beans). **CAVENDISH** offers a variety of European and Caribbean dishes. *All are located in the Centro Comercial Punta Tangolunda*, and all are elegant and rather expensive.

In La Crucecita, **EL GRILLO MARINERO**, *corner of Carrizal and Macuhitle*, and **EL DELFÍN**, *Gardenia at Ocotillo*, both serve fresh seafood at moderate prices; some tables are on outdoor terraces. **DON WILO**, *facing the zócalo* with balconies upstairs, offers Oaxacan regional specialties and pizza. **OASIS**, *on Flamboyán street near the zócalo*, has a menu that includes sandwiches and sushi. **MARÍA SABINA**, *nearby*, and **PALMA REAL**, *Gardenia at Ocotillo*, offer a variety of regional meat and seafood dishes. **LA TROPICANA** *has an outdoor terrace facing the zócalo* and a varied menu.

**PIZZERÍA IL BUON MANGIARE**, *Gardenias at Palo Verde*, serves you-know-what. **EMBAJADA JAROCHA**, *on the same corner*, has an outdoor terrace and inexpensive Veracruzan seafood dishes. **EL MANGUITO TODO NATURAL**, *facing the zócalo*, offers vegetarian dishes and fruit juices. There are many more restaurants around the *zócalo* and in the neighboring streets.

In Bahía de Santa Cruz, **VE EL MAR**, *facing the beach near the inner basin*, has a varied menu concentrating on seafood. A cluster of more modest spots close by, among them **GISEA**, **ROSY** and **FRANCIS**, offer fresh fish and seafood at moderate prices. *Nearer the center of the beach*, several other small restaurants, among them **GELA** and **3 HERMANOS**, are open from morning to early evening and offer tasty local dishes.

# SHOPPING

The area around Huatulco is not noted for handicrafts (*artesanías* in Spanish), but selections of weavings, leather goods, clothing, jewelry and other items from the central valleys of Oaxaca state and from around Mexico and Guatemala are readily available.

Besides the boutiques found in several of the bigger hotels, shoppers may wish to explore the **Centro Comercial Punta Tangolunda** *near the golf course* or the **Centro Comercial Oaxaca** *facing the zócalo* (central plaza) in La Crucecita. Both are small shopping centers with shops offering carefully selected items. Several more handicrafts shops are scattered around the area near the *zócalo*.

For a more rustic atmosphere and often cheaper prices, visitors may try the **Mercado de Artesanías de Santa Cruz**, *located by the plaza near the bay of the same name*, or **Mercado 3 de Mayo**, *the main public market in La Crucecita, situated on Guamuchil street near the zócalo*.

# ENTERTAINMENT & NIGHTLIFE

At the **Club Méditerranée** and at the **Hotel Royal Maeva**, guests are treated to musical shows or short theatrical performances each evening as part of the entertainment package included in their room rates. The biggest discotheque in Huatulco is **Magic Circus** *in Bahía de Santa Cruz*. It has a cover charge and does not open until late in the evening. Another is **Disco Club Tequila**, *facing the zócalo in La Crucecita*.

# EXCURSIONS

Most of the bigger hotels in Huatulco have tour desks offering a variety of excursions. As well, **Viajes y Excursiones García Rendón** has offices at Bugambilias and Octotillo streets in La Crucecita.

The most popular tours by far are **boat trips** around the nine bays. These vary in length and price. Some travel to all nine bays, others to just a few; some stop an hour or two for lunch or a swim, others don't. The **Sociedad Cooperativa Turística Tangolunda** operates boat tours from the basin at Bahía de Santa Cruz.

Fonatur, the government agency coordinating the development of Huatulco, has plans to tart up the village of **Santa María Huatulco**, *35 km northwest of the resort area*, turning it into an authentic Oaxaca village for the pleasure of tourists. We can hardly wait.

Other tours take visitors by road to **Puerto Ángel** and **Zipolite**, or to the **Manialtepec lagoon** *west of Puerto Escondido* for nature tours of an area rich in birdlife.

## PRACTICAL INFORMATION

### Airlines
• **Mexicana**, *at the airport, phone (958) 40208 or 40228, or at Hotel Castillo Huatulco, Bahía de Santa Cruz, phone (958) 70243*
• **Aeroméxico**, *at the airport, phone (958) 40328 or 40335*
• **Aeromorelos**, *phone (958) 10336*
  For an **airport van**, *phone (958) 10055, ext. 835.*

### Car Rentals
• **Budget** has four offices: *Hotel Royal Maeva, Tangolunda, phone (958) 10000, ext. 729; Posada Binniguenda, Bahía de Santa Cruz, phone (958) 70077, ext. 420; corner of Ocotillo and Jazmín, La Crucecita, phone (958) 70034 or 70010; and at the airport, (958) 70368 or 70388*
**Dollar**: *Sheraton hotel, Tangolunda, phone (958) 10055, ext. 878; Holiday Inn Crowne Plaza, Tangolunda, phone (958) 10044; and at the airport, phone (958) 40277*
**Hertz**: *represented at Flamboyán 13 in La Crucecita, phone (958) 70751*

### Currency Exchange
Three banks, **Bancomer**, **Banamex**, and **Comermex**, are located *near one along Boulevard Santa Cruz, Bahía de Santa Cruz, open 9 am to 1:30 pm weekdays only.* Rates are better than at most hotels. Visa and Mastercard cash advances are available.

### Golf
There is an 18-hole course *near Bahía de Tangolunda.*

### Laundry
Same-day service is available at **Lavandería Carrizal** *at Carrizal and Flamboyán streets near the zócalo in La Crucecita.*

### Newspapers
Mexican newspapers and foreign magazines are available in several of the bigger hotels and at **Publicaciones Huatulco**, *corner of Gardenia and Yuca in La Crucecita.*

# PUERTO ESCONDIDO

> *Puerto Escondido lies along Highway 200.*

Memories of **Puerto Escondido** extend back to the time not very long ago (we're talking mid-1980s) when the only aircraft serving the local landing strip was an ancient DC-3 that came lumbering in each morning from Oaxaca, flying not over but between the mountains that lie along the way. Passengers who disembarked next to the tiny, palapa-roofed terminal building would be whisked along a narrow road overlooking a long curved bay with a cluster of modest hotels (and one or two less modest ones) lining the beach below. The atmosphere was relaxed. Tourists would mingle with townspeople and fishermen, whose daily catches landed on dinner plates just hours later. The main beach was big and uncrowded, and a much bigger beach nearby was practically deserted. The sunsets were magnificent, and the evenings were calm and sultry.

Much of what made Puerto Escondido special to earlier visitors is still intact. The town has grown, the number of hotels has increased, and package tourists have begun to arrive, but the pace of growth has been gradual enough for the place to retain much of its character. Much of Avenida Pérez Gasga, the main street running parallel to the beach, is closed to motor traffic, and small hotels have sprung up along **Playa Zicatela**, a long beach with high waves favored by surfers. The ambiance, however, remains casual and somewhat bohemian. Hotel prices span a broad range, and there is a decent choice of restaurants.

## ARRIVALS & DEPARTURES

### By Air

There are no scheduled international flights to Puerto Escondido, although the occasional charter flight does find its way there. Mexicana flies five times weekly (daily during certain periods) from Mexico City, and Aeromorelos flies daily from Oaxaca. The airport code is PXM. The airport lies just 5 km northwest of town. Collective vans provide door-to-door service from the airport. To return to the airport, taxis are your best bet; the fare is only $3.

The Huatulco airport offers more frequent service to and from Mexico City. It lies about 1 1/2 hours by road from Puerto Escondido and can be reached inexpensively by bus or for about $50 by taxi.

### By Bus

Each bus company has its own terminal in Puerto Escondido. The most important is the Estrella Blanca terminal, just above the highway. Most of the others are clustered nearby. Estrella Blanca operates under several different names. It provides deluxe overnight service to and from Mexico City's southern terminal (12 hours, $36). It has first-class buses to or from Acapulco (7 hours, $17) 10 times daily, with daytime and overnight service, as well as second-class service (8 hours, $14) with hourly departures from early morning to late afternoon. Three of the first-class departures continue to Zihuatanejo and beyond.

First-class buses go hourly to Pochutla and Huatulco from early morning to early evening, and there are eight daily departures to Salina Cruz, with connections to Chiapas. Minibuses go several times an hour to Pochutla, with some continuing to Huatulco.

Estrella del Valle has eight daily round trips between Oaxaca and Puerto Escondido (7 hours, $9-$13). It operates from the second-class terminal in Oaxaca and from a building on Avenida Hidalgo in Puerto Escondido. Additional second-class service between Oaxaca and Puerto Escondido is provided by Transportes Oaxaca-Istmo. Cristóbal Colón has two daily first-class departures to Salina Cruz, with connections to Oaxaca or Chiapas.

**By Car**

Puerto Escondido lies along Highway 200, which runs parallel to the Pacific coast from the Guatemalan border to Acapulco and beyond. From Oaxaca, an all-paved route goes via Miahuatlán and Pochutla. There is also a more direct but only partly paved road via Ejutla. Both provide rugged mountain scenery.

## ORIENTATION

Puerto Escondido is bisected by Highway 200, which was in the process of being widened to a four-lane boulevard within town. Below the highway lie the beaches, most of the hotels, and **Avenida Pérez Gasga**, a lively pedestrian street lined by restaurants, hotels, shops and travel agencies, as well as a bank and exchange dealer. Above the highway lies the real town, where most of the townspeople live and shop. That's also where the public market and the bus terminals are located.

The main beach, known as **Playa Principal** (the eastern part of the beach is sometimes called **Playa del Marinero**), *faces the central bay* and lies close to many of the hotels and to Avenida Pérez Gasga. Since this is a sheltered bay, waves are quite gentle. The beach is not illuminated at night and is better avoided then.

*To the east, separated from the main beach by a cluster of large rocks*, is **Playa Zicatela**, which is long, vast and uncrowded. It is also unshaded. *At the western end, close to town*, is a cluster of small hotels and restaurants. High waves make this beach popular with surfers, and international competitions have been held here. Swimmers should beware of the undertow, which causes several drownings each year. There is some nude bathing toward the far end of this beach.

*To the west of town* is a small beach in a sheltered bay called **Puerto Angelito**, beyond the lighthouse that is plainly visible from the main beach. It is popular with local families and can get crowded on weekends.

It can be reached by foot, by taxi, or by boat from the main beach. Watch for small boats disgorging or embarking passengers.

*Further west* is **Playa Bacocho**, a long beach with rough waves, a strong undertow, and several big hotels perched on a bluff high above. *Between Puerto Angelito and Bacocho* lies tiny **Playa Carizalillo**.

Most trips within town and the area near the main beach are short enough to be done on foot. For longer trips, taxis are abundant and charge $2 to $3. The airport lies 5 km northwest of town.

## WHERE TO STAY

Hotels in Puerto Escondido span a broad part of the price range, with most hotels in the middle or lower part of the range. The bigger, more expensive hotels are clustered in a suburban subdivision west of town known as **Bacocho**, situated high above and well inland from the beach of the same name.

Visitors who prefer smaller, more modest hotels will be doubly rewarded, for they will find themselves closer to the beaches, restaurants and shops. A number of middle- and lower-priced hotels are clustered near the main beach or along the streets above, and a few others line **Playa Zicatela**, just to the east. Zicatela is especially popular with surfers. There are several hotels also along the highway or in town above the highway, but with one or two exceptions they are not very pleasant or convenient.

### Hotels near the main beach

**HOTEL SANTA FE**, *Calle del Morro between Playa del Marinero and Playa Zicatela, phone (958) 20266 or 20170, fax (958) 20260; 47 rooms, 18 more under construction; high season: $62 single, $72 double; low season, $43 single, $50 double; VI-MC-AE, discounts for payment by cash or travelers' check.*

Set astride two beaches, this congenial hotel draws many repeat visitors. Built in modular form, it shows Moorish and Spanish architectural influences, with good use of painted tile and stone. Rooms are big and nicely decorated; all have air conditioning and fans. Some are up two flights of steps. Most have sea views. There is a pleasant sitting area near the pool and a big palapa-shaded dining room facing the sea, with a fish, seafood and vegetarian menu.

The hotel also handles eight spacious bungalows next door, which go by the name **BUNGALOWS SANTA CRUZ**. *The price for two people is $77 in high season and $54 in low season.*

**EL TABACHÍN**, *next door to the Hotel Santa Fe, phone (958) 21179; 8 apartments, $45 to $65 in high season, $35 to $55 in low season, more for penthouse, no cards.*

Each apartment is lavishly furnished with marble floors, full kitchen, air conditioning and fans. They provide excellent value. Some can accommodate up to four people. As well, there are a roof garden and small pool. The owners also offer luxury lodgings near Nopala, an ancient village in the mountains about two hours from Puerto Escondido.

**HOTEL FLOR DE MARÍA**, *on an unnamed street near Playa del Marinero, phone (958) 20536; 20 rooms, $18 single, $27 double, VI - MC - AE.*

Located on a small, unnamed street running between the highway and Playa del Marinero, this pretty hotel offers exceptional value. Run by an Italian-born Canadian couple, it has a homey central courtyard and makes imaginative use of color. Rooms are big, each with two double beds and a ceiling fan. There are a small rooftop pool and bar. The restaurant, open daily except Monday, offers excellent Italian cooking.

**HOTEL PARAÍSO ESCONDIDO**, *Calle Unión 10, near the top of Avenida Pérez Gasga, phone (958) 20444; 20 rooms, $45 single, $54 double, VI - MC - AE.*

This fascinating spot is part hotel, part museum. A 1929 Ford Model A is parked near the entrance. Stone carvings, painted codices and other bits of artwork are scattered about. There are also a lookout with a hanging bridge, a cloister with a view over the sea, and a colonial-style chapel. Each room is a little different. All have terraces and original artwork, including wood carvings, indigenous paintings, and painted tiles and glass. The terraces of the upstairs rooms provide excellent views of the sea. All rooms are air conditioned, and there are a restaurant and pool. The hotel is a few minutes' walk from the beach.

**HOTEL MAYFLOWER**, *Andador Libertad just above Avenida Pérez Gasga, (958) 20367; 12 rooms; high season $18 single, $23 double; low season $14 single, $18 double; VI - MC.*

This modest spot on a quiet side street not far from the beach offers very good value. Bright, pleasant rooms all have balconies and make good use of tiles. Several have sea views. The hotel also provides dormitory space at $5 per bed. The German-born owner is very helpful with advice for travelers, and she offers private tours.

**HOTEL CASA BLANCA**, *Avenida Pérez Gasga, phone (958) 20168; 19 rooms, $24 single, $27 double, VI - MC - AE.*

This pleasant hotel, not far from the beach, has a pool and bright rooms with white tile floors, whitewashed walls, and cheery bedspreads and curtains. Most have balconies, but some face a narrow garden and wall.

**HOTEL LOREN**, *Avenida Pérez Gasga up the hill from the pedestrian zone, phone (958) 20591; 23 rooms; high season $30 single, $36 double; low season $15 single, $21 double; VI - MC.*

Bright, pleasant, simple rooms with fans are set in a pair of three-story buildings. There are sea views from the upper floors.

**HOTEL BARLOVENTO**, *Calle Álfaro, phone (958) 20220; 16 rooms; high season $36 single, $45 double; low season $30 single, $36 double; VI - MC.*

A group of pink buildings and a pool are terraced on a hillside in a somewhat remote spot near the lighthouse, a few minutes' walk from Puerto Angelito. The approach is partly by dirt road. Rooms are air conditioned and have stone walls and bright bedspreads.

**HOTEL RINCÓN DEL PACÍFICO**, *Avenida Pérez Gasga, phone (958) 20056 or 20101; 28 rooms, $22 single, $27 double, suites $36 single, $45 double, VI - MC.*

This two-story L-shaped building extends from the pedestrian street to the beach. Rooms have fans and simple furnishings but need maintenance. Suites lie directly on the beach; they have air conditioning and somewhat better furnishings.

**HOTEL LAS PALMAS**, *Avenida Pérez Gasga, phone (958) 20230 or 20303; 38 rooms; high season $29 single, $39 double; low season $18 single, $24 double; VI - MC - DC.*

This three-story U-shaped building extends from the pedestrian street to the beach. Rooms have fans. They are simple and comfortable, but could use some touching up.

**HOTEL NAYAR**, *Avenida Pérez Gasga up the hill from the pedestrian zone, phone (958) 20113 or 20319; 41 rooms; high season $22 single, $27 double; low season $20 single, $24 double; $6 extra for air conditioning; VI - MC.*

Rooms are simple and a bit tired-looking, and only a few have sea views. The hotel has a pool and restaurant. There are two entrances; use the upper entrance to avoid a long series of steps.

**HOTEL VIRGINIA**, *Calle Álfaro, phone (958) 20176; 12 rooms; high season $18 single, $25 double; low season $12 single, $15 double; no cards.*

This simple place on a small road just off the upper portion of Pérez Gasga offers plain rooms with fans.

**BUNGALOWS VILLA MARINERO**, *entrance from the highway, phone (958) 20716 or 20180; 16 bungalows; prices vary, depending on the size of the unit; high season $21 single up to $70 for four people; low season $15 to $53; no cards.*

The grounds, not very well kept, sprawl from the highway all the way down to the beach. All units have private terrace, kitchenette and fan. Most are simply furnished, and some need freshening up. Several of them are quite dark.

**HOTEL CASTILLO DE REYES**, *Avenida Pérez Gasga, phone (958) 20442; 17 rooms; high season $22 single, $30 double; low season $12 single, $15 double; no cards.*

This hotel, some way up the hill, has big rooms with fans. Rooms face an ugly concrete terrace.

**CABAÑAS NEPTUNIO**, *Avenida Pérez Gasga, phone (958) 20327; cabins: high season $15 single or double, low season $6; camping and trailers: high season $5 per person plus $5 per vehicle, low season $3; no cards.*

Tiny thatched huts with shared bath are scattered over a sprawling, sandy, tree-shaded area. They have mattresses but no sheets. A trailer park and campground are off to one side. The beach is nearby.

### Hotels along Playa Zicatela

**HOTEL ARCOIRIS**, *Playa Zicatela, phone (958) 20432; 24 rooms, $22 single, $28 double, VI - MC.*

Two low-slung white stucco buildings provide big rooms with red tile floors, whitewashed walls, wooden furniture, and fans. Each has a private terrace. Some have full kitchens ($28 single, $35 double). The grounds are lushly vegetated, with a big pool. The restaurant is upstairs and faces the sea.

**BUNGALOWS ACALI**, *Playa Zicatela, phone (958) 20778; 14 cabins, high season $22 single, $30 double; low season $15 single, $21 double; no cards.*

Cabins are set amid tropical vegetation and have a rustic feel, with wooden interiors, Aztec bedspreads and fans, with a palm-shaded pool.

**ART AND HARRY'S SURF INN**, *Playa Zicatela, no phone; 7 rooms, high season $24 single or double, low season $18, no cards.*

This casual spot is popular with surfers, offering simple rooms painted sky blue, each with mosquito netting and fan. Some of the downstairs rooms are a little dark. The big, bright palapa-shaded restaurant and bar has a campy feel and faces the sea.

**CABAÑAS ROCKAWAY**, *Playa Zicatela, phone (958) 20668; 12 cabins, high season $12 per person, low season $9 per person, no cards.*

Simple thatch-roofed cabins sleep up to four, with fans and mosquito nets. There is a pleasant palm-shaded pool. The restaurant is open only in high season.

**BUNGALOWS Y CABAÑAS ACUARIO**, *Playa Zicatela, phone (958) 20357; 20 rooms and cabins, high season $21 to $30, low season $18 to $24, no cards.*

A cluster of small buildings, including some individual cabins, is set on poorly kept grounds. Rooms vary in size and decor; most are simply furnished, and some have kitchenettes.

### Hotels in Bacocho

**HOTEL POSADA REAL**, *Fraccionamiento Bacocho, phone (958) 20237 or 20133, fax (958) 20192, reservations in US or Canada (800) 528-1234; 100 rooms, high season $94 single or double, low season $64, VI - MC - AE - DC.*

This Best Western affiliate consists of two modern low-rise buildings with stucco and stone exteriors and green and white decor in the rooms, all of which are air conditioned. The hotel has several pools, two restaurants, three bars, a beach club, satellite television, a travel agency, car rentals and room service. Most rooms offer at least a glimpse of the sea. The beach, a few minutes' walk down a long stairway, is broad and uncrowded, although the waves can be rough. Other hotels in Bacocho are further from the beach.

**HOTEL FIESTA MEXICANA**, *Fraccionamiento Bacocho, phone (958) 20150 or 20115; 100 rooms, high season $75 single or double, low season $45, VI - MC - AE.*

This pale orange building is set on lavishly wooded grounds, with a big pool. Rooms are big, bright and air conditioned, but quite plain. The hotel has two restaurants, a lobby bar and discotheque. The beach is some distance away.

**HOTEL ALDEA DEL BAZAR**, *Fraccionamiento Bacocho, phone (958) 20508, 47 rooms, high season $99 single or double, low season $79, VI - MC - AE.*

This two-story white building is distinguished by its Arabesque arches. It has big air conditioned rooms decorated in white and orange, a big unshaded pool with a concrete terrace, and lackadaisical service. The beach is some distance away.

**HOTEL SUITES VILLA SOL**, *Fraccionamiento Bacocho, phone (958) 20061 or 20382, fax (958) 20451; 108 rooms, high season $76 single or double, low season $60, VI - MC - AE.*

Five buildings are clustered around a pool, with music blaring loudly. Rooms are big but startlingly plain, with bare brick walls even in the master suites. Some rooms are up two flights of steps. The beach is some distance away.

### Center of town

**HOTEL LUZ DEL ÁNGEL**, *1ª Calle Norte near Avenida Oaxaca, phone (958) 20868, fax (958) 20122; 35 rooms; $18 single, $24 double with fan; $26 single, $32 double with air conditioning; no cards.*

Located near the bus terminals, this hotel offers big, bright, clean, simple rooms with television and telephone. Probably the best hotel in the center of town, it lies about ten minutes' walk from the beach.

## WHERE TO EAT

Puerto Escondido has good places to eat, and prices are generally moderate. The pedestrian-only portion of Avenida Pérez Gasga has a cluster of restaurants, and anyone strolling there can usually find a place they like.

The open-air restaurant of the **HOTEL SANTA FE**, *facing the sea between Marinero and Zicatela beaches*, is one of the better and more expensive places to eat in Puerto Escondido. There is no meat on the menu, which concentrates instead on fish, seafood and tofu dishes. Another hotel restaurant, at the **FLOR DE MARÍA** *nearby*, has excellent Italian dishes at reasonable prices. (It is closed Monday.)

*Along Pérez Gasga*

**PERLA FLAMEANTE** is an upstairs, palapa-shaded restaurant *near the eastern end of the pedestrian zone* with a full menu and a good selection of fresh fish and seafood at moderate prices. **MERGEO'S** and **7 REGIONES**, *both nearby*, offer seafood and *antojitos* such as tacos and enchiladas.

**BANANAS**, set in a garden with a series of palapas, offers light meals, salads and fruit drinks. *Toward the western end of the pedestrian zone*, **LA SARDINA DE PLATA** offers original preparations of steak and seafood in more elegant surroundings and at higher prices. **NAUTILUS** has good fish and seafood, along with a few German dishes, and well-priced full-course lunches. **LA GOTA DE VIDA**, *just beyond the pedestrian zone*, offers vegetarian dishes and juices.

*Along Playa Zicatela*

**ART AND HARRY'S BAR & GRILL** is a casual spot for a sunset drink and dinner. The signature dish is lobster linguini. Posters from Molson Breweries hint at the owners' nationality. *Nearby*, **BRUNO'S RESTAURANT** offers fish, seafood and pasta dishes beneath a big palapa shelter. *Next door*, **CIPRIANO'S PIZZA** prepares its wares in a brick oven.

*Along the eastern end of the main beach*

**RESTAURANT LIZA** offers fresh fish and steaks beneath a big palapa shade, while **RESTAURANT NEPTUNIO** specializes in seafood, pasta and pizza. *Nearby, on a side street facing the Hotel Flor de María*, **PANADERÍA CARMEN** has a good selection of breads and pastries.

## SHOPPING

A number of souvenir and handicrafts shops line the pedestrian-only portion of **Avenida Pérez Gasga**, and there are many market-type stalls, open into the evening, along the side street linking the eastern end of this pedestrian mall to the beach. Offerings range from lurid T-shirts to fine weavings and leather goods. Handicrafts production here is scarce, but items come in from elsewhere in Oaxaca and even from Guatemala.

## ENTERTAINMENT & NIGHTLIFE

Public entertainment in the evening is limited largely to eating, drinking, and strolling along the **Pérez Gasga** pedestrian street. One or two of the hotels along Playa Zicatela show films on video.

## EXCURSIONS

Several tour companies with offices along the Pérez Gasga pedestrian street offer a variety of group excursions. They include **Turismo Rodimar**, **Agencia de Viajes Erickson**, and **Viajes y Excursiones García Rendón**. They are easy to spot with their big signs out on the street. In Bacocho, there is a tour agency in the lobby of the Hotel Posada Real.

The most popular excursions are **bird-watching** tours in **Manialtepec lagoon** *about 20 minutes west of Puerto Escondido* and **Chacahua lagoon** and **national park,** *which is nearly two hours west.* Prices average about $30 per person. More information is provided on pages 54-55. These excursions can be difficult to arrange on an individual basis because of the need for a boat and the value of a guide, although it is often possible to rent canoes at either site.

Tour agencies also offer excursions to **Huatulco**, the resort development *two hours east of Puerto Escondido* with its series of nine bays.

**Nopala**, an ancient Chatino Indian village *in the mountains northwest of Puerto Escondido,* is interesting as a one-day or overnight excursion. Besides the town with its market and pre-Columbian stelae, visitors can see pottery in a nearby village as well as coffee-growing country and cloud forest. Accommodations are offered in a luxury ranch house near the town. Information is available from tour agencies and from El Tabachín, next to the Santa Fe hotel. **Juquila**, *further northwest*, is noted for its church, Chatino handicrafts, and nearby waterfalls.

**Atotonilco hot springs** can be reached on horseback in one hour from a point near Manialtepec lagoon. Visitors can relax in the thermal waters and swim in a nearby river. Tour agencies can make arrangements. **Jamiltepec**, *about two hours west of Puerto Escondido*, is noted for its colonial church and for the Mixtec Indian clothing and masks sold at the market. Sunday is the busiest day.

# PUERTO ÁNGEL

> *Puerto Ángel lies along the Pacific coast 13 km south of Pochutla, which lies near the junction between Highway 200 running parallel to the coast and Highway 175, which descends through the mountains from Oaxaca.*

Just as Puerto Escondido seems low-key compared to the glitzier Huatulco, **Puerto Ángel** seems quiet and remote when compared to Puerto Escondido. Puerto Ángel (pronounced AN-khel) is really just a fishing village and naval port with a bit of tourism tacked on. The nearest bank is in Pochutla.

Puerto Ángel has a small beach in town. Just east of **Zipolite**, where the beach is bigger and clothing optional; the accommodations are more primitive. Also close by is **Pochutla**, a busy, dusty town near an important highway junction. Some people choose to spend the day at Zipolite and the night at Puerto Ángel, which has better accommodations. There are several undeveloped beaches on the other side, to the east of Puerto Ángel. The town itself is flat near the waterfront but quite hilly beyond.

## ARRIVALS & DEPARTURES

### By Air

Puerto Ángel lies near the junction between Highway 200 and Highway 175, which is 41 km west of Huatulco and 69 km east of Puerto Escondido, both of which have regular air service. The Huatulco airport is quite close to Pochutla. Passengers arriving at Puerto Ángel by bus nearly always have to connect in Pochutla.

### By Bus & Taxi

Buses between Pochutla, Puerto Ángel and Zipolite run at 20-minute intervals from early morning to early evening. Most have little space for baggage. Taxis are readily available.

### By Car

The road between the highway junction and Puerto Ángel is quite hilly. As you descend into town, the bay looms into view. Toward the right is Playa Panteón, a small beach with calm waters and several fish restaurants. The road curves past Playa Panteón and continues on toward Zipolite, 5 km further.

### DECISIONS, DECISIONS ...

*Hotels in Puerto Ángel are mostly in the budget or lower intermediate range. They do not have direct telephone lines. Calls pass through a central switchboard and have to be transferred. Street addresses are not often used.*

## WHERE TO STAY

**HOTEL LA CABAÑA**, P*laya del Panteón, phone (958) 40395 to 40399, extension 128; 21 rooms, high season $24 single or double, low season $18, VI - MC.*

This hotel, just across from the beach, is livened by exuberant plants. Rooms on the street side are brighter and not noisy; they each have private terraces. All rooms are pleasantly furnished, with fan.

**HOTEL ÁNGEL DEL MAR**, *uphill from Playa del Panteón, phone (958) 40395 to 40399, extension 100 or 162; 42 rooms, high season $37 single or double, low season $24, VI - MC - AE.*

Perched proudly on a hilltop with splendid views of the bay and a pleasant sea breeze, this hotel had fallen into decay but is recovering slowly under a new manager. Rooms are simple, with fans, and have magnificent views. It can be a long climb, and taxis are suggested at night for security reasons. The hotel has a restaurant.

**HOTEL LA BUENA VISTA**, *on a back street up the hill behind Playa del Panteón (ask for the hotel by name), phone (958) 40395 to 40399, extension 112; 15 rooms, $16 to $23 in low season, more in high season, no cards.*

Reached by a long series of steps from the street, this hillside hotel has superb views of the bay from its hammock-filled terraces. Rooms are small and pleasant, with fans. The hotel has a restaurant.

**POSADA RINCÓN SABROSO**, *Calle Miramar near the center of town, no phone; 8 rooms, $12 to $18 according to season, no cards.*

This spot has a thoroughly bohemian atmosphere, with hammocks everywhere. It is situated up a long flight of steps, but views are partly obscured by heavy vegetation. Rooms are simply but decently furnished.

**CASA DE HUÉSPEDES CAPY**, *near Playa del Panteón, up a flight of stairs from the street, phone (958) 40395 to 40399, extension 126; 10 rooms, $7 to $9 single, $11 to $14 double, no cards.*

Rooms, with fans, are somewhat dark and musty but all right for the price. There are good views of the sea and a restaurant.

**HOTEL SORAYA**, *Calle José Vasconcelos in the center of town, phone (958) 40395 to 40399, extension 116; 31 rooms; high season $24 single, $33 double; low season $19 single, $22 double, no cards.*

This big, mustard-and-white, motel-style building is planted smack in the center of town. Rooms are big and rather bare, but there are good views.

## WHERE TO EAT

Three or four simple palapa-shaded restaurants set in a row *along Playa Panteón* offer fresh fish and seafood in a variety of preparations at reasonable prices. The restaurants at **HOTEL LA BUENA VISTA** and **CASA DE HUÉSPEDES CAPY** are slightly more expensive but offer good views and pleasant breezes in the evening.

# ZIPOLITE

*Zipolite lies 5 km east of Puerto Ángel.*

It is only a few years since **Zipolite** has been connected to the outside world by paved road, and even less time since accommodations evolved beyond simple huts with hammocks and outhouses, although lodgings are still quite rudimentary for the most part.

Zipolite is noted primarily for its long, broad beach where nudity is common and accepted, especially toward the western end of the beach – the far end as you approach from Puerto Ángel, 5 km to the east. The beach is also noted for its big waves and strong undertow; caution is advised. The village is small but very spread out.

*About 6 km west of Zipolite*, reachable by taxi or on foot, much of the way along virgin beach, is the tiny village of **Mazunte**, which can also be reached by a 10-km dirt road from the main highway. Mazunte was infamous in the past for the slaughter of turtles, whose skin and meat could be sold, but since 1994 it has been home to the **Centro Mexicano de la Tortuga**.

This is a museum and research center devoted to improving knowledge of turtles and working to save rare species from extinction. The research center houses laboratories and incubation cells as well as extensive documentation. The museum contains numerous aquariums and enclosures with marine and land turtles. It also has an exhibition hall, a botanical garden with cactus native to the region, a cafeteria and a gift shop. *Opening hours (subject to change) are Tuesday to Saturday 10:30 am to 5 pm and Sunday 10:30 am to 3 pm Admission is $3.*

## ARRIVALS & DEPARTURES

Buses between Pochutla, Puerto Ángel, and Zipolite run at 20-minute intervals from early morning to early evening. The 5-km road from Puerto Ángel is now paved.

## WHERE TO STAY

As mentioned, accommodations in Zipolite are rather limited, consisting mostly of simple huts where hammocks can be hung for a couple of dollars a night, but there is now a small hotel with several rooms equipped with private bath. Civilization has arrived!

**CASA DE HUÉSPEDES LOLA'S**, *toward the eastern end of the main beach, no phone; 14 rooms, $12 to $21 with private bath, according to season, $8 to $12 without private bath, no cards.*

Rooms have fans and very basic furnishings. The hotel has a restaurant and bar with good fish and seafood dishes, and a generator to supplement the unreliable electricity supply.

**SHAMBHALA**, also known as **CASA GLORIA**, *lies at the western end of the beach perched on a hilltop.* It offers a few small and rather primitive rooms without private bath for a few dollars a night and a large common area to hang hammocks. It is noted for its vegetarian restaurant and for its views over the beach and sea.

## WHERE TO EAT

Several palapa-shaded restaurants line the beach, among them **LA CHOZA**, which has tasty and creative fish and seafood dishes but rather slow service. **LOLA'S**, near the eastern end of the beach, can be recommended, as can **SHAMBALA**, up a series of steps at the western end of the beach, with a selection of vegetarian dishes.

# POCHUTLA

*Pochutla lies 13 km north of Puerto Ángel.*

**Pochutla** is a hot, bustling, rustic town that lies near several tourist towns but makes absolutely no concessions to tourism. It's an important transit point for bus passengers, though there's little reason to linger except to change money at the bank or to catch a glimpse of the rather plain *zócalo* (central plaza) and church one block behind the main street.

Pochutla is 42 km west of Huatulco, 70 km east of Puerto Escondido, and 249 km south of Oaxaca. The highway junction is 1 km south of town.

## ARRIVALS & DEPARTURES

Buses leave from several small terminals scattered along a three-block stretch of the main street. Small buses run several times hourly to Puerto Escondido, Huatulco, Puerto Ángel and Zipolite. Estrella del Valle and Transportes Oaxaca-Istmo provide second-class service to Oaxaca (6 hours) many times daily. Estrella Blanca has numerous first-class and second-class departures to Acapulco (8-9 hours) as well as overnight first-class service to Mexico City (13 hours). Cristóbal Colón has daytime and overnight first-class departures to Tuxtla Gutiérrez (10 hours) and San Cristóbal de las Casas (12 hours). Numerous second-class buses go to Salina Cruz, where there are additional connections for Chiapas.

## WHERE TO STAY

If you choose to stay overnight, your best bets are **HOTEL IZALA** *along the main street* or **HOTEL POCHUTLA** *on Calle Madero near the zócalo*. Both are simple, clean and friendly, with rates running between $11 and $18.

## WHERE TO EAT

**RESTAURANT LOS ANGELES**, *on Calle Igancio Allende between the Bancomer branch and the zócalo*, has good seafood cocktails and excellent fish soup. There are other restaurants facing the *zócalo*.

# 15. GUERRERO

The state of **Guerrero** is certainly less well known by name than its premier city, the port of **Acapulco**. Guerrero's long Pacific coastline gave rise first to Acapulco and, much later, to the twin resorts of **Zihuatanejo** and **Ixtapa** further up the coast, pockets of prosperity in an otherwise bone-dry, dirt-poor and mostly mountainous state.

In the northern part of the state, two-thirds of the way from Acapulco to Mexico City, an 18th century mining boom in **Taxco** bequeathed a delightful hillside town where tourism long ago replaced mining as the key industry.

## ACAPULCO

*Acapulco is linked to Mexico City by a new four-lane highway.*

For years the name **Acapulco** was synonymous with the romance and the glamour of travel. The city is set around a broad, sweeping bay on the Pacific coast, and travelers today and even after many visits are struck by the magnificence of **Acapulco Bay** as they approach from the surrounding hills. As you come nearer, your pleasure may be dimmed by the city's untidy sprawl and, sometimes, by a hint of smog. Even so, that first glimpse of Acapulco Bay is bound to leave a lasting impression.

Acapulco is now a mature resort, as they say in tourism industry jargon, which is a polite way of stating that it has been around a long time and has grown the point where it no longer displays the sort of dynamism that characterizes some younger resorts. Some parts of Acapulco, and certain hotels, have aged less than gracefully and now cater to a thriftier category of visitors than they did in their heyday. The number of visitors to Acapulco has held steady although the mix has changed, with more Mexicans and not quite as many foreigners. Now close to three-quarters of visitors are Mexican.

Acapulco's defenders point out, correctly, that the place has soul, that it has spirit, that is has character. This does not mean it has always shown foresight. Some past mistakes have been corrected, however. Fecal contamination that once earned the unhappy moniker Cacapulco has been all but eliminated by the simple (though less than ideal) expedient of pumping sewage far out to sea. Itinerant vendors who used to be a scourge on beaches and main streeets have been ordered to relocate to three new markets.

Money, both public and private, is being spent to build for the future. Several hotels have been fully renovated, and even in the 1990s new luxury hotels are appearing. It would seem premature to give Acapulco up for dead.

## THE OLD & THE NEW

Comparisons are bound to arise between Acapulco and Cancún, its upstart rival on Mexico's Caribbean coast, so let's just jump right in. Each is big very big in tourism terms, with somewhere in the vicinity of 20,000 hotel rooms. Cancún hotels are newer and more luxurious on average, with a majority of rooms earning Mexico's five-star rating. Acapulco has a broader range of accommodations, from the super-deluxe to the truly dismal, with plenty of middle-range hotels for the discerning traveler.

It's not just the hotels that are more varied. The city itself has both its new and old districts, each with a special character. Quite apart from the areas away from the beach (where the vast majority of Acapulqueños live, eat and shop but where few tourists venture unless they are headed for the bus terminals, rock-bottom lodgings or the red light district), there are four distinct zones.

East of the city, and the area nearest the airport, is **Punta Diamante**, home to the swankest, most lavish and, needless to say, most expensive resort hotels. More central, set around the beach-fringed rim of Acapulco Bay, is an area tourism authorities call **Acapulco Dorado** (*dorado* means golden), where many big hotels and associated tourism activity are concentrated. A bit further west is **Old Acapulco** (sometimes called *Acapulco tradicional*) containing the old heart of the city and some interesting hotels set atop dramatic cliffs, down by **Caleta beach**, or in a warren of small streets just west of the central plaza. Finally there is **Pie de la Cuesta**, a beach area just a short bus or taxi ride west of the city, with a distinctly rustic character, a string of mostly small hotels, and fabulous sunsets.

Acapulco is clearly a more Mexican place than Cancún. Although many, many restaurants and shops cater to American and other foreign tastes, you're rarely in doubt as to which country you're in. A big city in its own right, its population is nearing two million, with a local economy that remains excessively dependent on tourism. As the biggest city in barren Guerrero state, Acapulco has long been a magnet for families from poverty-ridden villages, which helps explain its dismaying growth. You need step only a few blocks from glitzy beachfront resorts to find yourself squarely in the Third World.

Acapulco has the usual panoply of urban problems, but it also offers urban pleasures, such as walking. The **Costera Miguel Alemán**, the broad boulevard running parallel to the beach and named after a former Mexican president, is a hive of activity day and night. Here you can step out of your hotel and stroll for many blocks past great numbers of eating places, shops, services and Acapulco's legion of late-night discotheques. Or you can head over to the *zócalo*, the lively central plaza in the old part of town, and witness the continuing spectacle as you sip something cool or have your shoes shined.

Now for some other pluses and minuses. Acapulco beaches do not have the extra-pale sand or turqoise waters of Cancún, but Acapulco is endowed with real scenery, and its weather is more reliable, with an average of only five sunless days per year. No Mayan ruins or top-notch snorkeling are found nearby, but there are other excursions to keep visitors busy, some of which are outlined below. And if cost is a big factor, Acapulco wins hands down.

**ACAPULCO BAY**

Acapulco also has plenty of history. Its name comes from Nahuatl Indian words meaning *Place of the Reeds*, and archaeologists believe the area has been inhabited for more than two thousand years. Spanish explorers first arrived in 1512, and soon afterward Acapulco became a staging post in the trade between Asia and Spain.

Merchandise arriving from the Philippines or China was landed here and taken on muleback up to Mexico City and then over to the port of Veracruz on the Gulf of Mexico for shipment to Europe. As this trade flourished, Acapulco became the target of pirate attacks in the 17th and 18th centuries. It declined in the years following Mexican independence and lost the chance of recovering its role as a commercial port when railways were built instead to rival ports on the Pacific.

Acapulco showed new signs of life when the ancient mule trail from Mexico City was converted to a highway in the 1920s, although it was unpaved for decades and required an arduous 16-hour journey. In 1954 the highway was paved, the new international airport opened, and Acapulco boomed. It became a haunt of jet-setters from the US, including many Hollywood luminaries, and it flourished in the 1960s and 1970s as mass tourism came into its own. Recent years have not been as kind to Acapulco, but the place has been tarted up, and the opening in 1993 of a new four-lane highway that shortened the trip from Mexico City to just four hours has created new flows.

If you have decided to visit Acapulco, read on. This *grande dame* of Mexican resorts is no plastic cut-out. Its sheer size can add to the challenge of a visit but also helps account for its spirit and soul. We'll help you try to enjoy it.

## ARRIVALS & DEPARTURES

### By Air

Acapulco's **international airport** (airport code ACA) lies about 20 km east of the city and is served by many scheduled and charter flights. American Airlines has direct flights from Dallas, Continental from Houston and Delta from Los Angeles.

Aeroméxico, Mexicana, and TAESA fly from several US points with stops or connections. The Mexican carriers fly frequently to and from Mexico City, where many itineraries require connections. A few go via Guadalajara, but there is a paucity of direct flights between Acapulco and most other points in Mexico. Oaxaca has been served on an on-again, off-again basis. Charter flights operate from several points in the US, Canada and Europe, particularly during the winter season. Tickets on these flights can normally be purchased only through travel agents, and usually only for roundtrip travel from the country of origin.

Airport vans meet incoming flights and charge about $6 per passenger to almost any hotel in Acapulco. To arrange a hotel pickup for the trip back, call Transportaciones Aeropuerto at (74) 852332. Taxis from central Acapulco to the airport charge about $16 per car. Buses pass along the highway near the airport, but this requires some walking and is not recommended if you are traveling with heavy baggage or after dark.

**NOTE:** if you are going to Pie de la Cuesta, you can take the airport van only to central Acapulco and must take a taxi or bus the rest of the way; ditto for the return.

### By Bus

Acapulco has two intercity bus terminals, the Estrella de Oro terminal along Avenida Cuauhtémoc (pronounced kwow-TAY-moc) a few blocks from the Costera, and a newer, bigger and busier terminal deeper in town along Avenida Ejido (pronounced ay-KHEE-do) serving all other long-distance bus lines. If you arrive in Acapulco at the new terminal, fixed-priced tickets are sold for taxis to various points in town. This is safer but usually more expensive than flagging a taxi in the street. Both terminals are served by local buses, but carrying baggage and finding your way can pose real challenges.

Frequent service is provided from both terminals for the four-to-five-hour trip to or from Mexico City's southern terminal at fares ranging from $22 to $37, depending on the degree of luxury you are looking for. The most expensive buses provide three-across seating rather than the usual four-across plus attendants serving drinks and sandwiches. Service is more frequent from the new terminal, which taxi drivers know as the Estrella Blanca terminal from the name of the biggest bus company operating there. This company also operates under the names Flecha Roja, Cuauhtémoc, Turistar and Gacela. Besides service almost hourly throughout the day, there are many overnight services to or from Mexico City. If you are traveling on a weekend or during a busy holiday period, it is best to book ahead. All seats are reserved, and you can usually choose your seat from a computerized chart.

Buses run north from both terminals to intermediate points including Chilpancingo, Taxco and Cuernavaca as well as northwest to Zihuatanejo. Once again, service is more frequent from the Estrella Blanca terminal, with express buses leaving on the four-hour trip to Zihuatanejo (fare $11) almost hourly in the morning and afternoon. Avoid the local service to Zihuatanejo unless you are planning an intermediate stop.

Direct service is also available from both Acapulco terminals to Mexico City's northern terminal with continuing service or connections to points throughout central and northern Mexico. For western and northwestern Mexico all the way to Tijuana, there are two daily departures from the Estrella Blanca terminal. From the same terminal, buses leave almost hourly around the clock to Puerto Escondido (6 to 8 hours, $14 to $17), with many continuing to other points along the Oaxaca coast including Huatulco (8 to 11 hours, $18 to $22). Express services are faster, more comfortable and only slightly more expensive. If you are headed for Chiapas, connections are available at Salina Cruz.

*For information in Acapulco (in Spanish only), call Estrella Blanca at (74) 833070 or 821100, or Estrella de Oro at (74) 858705 or 859360.*

**By Car**

The new four-lane highway from Mexico City makes it a whole lot easier and faster to get to Acapulco, only four hours, but the tolls, at the time of writing, come to a staggering $77 in each direction. It is little wonder that most traffic sticks to the slower and more dangerous federal highway. Route 200, the coastal highway, reaches Acapulco from the northwest and continues all the way to the Guatemalan border. This road is narrow and curvy but in reasonably good shape.

Because of occasional banditry, drivers are cautioned to avoid night travel in Guerrero state on all but the busiest roads.

## ORIENTATION

The central part of Acapulco is set around a big bowl-shaped bay and surrounded by high hills. The majority of tourists stay at hotels along or near the Costera Miguel Alemán, a broad and busy boulevard running parallel to the main beach and often referred to simply as the Costera. Many restaurants and shops are close by. The main beach is long and continuous, but portions of it are called by various names. The airport is located east of the city, and some of the swanker resorts lie between the city and the airport.

The *zócalo*, the central plaza in the older part of town, lies near the western end of the Costera. Several hotels are located in this area as well as in a hilly zone called La Caleta, a peninsula that juts out and forms the western boundary of Acapulco Bay. On the western side of this peninsula are Playa La Angosta and La Quebrada, where the cliff-divers perform their act. A more rustic beach area called Pie de la Cuesta lies about 10 km northwest of the city.

For general tourist information, the state tourism office has helpful, multilingual staff. They are located along the Costera in a white building on the beach side facing Hornos Beach, between the Gigante supermarket and the Hotel do Brasil. They can also help you lodge an official complaint if you feel you have been wronged by a merchant, taxi driver or some other party. They are open 9 am to 2 pm and 4 pm to 8 pm,

Monday to Friday only. Staff at most hotels can also help with general information.

Taxis are often the best way of getting around the city, especially at night. Taxi meters are not used in Acapulco. If you have doubts about the fare, inquire before embarking. Fares within the central part of the city are usually no more than $3, although to Pie de la Cuesta or the resorts at Punta Diamante it can be much more. The bigger taxis parked outside some of the luxury hotels charge higher fares than the taxis in the street.

There are numerous bus routes in Acapulco. The most useful route for most visitors runs almost the entire length of the Costera Miguel Alemán, from La Caleta in the west, past the *zócalo*, the beach and most of the big hotels, terminating at a point near the naval base in the east (thus the word *base* often painted on the windshield). The fare is 30 cents on most buses. The same route is served by buses marked *preferencial*, with air conditioning and more spacious seating, for a fare of 60 cents.

Service is frequent, every two or three minutes until mid-evening, and then it drops off sharply, ending at about midnight. Buses run to Pie de la Cuesta several times an hour until about 8 pm. They cost 30 cents and can be caught near the *zócalo* across from the Sanborns department store.

## WHERE TO STAY

Acapulco has hundreds of hotels, big and small. The most lavish resort hotels are situated in **Punta Diamante**, between the airport and the city. Many of the medium- and upper-priced hotels are located along or near the **Costera Miguel Alemán**, which runs parallel to the beach through the central part of the city, and there are medium- and lower-priced hotels further west in the area around the *zócalo*, around **La Caleta**, or much further out in **Pie de la Cuesta**, a rustic area overlooked by most visitors. There are cheaper hotels in the areas around the municipal market and the new bus terminal, but for the most part these are not places where, to put it delicately, you would want your sister to stay.

If you arrive without a hotel reservation, you can try phoning hotels mentioned below or just heading there directly. Alternatively, there are hotel booking offices at the airport and at both bus terminals, open until late evening. These offices deal with a limited number of hotels and will want to steer you somewhere that pays them a high commission, but you can often get good deals all the same. They normally offer a choice of hotels in several price categories.

As a last resort, you can ask a taxi driver for a hotel recommendation. Many drivers have standing arrangements with particular hotels and get commissions for any guests they bring in. These aren't always the most appetizing places, but if it's late at night and you don't feel like wandering around with your baggage, you can spend the night at one of these places and look for something more appealing in the morning.

There are literally hundreds of hotels in Acapulco, and the list below is very partial. Many of the bigger, more expensive hotels have a certain sameness about them, and only a few are mentioned. Many also charge substantially higher rates to individuals than to groups booked through tour wholesalers. At the smaller hotels, rates for individuals tend to be more realistic, and the hotels themselves often have more character.

### Punta Diamante

**CAMINO REAL ACAPULCO DIAMANTE**, *Carretera Escénica km 14, phone (74) 812010, fax (74) 812700, US and Canada reservations (800) 272-1107; 156 rooms, $195 single or double, VI - MC - AE - DC.*

This new and secluded hotel has a bright, airy lobby in traditional style adjoining a comfortable lounge facing the sea. Rooms, all air conditioned, are set in two buildings along a terraced hillside, and each has a sea view and terrace, with warm colors and plenty of marble and wood. Three pools are set on different levels with a small sliver of private beach below and bigger beaches nearby. The hotel lies down a steep, winding road from the highway. It has a tennis court and two restaurants.

**HOTEL LAS BRISAS**, *Carretera Escénica, phone (74) 841580, fax (74) 842269, US and Canada reservations (800) 228-3000; 265 rooms, high season, $259 and up, service included, VI - MC - AE - MC.*

This very expensive and very romantic spot, with pink and white bungalows set on a terraced hillside above the highway, all with stunning views of Acapulco Bay, remains popular with American honeymooners. Staff far outnumber guests, and service is very attentive at this Westin affiliate. Some bungalows have shared pools and others have private pools for $110 more. Suites are priced at stratospheric levels. A fleet of pink and white jeeps takes guests up and down a winding roadway between their lodgings and the various services, which include three restaurants and five tennis courts. Rooms are spacious with patios facing the bay, marble floors, stone walls and decor in pastel shades. All have air conditioning, but the sea breezes render this unnecessary. The hotel has a beach club 3 km away, with transportation at 20-minute intervals.

Two other hotels in the Punta Diamante area, the **ACAPULCO PRINCESS**, *phone (74) 691000, fax (74) 791015*, and its sibling the **PIERRE MARQUÉS**, *phone (74) 842065 or 842044, fax (74) 848554*, are reputed for the lavishness of their amenities. *They lie near one another on Playa Revolcadero, and the US reservations number for both is (800) 223-1818.*

At the **Acapulco Princess**, high season rates for normal rooms range from $286 for one person and a golf course view to $363 for two persons and a sea view, including two obligatory meals; low season rates are $176 to $198, without meals. Rates at the **Pierre Marqués** are about 20 per cent less. They share two 18-hole golf courses and between them have countless pools, tennis courts, restaurants, bars, shops and a discotheque. The jungle- and waterfall-draped pool near the lobby at the Princess is quite spectacular. Decor at both hotels is cheerful, with rattan furniture. Rooms are spacious and air conditioned.

### Acapulco Dorado

**HOTEL ELCANO**, *Costera Miguel Alemán 75, phone (74) 841950, fax (74) 842230; 180 rooms, $125 single or double, $182 during peak holiday periods, VI - MC - AE - DC.*

This freshly renovated seafront hotel is decorated in blue and white with original murals and paintings. Rooms are comfortable, spacious and air conditioned, and all have sea views. The hotel has two restaurants and an elaborate pool and beach area.

**VILLA VERA HOTEL & RACQUET CLUB**, *Lomas del Mar 35, phone (74) 840333, fax (74) 847479, US reservations (800) 223-6510 or 525-4800; 80 rooms and villas, high season $165 and up, single or double, low season $132 and up, VI - MC - AE - DC.*

This secluded hillside hotel recalls the days when well-heeled visitors to Acapulco preferred to view the bay from above and enjoy the sea breezes that reach the higher elevations. Rooms and villas are set on a series of terraces amid tropical vegetation. Views of the bay are partly obstructed by high buildings that have gone up since. Some of the villas have private pools (high season $335, low season $281), and all offer a sense of privacy. The hotel has a big main pool, jacuzzi, lavish open-air restaurant and four tennis courts, including two clay courts. An arrangement with the Hotel Elcano allows for the use of beach facilities.

**HYATT REGENCY ACAPULCO**, *Costera Miguel Alemán 1, phone (74) 691234, fax (74) 843087, US and Canada reservations (800) 233-1234; 690 rooms, high season $209 single or double, low season $143, VI - MC - AE - DC.*

This tall, nondescript hotel lies at the eastern end of Acapulco Bay and offers fine views of the bay with the city and hills behind. It is the first hotel actually in the city on the way from the airport. Some rooms on the lower floors or the corners lack sea views and are priced at $131 in high season, $88 in low season. The hotel has an array of pools, restaurants and bars, including a swim-up bar and a 24-hour restaurant. Its clients include observant Jews, drawn by its kosher restaurant and chapel with daily services.

**AUTO-HOTEL RITZ**, *Avenida Wilfrido Massieu near the Costera, phone (74) 858023 or 858127, fax (74) 855647; 100 rooms, high season $63 single or double, low season $56, VI - MC - AE - DC.*

This hotel, a couple of minutes' walk from the beach, is among the better values near the central part of the Costera. Rooms are plain and views are uninteresting, but the pool area is pleasant and parking is free.

Several other hotels along the main strip provide reasonable value in the middle of the price range. Rates, for single or double occupancy, are subject to change. Most lie near the beach but not directly along it, and most have modern, boxy architecture and average levels of comfort.

They include **HOTEL DO BRASIL**, *Costera 266, phone (74) 854600 or 854545, 18 stories, bay views from upper floors, $50*; **HOTEL MÓNACO**, *Costera 137, phone (74) 856415 or 856467, motel-style, pool, quiet, $40*; **HOTEL COPACABANA**, *Tabachinas 2, phone (74) 843155 or 843260, in front of the Centro de Convenciones, $58*; **HOTEL ACAPULCO SOL**, *Costera 53, phone (74) 851918 or 851759, $42*; **HOTEL ACAPULCO IMPERIAL**, *Playa Hornos next to Comercial Mexicana, phone (74) 851918 or 851759, $56 including breakfast for two*; and **ROMANO DAYS INN**, *Costera 2310, phone (74) 845332, $66.*

There is one trailer park right in town, **PLAYA SUAVE**, *on Vasco Núñez de Balboa, one block north of the Costera between Diego Hurtado de Mendoza and Capitán Malespina, phone (74) 851464 or 863160.*

### La Caleta

**HOTEL LOS FLAMINGOS**, *Calle López Mateos, La Caleta, phone (74) 820690 to 820692, fax (74) 839806; 46 rooms, high season $72 single or double, low season $55, more for superior rooms, VI - MC - AE.*

This is quite simply the most romantic hotel in Acapulco. It recalls the the era of Errol Flynn and Lana Turner, when Acapulco was a favorite hideaway of Hollywood stars and many stayed at this hotel. Johnny Weissmuller (Tarzan) actually lived here for many years; hotel staff enjoy pointing out his circular villa. The hotel's pink and white villas (yellow and white on the inside, with bright floral bedspreads) and its beautifully landscaped grounds are perched on a hill overlooking the bay. It is *the* place to stay for anyone interested in Hollywood memorabilia, and it will please visitors whose vacation does not center around the beach, although Caleta beach is a few minutes' walk from here. Most rooms have magnificent sea views. Sea breezes provide ample ventilation. A few rooms face away from the sea and are air conditioned. The hotel has a restaurant, a small pool and attentive staff.

**HOTEL PLZA LAS GLORIAS EL MIRADOR**, *Plazoleta La Quebrada, phone (74) 831221 or 831155, fax (74) 82456; 130 rooms, high season $104 single or double, low season $75, VI - MC - AE - DC.*

This hotel is next to La Quebrada, where Acapulco's famous cliff-divers do their thing, and in the evening it offers buffet dinners with a view of the show. Rooms have bright, comfortable sitting areas, air conditioning, and cliffside sea views; they are terraced on a steep hillside and reached by a pair of funicular railways. The hotel has two restaurants, two bars and three pools, including a salt-water pool. There is no direct beach access, but guests may use a nearby beach club.

**HOTEL CALETA ACAPULCO**, *Cerro San Martín, La Caleta, phone (74) 839940, fax (74) 839125; 261 rooms, $66 single or double, higher during holidays, VI - MC - AE - DC.*

Set on a small promontory and surrounded by water on three sides, this is another Acapulco oldie. In the last few years it has undergone several changes of ownership and management, coming most recently under the control of Spain's Meigas resort group. Big rooms, set in two wings, have private terraces, magnificent views, air conditioning and 1950s-style furnishings. Grounds are landscaped in a pleasingly old-fashioned way.

**HOTEL GARZAS INN**, *Costera Miguel Alemán 26, La Caleta, phone (74) 820570, fax (74) 820573; 78 rooms, $31 single or double, higher at peak holidays, VI - MC - AE.*

This eight-story atrium-style hotel faces Caleta beach and has bright, airy, newly renovated rooms with fan and kitchenette. About half have sea views. Those facing the street are noisy during the day but quiet at night.

**HOTEL LINDA VISTA**, *Playa Caleta, phone (74) 822783, fax (74) 825414; 43 rooms, $24 single or double with fan, $36 with air conditioning, VI - MC - AE.*

Set on a hillside in front of Playa Caleta, this hotel has sea views from the upper floors. Rooms are furnished like an old US motel.

**HOTEL NAO**, *Camino Viejo a Caleta, phone (74) 838710; 110 rooms, $18 single, $24 double, VI - MC - AE.*

This simple hotel lies near the beach but does not have beach views. Rooms have fans.

**HOTEL CASA BLANCA**, *Cerro de la Pinzona, La Caleta, phone (74) 821212 to 821215, fax (74) 821517,* and **HOTEL REAL DEL MONTE**, *directly across, phone (74) 832880 or 837666; 300 rooms in total, $40 single or double, VI - MC - AE - DC.*

Under joint ownership, these hilltop hotels provide splendid views in every direction. Unfortunately, both suffer from lack of upkeep. Rooms are big but musty.

### Near the Zócalo
**HOTEL MISIÓN**, *Felipe Valle 12, phone (74) 823643; 26 rooms, $14 single, $24 double, no cards.*

This family-run hotel three blocks west of the *zócalo* is situated in a three-story colonial-style building with simple but pleasant rooms set around an attractive, tree-shaded courtyard, where breakfast is served on weekends and a Guerrero-style barbecue is offered on Thursday afternoons.

**HOTEL MAMA HÉLÈNE**, *Benito Juárez 12, phone (74) 822396, fax (74) 838697; 18 rooms, $12 per person, no cards.*

This simple hotel, also known as Casa Hélène, is run by a Frenchwoman who also speaks Spanish and English. It attracts many younger travelers and has a friendly atmosphere.

**CASA DE HUÉSPEDES CALIFORNIA**, *La Paz 12, phone (74) 822893; 24 rooms, $12 single, $18 double, higher at holidays, no cards.*

Rooms are clean but simple. Many face a tree-shaded but concrete-covered courtyard. Rooms near the street are noisy.

If you don't find rooms at these hotels, there are several other modestly priced hotels in the same general area.

### Pie de la Cuesta

All hotels below are situated near the beach. Swimmers should beware of a strong undertow.

**VILLA NIRVANA PLAYA**, *phone (74) 601631; 6 rooms, high season $24-$30 single or double, low season $18, no cards.*

This friendly spot is one of the best values around. Rooms are simply but pleasantly furnished, with colorful wall hangings and fans. Some have kitchenettes, and there is a small restaurant. The grounds are attractive, with a pool in a palm-shaded area.

**HOTEL PUESTA DEL SOL**, *phone (74) 600412; 24 rooms, $23 single or double, no cards.*

This is another very good value, with a tennis court, restaurant and palm-shaded pool. Situated about 100 meters from the main road, it consists of a cluster of low-rise buildings separated from the beach by a low wall. Some have kitchenettes or terraces overlooking the sea.

**HOTEL UKAE KIM**, *phone (74) 602187, fax (74) 602188; 20 rooms, $45 to $60 single or double, higher at holiday periods, VI - MC.*

A pair of two-story buildings face each other across a narrow, tree-shaded passage. Split-level rooms have cushioned seating areas, lots of painted tile, mosquito netting and fans. The restaurant, bar and pool lie on a terrace facing the beach and the sunsets. Service can be a bit sluggish. Room rates vary according to the distance from the beach,

**HOTEL CASA BLANCA**, *phone (74) 600324; 13 rooms, high season $24 single or double, low season $18, higher during holidays, no cards.*

This folksy spot has a restaurant and simply furnished rooms with area rugs.

**HOTEL LA CABAÑITA**, *phone (74) 600052; 7 rooms, $15 single or double, VI - MC.*

Rooms are simply furnished, with fans.

**HOTEL QUINTA BLANCAS**, *phone (74) 600311; 15 rooms, $9 single or double, no cards.*

Rooms are very simple, with fans.

**HOTEL QUINTA CARLA**, *no phone; 6 rooms; high season $21 single, $30 double; low season $12 single, $15 double; no cards.*

This is one of the first hotels you see as you arrive from Acapulco. It is better to avoid its shabby, overpriced rooms.

**HOTEL PARADOR DEL SOL DE ACAPULCO**, *Carretera a Barra de Coyuca km 5, phone (74) 602003 to 602006, fax (74) 601649; 150 rooms, $68 single, $120 double, $18 extra for children under 12, including meals, tips and activities; VI - MC - AE.*

Formerly called Hotel Acapulco Villas, this all-inclusive resort hotel is situated on an isolated site far from the other hotels in Pie de la Cuesta and is in a different category altogether. To get there, continue west beyond the military base and airstrip. The hotel faces Coyuca lagoon on one side and an ocean beach on the other, with very extensive grounds bisected by the road and dotted with 75 terra cotta and red-tile villas. The rooms, two to a villa, have pastel and dark blue decor with wood ceilings, fans and air conditioning. Amenities include a restaurant, three bars, a discotheque, two pools, a gym, tennis court, nine-hole golf course, and soccer and basketball courts. Packages for day visitors include breakfast, lunch, drinks, tips and the use of all facilities for $18. An evening package includes supper, drinks, tips and entry to the discotheque for $23.

## WHERE TO EAT

Acapulco has countless restaurants catering to all sorts of tastes. If you are staying at a hotel along or near the Costera Miguel Alemán, you need not walk more than a few minutes to encounter dozens of them, some casual and inexpensive, others more formal. The area around the *zócalo* and just to its west is a good place to go restaurant hunting. Many restaurants there offer seafood dishes or regional specialties such as *pozole* (a hearty soup containing large-grained corn and meat, a meal in itself) at moderate prices. And all along the beach at Pie de la Cuesta are simple, palapa-shaded restaurants offering fresh fish lunches in a very relaxing setting.

Here is a dark little secret about fish and seafood in Acapulco: most of it comes from elsewhere, since the surrounding sea has been largely fished out. Some hotels even bring in their fish and seafood frozen from Mexico City!

For genuinely fresh seafood, **MI BARQUITA**, *López Mateos 30, on Playa La Angosta in the Caleta area*, is favored by *Acapulqueños*, as are **PACO'S**, *nearby at La Quebrada 36*, and **JULIUS**, *along Avenida Wilfrido Massieu about four blocks north of the big Salinas y Rocha store*. In the area west of the *zócalo*, **MARISCOS MILLAS**, *at the corner of Emilio Carranza and Teniente Anzueta*, has very good and inexpensive seafood dishes; it closes early. Other good seafood spots nearby include **LA SIRENITA**, *Teniente Azueta 1*, and **EL AMIGO MIGUEL**, *Benito Juárez 16*, which also has a branch on the Costera between the tourism office and Restaurant Bella Italia.

   **LA FLOR DE ACAPULCO**, *facing the zócalo*, is a landmark restaurant with a broad menu and moderate prices. **EL ZORRITO**, *along the Costera across from the giant Hotel Acapulco Plaza*, is open 24 hours a day and offers Mexican favorites such as *Tampiqueño* steak, enchiladas, and a variety of tacos at moderate prices. **EL FOGÓN**, *right next door*, is a similar spot. Restaurants specializing in *pozole* include **EL AMIGO JUAN**, *on Benito Juárez west of the zócalo* (very cheap), and **LULÚ**, *uptown at Ruiz Cortines and Cuauhtémoc*.

   For charcoal-grilled steaks, recommendations include **LA TABLITA**, *Costera 82*, and **LA MANSIÓN**, *just across at Costera 81*, both formal, expensive and very good. **SIROCCO**, *on the Costera across from the Aurrerá supermarket*, is an elegant and highly regarded spot for Spanish specialties, including *paella* and *fabada*.

   For something casual and familiar, there is no shame in eating at a chain restaurant. **DENNY'S** has several branches in Acapulco, as do its Mexican counterparts such as **VIPS** and **CALIFORNIA**. The usual pizza and hamburger joints are also quite evident. **100% NATURAL** is an Acapulco-based chain with a menu leaning heavily to salads and fruit juices, but it also offers meat dishes and a variety of Mexican *antojitos* such as enchiladas. It has many branches.

## SEEING THE SIGHTS

   The *zócalo*, or **central plaza**, lies at the heart of the old section of Acapulco, near the western end of the Costera Miguel Alemán. It is a big, breezy, tree-shaded plaza, with cafés, restaurants, and newsstands, and a good place to catch a slice of life. It bustles day and night, with hundreds of people passing through and shoeshine men and musicians plying their trades. On weekends it is sometimes converted to a fairground. Several banks and department stores lie nearby, and in the streets to the west are several good and inexpensive seafood restaurants. At one end of the plaza is the modern **Nuestra Señora de la Soledad** church, notable for its white exterior and its blue and yellow domes.

   The **Museo Histórico de Acapulco** is situated in the 18th century **Fuerte de San Diego** (*fuerte* here means fort), *perched on a low hilltop overlooking the Costera and the harbor on a small promontory between the zócalo and the modern part of Acapulco*. The fort was built originally in the 16th century to repel pirate attacks and was rebuilt after a devastating earthquake in 1776. This is a storybook stone fort, complete with cannon. Exhibition rooms are set around a central patio and depict Acapulco in the pre-Hispanic period, in the era of evangelization, and in the heyday of the maritime trade. Another room displays several cannon. *Visitors are admitted daily except Monday from 10:30 am to 4:40 pm. Entry is $4 but is free on Sunday (free every day to people over 60).*

**Pie de la Cuesta** (pronounced PYAY-day-la-QUES-ta) is a beach area *10 km northwest of Acapulco* that seems worlds apart. The tranquility is broken only by the rolling of the surf (swimmers should beware of a strong undertow), and the many small, palapa-shaded restaurants that dot the beach offer fish and seafood at inexpensive prices. Restaurants provide lounge chairs on the beach free of charge if you order a meal, or about $1 otherwise. Pie de la Cuesta is famous for its sunsets, and some people choose to stay at hotels here. It is linked several times an hour by buses, which can be caught across from the Sanborns department store near the *zócalo* in Acapulco.

**Isla Roqueta**, *reached by a ten-minute boat ride from the pier between Caleta and Caletilla beaches*, has beaches, many restaurants, and a tiny zoo. **Magico Mundo Marino**, *situated on a small point between Caleta and Caletilla beaches*, has aquariums with many species of tropical fish. It also has a pool, a small nautical museum, and several restaurants. *Open daily 9 am to 6 pm Admission $8 for adults, $5 for children under 13.*

**Parque Papagayo** is a big, beautifully wooded amusement park toward the western side of town with rides for children, a roller skating rink, and a lagoon with pedalboats for rent. It also has a large aviary (well worth it for adults) and a model of a Spanish galleon. The Costera tunnels beneath the park to allow direct access to the beach. The park is open day and night, and admission is free. The **Centro Internacional para Convivencia Infantil**, usually known as **CICI**, is a water park for children, *located along the eastern part of the Costera near the monument to Christopher Columbus.* It has water slides, a big pool with wave makers, a small aquarium, and seal and dolphin shows. *Open daily 10 am to 6 pm; admission $9, slightly less for children under 11.*

Several companies offer **yacht cruises** around Acapulco Bay and the surrounding area. They include **Yates Hawaianos**, *phone (74) 820785 or 831808*, which provides three-hour daylight cruises for $14, and **Kon-Tiki**, *phone (74) 846140*, whose three-hour cruises include drinks and music for $18. Both leave from piers near the *zócalo*, and both also offer dinner cruises, at higher cost. Hours vary according to season.

## ENTERTAINMENT & NIGHTLIFE

A venerable Acapulco tradition are the **cliff-divers**, called *clavadistas*, who jump from the cliffs at **La Quebrada**, on the same peninsula as Caleta beach but on the other side, reached by a road that climbs steeply from the zócalo. *Shows are presented each day at 1:30 pm and hourly from 7:30 pm to 10:30 pm. Admission to the observation deck is $1.50.*

Alternately, the **Hotel Plaza Las Glorias El Mirador** has a dining area facing the cliffs. Dinner, the cliff-diving show and one drink cost $33. The divers jump from heights of more than 40 meters (130 feet) into a narrow, rocky expanse of pounding suf, and their timing has to be precise so that they hit the water just at the moment that a wave comes in. For the last show of the evening, they carry flaming torches.

Acapulco is also famed for its **discotheques**, which were all the rage through the 1970s and 1980s but have started to wane slightly as their clients age or go deaf. Most open only after 10 pm and stay open until shortly before dawn. Things get lively around midnight. All have cover charges, which may or may not include drinks, and all are vulnerable to the vagaries of fashion.

Among the more popular discos are **Extravaganza** and **Fantasy**, *both along the Carretera Escénica near the Hotel Las Brisas*; **News**, *Costera 12*, and **Baby'O**, *Costera 22, both near the naval base*; and **Le Dome**, *Costera 4175 at the far end*. **Salón Q**, *Costera 23*, **Nina's**, *Costera 41*, and **Afroantillanos**, *Juan de la Cosa 32 near the Costera*, all have live salsa bands, providing a welcome change from the thumping disco beat which comes on between sets. **Disco Beach**, *facing Playa Condesa*, has live rock bands. **B & B Disco**, *along Gran Vía Tropical, La Caleta*, appeals to an older crowd with hits from past decades and a separate dance floor with romantic music.

As well, Acapulco has its share of **strip shows**. These include **Las Chicas** and **Tabares**, *off the Costera near the statue of La Diana*, and **Foxis Club**, *near the Hotel Acapulco Plaza*. For something truly raunchy, try *La Huerta or the 24-hour Bar Arcelia, in the back streets behind the Estrella Blanca bus terminal*. For your safety, arrive and leave only by taxi.

For **classical music** lovers, monthly chamber music concerts are held at the Hotel Ritz Acapulco (not the same as the Auto-Hotel Ritz). *For information, call Fernando Ibarra, president of Cultural Musical de Acapulco, at (74) 838841.*

## SHOPPING

Whether your tastes run to lurid T-shirts or to fine handicrafts, you will be well catered to in Acapulco. Shopping venues range from climate-controlled malls to open-air bazaars. The two biggest markets are the **mercado municipal**, *just north of Avenida Cuauhtémoc a few blocks east of Áquiles Serdán*, and the **mercado de artesanías** (*artesanías means handi-crafts), north of the Costera about midway between Papagayo Park and the Fuerte de San Diego.*

The municipal market concentrates on day-to-day items ranging from tomatoes to plastic pails, but it also has a big section selling flowers and a range of lower-priced handicrafts including basketware, embroidered blouses and simple items of jewelry. It is sprawling, untidy and full of life, bustling from early morning to mid-afternoon.

The handicrafts market aims squarely at foreign tourists. It is more orderly, not nearly as claustrophobic, and a little more expensive. It also keeps later hours, with many stalls open until 9 pm Besides the usual array of T-shirts and other souvenirs, you will find a broad selection of serapes, rugs, wall hangings, tablecloths, leather goods of every description, glassware, silver jewelry (look for the .925 symbol if you want to buy sterling silver), straw hats, assorted basketware, a wide variety of ceramic objects, hand-painted wooden items, ceremonial masks, and much more. Prices tend to be lower than at the shops in the hotels or along the Costera, but you have to be prepared to bargain

More elegant shopping, including international brand-name boutiques, is found along the Costera, especially in the area around the **Hotel Fiesta Americana Condesa**, and in the enclosed shopping centers (nine at last count) that have sprung up near some of the larger hotels along the Costera. The **Acapulco Princess** east of the city has its own mall.

The itinerant vendors who used to pester tourists along beaches or streets have been herded into a series of flea markets, mostly scattered along the Costera. The variety is not what you'll find at the *mercado de artesanías*, but there are some interesting items nonetheless.

## EXCURSIONS

A popular excursion from Acapulco is to the former silver-mining town of **Taxco**, *272 km to the north*, noted for its picturesque cobbled streets and numerous jewelry shops. Taxco is described at length later in this chapter. It is easy to reach by car, bus or organized tour. The trip takes about three hours in each direction (slightly longer by public bus). Some visitors prefer to stay there overnight so that they can see a bit more. It is best to go on weekdays: Taxco can get quite crowded on Saturdays and Sundays.

An interesting Sunday excursion is to **Chilapa**, with its enormous and thoroughly authentic weekly market, which provides a wonderful glimpse of rural Mexico. *Chilapa lies 57 km east of Chilpancingo, which in turn is 133 km north of Acapulco.*

The trip from Acapulco to Chilapa takes a little over two hours in each direction by car or three hours by bus. First-class buses go at half-hour intervals from the Estrella Blanca terminal to Chilpancingo, with connections there to the second-class buses that run to Chilapa at 20-minute intervals on Sundays. (Estrella de Oro leaves you at the wrong terminal in

Chilpancingo.) Some tour companies in Acapulco provide organized visits. For a description of the market and other attractions, see the short section below on Chilpancingo and Chilapa.

Nearer Acapulco, **Hacienda de Cabañas** is a popular getaway spot among *Acapulqueños*. This is a small seaside village with fine beaches and simple restaurants serving fresh fish. *It is reached by a dirt road running 8 km south from Highway 200 from a cutoff about 75 km west of Acapulco, near the town of San Gerónimo.* Only by car is it practical: you can take a bus to San Gerónimo and a taxi from there, but getting back can be a problem.

## PRACTICAL INFORMATION

### Airlines

For information, reservations or reconfirmations in Acapulco, call:
- **American Airlines**: *841734 or 841814*
- **Continental**: *669064 or 669051*
- **Delta**: *840466 or 840797*
- **Aeroméxico**: *851600 or 851625*
- **Mexicana**: *846890 or 840317*
- **TAESA**: *864576 or 864577*

If you come on a **charter flight**, your travel agent will probably have given you an information sheet including a number to call for reconfirmations. If you need an **airport van**, call **Transportaciones Aeropuerto**, *(74) 852332.*

### Car Rentals

Several car rental companies, among them **National, Dollar, Avis,** and **Hertz,** have counters at the airport, along with local firms **Economóvil, Quick,** and **Saad.**

Among car rental counters at hotels in town are:
- **National**: *the Hotel Presidente (phone 848234)*
- **Economóvil**: *the Hotel Condesa Acapulco (phone 841819 or 842727) and the Hotel Acapulco Plaza (phone 858050 or 859050)*
- **Dollar**: *the Hotel Hyatt Regency (842888, ext. 853) and Hotel Acapulco Princess (phone 803100)*
- **Flash**: *the Hotel Bali-Hai (phone 856622)*

*Several other car rental offices are located along the Costera Miguel Alemán, including:*
- **Budget**: *phone 810592 or 810596*
- **Saad**: *phone 843445 or 845325*
- **Hertz**: *phone 858947 or 856942*
- **National**: *phone 848234*

**Consulates**
- **Britain**: *Hotel Las Brisas, phone 841650 or 846650*
- **Canada**: *Hotel Club del Sol, phone 856621*
- **US**: *Hotel Club del Sol, phone 857207*

Several other European countries also have consulates or honorary consulates in Acapulco.

**Telephone Code**

All telephone numbers shown here have the city code 74.

**Tourist Information**

The **state tourism office**, *open 9 am to 2 pm and 4 pm to 8 pm Monday to Friday only, is located along the Costera Miguel Alemán in a white building on the beach side facing Hornos Beach, between the Gigante supermarket and the Hotel do Brasil.* Staff is very helpful.

# CHILPANCINGO & CHILAPA

*Chilpancingo is the capital of Guerrero and lies in the center of the state, 133 km north of Acapulco, 138 km south of Taxco and 277 km south of Mexico City.*

*Chilapa lies 57 km east of Chilpancingo, connected by a winding mountain road with good views of the surrounding valleys.*

## ARRIVALS & DEPARTURES

**Chilpancingo** is served by Estrella Blanca (operating under several different nam es) and Estrella de Oro bus lines, leaving from different terminals. For travel to **Chilapa,** second-class buses leave from Chilpancingo's Estrella Blanca terminal at 20-minute intervals on Sundays, at 30-minute intervals other days.

## WHERE TO STAY IN CHILPANCINGO

**HOTEL POSADA MELÉNDEZ**, *Benito Juárez 50 across from the Estrella de Oro bus terminal, phone (747) 22050 or 23087, $24 single, $30 double, VI - MC.*

A friendly place in the style of an old-fashioned grand hotel, with a big pool set in a garden, a restaurant, and 35 simply furnished rooms.

**CONJUNTO TURÍSTICO JACARANDAS**, *Avenida Ruffo Figueroa, phone (747) 24444, $35 single, $51 double, VI - MC - AE.*

Located on a hillside on the outskirts of town, this is a more lavish but less appealing place, with two cinemas, discotheque, restaurant, big pool, and 60 air-conditioned rooms furnished in modern style.

**HOTEL PRESIDENTE** and **HOTEL MARINA** are cheaper, noisy spots *on Avenida Guerrero near both bus terminals.* **HOTEL DEL PARQUE,** *Colón 5 near the zócalo, phone (747) 23012 or 21285; $39-$48, VI - MC - AE,* is a modern spot. Its 29 rooms are pleasantly furnished but small, dark and overpriced.

## WHERE TO STAY IN CHILAPA

**HOTEL BELLA VISTA,** *near the cathedral,* and **HOTEL LAS BRISAS,** *near the entrance to the town,* are simple, inexpensive places.

## WHERE TO EAT IN CHILAPA

**RESTAURANT SALÓN FAMILIAR DOÑA PAULINA,** *on Avenida José María Andraca behind the cathedral,* is a friendly spot with tasty regional specialties. Meals are also served at some stalls in the market.

## SEEING THE SIGHTS

**Chilpancingo** is of limited interest to tourists, but the area around the *zócalo,* the **central plaza,** is now a lively pedestrian zone. Nearby are the 18th century **Asunción** church, where Mexico's declaration of independence was drafted, the **Casa de las Artesanías,** with displays of silver jewelry and textiles, and the modern **Palacio Municipal,** with murals by Mexican painters Luís Arenal and Roberto Cueva del Río. Four km outside Chilpancingo lie the **Grutas de Juxtlahuaca,** a series of 19 caverns adorned with stalagmites and stalactites.

**Chilapa** is famous for its **Sunday market,** which brings together thousands of buyers and sellers from neighboring towns and villages. The market spills out from the tree-shaded central plaza to envelop many neighboring streets. Most stalls offer farm produce or cheap manufactured goods, but some deal in fine regional handicrafts, including elaborate basketware items, hand-painted wood and *papier mâché* objects, jewelry, chairs made of wood and palm fronds, long home-made candles, straw mats, flowers and *sombreros* from a local factory. This market is utterly authentic, and not many tourists have discovered it yet, although organized groups have begun arriving from Acapulco. It is best to arrive in the morning; things start to wind down by early afternoon.

**Asunción de María** cathedral, facing the central plaza in Chilapa, is one of the biggest churches in Mexico. It is a modern concrete building imitating the Gothic style, erected on the site of an earlier wooden church that was destroyed by fire. It has an unfinished look, but inside are paintings depicting the stations of the cross and other moments in the life of Christ. Stained glass windows honor the patron saints of various towns in Guerrero state. Chilapa has an intense religious life, and there are 16 annual festivals.

# ZIHUATANEJO & IXTAPA

> *The twin resorts of Zihuatanejo and Ixtapa are nestled along the Pacific coast about 240 km northwest of Acapulco.*

Separated by a rugged promontory jutting into the sea,**Zihuatanejo** and **Ixtapa** offer two very different worlds.

**Zihuatanejo** (pronounced zee-wa-ta-NAY-kho) is an old fishing village that retains some of its early charm despite its growth into a busy tourist town. There are several fine beaches, including one right in town called **Playa Principal**. Two bigger, broader beaches, **Playa La Madera** and **Playa La Ropa**, are set in gorgeous bays on the outskirts. Accommodations range from the cheap and funky to the very exclusive.

Around the point, **Ixtapa** (pronounced eeks-TA-pa) is a modern resort developed by Fonatur, the same government agency that built Cancún. Ixtapa is more homogeneous and very suburban in feel. Its central area consists of a string of big, standard-issue beachfront hotels with clusters of shops and restaurants set across a broad, garden-lined boulevard.

Zihuatanejo and Ixtapa both will appeal to travelers who prefer a mid-sized resort town, more intimate than mega-resorts like Cancún and Acapulco, yet big enough to offer airline service and a decent choice of hotels and restaurants. The beaches are uncrowded, sunless days are rare, and the water stays warm year-round, although waves can be rough on the Ixtapa side. There's not much to do here besides beachcombing, but if you're looking mostly for a place to relax, you won't go far wrong here.

## ARRIVALS & DEPARTURES

### By Air

Zihuatanejo and Ixtapa share an international airport (airport code ZIH) located about 20 km northeast of either place, about 2 km off highway 200. Aeroméxico and Mexicana each have several daily flights from Mexico City plus service from Guadalajara. There are few nonstop international flights apart from Delta Airlines' service from Los Angeles and an assortment of charter flights from points in the US and Canada, most of them operating in the winter only. Collective vans meet each flight and provide economical transportation from the airport to any point in Zihuatanejo or Ixtapa. Returning to the airport, taxis are your best bet.

### By Bus

Estrella Blanca and its associated companies, which go by names including Turistar, Cuauhtémoc and Flecha Roja, operate from a large terminal along Highway 200 on the outskirts of Zihuatanejo. They offer first-class service to Acapulco nearly every hour from 6 am to 6 pm ($10, four hours). Leaving from Acapulco, departure times are mostly 30 minutes after the hour, starting at 6:30 am. Second-class service ($8, five to six hours) runs at half-hour intervals beginning around 5 am.

At Acapulco there are frequent connections to or from Mexico City (southern terminal) and other points. Direct services between Zihuatanejo and Mexico City via Acapulco ($27-$36, eight to nine hours) operate mostly overnight, with several departures between 6 pm and 10 pm. As well, overnight first-class buses connect Zihuatanejo with Puerto Escondido and Huatulco. To or from points to the northwest, second-class service to Lázaro Cárdenas ($3, two hours) runs at half-hour intervals. One or two first-class buses go all the way to Tijuana.

Estrella de Oro offers competing service to Acapulco and Mexico City from a small terminal on Paseo del Palmar. Service is less frequent than with Estrella Blanca but includes premium-class Diamante service overnight to Mexico City for $48 with extra-big seats, full leg rests, and refreshments on board.

Autobuses Zinacatepec operates to and from Mexico City by the slower but more scenic route via Ciudad Altamirano and Toluca, with three daytime departures and two overnight runs. This company operates from the western terminal in Mexico City and has its own small terminal in Zihuatanejo near the Estrella Blanca terminal.

### By Road

Zihuatanejo and Ixtapa lie along Highway 200, the main route along the Pacific coast. Travel time to or from Acapulco is a little over three hours. The road is quite curvy and is referred to as the coastal highway, although most of the way it runs some distance inland. An alternative route to Mexico City runs northeast via the dusty farming town of Ciudad Altamirano. This road is more of an adventure: the countryside is mountainous and quite solitary, with few gas stations or villages along the way, and there are added dangers from rockslides and bandits. It is safer by bus than by car.

## ORIENTATION

Zihuatanejo and Ixtapa lie about 10 km apart and are connected by a road that runs well inland. The center of Zihuatanejo is laid out in a grid pattern and is quite compact. **Playa Madera** is easily reached by a footpath near the shore, and **Playa La Ropa** lies further along in the same direction. To Playa La Ropa is a long walk; taxis are a better bet. There are many restaurants and shops in the center of Zihuatanejo and several restaurants along Playa La Ropa. Further in the same direction is **Playa Las Gatas**, popular with snorkelers.

The central area of Ixtapa is bisected by a broad boulevard running parallel to the shore with a string of hotels on one side along the main beach, called **Playa Palmar**. On the other side are clusters of shops and restaurants, as well as a golf course. The Club Med and a couple of newer hotels are situated on **Playa Quieta** or **Playa Linda**, off to one end, while the Westin is on the smaller **Playa Vista Hermosa**, at the other end. Many condominium developments are situated near the road to Zihuatanejo, well away from the beach.

The **tourism office in Zihuatanejo** is located in the town hall (*palacio municipal*) *on Juan Álvarez street near the waterfront, open 9 am to 3 pm and 6 pm to 8 pm weekdays, 9 am to 2 pm Saturdays*. Staff can provide maps but don't seem very knowledgeable.

The **tourism office in Ixtapa**, *opposite the Presidente hotel, phone (753) 31967 or 31968, open 9 am to 2 pm and 4 pm to 7 pm weekdays only*, is run by the state government and is more helpful.

Small buses run frequently between Avenida Morelos, a few minutes' walk from the beachfront promenade in Zihuatanejo, and the main boulevard in Ixtapa. The fare is 30 cents. Taxis charge about $5; they are not metered, and you may want to check the fare before embarking. Between the center of Zihuatanejo and Playa La Ropa, there are no buses; taxis cost $1.50 to $3. From the airport, collective vans take you directly to your hotel. To return to the airport, taxis charge about $9. From the bus terminals, taxis are your best way of getting to the center of town or the beaches, especially if you have baggage.

## WHERE TO STAY

Nearly all hotels in Ixtapa are in the upper-middle to upper price range and offer the usual amenities, including spacious rooms with air conditioning, big pools, a range of sporting activities, and a choice of restaurants and bars. On the Zihuatanejo side, prices are mostly lower, but that's also where you'll find the region's two most exclusive resorts.

Most hotels in Ixtapa cater to people arriving on package tours, and several of them operate on the all-inclusive formula, with meals and many activities included in room rates. Rooms booked on an individual basis tend to cost considerably more than as part of a package tour. Standard undiscounted rates appear below.

Zihuatanejo hotels are more varied in size, comfort, amenities and price. Usually there is little gap between posted prices and what most people pay. All hotels mentioned here face the beach or lie within several minutes' walk of the beach. Addresses of beachfront hotels consist simply of the name of the beach. Taxi drivers know them all.

*Center of Zihuatanejo*

**HOTEL ÁVILA**, *Juan Álvarez 8, phone (753) 42010; 27 rooms, high season $42 single, $48 double, ocean view $12 more, low season $6 less, VI - MC - AE.*

This beachfront hotel also lies in the center of town. Rooms facing the beach have spacious terraces. Those facing the street have balconies. Rooms have white tile floors and simple furnishings.

**POSADA CITLALI**, *Vicente Guerrero 3, (753) 42043; 20 rooms, $21 single, $27 double, no cards.*

A friendly place half a block from the beach. Rooms are small but comfortable; there are pleasant open-air lounges where guests can mingle.

**HOTEL SUSY**, *Vicente Guerrero at Juan Álvarez, phone (753) 42339; 16 rooms, $17 single, $26 double, VI - MC - AE.*

Not as pleasant as the Posada Citlali next door but still a good value.

**HOTEL ZIHUATANEJO CENTRO**, *Augstín Ramírez 2, phone (753) 43661, fax (753) 42669; 69 rooms, high season $54 single or double, low season $42; VI - MC - AE.*

This hotel is set on a quiet side street a couple of blocks from the beach, but the inner courtyard has been turned into a parking lot. Furnishings are motel-style, and there is a small pool.

**PUERTO MÍO HOTEL MARINA RESORT**, *Playa del Almacén, phone (753) 42748 or 43624, fax (753) 42048; 20 rooms; high season $198 single or double, breakfast included; low season $138, no meals included; VI - MC - AE.*

Situated on a peninsula at the edge of town, this hotel has dramatic views of the bay and surrounding hills. A marina lies on one side and a small rocky beach on the other. Grounds are attractive with plenty of tropical vegetation, and there is a long, narrow pool. Rooms have pink and white decor with brightly colored cushions and plenty of painted tile.

**HOTEL RAÚL TRES MARÍAS CENTRO**, *Juan Álvarez 52, phone (753) 42977; $18 single, $24 double, higher at Christmas, VI - MC - AE.*

This small hotel, in the center of town on a street running parallel to the beach, is furnished very simply. There are sea views from the third-floor balconies facing the street.

**HOTEL RAÚL TRES MARÍAS NORIA**, *Colonia Lázaro Cárdenas, phone (753) 42191 or 42591; 25 rooms; high season $15 single, $24 double; low season $11 single, $15 double; no cards.*

Lodgings here are quite rudimentary. A footbridge across a narrow inlet leads to the center of town.

**VILLA DEPORTIVA JUVENIL**, *Paseo de las Salinas, phone (753) 44662; 64 beds, $5 per person, no cards.*

This youth hostel, a few minutes' walk from the center of town, is open to people of all ages and has no curfew. Accommodation is in dormitories, and the sexes are segregated.

**HOTEL IMELDA**, *Catalina González 11, phone (753) 43199; 40 rooms, $30 single, $36 double, VI - MC.*

This hotel lies several blocks from the beach. Service is unfriendly, and rooms are very ordinary.

### Playa La Madera

**BUNGALOWS PACÍFICOS**, *phone (753) 42112; 6 rooms, high season $50 single or double, low season $45, no cards.*

This tiny, plant-filled place draws many return guests. The owner, Señora Anita Hahner, speaks German, English and Spanish and has a keen knowledge of archaeology. Each room has a private terrace facing the sea and a kitchenette. Ventilation is provided by sea breezes and fans. There is a long series of steps to the beach.

**HOTEL IRMA**, *phone (753) 42025 or 42105, fax (753) 43738; 75 rooms, high season $90 single or double, $54 low season, VI - MC - AE - DC.*

This hillside hotel has a pool, a restaurant and friendly service. Thirty of its rooms face the sea and have excellent views. Some rooms are air conditioned, while others have fans.

**HOTEL VILLAS MIRAMAR**, *phone (753) 42106 or 42616; 18 rooms, high season $66 single or double, low season $45; VI - MC - AE.*

This friendly hotel is situated near the beach and has two sections, each with a pool. Rooms are big and air-conditioned. Some are a little dark, but they are painted in bright pastel shades. The restaurant is not open for supper.

**HOTEL PALACIOS**, *phone (753) 42055; 25 rooms, high season $41 single or double, low season $21-$30, no cards.*

Next door to Villas Miramar, this hotel has simple rooms, most with fan. Only a few have sea views. There is a small pool.

**HOTEL BRISAS DEL MAR**, *phone (753) 42124; 22 rooms, high season $20 single, $30 double, low season $18 single, $27 double, VI - MC.*

This family-oriented place has rooms that can accommodate up to seven people (extra charge). Rooms are big, most with sea views and kitchenettes. All have fans, terraces and simple furnishings. Upkeep could be better; there are some broken floor tiles, for example.

**BUNGALOWS SOTELO**, *phone (753) 43545; 10 rooms, $57 single or double, no cards.*

Ten big, pleasant, brightly colored (some might say garish) rooms are terraced on a hillside. Service is inattentive.

### Playa La Ropa

**HOTEL VLLA DEL SOL**, *phone (753) 42239 or 43239, fax (753) 42758 or 44066, US or Canada reservations (800) 223-6510; 36 suites, high season $198 to $506, low season $143 to $363, VI - MC - AE.*

Staff outnumber guests at this very lavish beachfront hotel, with a reputation for personal attention. Suites are set in a series of two-story beige adobe villas situated amid meticulously landscaped tropical gardens. The bigger suites each have two bedrooms, two bathrooms, private terraces and whirlpool or private mini-pool. All have living rooms, air conditioning, ceiling fans, and bathrooms with painted tiles. Amenities include a palapa-shaded bar and dining area with classical music in the evening, two pools, palm-shaded beach chairs, two tennis courts, and secretarial services.

**HOTEL LA CASA QUE CANTA**, *phone (753) 42722 or 42782, fax (753) 42006, US reservations (800) 432-6075; 18 suites, most priced in high season at $259 to $275 single or double, low season $209 to $220, VI - MC - AE - DC.*

Perched above the northern end of Playa La Ropa, this is one of the prettiest hotels in Mexico, with exquisite attention to detail. Ochre-colored, thatch-roofed villas, along with a pool and open-air restaurant, are terraced on a landscaped hillside. Rooms are very big rooms and have panoramic views. Two have private pools. Fine furniture and Mexican art are found in rooms and common areas. Ventilation is provided by sea breezes and fans. La Casa Que Canta means, literally, the singing house. There have been some complaints about service, however.

**HOTELES SOTAVENTO & CATALINA**, *phone (753) 402032 or 42033, fax (753) 42975; 125 rooms, high season $69 single, $74 double, low season $54 single, $59 double, a few rooms priced more cheaply. VI - MC - AE - DC.*

These two hotels are under joint management, with shared reception area and restaurant. Situated next to each other, both are terraced into a hillside high above the beach, with excellent views. They have pleasant breezes but long climbs from the beach. Although older, the Catalina was renovated a while ago and looks fresher, with painted tiles and Mexican art. Some passageways are dark, however. Both have big whitewashed rooms with ceiling fans and broad terraces (with hammocks) facing the sea. Furnishings in the Sotavento are looking tired. Both have cheaper rooms, priced at $40 to $49 in high season and $33 to $36 in low season. Those in the Sotavento are in the back of the building with no sea view, while four of the cheaper rooms in the Catalina have terraces and views, providing excellent value.

**HOTEL FIESTA MEXICANA**, *phone (753) 43636 or 43776; 61 rooms, Christmas $110 single or double, regular high season $70, low season $55, VI - MC - AE - DC.*

Most rooms are set around a pool courtyard; a few face the sea. Furnishings are quite ordinary, and some rooms are a little dark. All have air conditioning and mosquito nets. The hotel offers beach chairs beneath palapas or palms and a palapa-shaded beachfront restaurant.

**VILLAS LAS URRACAS**, *phone (753) 42049 or 42053; 14 cabins, high season $51 single or double, low season $45, no cards.*

This spot is popular with long-staying guests who return each year. Cabins are plain and rather dark but have separate living rooms, fully equipped kitchens and big porches, facing a lush garden.

**BUNGALOWS PALACIOS**, *phone (753) 42631 or 44616; 17 cabins, high season $59 for up to 4 people, low season $50, no cards.*

Bedrooms have two double beds, and there are separate living rooms and kitchens. This rather plain spot is set in from the beach.

**HOTEL CALPULLI**, *phone (753) 42166; 44 rooms, beachfront rooms $50, rooms away from the beach $27, VI - MC.*

Rooms are bare, with paint peeling. There is a pool.

**HOTEL OMAR**, *phone (753) 43873; 16 rooms, $18 single, $23 double, VI - MC.*

Scruffy, bohemian and cheap, this place has basic decor and broad terraces facing the sea.

Houses a few minutes' walk from the beach and sleeping up to six people are available for rental. *For information, contact Grace Relfe in Zihuatanejo, fax (753) 42790 or 42811, or Karen Arthur in San Francisco, phone (415) 868-0263.*

### Ixtapa

**WESTIN RESORT IXTAPA** *(formerly the Camino Real), Playa Vista Hermosa, phone (753) 32121, fax (753) 30751, US and Canada reservations (800) 228-3000; 428 rooms, high season, $143, single or double; low season, $105; VI-MC-AE-DC.*

This hotel is surrounded by tropical forest and terraced into a hillside. Set on an isolated site reached by a stone-paved road, the building has an ochre exterior and makes extensive use of tiles and painted stucco inside. The lobby features bold columns with the sea on one side and the forest on the other. Rooms are rather small, but each has a large private outdoor terrace with a hammock. The four interconnected pools have waterfalls and spouts. The beach has striking rock formations and rough waves. The lobby bar is superb for sunsets.

**HOTEL KRYSTAL IXTAPA**, *Playa Palmar, phone (753) 30333, fax (753) 30216, US or Canada reservations (800) 231-9860; 254 rooms, high season $187 single or double, low season, $127, VI - MC - AE - DC.*

Rooms in this beachfront hotel are freshly renovated in pastel shades, and all face the sea. The hotel has a large pool area and the biggest convention facilities in the region.

**HOTEL OMNI IXTAPA**, *Playa Palmar, phone (753) 30003, fax (753)*

*31555; 271 rooms, high season $186 single or double, low season $126, VI - MC - AE - MC.*

Rooms in this new hotel all face the sea and are decorated in modern Mexican style, with pastel shades. The lobby is enormous, and the pool area is big. The usual lounge chairs and palapa shades are provided on the beach.

**HOTEL PRESIDENTE IXTAPA**, *Playa Palmar, phone (753) 30018, fax (753) 32312, US reservations (800) 447-6147; 315 rooms, high season VI - MC - AE - DC.*

This is one of several beachfront hotels to adopt the all-inclusive formula, with all meals and most drinks and sporting activities included in the room rate. Rooms are big and comfortable, with air conditioning and television. Most are in a high tower, while suites are in villas near the beach. Pools, beach chairs, two tennis courts, three restaurants, two bars and numerous recreational activities are available for guests.

Other hotels along Playa Palmar include the **SHERATON IXTAPA**, **ARISTOS, DORADO PACÍFICO, FONTAN IXTAPA** and **HOLIDAY INN SUNSPREE RESORT**. These look-alike hotels provide high levels of comfort and similar amenities. Some, including the Sheraton and the Fontan, offer all-inclusive packages as an option. The **POSADA REAL** is somewhat smaller and less expensive than the others. **CLUB MÉDITERRANÉE**, on Playa Quieta, is an all-inclusive resort with a broad range of organized activities and rooms set in low-slung buildings.

**QUALTON CLUB IXTAPA**, *Playa Linda, phone (753) 31985, fax (753) 31583; 190 rooms; high season $121 single, $198 double; low season $99 single, $154 double; meals, drinks and activities included; VI - MC - AE -DC.*

This all-inclusive resort (formerly the Hotel Playa Linda) offers activities including tennis, windsurfing, sailboarding and the use of a gymnasium. Rooms are air conditioned, many with sea views, and are set in a series of two-story buildings. The water is calm and well suited to windsurfing. The beach is long and sandy but quite dark.

## WHERE TO EAT

The temptation is great, when staying at one of the big resort hotels in Ixtapa, to dine at a hotel restaurant, especially if you're on the all-inclusive plan and your meals are already paid for. It's probably not a bad idea, however, to poke around elsewhere at least once or twice during your stay and try something a little different. While there is certainly good eating in Ixtapa, restaurants on the Zihuatanejo side are often just as good and tend also to be more authentic and less expensive. Besides, there's a lively street scene in the evening.

### In Zihuatanejo

In the center of Zihuatanejo, several restaurants line the beachfront promenade called **Paseo del Pescador**. Some of their touts are quite aggressive; a sensible way to deal with these people is to avoid any place they try to steer you to.

Among the better of these restaurants is **LA SIRENA GORDA**, *next to the pier*, is very good for fish, seafood and a view of waterfront activity; it is also open for breakfast. **CAFÉ LA MARINA** is less simple than it looks, with some interesting European and Mexican fish and seafood dishes and pizzas. **CASA ELVIRA**, *also along the Paseo del Pescador*, has good fish dieshes and traditional Mexican meals. Just behind, *on Avenida Juan Álvarez*, **GARROBOS** is known for seafood served in a variety of fashions, including brochettes and tacos.

**COCONUTS**, *on Paseo Agustín Ramírez*, offers lush tropical surroundings, a sumptuous choice of fish, seafood and meat dishes, as well as pasta and salads, and rather high prices. **EL MANGO** is very good for traditional Mexican dishes and juices. **TAMALES Y ATOLES ANY**, *on Calle Nicolás Bravo*, is another casual spot for Mexican favorites and is noted in particular for its wide variety of cornmeal tamales.

**PUNTARENAS**, an old family-run spot *just beyond the footbridge at the end of Avenida Juan Álvarez*, is open until early evening with good fish dishes and Mexican specialties. **LA MESA DEL CAPITÁN**, *on Calle Nicolás Bravo*, serves overpriced seafood and steaks in nautical surroundings. **PIZZERÍA EMILIO'S** *on Calle Vicente Guerrero* bakes its wares on a wood fire. **TEOTZINTLE**, *on the road to Acapulco just beyond the gas station*, is an inexpensive place noted for regional dishes, including the large-grain corn and meat soup known as *pozole* served on Thursday. Several small, inexpensive, open-air restaurants in the center of town served chichen grilled on a spit.

*Along Playa La Ropa*, **LA PERLA** and **LA GAVIOTA** are casual, palapa-shaded beachfront restaurants with wonderfully fresh fish and seafood in a variety of preparations at moderate prices. A couple of simpler and less expensive places lie further along the beach. **EL CANTO DE LA SIRENA** *in Hotel La Casa Que Canta* offers superb views over the bay, fine European and Mexican cuisine, and steep prices. At **VILLA DEL SOL** as well, the atmosphere is refined, the food is excellent, and prices are very high.

*Near Playa La Madera*, **RUBÉN'S** is a casual spot with good hamburgers and baked potatoes. *On Playa Las Gatas*, **LA MARINERA** has good seafood dishes.

### In Ixtapa

Most restaurants here are situated in the big hotels and tend to be quite expensive. Among free-standing restaurants are **RAFFAELO**, *in the Centro Comercial Galerías across from the Hotel Dorado Pacífico*, and **DA BAFFONE**, *in the Centro Comercial La Puerta opposite the Hotel Presidente*, each with selections of pastas and other Italian dishes at moderate prices.

**VILLA SAKURA**, *in the Centro Comercial Ixtapa*, is big and fairly expensive, with Japanese specialties, including sushi. **LE MONTMARTRE**, *in the Centro Comercial Galerías*, offers French cuisine in a formal setting. For something lighter, **FIGARO'S**, *in the Centro Comercial Los Patios*, has pizzas, hamburgers and tacos. **LOS HUARACHES**, *almost next door*, offers a variety of Mexican *antojitos* such as tacos, quesadillas, melted cheese and *tortas*, which are elaborate sandwiches.

**EL TACONZITO**, *in the Centro Comercial La Puerta*, specializes in pastas, pizzas and, as the name suggests, tacos, including seafood tacos. **PIZZERÍA MAMA NORMA**, *across from the Hotel Presidente*, has guess what. **BOGART'S**, *in the Hotel Krystal*, is heavily hyped, lavishly decorated in Moroccan motif, expensive, and not at all good.

## SEEING THE SIGHTS

The sights consist mostly of the beaches, nestled between scenic bays and mountains. In the opinion of many visitors, **Playa La Ropa** is the most attractive, big, broad, sandy and washed by gentle waves. **Playa Las Gatas**, just beyond La Ropa and reachable only by boat, is favored by snorkelers and divers. It has several dive shops and small restaurants. With its calm waters, it is a suitable place for children to swim. Boats run frequently from the pier in the center of Zihuatanejo.

**Isla Ixtapa** is a wildlife preserve and also has three beaches, noted for snorkeling and diving, and several small restaurants. Boats for the five-minute trip leave regularly from Playa Quieta just north of Ixtapa.

The area around the pier in the center of Zihuataneho is a good place to watch **fishermen** bring in their catches. The busiest times are around 7 am and again around 11 am.

**Museo Arqueológico de la Costa Grande** is located in a new stone building near one end of the Paseo del Pescador in Zihuatanejo. It displays a collection of ancient stone carvings and pottery from several eras, found in the western part of Guerrero state. *The museum is open daily except Monday from 10 am to 6 pm Admission is $1.20.*

## SHOPPING

**Ixtapa** is where much of the shopping is concentrated, with an almost continuous row of shopping centers along **Boulevard Ixtapa** opposite the hotels. Most shops sell clothing, jewelry or Mexican handicrafts, including hand-painted ceramic objects, wall hangings, leather goods, ceremonial masks, sarapes, hammocks and other items. There is enough competition to keep prices reasonable.

In **Zihuatanejo**, a handicrafts market *extends several blocks along Calle 5 de Mayo* with a selection of all of the above classes of items. It is often necessary to bargain. There are many shops along **Juan Álvarez**, **Cuauhtémoc**, and **Galeana** streets and also along the **Paseo del Pescador**. **Coco Cabañas**, *on Calle Vicente Guerrero opposite the Posada Citlali*, offers a selection of top-quality regional handicrafts.

## ENTERTAINMENT & NIGHTLIFE

Good spots to witness a spectacular sunset while sipping something cool include the **BAY CLUB**, *along the road leading to Playa La Ropa*, and the main bar in the **WESTIN RESORT IXTAPA**. The Bay Club has musicians some evenings.

Ixtapa is well endowed with discotheques. They generally are open from late evening until a couple of hours before dawn. All have a cover charge, which sometimes includes drinks. Some have a dress code barring shorts, jeans and T-shirts. Discotheques include **MAGIC CIRCUS** and **CHRISTINE'S**, *both near the Hotel Krystal*, and **EUFORIA**, with an erupting volcano, *in front of the Hotel Posada Real*.

## PRACTICAL INFORMATION

**Airlines**
• **Aeroméxico**: *(753) 42018*
• **Mexicana**: *(753) 32208*
• **Delta**: *(753) 43386*

**Car Rentals**
Cars are available at the airport and at several of the bigger hotels in Ixtapa.

**Currency Exchange**
There are several banks in the center of Zihuatanejo and a branch of **Bancomer** *in the Centro Comercial La Puerta in Ixtapa. The banks are open 9 am to 1:30 pm Monday to Friday.*

**Golf**
The 18-hole **Palma Real** course in the hotel zone in Ixtapa is open to the public. Information is available at any of the bigger hotels.

**Horseback Riding**
**Rancho La Manzanilla** *near Playa La Ropa* offers horses and guides which can take visitors through the hills and down to Playa Las Gatas.

## Laundry

There are two laundries *near the corner of Catalina González and Cuauhtémoc in Zihuatanejo.* Both offer same-day service.

## Motorbike rentals

**Hola Renta Motos**, *at Centro Comercial El Portal, Ixtapa.*

## Tourism Information

**Zihuatanejo**: *Palacio Municipal, Calle Juan Álvarez near the waterfront, open 9 am to 3 pm and 6 pm to 8 pm weekdays, 9 am to 2 pm Saturdays.*

**Ixtapa**: *opposite the Presidente hotel, phone (753) 31967 or 31968, open 9 am to 2 pm and 4 pm to 7 pm weekdays only.*

# TAXCO

*Taxco lies along the old Mexico City-Acapulco highway, about two hours' drive from Mexico City.*

**Taxco** (pronounced TASS-co) is an enchanting old silver-mining town that spreads up and down the hillsides in a jolly, twisting maze of cobbled streets and cheerful, whitewashed stucco buildings.

Its history is one of decline and rebirth. Spanish conquistador Hernán Cortés ordered the development of the silver mines in the 16th century, but they later fell into decay. In the 18th century, a Frenchman with the Mexicanized name Juan de la Borda revived the mining industry, and many buildings in the center of Taxco date from this period. Again, the mines fell into decay, never to recover fully. Today one silver mine remains in operation, and just barely. In the 1930s New Orleans artisan William Spratling set up an apprentice shop for the production of silver jewelry, using designs that often predated the Spanish conquest. This provided the town's third great impetus.

Tourism is now the most important industry, and it's easy to see why. The town and its surrounding hills are really quite captivating. As well, there are several museums and festivals. And Taxco is famed worldwide for its silver jewelry. The town is chock-a-block with jewelry shops. It is also noted for its religious processions during Holy Week, the period leading up to Easter.

Situated near the northern edge of Guerrero state, Taxco makes an easy day excursion from Mexico City two hours away, although many visitors may choose to stay longer. It can also be visited in a single day from Acapulco, but this is tiring; it makes more sense to stay overnight. The town tends to be very crowded on weekends and at peak holiday periods.

Visitors who come in midweek will have the place almost to themselves and will be served better at hotels and restaurants.

Fireworks and firecrackers are very popular in Taxco and form part of some religious ceremonies. Sometimes it may sound as if a huge gun battle has broken out. Visitors have no cause for alarm.

## ARRIVALS & DEPARTURES

### By Bus

Two bus companies connect Taxco with Mexico City to the north and Acapulco to the south. Each has its own terminal in Taxco, situated a few blocks apart along the highway, also known as Avenida Kennedy, that winds its way around the eastern edge of the city. Both terminals have reasonable seating areas.

Estrella Blanca, which also operates under the names Flecha Roja and Cuauhtémoc, provides hourly express service on the two-hour trip to or from Mexico City (southern terminal), with the last departures in either direction at about 8 pm. Buses offering varying levels of comfort go at different hours, and fares range between $5 and $9. There are eight daily departures to or from Acapulco (3 1/2 hours, $11-$14) via Iguala and Chilpancingo. The Estrella Blanca terminal is also the base for many second-class services, including local service twice hourly to Cuernavaca and about once an hour to Ixtapan de la Sal, with some buses continuing to Toluca.

Estrella de Oro has five daily first-class buses connecting Taxco with Mexico City and four to or from Acapulco.

### By Car

Taxco lies along the old Mexico City-Acapulco highway but is by-passed by the newer multi-lane highways, to which it is linked by roads that zigzag about 35 km through the hills in between. Coming from Acapulco or Chilpancingo, it is best to take the exit for Iguala and the direct road to Taxco from there. From Zihuatanejo it is probably better to go via Acapulco rather than taking what, on the map, looks like a shorter route via Ciudad Altamirano. This latter route goes through some very rugged and solitary countryside.

## ORIENTATION

Taxco, with its hilly, winding streets, is a difficult place to establish bearings. It is also a difficult place to find useful maps, but even good maps gives only a partial idea of the city's layout. Whichever highway you arrive on, you'll end up along Avenida Kennedy, a winding road which skirts the eastern part of the city. Several streets, among them Calle La Garita in the north (if you're coming from Mexico City) or Calle Pilita in the south will take you uphill to the central part of the city.

The main square is the Plaza Borda, also called the *zócalo*. It faces Santa Prisca church and lies at the center of a maze of narrow, cobbled streets radiating in several directions. Several *plazuelas*, or small plazas, are situated nearby, notably the Plazuela de San Juan.

The best way to discover Taxco is on foot. Most streets are steep and narrow, not really well suited to motor traffic. Most have one-way traffic, making for confusing detours for cars. Some passages are open to pedestrians only. Even if you arrive by car, it makes sense to park your vehicle and then walk around the center of town. From the bus terminals or the outskirts, taxis and minibuses are cheap and plentiful.

There is a **tourism information office**, *open irregular hours, in the convention center near the northern approach to the city at a spot called Los Arcos where an old aqueduct arches over the roadway.* Some booths purporting to provide tourism information are really just come-ons for silver shops. For **currency exchange**, there are several banks around town and two *casas de cambio* next to Plazuela de San Juan open weekdays until 8 pm and Saturdays until 3 pm.

**THE STREETS OF TAXCO**

## WHERE TO STAY

Hotels in Taxco are often deluged with one-night weekend visitors from Mexico City and almost bereft of customers the rest of the week. It doesn't take a wizard to figure out that this creates a revenue shortfall, and some spots have responded by neglecting maintenance.

Most, though, manage to keep things in reasonable shape. Hotels in the center of town are all in the middle or lower price range, while the more lavish hostelries are away from the center. Many hotels have excellent views of the city and nearby hills.

### In or near the town center

**HOTEL SANTA PRISCA**, *Cena Obscuras 1, phone (762) 20080 or 20980, fax (762) 22938; 32 rooms, $24 single, $35 double, VI - MC - AE. S*

Situated in a quiet corner near the Plazuela de San Juan, this colonial-style spot has pleasantly furnished rooms set around a beautiful garden terrace. The hotel has a restaurant, bar, library and patio with city views.

**HOTEL AGUA ESCONDIDA**, *Plaza Borda 4, phone (762) 20726 or 20736, fax (762) 21306; 50 rooms, $27 single, $41 double; VI - MC.*

This big, old-fashioned place is very centrally located and has quiet, comfortably furnished rooms, indoor parking, a pool, and terraces with excellent city views.

**HOTEL POSADA SAN JAVIER**, *Estacas 1, phone (762) 23177 or 20231, fax (762) 22351; $20 single, $27 double, VI - MC - AE.*

This is a quiet, midtown oasis with a lush garden, pool and parking, but some rooms are a little dark and furnishings are tired. It was formerly known as Hotel Las Palmas.

**HOTEL EL MESÓN DE LOS ARCOS**, *Juan Ruiz de Alarcón 2, phone (762) 21836; 36 rooms, $18 single, $27 double, VI - MC.*

Situated in a 17th-century building down the hill from the Plaza Borda, this hotel has wood-beamed ceilings, a pleasant courtyard, and colonial-style decor. Rooms in back are quieter.

**HOTEL POSADA DE LOS CASTILLO**, *Juan Ruiz de Alarcón 3, phone (762) 21396 or 23471; 15 rooms, $20 single, $27 double, VI - MC.*

Right across the street, this hotel also has a colonial ambiance. Again, rooms in back are quieter.

**HOTEL CASA GRANDE**, *Plazuela de San Juan 7, phone (762) 21108; $12 single, $16 double, higher at Christmas and Holy Week, VI - MC.*

This spot is well situated and has simple, very small rooms.

**HOTEL EL TASQUEÑITO**, *Calle Pedro Martín, phone (762) 20623, fax (762) 25737; 28 rooms, $15 single, $21 double.*

Situated on a quiet back street, this friendly place offers simply furnished rooms.

**HOTEL MELÉNDEZ**, *Cuauhtémoc 6, phone (762) 20006; 33 rooms, $15 single, $24 double, VI - MC.*

This centrally located hotel is basic and run-down.

**HOTEL RANCHO TAXCO VICTORIA**, *Carlos J. Niuri 5, phone (762) 20210, fax (762) 20010; 74 rooms, $30 single, $36 double, VI - MC - AE.*

This hotel, with rooms divided between four buildings, has good views from its upstairs terraces, but it is well past its prime. Maintenance is poor, and the furnishings look tired.

**HOTEL ESTELAR**, *Segunda de Reforma, phone (762) 21341; 30 rooms, $24 single, $36 double, VI - MC.*

We mention this dark, gloomy concrete shell, situated near the highway next to a soft drink warehouse, only because some taxi drivers bring unsuspecting visitors here. It is a charmless, overpriced place; some rooms have no outside window.

### Hotels away from the center

**HOTEL POSADA DE LA MISIÓN**, *Cerro de la Misión 32, phone (762) 20063 or 20533, fax (762) 22198; 150 rooms, $90 single or double, VI - MC - AE - DC.*

This sprawling place along the highway not far from the center of town has five sections built between 1940 and 1990, with good views everywhere and a big colored stone mural by Mexican artist Juan O'Gorman facing the pool. The hotel has two restaurants, two bars and three conference halls. Many rooms have carved wooden door and bedsteads, and a few are wheelchair-accessible, a rarity in Mexico

**HOTEL MONTE TAXCO**, *Fraccionamiento Lomas de Taxco, phone (762) 21300 or 20301, fax (762) 21428; 156 rooms, $97 single or double, slightly higher in peak holiday periods, VI - MC - AE - DC.*

This is the most lavish spot around. It sits atop a hillside just outside town with gorgeous views on all sides. It can be reached by road or by aerial cable car, which is a tourist attraction in itself. This is a full resort hotel, with tennis courts, nine-hole golf course, horseback riding, swimming pool, gymnasium, sauna, steam baths and massages. It also has an art gallery, three restaurants and a discotheque. Rooms are set in two buildings, and nearly all have splendid views.

**HOTEL DE LA BORDA**, *Cerro del Pedregal, phone (762) 20225 or 20226, fax (762) 20226; 120 rooms, $55 single or double, VI - MC - AE.*

This spacious, old-fashioned hotel with big indoor and outdoor lounges has many colonial touches in its decor. It is perched on a hill just across the highway and has good views over the town. Unfortunately, parts of this otherwise pleasant place are crumbling because of weak maintenance, and many rooms are out of service. There are a pool and restaurant.

**HOTEL HACIENDA DEL SOLAR**, *off the highway south of town, phone (762) 20323; 22 rooms, $74 single, $102 double, VI - MC - AE.*

Rooms are well furnished and divided among four buildings set on extensive grounds on an isolated hillside site. The hotel has a pool, tennis court, an elegant restaurant and splendid views. De luxe rooms and suites are available at higher cost.

**HOTEL LOMA LINDA**, *Kennedy 52, phone (762) 20206 or 20753, fax (762) 25125; 60 rooms, $30 single, $38 double, VI - MC - AE.*

This friendly, sprawling, motel-style spot along the highway has a large parking area, pool, children's playground, and restaurant. All rooms have private terraces with mountain views; a few also have city views.

## WHERE TO EAT

Several good restaurants are located on or near the Plaza Borda in the heart of Taxco. Others are located by the Plazuela de San Juan. Menus tend to emphasize meat dishes, but seafood and pasta can also be found, and pizza has become quite popular. The town gets crowded on weekends and holidays, with many day visitors from Mexico City, and restaurants are very busy at lunch. Since places start to fill up shortly after two o'clock, a simple expedient is to arrive earlier.

*Overlooking Plaza Borda,* **BAR-RESTAURANT PACO** has a broad menu including oysters and a variety of salads. **CIELITO LINDO** has excellent meat dishes and Mexican *antojitos* as well as good views of the plaza. *Nearby,* **LA PARROQUIA** and **EL MIRADOR** also have good views but rather ordinary food. **LA HACIENDA**, *in the Hotel Agua Escondido just off Plaza Borda*, has very good breakfasts and regional dishes, including a breakfast dish called *aporreado guerrerense*, consisting of slivers of beef in a spicy sauce. Full-course lunches and suppers are reasonably priced.

*Across the plaza,* **SEÑOR COSTILLA'S** is noisy and expensive but seems popular anyway; it specializes in ribs and chops. *In the same building,* **PIZZERÍA MARIO** is quite tiny but has a terrace with good views. *Just down the hill on Benito Juárez, near the Palacio Municipal,* **LA TABERNA** offers pizzas, pastas and other dishes in pleasant surroundings.

**CAFÉ-BAR LA CONCHA NOSTRA**, *facing Plazuela de San Juan, through the same doorway as the Hotel Casa Grande*, has a huge collection of masks at the entrance, a view over the *plazuela*, and a menu concentrating on pizzas. **HOSTERÍA EL ADOBE**, *also overlooking the plazuela*, is a small, cozy place, also decorated with masks, with a wider menu including *antojitos*, meats, and seafood. Three small restaurants *on Calle Hidalgo just off Plazuela de San Juan*, **ETHEL**, **SANTA FE** and **DON ANDRÉS**, offer a variety of inexpensive regional dishes and *antojitos* in simple surroundings. Restaurant de Don Andrés is more elegant than the other two and also slightly more expensive.

**LA VENTANA DE TAXCO**, *situated on the grounds of the Hotel Hacienda del Solar just south of Taxco*, is an elegant restaurant with superb city views and a good variety of Mexican and Italian dishes. Prices on the menu are expensive and do not even include tax. For big appetites, the **HOTEL MONTE TAXCO** has big weekend buffets in its main dining room and *à la carte* service at its other, more exclusive restaurants.

## SEEING THE SIGHTS

The best way to see Taxco is simply to walk around the steep maze of cobbled streets in the center of town and to enjoy views that change at every corner. The stone-paved **Plaza Borda**, also known as the *zócalo, is situated in the heart of the city*. Part of the plaza is choked by motor traffic. It faces the **Iglesia de San Sebastián y Santa Prisca**, an ornate 18th century church built with wealth from the silver mines and usually known simply as Santa Prisca. The church's pink stone exterior is intricately sculpted with religious figures and decorations in a blend of Spanish baroque and roccoco styles. Inside, the altarpieces are covered in gold leaf, and there are several big paintings.

To the right of the church is an alleyway where regional handicrafts are sold from tiny stalls. The **public market** lies near the bottom of this alleyway. Many other colonial churches are scattered around town. Several small plazas, known as *plazuelas*, are situated near Plaza Borda. Among them are **Plazuela de Bernal** *a short hop north*, and **Plazuela de San Juan**, *to the south*. The *plazuela* in front of **Guadalupe church**, *up a hill to the west of Plazuela de Bernal*, offers panoramic views of the town and the surrounding countryside.

Museum-goers can keep busy for several hours. **Museo Guillermo Spratling** (Guillermo is the Spanish equivalent of William), *one block below the zócalo behind Santa Prisca church, is open daily from 10 am to 3 pm; admission $3, children free*. It displays archaeological objects from several regions of Mexico, including a large Olmec collection. Contemporary paintings are displayed in the basement. **Casa Humboldt**, *down Calle Juan Ruiz de Alarcón, is open Tuesday to Saturday from 10 am to 5 pm and until 3 pm Sunday; admission $3*. It presents objects from various periods in Taxco's history, including religious items found in storage during the 1988 restoration of Santa Prisca church.

**Museo Gráfico de la Historia Social de Taxco**, *just around the corner, open 9 am to 3 pm and 6 pm to 7:30 pm, closed Tuesday evening and all day Wednesday; admission $1*, displays photos of Taxco from early in the 20th century. **Museo de Platería**, *entrance on Plaza Borda near Señor Costilla's restaurant, open daily 10 am to 5 pm; admission $1, children free*, is an elaborate exhibition of silver objects and of the history of the silver industry in Mexico.

The **aerial cable-car** (*teleférico*) ascending to the Hotel Monte Taxco runs 800 meters with a vertical rise of 173 meters, with superb scenery along the way. *It operates from 7:15 am to 7 pm; roundtrip tickets are $3, half-price for children. The base is near Los Arcos toward the northern edge of town (reachable by taxi or minibus).*

## SHOPPING

Taxco is known worldwide for its silver jewelry, and the town is heavily sprinkled with jewelry shops. On a short stroll it is easy to find dozens of them. Many workshops are located here, although prices are not always lower than in Mexico City. A little bargaining may be required. To be certain of getting sterling silver, look for the .925 stamp, indicating that the item is 92.5 per cent silver. (Forgers are sent to prison.) Other items may be silver-plated or made of *alpaca*, a cheaper metal alloy. Many jewelry shops also offer gemstones and other articles. Several are clustered in the **Patio de las Artesanías** *on Plaza Borda near Santa Prisca church, or on the Plazuela de Bernal one block away*, including **Los Castillo Plateros**, with its lavish displays and workshops.

A variety of regional handicrafts can be found in Taxco, including hand-painted gourds and boxes, basketware, bark paintings and small ceramic objects from nearby parts of Guerrero state. Some of these may be found in the alleyway next to Santa Prisca church cathedral or in the public market, which can be entered from the bottom of this alleyway.

### FESTIVALS & FAIRS

*Taxco is noted for its **Holy Week processions**, beginning on Palm Sunday, a week before Easter. There are candlelight processions most nights and special ceremonies at churches in town and in the neighboring villages, from where some penitents set out by foot on multi-day voyages carrying heavy wooden crosses. This is a busy holiday period, and hotels tend to be full. A few weeks earlier, neighborhood and village celebrations mark the beginning of Lent with music and fireworks.*

*On January 18, the day of **Santa Prisca**, and January 20, the day of **San Sebastián**, Taxco's patron saints, there are music, fireworks and dances in the Plaza Borda. The annual blessing of the animals takes place at the entrance to the church on January 17. There are many other religious celebrations throughout the year. The **Feria de la Plata**, a week-long silverwork fair, is held in late November or early December and is accompanied by concerts and rodeos.*

## ENTERTAINMENT & NIGHTLIFE

For evening entertainment, the **Hotel Monte Taxco** has advertised a 10 pm show (daily except Sunday, admission $15) featuring the **Voladores de Papantla**, who spin in the air around high poles. Taxco has a handful of low-key **discotheques** that really come to life only on weekends. These include **Disco Escupar Artes**, *off the Plaza Borda*, and **Tequila's Disco** and **Salsa Romántica**, *both along Avenida Kennedy*.

## EXCURSIONS

The **Grutas de Cacahuamilpa** (pronounced CA-ca-wa-MIL-pa) are an elaborate series of caves *28 km north of Taxco, just off the well marked road leading to Ixtapan de la Sal*. By second-class bus, Tres Estrellas del Centro goes hourly from the Estrella Blanca terminal in Taxco, taking 45 minutes and leaving passengers at a junction ten minutes' walk from the entrance.

Visitors can see huge caverns, with the requisite stalactites and stalagmites in their weird and wonderful formations. Everyone must go in groups accompanied by a guide (Spanish only). *Tours leave the entrance hourly from 10 am to 5 pm, and tickets are $5.* There can be long waits on weekend afternoons. (If traveling by bus, go early to avoid returning after dark.)

Guides take visitors on a one-hour tour two kilometers into the caves, and then it is a half-hour to return to the entrance. Visitors should be prepared for slippery footing, high humidity and a good test of their night vision. A restaurant and gift shops are at the entrance, and there are toilets inside the caves themselves.

# INDEX

*Bold type designates main references*

## FROM THE PUBLISHER

Our goal is to provide you with a guide book that is second to none. Please remember, however, that things do change: phone numbers, prices, addresses, quality of food served, value, etc. Should you come across any new information, we'd appreciate hearing from you. No item is too small for us, so if you have any recommendations or suggested changes, please write to the author care of Open Road.

The address is:

Eric Hamovitch
c/o Open Road Publishing
P.O. Box 11249
Cleveland Park Station
Washington, DC 20008

# TRAVEL NOTES

# TRAVEL NOTES

# TRAVEL NOTES

# TRAVEL NOTES

# TRAVEL NOTES

# YOUR PASSPORT TO GREAT TRAVEL FROM OPEN ROAD PUBLISHING

## OUR CLASSIC CENTRAL AMERICA GUIDES!!!

**COSTA RICA GUIDE** by Paul Glassman, 5th Ed. Glassman's classic travel guide to Costa Rica remains the standard against which all others must be judged. Discover great accommodations, reliable restaurants, pristine beaches, and incredible diving, fishing, and other water sports. Revised and updated. **$14.95**

**BELIZE GUIDE** by Paul Glassman, 6th Ed. This guide has quickly become the book of choice for Belize travelers. Perhaps the finest spot for Caribbean scuba diving and sport fishing, Belize's picture-perfect palm trees, Mayan ruins, tropical forests, uncrowded beaches, and fantastic water sports have made it one of the most popular Caribbean travel destinations. Revised and updated. **$13.95**

**HONDURAS & BAY ISLANDS GUIDE** by J.P. Panet with Leah Hart and Paul Glassman, 2nd Ed. Open Road's superior series of Central America travel guides continues with the revised look at this beautiful land. **$13.95**

**GUATEMALA GUIDE** by Paul Glassman, 9th Ed. Glassman's treatment of colorful Guatemala remains the single best source in print. **$16.95**

## SEE EUROPE & ASIA WITH OPEN ROAD!

**PARIS GUIDE** by Robert F. Howe and Diane Huntley. See the City of Light as never before. Howe & Huntley take you to their favorite haunts, lead you to great values, and help you discover the beauty, fun, and romance of Paris. **$12.95**

**FRANCE GUIDE** by Robert F. Howe and Diane Huntley. Discover the majesty and splendor of France, from chateau country in the north to the beaches of the south, from windswept Brittany on the Atlantic to the fields and villages of Alsace-Lorraine. All regions are covered, including updated material on Paris. Extensive food and wine section explains in great detail all about the incredible cuisine and wines of La Belle France. **Spring 1995, $16.95**

**CHINA GUIDE** by Ruth Lor Malloy, 8th Ed. At 704 pages, this is the most comprehensive guide to the new China you'll find. Detailed travel planning information, including Chinese phrases, tips on Chinese food, best ways to get around, and much more, plus insider material on Beijing, Shanghai, Xi'an, Guangdong, and the more remote areas along the Silk Road and Tibet. **$17.95**

**HONG KONG & MACAU GUIDE** by Ruth Lor Malloy and Linda Malloy. Visit Asia's most dynamic and energetic city, Hong Kong, and the former Portuguese colony, gambling mecca, and car racing paradise of Macau, with former residents and China experts Ruth and Linda Malloy. All new material on hotels, restaurants, excursions, sight-seeing, and especially shopping! **$13.95**

## TRAVEL AMERICA'S OPEN ROAD!

**AMERICA'S MOST CHARMING TOWNS & VILLAGES** by Larry Brown. *The* book everyone's talking about! Larry Brown shows you the 200 most charming and quaint towns in America – all 50 states included. Great coverage of each town includes local sights, interesting historical notes, directions, and up-to-date information on where to stay and eat. **$14.95**

**WALT DISNEY WORLD AND ORLANDO THEME PARKS** by Jay Fenster. *The* complete guide to Disney World and all of Orlando's great theme parks (including Sea World, MGM Studios, Busch Gardens, Church Street Station, Spaceport USA, and more), shows you every attraction, ride, show, shop, and nightclub they contain. Includes 64 money-savings tips for hotel, airfare, restaurant, attractions, and ride discounts. **$12.95**

**LAS VEGAS GUIDE** by Ed Kranmar & Avery Cardoza, 2nd Ed. The most fun guide to Vegas, plus expert gambling advice from insider Avery Cardoza, the world's foremost publisher of gambling books. Get the latest scoop on hotels, theme parks, restaurants, shopping, wedding chapels, area excursions, things to do with kids, and much more! **$12.95**

## IF YOU LIKE GOLF, YOU'LL LOVE OUR GOLF GUIDES!

**FLORIDA GOLF GUIDE** by Jimmy Shacky. **$14.95**

**GOLF COURSES OF THE SOUTHWEST** by Jimmy Shacky. Featuring courses in Arizona, New Mexico, and Nevada. Includes accommodations and things to do. **$14.95**

**NEW YORK & NEW JERSEY GOLF GUIDE** by Jimmy Shacky. Includes accommodations and things to do. **$14.95**

Each golf guide gives you all necessary course information presented in an easily accessible format. Greens fees, yardage, course and slope ratings, tee times, course type, architect, local pro, price, total holes, facilities and amenities, and much more!

## PLEASE USE ORDER FORM ON NEXT PAGE

# ORDER FORM

Name and Address: _____

_____

_____

_____ Zip Code: _____

| Quantity | Title | Price |
|----------|-------|-------|
|          |       |       |
|          |       |       |
|          |       |       |
|          |       |       |
|          |       |       |
|          |       |       |
|          |       |       |

Total Before Shipping _____

Shipping/Handling _____

**TOTAL** _____

**Orders must include price of book <u>plus</u> shipping and handling**. For shipping and handling, please add $3.00 for the first book, and $1.00 for each book thereafter.

Ask about our discounts for special order bulk purchases.

*ORDER FROM:* **OPEN ROAD PUBLISHING**

**P.O. Box 11249, Cleveland Park Station, Washington, D.C. 20008**